THE VICTORIANS
AND ANCIENT GREECE

The
VICTORIANS
and
ANCIENT GREECE

Richard Jenkyns

Harvard University Press
Cambridge, Massachusetts

Library of Congress Catalog Card Number: 81-81474

ISBN 0-674-93686-8 (cloth)

ISBN 0-674-93687-6 (paper)

PREFACE

'The history of the Victorian age will never be written,' Lytton
Strachey declared, fixing that tangled and exuberant epoch with the
cold, clever eye of a disenchanted generation: 'we know too much
about it. For ignorance is the first requisite of the historian—
ignorance which simplifies and clarifies; which selects and omits . . .'
During the sixty years since those words were penned the labours of
countless researchers have made such ignorance harder and harder to
come by, and a total history of the nineteenth century, with each
aspect given its due place and proportion, seems more than ever
impossible. It may be better to take one element in the history of the
period, to trace its unity and diversity at different times and in
different places, to hope that in this way a partial study may shed
some light, however oblique and uncertain, upon a larger whole.
This book takes one such element. It is concerned with the influence
of ancient Greece upon Victorian England, and here it includes ideas
and institutions which were not really derived from Greece but to
which some Victorians chose to give a Hellenic colouring. It also
deals in a lesser degree with Victorian interpretations of Greek art
and society; naturally the two subjects—the influence of Greece upon
England, the English attitude to Greece—are intimately linked. I
mention both important and unimportant people, the former for the
part that they played in giving the age its character, the latter because
they often reflect that character more simply than their more eminent
contemporaries. I am not writing a history of scholarship, and professional scholars appear only if they widely influenced Victorian
culture, or else may be used to illustrate it.

   In one sense our ignorance has much increased since Strachey
wrote. As time separates us from the Victorians, the difficulty of
imagining how they thought and felt grows greater. Twenty years
ago a fair number of British schools were offering what was in
essence a Victorian classical education, with the emphasis on the
detailed reading of texts and the composition of prose and verse in

both Latin and Greek. Those who were put through this mill
fortuitously acquired some understanding of how part of a Victorian
gentleman's mind was furnished. Today there can be very few schools
that still use the old system, perhaps none. In many cases we perceive
where our ignorance of the past lies; we appreciate the effort of
imagination needed to understand why such issues as, say, the
emancipation of women or the interpretation of the thirty-nine
articles were so intensely controversial. But few people suspect the
extent to which the ancient world, and especially Greece, influenced
the Victorians. I wish, in fact, to make ambitious claims for my
subject; Hellenism may sound a mandarin topic, and so in a way it is;
yet ancient Greece preoccupied many of the finest minds of the last
century, and thus, directly and indirectly, it became a pervasive
influence, reaching even to the edges of popular culture. Even those
who hated the Greeks or detested the system of classical education
were affected willy-nilly. Unless we realize how much the Victorians
thought about Greece, we will not fully understand them.

I have been concerned to lower the barriers between literary
criticism, art history, the history of ideas, and so forth. Of history in
the more conventional sense this book contains comparatively little.
The story of nineteenth-century education is one about which whole
volumes have been written, and what I have said about it is not
intended to do more than sketch a background. In parts of the book I
have leapt back and forth from one decade to another, since one of
my purposes has been to suggest the persistence of certain themes
and ideas in differing places and in disparate people. That sense of
process, of steady and continuous change as year succeeds to year,
which to many seems to be the very essence of history, is not
prominent in much of my book; none the less, I do have beliefs about
the way in which Hellenism waxed and waned as a force in British
culture, and I hope that as the book proceeds a pattern half emerges
into the light, which is as far perhaps as a pattern of this kind ought
to emerge. The Victorian age was nothing if not complex and
diverse; I have sought to show Hellenism caught up and enmeshed in
that complexity. Though I have resisted the temptation to end with a
chapter of magisterial summation, in the course of the book I have
tried constantly to suggest shapes and tendencies, without excessive
emphasis. I do not claim to account for all that I describe; it is a
shallow kind of history that purports to explain everything.

Although I have looked back to the eighteenth century and forward to the twentieth, my central concern has been with the Victorian
age. All 'periods' are artificial concepts, but like many others I would

prefer to think in terms of two periods, the one stretching from 1832 to the 1870s, the other from the 1870s to the First World War. But the word 'Victorian' is too well established to be abandoned, and its very looseness may even be of some use, since statements about 'the Victorians' cannot pretend to be more than crude generalizations. The Victorians were many millions of individual human beings, born in different generations and living through times of rapid and profound change; still, I have sometimes spoken about Victorian ideas or Victorian characteristics where the alternative would have been cumbrous periphrasis. And to adapt a phrase from J. L. Austin, one might in any case be tempted to call over-simplification the occupational disease of historians if it were not their occupation. In talking about the ancient world, where I have not concealed my own views, I have stated them with dogmatic brevity; any other method would have been tedious and confusing. When quoting, I have transliterated Greek words except in a very few cases where the Greek script is an essential part of the author's meaning.

I owe a great debt to the Warden and Fellows of All Souls College, Oxford, for electing me to the fellowship which enabled this book to be written. Oswyn Murray has been a constant source of advice and encouragement; John Clive read most of the book in draft and made valuable suggestions; Edna Laird typed and retyped with inexhaustible patience. Other debts are more intangible. I hope that it will not seem too grudging in me to have cited secondary sources as references only; the reasons for this austerity I leave my readers to consider. I have been influenced by my teachers both at school and university, probably more than I realize; for the defects in what follows they are of course partly responsible. I dedicate the book to my parents.

CONTENTS

LIST OF ILLUSTRATIONS

I

THE ORIGINS OF
HELLENISM

Late in the evening of March 17th, 1751, a boat carrying two British travellers anchored at a small port in the Levant. When the sun rose on the following morning, they could see several miles away through the luminous and as yet unpolluted air a flat-topped hill of moderate height crowned with a picturesque jumble of buildings, some Christian, some Muslim, some the relics of a yet older civilization. What they saw was a provincial town in an unimportant part of the Ottoman Empire; yet this was their goal, the fulfilment of three years of planning and contrivance: they were in sight of Athens.[1]

James Stuart and Nicholas Revett had met a few years earlier in Rome, the Niobe of nations and the finishing-school of the English aristocracy, where they both seem to have supported themselves by acting as guides to wealthy compatriots anxious to admire the sublimities of the eternal city in the correct manner.[2] In 1748 they conceived the scheme that was to make their reputations: to visit Athens and make accurate drawings of the ancient remains. They were fortunate in their patrons; Sir James Gray, the British resident in Venice, raised funds for them, and the British ambassador in Constantinople used his influence with the Porte.[3] Stuart and Revett spent two years in Athens; when they returned to England they had a fuller and more accurate knowledge of ancient architecture than anyone had possessed since the days of the Roman Empire. In an age which valued classical correctness next to godliness, and not seldom above it, that knowledge was beyond price. Plans were made to publish their discoveries in a series of folio volumes, and subscriptions invited from the worlds of scholarship and fashion. In 1758

Stuart designed a Doric temple at Hagley Park; it was the first building of the Greek Revival in all Europe.

The first half of the eighteenth century was England's 'Augustan' age, when the writers of Rome were held up as models. But the original Augustans had been imitators too, and proud of it: Virgil boasts that he is the first to sing the verses of Theocritus in Latin, Horace that he has shown the quality of Archilochus and Alcaeus to Rome.[4] The Roman poets never forgot that they stood in the shadow of a giant; their fingers were always pointing behind them to the glories of the Greek past, and an admiration for Latin literature leads naturally to a respect for the authority of the Greeks. Stuart, careful to justify his enterprise in Augustan eyes, quoted Horace's famous tag about captive Greece taking her conqueror captive and cited a variety of Latin writers to show that Athens must be allowed to surpass Rome 'for the beauties of a correct style'. This city had been the most renowned in Greece 'for the culture of every Art'. 'We therefore resolved to examine that Spot . . .: flattering ourselves, that the remains . . . would excel in true Taste and Elegance every thing hitherto published.'[5] Taste and Elegance—the propriety of the concept and the seemliness of the expression sound typically Augustan; but in some respects Stuart and Revett's project was less conventional. The stirrings of romantic sentiment can be sensed beneath their smooth prose:[6]

> There is perhaps no part of Europe, which more deservedly . . . excites the curiosity of the Lovers of polite Literature than . . . Attica, and Athens its capital City: whether we reflect on the Figure it makes in History, on account of the excellent men it has produced in every Art . . . or whether we consider the Antiquities which are said to be still remaining there . . . the most perfect Models of what is excellent in Sculpture and Architecture.

'Where'er we tread, 'tis haunted holy ground';[7] it was Byron, some sixty years later, who was to articulate this sentiment unforgettably and to associate it indelibly with Greece, but Stuart and Revett helped to kindle the spark, and even Johnson caught something of the glow. His visit to Iona moved him to declare, 'That man is little to be envied, whose patriotism would not gain force upon the plain of Marathon.'[8]

Johnson spoke hypothetically: the plain of Marathon must have seemed almost as remote from Inner Temple Lane as the kingdom of Cathay. Stuart and Revett's expedition, indeed, was an adventure.

The reason why Greek antiquities had been neglected was, as they caustically observed, obvious: 'Artists capable of such a Work, have been able to satisfy their passion . . . for Fame or Profit, without risking themselves among such professed Enemies to the Arts as the Turks are. The ignorance . . . of that uncultivated people,' they added, 'may perhaps, render an undertaking of this sort, still somewhat dangerous.' They were right. They were ambushed by corsairs, they were forced to decamp from Athens by the disturbances that followed the death of the Chief of the Black Eunuchs; constantly they risked death from disease or the knife.[9] They were not only scholars and artists, therefore, but explorers too, and they went not only to recover the classic glories of Hellas but also to observe the scenery and the inhabitants; their engravings are enlivened by scenes of modern Athenian life, featuring bearded Turks and Grecian maidens and even a Capuchin contemplating a skull like a latter-day Jerome. Their picture of the 'Doric Portico' shows storks building their nests on the pediment, Stuart (or Revett) mounting his horse, and the French consul sitting between a Turk and a Greek 'for the Sake of exhibiting the different Habits of this Country'. Indeed, the artist ventured on a topographical impropriety: 'The Liberty has been taken of turning this Fountain somewhat from its real Position, so as to give the Reader a View of this kind of Turkish Fabrick.'[10] Stuart and Revett were collectors of *choses vues*; they had come to study the sublimities of Hellas, but they kept an eye open for the minor pleasures of Levantine life.

What is more, they actually *liked* the Greeks, and especially praised the modern Athenians for their genius, courage and sagacity: 'They want not for artful Speakers and busy Politicians . . . and it is remarkable enough, that the Coffee-House which this species of Men frequent, stands within . . . the ancient Poikile.' These words associate, perhaps for the first time, memories of the old Athenian democracy with the struggle of the modern Greeks against Ottoman oppression. In addition to their other achievements, Stuart and Revett have some claim to be considered the unconscious founders of English philhellenism (philhellenism being the love of modern Greece and its people as distinct from Hellenism, which is an interest in the ancient Greeks). Stuart explained that their second volume would 'treat of Buildings erected while the Athenians were a free people, chiefly during the administration of that great statesman Pericles.'[11] Again the philhellene tone is unmistakable.

In 1751 they were elected to the Society of Dilettanti, an honour which brought them into contact with a curious milieu. Eventually the

Society would be able to claim among its past members a murderer and seven Prime Ministers; but it was originally more purely rakish. When the Dilettanti published the *Ionian Antiquities* they were very bland: 'It would be disingenuous to insinuate that . . . the Promotion of Arts was the only Motive for forming this Society . . . Social Intercourse was, undoubtedly, the first great Object in view.' Horace Walpole was blunter: 'The nominal qualification for membership is having been in Italy, and the real one, being drunk.'[12] The members' interest in the fine arts was often of a salacious kind. One of them was painted caressing a bronze Aphrodite, another as a friar adoring the Medici Venus in a blasphemous parody of the mass. Sexual rebellion, licentiousness, and that strange species of religious revolt which is almost a sort of religiosity, fired by a prurient fascination for the object of its attack, were features of English Hellenism that were soon to disappear; or rather to lie dormant, for lubricity and a febrile religiosity were both to be elements in the decadent and decaying Hellenism of the later Victorian age.

What most of the Dilettanti had in common was an urge to kick against the conventions. Many of them were enemies of Sir Robert Walpole's ascendancy, not through ideological conviction, but because of the natural dislike of the young for the old, the corrupt and the successful; but Walpole's defeat and death failed to shake the Whig establishment, and its opponents were driven to look elsewhere for an outlet. For any traveller the Turkish Empire answered to the requirements that Afghanistan and Nepal have been used to satisfy more recently. Everyone of consequence had been to Italy ('A man who has not been in Italy,' said Johnson, 'is always conscious of an inferiority'), but Greece offered the charm of novelty; it was near enough to be accessible, remote enough to be exotic, with a soupçon of danger to add spice to the adventure. And to the Dilettanti Greece offered another opportunity: even though the Whig oligarchy were unassailable politically, they might be vulnerable to aesthetic attack; Greek art could be used to overthrow the Palladian style that they favoured—if only one knew what Greek art was like.

And so, half by accident, the Dilettanti became discoverers. Lord Sandwich is best known for putting a piece of meat between two slices of bread; more remarkably, he kept a mistress who was murdered by a clergyman, an unusual occurrence even in the Age of Reason; more important, he travelled in 1738–1739 around the Aegean, returning with a shipload of antiquities. When Lord Charlemont toured Greece ten years later, he took with him an artist to make drawings of the monuments. When Sir James Gray met Stuart and Revett, it was

natural that he should favour their project. In proposing their
election to the Society, however, he was taking a less obvious step.[13]
Hitherto the members had been rich and aristocratic, but henceforth
an increasing proportion of them would be scholars, students and
artists; the Society had started its long slide into respectability. The
effect on the history of taste was considerable: Greek culture became
à la mode; art, archaeology, history and philology would have a
nucleus around which they could gather, each stimulating interest in
the others. Future members of the Society would include the
philologist Wood, the historian Mitford, the arbiters of taste Hope
and Payne Knight, the topographers Leake and Gell, the phil-
hellenes Guilford and Morritt, the painter West, the sculptor
Westmacott. All these men, despite their many dissimilarities, were
interested, in one way or another, in the heritage of ancient Greece;
so much was fresh, so much was undiscovered that Hellenism could
permeate a fine diversity of activities.

Stuart and Revett's arrival at Athens on that March day in 1751 is
a landmark in the history of taste. Before there had been amateur
zeal; to that excitement they added, in investigating Greece, a
seriousness and thoroughness that were new. Although they hoped to
change the current of taste, they went without preconceived ideas:
'We determined to avoid Haste, and System.' They were looking for
'the Antiquities which *are said* to be still remaining there'; and as for
the architectural decorations, 'These Sculptures we imagine will be
extremely curious.'[14] One realizes with a sense of shock that they are
referring to what we call the Elgin Marbles; they were opening up a
new world. The first volume of *The Antiquities of Athens* (1762)
enjoyed an immediate success, which was fully deserved, for it was
simultaneously an important work of scholarship and a magnificent
picturebook. To the student of architecture it was a revelation of an
unknown world; but the armchair traveller, too, was invited to tread
the soil of Greece along with the authors and join in the fun. Their
plate of the Philopappus monument bears a charming caption: 'On
the foreground Mr. Revett and myself are introduced with our
friends Mr. James Dawkins and Mr. Robert Wood; the last of
whom is occupied in copying the inscription. . . . Our Janizary is
making coffee, which we drank here; the boy . . . attends with our
cups and saucers.'[15] Stuart sounds almost like Uncle Fred showing off
his holiday snapshots; all the gaiety of eighteenth-century philhellenism is in those words, and yet there was purposefulness
underneath.

During the next quarter of a century the Adam style was

predominant, and few people today allow much importance to Stuart; but in the first half of the last century opinions were different. In 1842 Joseph Gwilt wrote that the 'chasteness and purity' which Stuart and Revett had brought to English architecture had eventually ousted 'the opposite and vicious taste of Robert Adam'. In 1847, James Elmes insisted that no event in the history of English architecture produced 'so sudden, decided and beneficial effect' as the works of Stuart. As late as 1854 Owen Jones declared that Stuart and Revett had 'generated a mania for Greek architecture, from which we are barely yet recovered'.[16] There is a core of truth in these claims. Robert Adam was in his way an original genius, but perhaps it was for this very reason that the Adam style led nowhere; its rich but elegant eclecticism was too distinctive to appeal to any architect of strongly individual character, too difficult to attract the common run of imitators. Stuart, by contrast, did not create a style of his own. He had gone to Athens to see what he could find, and in his work he presented his 'findings' to the public, giving the first and necessary impetus to a slow but large change in architectural taste. His nickname, 'Athenian' Stuart, was well deserved; his style was not 'Stuartish' but simply Greek.

For whatever reason, the volumes of the *Antiquities* were very slow in appearing. Since the first volume dealt only with minor works, it was not until its successor came out in 1787 that the public learnt the true appearance of the great Athenian masterpieces. Before this time, Stuart and Revett had had the field largely to themselves, and they were apparently content for the 'Grecian gusto' to exist as the favoured style of a few fashionable *cognoscenti*. Indeed, a strain of conscious dilettantism may be detected in their works. The Doric columns of Revett's church at Ayot St. Lawrence and portico at Standlynch are fluted only at the very top and bottom. There is no obvious reason why he should twice have adopted this curious design, except that he and Stuart had discovered it on Delos. It is as though he were saying, in the tones of a connoisseur, 'Look at what I found on my travels.' Stuart improved the grounds at Shugborough by sprinkling the landscape with 'antiquities', mostly adaptations of Attic originals. There is no unity of style or date between the monuments which he imitated: they were all Athenian, and that sufficed. Like a young nobleman bringing back paintings and marbles from the Grand Tour, Stuart treats the buildings of Athens as *souvenirs de voyage*, disposing them over the park like bibelots in a gigantic outdoor drawing-room. His treatment of the Arch of Hadrian suggests that this effect was consciously intended. The original arch in Athens stands on low ground, among buildings; Stuart placed his imitation on a rounded, grassy hillock, to be viewed from the house as an eye-catcher. In the afternoon the sun strikes through the wide gaps between the columns, casting upon the smooth bright grass a shadow of complicated and fascinating shape, streaked with gashes of sharp light. Forced to use the dark, gritty sandstone of northern England in place of the glistening marble of Pentelicus, he turned necessity to advantage by adding decorations in a bright white stone which contrasts effectively with the nutty brown coloration of the rest. The Tower of the Winds, unimpressively sited in Athens, was at Shug-borough placed in the middle of a lake. In the *Antiquities* Stuart had emphasized the importance of seeing and depicting buildings in their setting, and at Shugborough he must have been aware of what he was doing. For the first time in the history of Hellenism the Englishness of the English scene, green, northern and well watered, was consciously compared and contrasted with ancient Greece.

Among the members of the Dilettanti Society was the archaeolo-gist, philologist and politician Robert Wood, whose scholarly career, moving from architecture to literature, is a microcosm of the early history of English Hellenism. In 1751 he had drunk coffee with Stuart and Revett at the monument of Philopappus; then he had travelled eastward to study the temples of Baalbek and Palmyra. Wood was also a man of wide literary culture, and he took with him an extensive library of Greek authors. No previous visitor to this part of the world had possessed his wide knowledge of the ancient language: for the first time a modern traveller was able to steep himself in Greek literature amid Greek scenery. This novel experi-ence stirred within him a novel type of sentiment:[17] 'Circumstances of climate and situation, otherwise trivial, become interesting from that connection with great men . . . which history and poetry have given them: the life of Miltiades . . . could never be read with so much pleasure, as on the plain of Marathon . . . the Iliad has new beauties on the banks of the Scamander . . .' This conception of the special magic that places can acquire through their connection with great men and events, or through the associations breathed into them by poetry, is something still fresh in European thought. Stuart and Revett rediscovered Greek architecture, but Wood has a claim to be considered the first 'pilgrim' to Greece.

Homer, above all, haunted his thoughts. Pope had written mock-ingly to a friend in Constantinople, 'It is never to be repaired, the loss that Homer has sustained for want of my translating him in Asia.' But where Pope jested, Wood was serious: 'We proposed to read the

Iliad and Odyssey in the countries, where Achilles fought . . . and where Homer sung.'[18] Rambling about the Troad, Homer in hand, he became convinced that the poet had recorded its topography with exceptional accuracy. At the same time, his philological studies led him to another important conclusion: that Homer had been ignorant of writing. His *Essay on Homer* came out in 1767, went through five editions and was translated into four languages. In Germany it was to fall into the hands of a young philologist named Wolf, with momentous consequences for both scholarship and literature.

Pope had paid tribute to the 'Fire and Rapture' of Homer, contrasting his bold impetuosity with the elegance of Virgil.[19] But Pope's translation, whatever its merits, was not impetuous; Bentley's gibe was too accurate not to be remembered: 'A very pretty poem, but you must not call it Homer.' Pope excited interest in Homer, but ironically that very interest was to encourage the reaction against his own work. Wood attacked Pope on grounds that would now be called neoclassical: his aim was to 'justify the Original'. He blamed Pope for obscuring Homer's simplicity, and he proved his point by a devastating use of quotation.[20] Cowper set about a new translation of Homer, and associated his work with the reaction in the visual arts against rococo frippery, contrasting two French prints of scenes from the *Iliad* with an English one: 'In one of the former, Agamemnon addresses Achilles exactly in the attitude of a dancing-master turning miss in a minuet; in the latter, the figures are plain also. This is . . . the difference between my translation and Pope's.' He admitted that some of his lines have 'an ugly hitch in their gait, ungraceful in itself'; but they are 'made such with a willful intention'. 'Cowper . . . loves to be coarse,' was Macaulay's comment.[21]

An admiration for primitive art and society is a familiar element of later eighteenth-century taste. Rousseau praised the noble savage; Horace Walpole revived pointed architecture, which the renaissance had abusively called 'gothic'. Homer suited the taste for 'primitive' poetry; the reader who turned wearily from the Augustan perfection of Virgil looked inevitably to Virgil's grand original. At this period there was also a growing admiration for shaggy, uncultivated landscapes, and here too Homer had a part to play. Wood felt that the scenery of Ionia was marvellously unchanged from Homer's day; here nature was a delight, thanks to 'the elegant dishabille in which Homer and we found her'.[22] Thus a taste for Homer became intertwined with a romantic interest in topography and travel. Le Chevalier, indeed, pictured Homer as a romantic tourist like himself: 'Methinks I behold . . . Homer . . . doing . . . homage to the shade of Achilles. I see him walking with a . . . thoughtful mien, between the banks of the Simois and the Scamander. His eye . . . glances over the surrounding objects' (here a solemn footnote adds that if Homer was blind, he was not likely to have become so until old age); '. . . his imagination catches fire; the plan of the *Iliad* is formed.'[23]

This tells us more about the 1790s than about Homer. Le Chevalier had gone on pilgrimage to the scenes of the *Iliad*, and illogically pictures Homer himself paying homage to the imaginative power of his own poetry. He also started a controversy on which all sorts of people felt themselves entitled to hold an opinion. There could have been no better way of exciting interest in the *Iliad*; whichever side one was on, one was at least engaged in the question. He argued that Wood had got the site of Troy wrong, and proposed a new site. Jacob Bryant, free from any prejudice which a visit to the Troad might have engendered, retorted that the Trojan War had never taken place and that there was no city of Troy. The public was deluged with Vindications and Expostulations. As a controversy it had everything to recommend it: its followers could enjoy literary, historical and geographical speculation, taste the pleasure of armchair travel to distant climes, and indulge themselves with the ever delightful spectacle of learned men locked in acrimonious contention. Perhaps the most elegant (and best informed) contribution came from Richard Chandler, whose description of the Trojan War was gloriously bland: 'Homer has made us acquainted with some of the transactions, which happened during this interval.' Byron devoted a stanza of *Don Juan* to making fun of the contenders; but in the next stanza he dropped, for once, the flippant tone:

> High barrows, without marble or a name,
>   A vast, untill'd, and mountain-skirted plain,
> And Ida in the distance, still the same,
>   And old Scamander (if 'tis he), remain:
> The situation seems still form'd for fame—
>   A hundred thousand men might fight again
> With ease; but where I sought for Ilion's walls,
> The quiet sheep feeds, and the tortoise crawls.

Wood had sensed the nearness of the past at Troy; Byron, more eloquently, felt simultaneously the closeness of the past and its immeasurable distance from the present day. The paradox was to become familiar. Byron shared another of Wood's sentiments: 'It is one thing to read the Iliad . . . with Mount Ida above . . .; and another to trim your taper over it in a snug library—*this* I know.'

He tried to make fun of Bryant and his opponents, but the romance of Homer got the better of him. His language for a moment takes on the tone of religious apologetic; his belief in Homer's veracity is justified by faith: 'I've stood upon Achilles' tomb, And heard Troy doubted; time will doubt of Rome.'[24]

Even Robert Adam said he felt a desire to stand where Epaminondas had fought and Pericles counselled. When he published the *Ruins of . . . Spalatro* (1764), he admitted that he had been encouraged by Wood's volumes on Baalbek and Palmyra, adding, 'I am far from comparing my undertaking with that of Messieurs Dawkins, Bouverie, and Wood . . . I was not, like these gentlemen, obliged to travel deserts, or to expose myself to the insults of barbarians . . .'[25] The note of modesty, almost of apology, is significant. The thrill of exploration and the study of architecture were associated in the public mind: it is as though Adam ought to have found a few barbarians to insult him, and a desert or two to cross. This association of ideas was natural. Since the sixteenth century England had looked to Italy as the source of architectural inspiration, but access to this storehouse of wisdom was laborious and expensive: neither Wren nor Hawksmoor ever made the journey. However, the relative peace which Europe enjoyed for much of the eighteenth century and the steady growth in the wealth and power of Britain made continental travel increasingly easy. James Gibbs trained in Rome and this experience was found to give him an edge over other British architects of his time. Expediency as much as enthusiasm set Adam's feet upon classic ground.

In the preface to a folio of their designs (1778) the Adam brothers explained that architecture in Britain had improved in stages 'from the time, that our ancestors, relinquishing the gothick style, began to aim at an imitation of the Grecian manner, until it attained that degree of perfection at which it has now arrived'. This notion of a slow but successful struggle towards an ideal standard was the orthodoxy of the age. The belief that British architecture had steadily improved since the abandonment of the gothic style, combined firstly with a trust in the authority of ancient canons and secondly with the geographical isolation of Britain from lands where ancient buildings could be studied, made it inevitable that the progress of architecture should come to be seen as a sort of archaeological process, a gradual recovery of the true antiquity. But in that case, why stop at Italy? Vitruvius himself, as Stuart pointed out, looked to Greece as the fountainhead. The frontispiece of the Adams' folio depicted 'A Student conducted to Minerva, who points to Greece, and

Italy, as the Countries from whence he must derive the most perfect Knowledge & Taste in elegant Architecture.' The map to which she points is distorted to represent Greece directly below Italy; the moral is that the knowledge of correct architecture has progressed northward, from Greece to Italy, and from Italy—to England.

On the Continent, where the baroque and rococo styles had long been dominant, 'neoclassicism' took the form, in the first instance, of a theoretical and dogmatic reaction to their supposed excesses. In his *Essay on Architecture* (1753) M.-A. Laugier argued that buildings should be purely rational and functional; the rustic hut of primitive man was 'the model upon which all the magnificences of architecture have been imagined'.[26] Like Stuart and Revett's project, and like many of the most influential theories, Laugier's system was both conservative and radical; radical because it abolished pilasters, pedestals, false pediments and broken entablatures, conservative because the notion that architecture developed from the rustic cabin derives from Vitruvius. Other writers were quick to point out that the only way of combining the new purism with the old reverence for classical precedent was to go back to Greek models. And surely the Doric order, sturdy and plain, would prove to be the closest to Laugier's ideals. British architects came to Greek architecture by a more haphazard route; but they too were led towards the Doric order. When the Bodleian Library was erected early in the seventeenth century, its architect gave it a tower of five storeys, each decorated with columns belonging to one of the five orders: Tuscan, Roman Doric, Ionic, Corinthian, Composite. But one order, familiar to us, is missing: Greek Doric, which we know as 'Doric' pure and simple. Nowhere is the gulf between renaissance classicism and the Greek Revival more plainly visible: the Tower of the Five Orders is a self-conscious display of learning, but the first and grandest of the orders is absent, despite Vitruvius, and for the simple reason that not one example of it was known. The antiquarianism with which the progress of architecture had become associated in England was supposedly a pursuit of ever greater correctness, but in fact it put a premium on novelty: find a new type of classical architecture, and your reputation was made. The 'Etruscan' style, the elegances of Pompeii, the grandeur of Palmyra—all these were new discoveries, and all, at some time, enjoyed a vogue among architects. Now the principal novelty which Stuart and Revett found at Athens was the Doric order in its most perfect form. The Ionic order was favoured by Stuart himself and played an important role in the Greek Revival, but the Doric had the advantage of being more completely unfamiliar, and better suited to neoclassical ideals. There was also more scope for varying the dimensions of Doric buildings; the Ionic style was exceedingly pure and refined, but for that very reason a small deviation from the best proportions could be disastrous.

When the second volume of Stuart and Revett appeared, the public at last had an accurate representation of the masterpieces of Athenian Doric architecture. Now the pent-up force of Greek Revivalism burst forth; Latrobe, Harrison and Bonomi began to put up strong, original buildings in the new manner. For a little while, however, the advocates of the Greek style could still feel modestly *avant-garde*, for Sir William Chambers, who as Comptroller of the Works headed the architectural profession, launched a ferocious attack upon it; but he used such bad arguments that he strengthened his opponents' cause. Impudent young Reveley, who edited the third volume of the *Antiquities of Athens*, danced gaily round his elderly adversary: Chambers had alleged that the Parthenon was smaller than Saint Martin in the Fields, and Reveley gave the dimensions to refute him.

> Artists who . . . ever read Vitruvius [he continued with the maddening condescension of a young man certain that he is right], know that Saint Martin's Church . . . is . . . a very inferior imitation of the Greek Prostyle temple . . . Sir William seems to insinuate . . . that the Parthenon would gain . . . by the addition of a steeple. A judicious observer . . . would scarcely be more surprized were he to propose to effect this improvement by adding to it a Chinese pagoda.[27]

This last sentence was a good hit: Chambers had designed the pagoda at Kew.

Chambers had censured Doric buildings for their 'gouty columns' and 'disproportionate architraves'. Reveley's reply shows that the dispute was not simply about facts: he admired the very qualities that Chambers condemned. 'The entablature,' he agreed, 'is ponderous and its decorations few . . . and of a strong character.' 'Ponderous' is an epithet of praise. 'The Grecian Doric,' he continued, 'is by many censured for clumsiness.' But what matter? It possessed 'a masculine boldness', 'a solemn and majestic feeling', an 'awful dignity and grandeur'.[28] Here is the voice of the new generation: Stuart would not have used such romantic terms. Reveley's language reveals that the Greek style, oddly enough, might provide in architectural terms the thrill of agreeable horror that the reading public sought from the 'gothick' novel. The energetic grandeur of the

Greeks could breathe life and fire into the cold, smooth body of eighteenth-century classicism.

An interest in architecture and a taste for travel and topography were the dominant forces leading Englishmen towards Hellenism. Byron presented Greece to his public as a country where the beauty of art, the beauty of nature and the beauty of association were magically and uniquely combined. With this sentiment of pilgrimage there was mingled a spirit of almost boyish adventurousness which gradually faded as the century wore on; but in early Victorian times there must still have been many old gentlemen, like George Eliot's Mr. Brooke, with dim memories of past travels in a still half-unknown Greece. When Cockerell had become the leading architect of the last phase of the Greek Revival, did he recall that in his youth he had serenaded Byron in his boat near Athens, and run naked round the tomb of Patroclus?[29] To be young, and in Greece, had been very heaven.

Meanwhile the Germans were approaching the shrine by a different road. Like the English, they enjoyed speaking of Hellas in religious language, but in the manner less of pilgrims than of visionaries. Neither Winckelmann nor Lessing nor Goethe ever saw Greece for himself; and to the German mind Hellas became a sort of heavenly city, a shimmering fantasy on the far horizon. This emotion was one element in English Hellenism also; for Shelley, Athens was 'a city such as vision Builds from the purple crags and silver towers Of battlemented cloud'—a different picture from that of Byron, who disparaged the Attic scenery, and remarked that the Parthenon was very like the Mansion House.[30] Winckelmann, the father of German Hellenism, based his idea of the Greeks on their sculpture; gazing at the Laocoön in Rome, he decided, with a perversity so astounding that it amounts almost to genius, that this complex contorted *tour de force* of agonized expressionism showed that the essential qualities of all Greek art were noble simplicity and calm grandeur. Indirectly, through Goethe, Schiller and Schlegel, he was to have a great influence in England; but from 1807 onwards, when the Elgin Marbles were put on public display in London, the English had to try to reconcile his idea of Greek sculpture with the actuality. The reconciliation was imperfect, for though the marbles were certainly calm and grand, the fluidity of their modelling and the monumentality of the pedimental figures excited in their admirers a spirit of agitated romanticism. They filled Keats with a 'dizzy pain'; and Hazlitt wrote, 'The flesh has the softness . . . of flesh, not the . . . stiffness of stone. There is an undulation . . . on the surface, as the breath of genius moved the mighty mass.'[31] Indeed the combination of classic and romantic in the sculptures—much like that in Doric architecture—was in harmony with the spirit of the romantic age.

'De Greeks were Godes,' Fuseli shouted on first seeing the marbles. It was not only sculpture that inspired this feeling; Shelley called the Greeks 'glorious beings whom the imagination almost refuses to figure to itself as belonging to our kind', and Macaulay confessed that on this subject he loved 'to forget the accuracy of a judge, in the veneration of a worshipper'.[32] These reverential attitudes were to lead later to an uncritical sentimentality, but for the time being the Greeks were a strong inspiration. In the twentieth century those disaffected with their own society have been able to idealize fascist or communist systems; in the last century there were no such alternative societies in the civilized world, and ancient Greece performed the role that has been given more recently to Russia and China. For agnostics and atheists, Hellas was the supreme example of a non-Christian society that had reached the highest degree of humane civilization; for radicals Athens was the state that had come closest to political perfection. Paine saw 'more to admire, and less to condemn, in that great . . . people, than in anything which history affords'.[33]

This belief was not shared by contemporary historians. In 1786 John Gillies dedicated his history of Greece to the king with the assurance that the subject exposed 'the dangerous Turbulence of Democracy'; Mitford's more famous *History* (1784–1810) exhibited, in Macaulay's words, 'a marked partiality for Lacedaemon, and a dislike of Athens'. 'His great pleasure is in praising tyrants,' was the blunter comment of Byron, who admitted none the less that he was 'perhaps the best of all modern historians'. His virtues were 'labour, learning, research, wrath, and partiality. I call the latter virtues in a writer, because they make him write in earnest.' This was praising with faint damns indeed. Mill too confessed that as a child he had read Mitford with ever fresh enjoyment, despite his dislike of the writer's Toryism.[34] Mitford's greatest service, in fact, was to excite the wrath and partiality of his opponents. In the pages of the reviews Tories and liberals fought over Athens like Greeks and Trojans over the body of Patroclus. Thirlwall complained of 'the attempts, which for the last forty years have been systematically made . . ., for political and other purposes, to vilify the Athenians'.[35] Both he and Grote wrote their histories in part with a polemical intention, to destroy Mitford's legacy and vindicate their favourite city. Until the later eighteenth century Greek democracy had seldom aroused much enthusiasm; it was with delighted excitement that liberals and radicals discovered that they had allies far back in the past, and with eagerness that they rushed to defend these long dead friends from slander. Matthew Arnold was to write that in contemplating Greece 'our gaze . . . is fixed on Pericles rather than Epaminondas';[36] this now seems a truism, but it could not have been said in any century before the nineteenth.

'The battle of Marathon,' Mill declared, 'even as an event in English history, is more important than the battle of Hastings'. Marathon was the place where Byron dreamed that Greece might yet be free;[37] the association of the ancient Greeks with 'liberty' (a vague word) was strengthened and lent glamour by the struggle of the modern Greeks for independence. (The banditti who fought the Turks were not always sensible of these ancient associations: 'Who is this Achilles?' one of them asked. 'Has the musket of Achilles killed many?')[38] Christians and pagans, radicals and conservatives could all feel eager for the independence of the Greeks. Once they were free, the Greeks lost much of their glamour, and in the 1850s their discontent at the British alliance with Turkey in the Crimean War was to earn them much unpopularity, but in the early part of the century Hellenism and popular philhellenism went hand in hand, each stimulating the other.

The first part of the century is the great epoch of Grecian taste in literature, architecture, furniture, and even in dress ('Ross's . . . Grecian volute headdress, formed from the true marble models . . .').[39] It is easy for us to think of the Victorian age, with its Gothic enthusiasm, as a period of reaction against the Hellenism of an earlier generation; the Victorians themselves thought differently. 'We are all Greeks,' Shelley said, and this sentiment was to be echoed again and again throughout the century. Swinburne called Greece the 'mother-country of thought and art and action'; John Addington Symonds declared that all civilized nations were colonies of Hellas. As Kingsley explained in a book for children, 'You can hardly find a well-written book which has not in it Greek names, and words . . .; you cannot walk through a great town without passing Greek buildings; you cannot go into a well-furnished room without seeing Greek statues and ornaments, even Greek patterns of furniture and paper . . .' More remarkably still, Ruskin wrote in 1873, 'We have lost all inheritance from Florence and Venice, and are now pensioners upon the Greeks only.'[40]

To some Englishmen Hellenism seemed alien to the time and place in which they found themselves; the Gothic spirit appeared to be their natural inheritance. Others took the opposite view: Hazlitt thought that the Middle Ages seemed darker and older than 'the brilliant and well-defined periods of Greece and Rome', and at the other end of the century Wilde was to agree: 'Whatever . . . is modern . . . we owe to the Greeks. Whatever is anachronism is due to medievalism.'[41] The tension between these two views—and it is not uncommon to find both of them held by the same person—is central to Victorian Hellenism. Whatever a man's own opinion might be, it was hard for him to avoid the awareness that Greek influences were all around him. The range of nineteenth-century books that cannot be printed without the use of Greek type is extraordinarily wide; it includes Newman's *Apologia, Modern Painters, Culture and Anarchy,* Mill on Liberty, *Pendennis, Coningsby, Jude the Obscure, Don Juan, Tom Brown's Schooldays, Eric; or, Little by Little, Nightmare Abbey,* all but one of George Eliot's novels, even *Lorna Doone* and a couple of Gilbert and Sullivan's operettas. But this is a crude test to apply; often the ideas and actions which had been most deeply influenced by Greece were those that appeared the less Hellenic on the surface: Ruskin (for example) gained far more from the study of Greece than Landor, and indeed much of the work of (say) Tennyson or Hopkins or George Eliot was un-Greek on Greek principles. The Greeks themselves had been experimenters; and the best Hellenists had the power to transform what they took from Greece. In the middle of the Victorian age Hellenism was subtly pervasive; it was not the name of a fashion or a movement. True, there was always some tendency for people to use the Greeks as a means of confirming their own prejudgements, and when this tendency became dominant, Hellenism soon ceased to be a living force; but in the first instance the rediscovery of Greece was, like the discovery of Australia or of uranium, an event with varied potential and uncertain consequences. Keats said that to read Greek literature was 'to visit dolphin-coral in deep seas';[42] it was an exploration, and explorers do not always know what they will find or even whether they will like it.

One element in the Greek Revival was a scholarly purism. A second was the austere virility associated mainly with the Doric order. A third was the use of Greek forms, sometimes much altered, to produce an original, experimental type of architecture; in the work of Soane especially this verges on a 'stylelessness' that looks forward to the end of the century. A fourth element, prominent in the later stages of the Greek Revival, when it was already losing ground to the Goths, was an eclecticism which blended Hellenic forms with others derived from the Italian renaissance; Cockerell was the most accomplished exponent of this style, which again looks forward to the end of the century. A fifth was the use of Greek ornamentation on buildings that were still essentially Georgian in plan and proportion. This was by far the commonest pattern that the Greek Revival took, for who knew what Greek houses had really been like?—and the forms of Greek temples were not readily adaptable to domestic use.

In its grander and purer forms the Greek style in architecture never gained much popular affection, and in its commoner forms the Hellenic features were somewhat superficial. To its enemies, therefore, it seemed the product of hypocrisy. 'Do you seriously imagine, reader,' Ruskin asked, 'that any living soul in London likes triglyphs?—or gets any hearty enjoyment out of pediments?' Gothic buildings, however, were natural and lovable; Ruskin pointed out that British children enjoyed drawing pictures of medieval churches and castles; one did not catch them drawing Parthenon fronts.[43] Indeed, Pugin's advocacy of Gothic art was in large part patriotic: 'There is no need of visiting . . . Greece and Egypt to make discoveries in art. England alone abounds in . . . antiquities of surpassing interest.'[44] (He shocked Newman by insisting that St. Peter's itself was pagan; 'If only that dome would collapse!'[45] Given his way, he would have rebuilt it in the English Middle Pointed style, while the Apostolic Palace might now look like a very fair imitation of the St. Pancras Hotel.) As he said, the medieval cathedrals were the largest and most glorious buildings that Englishmen saw about them; they had Gothic bred into their bones. None the less, he also shared the feeling that the Greek style belonged naturally in the modern world; indeed, that was the basis of his objection to it. The illustrations to his *Contrasts* associate the 'new square style', symbolized by a carpenter's measuring instruments, with the drabness of modern industrial life, with its peelers and mechanics' institutes and mass production; his Gothic world, by contrast, is a realm of idealizing fantasy, filled with saintly monks and pious beadsmen.

The slender Gothic towers of New College rise above the solid Greek bulk of the National Gallery in the heart of Edinburgh. Both buildings were designed by W. H. Playfair; he took the view of the Greek Revivalists that Gothic was the more fragile and attenuated style. Pugin turned this view upside down; and the skimpy design and cheap construction of many recent buildings gave substance to his case. James Elmes confessed ruefully, 'We had converted Greek architecture into the most humdrum sort of design. Nay it . . . paralysed our powers of design . . ., so that the only alternative left was to escape . . . by plunging *headlong* into the Gothic and Italian styles.'[46] Elizabethan classicism had been ebulliently, inventively, sometimes magically wrong; the new Grecianism suffered perhaps from an excess of correctitude. Burke tells us that a constitution without the means of some change is without the means of its own preservation; and the like is true of an architectural style. Looking back in 1880, the judicious Lewis Day wondered how far the Gothic revival had owed its attractiveness to the 'possibility of achieving something like success'; 'Gothic work . . . does depend far less upon perfection of execution. . . . In the very perfection of Greek . . . art there is . . . something deterrent. . . . Dare we enter into rivalry where anything less than perfection is utter failure?'[47] Ruskin had put the matter in moralistic terms: the repetitiousness of Greek ornament was servile; it made the workman a slave.

Ruskin listed the characteristics of the Gothic builder as Savageness or Rudeness, Love of Change, Love of Nature, Disturbed Imagination, Obstinacy, Generosity. Today almost all these characteristics sound strikingly Victorian. The spirit of the age was all for exuberant fancy, profuse ornament and richness of detail; it was suffused with that 'love of complexity and quantity' which Ruskin detected in himself.[48] When he thought about Greek architecture he found himself painfully torn: on the one hand, he deeply admired the Greeks, and insisted that their literature ought not to be studied in isolation from their art; on the other, his theories exalted Gothic architecture and compelled him, so it seemed, to attack the classical manner. Architecture and ancient Greece were two of the chief preoccupations of his life; ancient Greek architecture brought them together, and they clashed. The tension is apparent in *The Seven Lamps of Architecture*; a judicious and not unfavourable account of Greek aesthetic principles, showing how they differed from Gothic, is interrupted by a sudden outburst. 'The Byzantines had truer sympathy with what God made majestic, than the self-contemplating and self-contented Greek. I know that they are barbaric in comparison; but there is a power in their barbarism . . . which . . . could not bury itself in acanthus leaves.' Ruskin seems to have shocked himself by this blasphemy against Hellas, for he later added a footnote: 'The bit about self-contented Greeks must be omitted. A noble Greek was as little content without God, as . . . St. Francis.'[49] Elsewhere, indeed, he spoke with veneration; no architecture, he declared, had so stern a claim to men's reverence as Venetian Gothic: 'I do not except even the Greek Doric.' This was high praise of the Greeks, and yet he felt bound to add a cautionary note: 'The Doric manner of ornament admitted no temptation; it was the fasting of an anchorite—the Venetian ornament embraced . . . all vegetable and animal forms; it was the temperance of a man, the command of Adam over creation.'[50] He prefers the Venetians on 'Protestant' grounds; like Milton, he cannot praise a fugitive and cloistered virtue. But he allowed that the Parthenon was one of the most perfect buildings in the world, and many of his criticisms of the Greek Revival were almost a tribute to the style that it imitated: 'The most familiar position of Greek mouldings is in these days on shop fronts. There is not a tradesman's sign , . . which has not upon it ornaments which were invented to adorn temples and beautify kings' palaces. There is not the smallest advantage in them where they are . . . they only . . . vulgarise their own forms.'[51] These are the terms, very nearly, in which he condemned the use of the Gothic style for railway stations; its purity should not be polluted by the sordid facts of steam locomotion. In *The Stones of Venice* he treated Greek architecture as both symbol and fountainhead: 'All European architecture . . . is derived from Greece through Rome. . . . The history of architecture is nothing but the tracing of the various modes . . . of this derivation . . . the Doric and the Corinthian orders are the roots, the one of all Romanesque massy-capitalled buildings . . .; and the Corinthian of all Gothic . . . there are only two real orders, and there can never be any more until Doomsday.'[52] His argument was that all capitals are in essence either convex or concave. The former are Doric, the latter Corinthian; the Greeks formed the pattern for all time. Yet even this compliment is backhanded, for in the sense in which there are five classical orders, based on certain canons of proportion and forms of decoration, there are, as he goes on to explain, thousands upon thousands of Gothic and Romanesque orders. In these latter styles every capital, every column creates its own order. So the Gothic style is infinitely more inventive than the Greek.

The conflict within Ruskin may stand as a symbol for the conflict that ran through the Victorian age as a whole. Throughout this time Greece engaged the enthusiasm of a splendid variety of disparate men. It is perhaps not surprising that such monuments of nineteenth-century energy as Gladstone and Macaulay should prolong the studies that they had pursued at school and university throughout their lives; but that Swinburne (say) should pore over Greek books with such passionate eagerness—Swinburne who jumped up and down on the top hats in the Arts Club, who skipped stark naked through the rooms of Tudor House—that is altogether more remarkable. We do not commonly turn to Wilde in pursuit of truth, but he was not far wrong when he wrote, 'It is really from the union of Hellenism, in its breadth . . ., its calm possession of beauty, with the passionate colour of the romantic spirit, that springs the art of the nineteenth century in England.'[53]

II

THE DEATH OF POETRY

I thought how markedly . . . these works participate in that quality of being—albeit marvellously—always incomplete, which is the peculiarity of all the great works of the nineteenth century, with which the greatest writers of that century have stamped their books, but, watching themselves at work as though they were at once author and critic, have derived from this self-contemplation a novel beauty.

Proust[1]

A YOUNG poet introducing his first large work to the world is wise to be modest, and it was perhaps natural that Keats should write in the preface to *Endymion*, 'I hope I have not in too late a day touched the beautiful mythology of Greece, and dulled its brightness.' But the diffidence was not assumed; the same theme invades the poem itself:[2]

> O fountained hill! Old Homer's Helicon,
> That thou wouldst spout a little streamlet o'er
> These sorry pages! Then the verse would soar . . .
>   . . . But all is dark
> Around thine agèd top, and thy clear fount
> Exhales in mists to heaven. Aye, the count
> Of mighty poets is made up . . .
> The world has done its duty. Yet, oh yet,
> Although the sun of poetry is set,
> These lovers did embrace, and we must weep
> That there is no old power left to steep
> A quill immortal in their joyous tears.

Keats is not speaking just of himself: there is no one at all, he claims, who can write great poetry any more. This failure of confidence may seem strange in the age of Wordsworth, Coleridge, Byron and Shelley, but it is an attitude that runs through much nineteenth-century literature. Its origins are in the experience of an earlier generation. 'By the general consent of critics,' wrote Johnson, 'the first praise of genius is due to the writer of an epic poem';[3] yet the eighteenth century produced no great epic poem, either in England or anywhere else. The critics called for epic, but the poets failed to provide it, and this failure was bound to produce a sense of defeat. Shelley wrote, 'The human mind attained to a perfection in Greece which has impressed its image on those faultless productions, whose very fragments are the despair of modern art.'[4] It was not a dead metaphor, that word 'despair'.

Thirty years before Keats even Goethe had felt the same oppression. In the spring of 1787 he had travelled south from Rome, crossed the Straits of Messina and journeyed on to Palermo. And there he had a revelation. Fifteen years before he had described Werther reading the *Odyssey* as he drank his coffee under the lime trees; now he was reading the poem in the holiday atmosphere of a Sicilian spring. He recited the story of Nausicaa aloud with rapture; as never before he seemed to realize all the glory of Homer's art. And yet Homer's greatness must also have been dispiriting to him, as events were to show. In 1795 F. A. Wolf published his *Prolegomena to Homer*. The contents were even drier than the title; yet probably this work had a greater impact than any other work of philology that has ever been written. What he did was to invent the Homeric question, which has dominated Homeric scholarship ever since, right up to the present day. He argued that neither the *Iliad* nor the *Odyssey* was the work of a single poet; instead, each was a collection of ballads composed by diverse bards. This theory thrilled Goethe: suddenly he was no longer crushed by the weight of Homer's greatness for the simple reason that Homer had never existed. Accordingly he embarked upon *Herman and Dorothea*, designed as a modern bourgeois equivalent of the *Odyssey*. Then, flushed with its success, he thought of retelling the story of the *Iliad*; but after writing a few hundred lines of his *Achilles*, he abandoned it in despair. Realizing that the *Iliad* is inimitable, he returned to the view that it was composed by a single poet. The oppression settled over him once more and never again did he attempt epic poetry. In his old age, when he was widely regarded as the greatest man alive in the world (a view that he seems to have shared), he declared that modern writers could create only heroines: 'Nothing can be done with the men. Homer has got all beforehand in Achilles and Odysseus, the bravest and the most prudent.'[5]

But perhaps the English romantics did produce a great epic after all. Quiller-Couch thought so: 'I believe *Don Juan* will someday be recognized for one of the world's few greatest epics,' he wrote. 'I am sure that it is, after *Paradise Lost*, our second English epic.'[6] How-

ever, *Don Juan* is only an epic in a peculiar sense. Byron too felt the
weight of past greatness crushing the strength out of the modern
poet. *Childe Harold's Pilgrimage* opens with these lines:

> O thou! in Hellas deemed of heavenly birth,
> Muse! form'd or fabled at the minstrel's will!
> Since shamed full oft by later lyres on earth,
> Mine dares not call thee from thy sacred hill
> Yet there I've wander'd by thy vaunted rill;
> Yes! Sigh'd o'er Delphi's long deserted shrine,
> Where, save that feeble fountain, all is still;
> Nor mote my shell awake the weary Nine
> To grace so plain a tale—this lowly lay of mine.

The great name of Hellas, resonant with ancient splendour, is contrasted with the 'poetrylessness' of the present age (to borrow
Matthew Arnold's graceless word); Byron associates the ruin of
Greece and the ruin of poetry together. In *English Bards and Scotch
Reviewers* he declares that once, when Homer and Virgil wrote, epic
poetry had been possible;[7] even so, all antiquity produced only two
great epics (he counts the *Iliad* and *Odyssey* as one poem). Now
epics are commonplace and debased: the mighty genius of Southey
has already produced no less than three, *Joan of Arc*, *Madoc* and
Thalaba ('Which,' Porson said, 'will be read when Homer and
Virgil are forgotten, but—not till then'). But even the industrious
Southey felt that the day of epic was passed, for he had written, as
Byron noted ironically, '*Madoc* disdains the degraded title of epic.'
   In *Don Juan* Byron found a solution—after a fashion:[8]

> My poem's epic, and is meant to be
>   Divided in twelve books: each book containing,
> With love, and war, a heavy gale at sea,
>   A list of ships, and captains, and kings reigning,
> New characters; the episodes are three:
>   A panoramic view of hell's in training,
> After the style of Virgil and of Homer,
> So that my name of epic's no misnomer.

This burlesque suggests that epic is an absurdity in the nineteenth
century, but it also opens the way for something new, a parody epic.
Don Juan is satire, but on a colossal scale; 'this epic satire', in
Byron's own phrase.[9] If Homer composed primary epic and Virgil

and Milton secondary epic, *Don Juan* could perhaps be called a tertiary epic. Byron makes fun of worn-out conventions: 'Hail, Muse! *et cetera.*—' is the insouciant beginning of Canto III.

Like Keats, he cannot resist bringing on the ghost of Homer:[10]

> The work of glory still went on
>   In preparations for a cannonade
> As terrible as that of Ilion,
>   If Homer had found mortars ready made;
> But now, instead of slaying Priam's son,
>   We only can but talk of escalade,
> Bombs, drums, guns, bastions, batteries, bayonets, bullets;
> Hard words, which stick in the soft Muses' gullets.
>
> Oh thou eternal Homer! Who couldst charm . . .
> By merely wielding, with poetic arm,
>   Arms to which men will never more resort,
> Unless gunpowder should be found to harm,
>   Much less than is the hope of every court . . .

This is comedy, black and grotesque though it be, but Byron has a serious point to make as well. As he says later, 'War's a brain-spattering, windpipe-slitting art', and poets no longer have the stomach to glorify 'the blaze Of conquest and its consequences, which Make epic poesy so rare and rich.'[11] Here he is concerned not with the oppressive weight of past poetry but with the oppressive horror of modern life. War is now ugly and unromantic, and the poetry of war must become unromantic too. When he began *Don Juan* Napoleon was still alive on St. Helena; Byron knew what he was talking about, and it is a pity that he was not heeded. As the long prosperous years of the Pax Britannica succeeded one another, the truth about war was forgotten, and in 1914 young officers went into battle with the *Iliad* in their knapsacks and the names of Achilles and Hector engraved upon their hearts. This time the disillusionment was to be lasting.

In his seventh canto Byron addresses Homer directly:[12]

> O thou eternal Homer! I have now
>   To paint a siege, wherein more men were slain,
> With deadlier engines and a speedier blow,
>   Than in thy Greek gazette of that campaign;
> And yet, like all men else, I must allow,
>   To vie with thee would be about as vain

As for a brook to cope with ocean's flood
But still we moderns equal you in blood;

If not in poetry, at least in fact;
And fact is truth, the grand desideratum!

Fact, fact, fact; we hear this complaint again and again in the nineteenth century. There were indeed other reasons for believing in the
poetrylessness of the modern world than the fear that everything
worth saying had been said already. Firstly, there was a feeling that
the new era was in intellectual terms a scientific age; that scientific
thought, hard, remorseless and factual, was draining the magic and
fantasy out of the world. More important still were the visible
consequences of the Industrial Revolution, which inspired emotions
that could only intensify as time went by: year by year, almost day
by day, Englishmen could see England growing uglier. Peacock
worked these ideas and emotions into a half serious, half humorous
essay called *The Four Ages of Poetry*; his aim was to show by analogy
with the history of Greece that to write good poetry was now
impossible. Poetry may be said to have four ages, he wrote: the ages
of Iron, Gold, Silver and Brass. The first poets were rude bards, but
then came the Golden Age, at a time when 'Nature is still un-
subdued . . . and men are not yet excluded from her observation by
the magnitude of cities.' At this period poetry has the whole field of
intellect to itself without rivals in history or science: 'It is the age of
Homer, the Golden Age of poetry. Poetry has now obtained its
perfection: . . . genius therefore seeks new forms . . . hence the lyric
poetry of Pindar . . . and the tragic poetry of Aeschylus and
Sophocles.' But in the fifth century poetry begins to give way to
prose: 'The maturity of poetry may be considered the infancy of
history.' At this point Peacock leaps forward four centuries: Virgil is
a 'silver' poet *par excellence*, recasting and polishing the poetry of the
Age of Gold (the metaphor gets rather confused here). Finally we
arrive at a Brass Age, which tries to get back to the Age of Gold but
produces only crude verbosity.

This is an intriguing example of the effect of Hellenism on a theory
about the modern world; the argument could not have been produced
before the neoclassical age, because it involves seeing the whole of
Latin literature as no more than an appendix to Greek. Now Greek
literary history does indeed have a peculiar simplicity. First come the
Homeric epics, followed by the age of lyric poetry, which begins in
the seventh century and reaches its climax with Pindar in the fifth.

At this point the great line of lyric poets comes abruptly to an end. The fifth century was above all the age of drama; a single city produced Aeschylus, Sophocles and Euripides, as well as the comic genius of Aristophanes; yet Greek tragedy comes to an end even more sudden and puzzling than that of lyric. The great age of prose overlaps with the age of drama. First come the historians Herodotus and Thucydides, then in the fourth century the philosophers Plato and Aristotle, and the orators, above all Demosthenes. In this century the Greek world produced no poet of eminence. Provided we do not look beyond the death of Alexander, Greek literary history does indeed seem to fall into four distinct periods, the ages of epic, lyric, drama and prose. But there is no good reason to suppose that the Greek experience obeys a universal law of human development. Latin literature cannot be sorted into such tidy pigeon-holes, and only by demoting it in favour of Greek could Peacock make his theory plausible.

However, his imagination is so dominated by ancient Greece that he attempts to force more recent literature into the same strait-jacket. Modern poetry, he argues, has also gone through four ages: first comes medieval romance; then Shakespeare and Ariosto; the third period runs from Dryden to Gray; and we are now in the fourth age. Therefore the modern 'return to nature' is necessarily bogus: 'In the origin and perfection of poetry all the associations of life were composed of poetical materials. . . . We know too well that there are no dryads in Hyde Park nor naiads in the Regent's Canal. But barbaric manners and supernatural inventions are essential to poetry.' So the modern poet, ignoring the achievements of historians and philosophers, is merely 'wallowing in the rubbish of departed ignorance'. These are revealing sentences. Peacock associates the advance of scientific knowledge with the prosaic drabness of the urban scene; in fact, we know equally well that there are no naiads in Dovedale or oreads on Helvellyn, but this does not occur to him. He praises progress and useful knowledge, but condemns modern literature wholesale: 'To read the promiscuous rubbish of the present time to the exclusion of the select treasures of the past is to substitute the worse for the better variety of the same mode of enjoyment.' Progress, in fact, means 'read more Greek'. The conclusion is surprising; and significant. Peacock anticipated the essay on Milton in which the young Macaulay analysed the obstacles which the advance of culture and civilization had erected in the path of the would-be epic poet: *Paradise Lost* was a success realized against almost impossible odds, and an achievement which could scarcely be repeated. Both essayists drew on ideas that were already in the air: Schiller had distinguished between naïve and sentimental poetry, Saint-Simon between the organic and critical periods of human history. The sense of belonging to a secondary age was strong throughout Europe, and only a painful distress at the practical effects of industrialization was distinctive of English writers.

Poe complained in a sonnet *To Science*,

> Why preyest thou thus upon the poet's heart,
>   Vulture, whose wings are dull realities? . . .
> Hast thou not dragged Diana from her car? . . .
> Hast thou not torn the Naiad from her flood,
> The Elfin from the green grass, and from me
>   The summer dream beneath the tamarind tree?

Clough expended his indignation more specifically upon the Industrial Revolution; like Peacock, and unlike ourselves, he enjoyed abusing canals:[13]

>   To live now
> I must sluice out myself into canals,
> And lose all force in ducts. The modern Hotspur
> Shrills not his trumpet of 'To Horse, To Horse!'
> But consults columns in a Railway Guide;
> A demigod of figures; an Achilles
> Of computation . . .

Disraeli's Grandison blames the weakening of the church and the rise of democracy; the age of faith is over, he says, and without religion there will soon be 'universal desolation': 'I do not believe there could be another Dante, even another Milton. The world is devoted to physical science.'[14] The difference in the explanations given for the failure of poetry is eloquent, for it shows how widely it was assumed, without question, that modern poetry had indeed failed.

Many of these condemnations were superficial, and may well have galled such poets as did not join in them. Mrs. Browning put a protest into the mouth of her heroine, the poetess Aurora Leigh:[15]

> The critics say that epics have died out
> With Agamemnon and the goat-nursed gods—
> I'll not believe it. I could never dream . . .
> That Homer's heroes measured twelve feet high.
> They were but men!—his Helen's hair turned grey

Like any plain Miss Smith's, who wears a front . . .
All men are possible heroes: every age . . .
Looks backward and before, expects a morn
And claims an epos.

Epos—the word is redolent of Carlyle, and sure enough, Aurora's
thoughts turn next in his direction:[16]

Ay, but every age
Appears to souls who live in it (ask Carlyle)
Most unheroic. Ours, for instance, ours!
The thinkers scout it, and the poets abound
Who scorn to touch it with a finger tip.

When we 'ask Carlyle', however, we find that he was not quite so
facile. Sharing the general doubt about the possibility of epic in his
own time, he jotted in his notebook, 'The old epics are great because
they . . . show us the *whole world* of those old days. A modern epic
that did the like would be equally admired. . . . But where is the
genius that can write it? . . . Is Art in the old Greek sense possible for
men at this late era? Or were not perhaps the founder of a religion
our true Homer at present? The *whole soul* must be illuminated.[17]
As he began the last section of his *French Revolution,* he called Homer
on to the stage to take a bow with him: 'Homer's Epos . . . is like a
Bas-relief sculpture: it does not conclude, but merely ceases. Such,
indeed, is the epos of Universal History itself.'[18] Earlier he had
asked, 'Are the true heroic poems of these times to be written with
the *ink of science*? Were a correct philosophic biography of a man . . .
the only method of celebrating him? The true history . . . the true
epic poem? I partly begin to surmise so.'[19] Epic might still be
feasible, but only in prose; it was a conclusion that gave little
consolation to the poets.

With an optimism that her verse hardly justifies, Mrs. Browning
decided that epic was still possible for the poet who was prepared to
set it in 'this live, throbbing age', which, as she bathetically
insisted,[20]

spends more passion, more heroic heat,
Betwixt the mirrors of its drawing rooms,
Than Roland with his knights, at Roncesvalles.
To flinch from modern varnish, coat or flounce,
Cry out for togas and the picturesque,
Is fatal—foolish too. King Arthur's self
Was commonplace to Lady Guenever;

And Camelot to minstrels seemed as flat
As Regent Street to poets.

The second of these sentences is possibly wise; the last displays a fatal superficiality. The notion that all times and places are equally commonplace, and are felt by those who live in them to be commonplace, is crude, although it was favoured by historical novelists. The opposite view, that certain ages are keenly aware of their own beauty and splendour, was brilliantly put by Ruskin; the chapter in which he contrasted the magnificence surrounding the young Giorgione in Venice with the squalor amid which Turner spent his London boyhood, if not totally convincing, is yet very largely so.[21] Mill similarly held that 'nothing contributes more to nourish elevation of sentiments in a people, than the large and free character of their habitations', and he contrasted 'the middle-age architecture' of Forde Abbey with 'the mean and cramped externals of English middle class life'.[22] In the last century, as today, one could compare, say, Oxford and Birmingham, and appreciate that the inhabitants of the former enjoyed a privilege which the others did not share. Aurora Leigh was unpersuasive.

  She was perhaps a little severe, too, in her criticism of the poets for retreating from the present time. After all, they had come under attack from the utilitarians, whose philosophy seemed to epitomise the hard, factual nature of modern life. Bingham wrote 'Mr. Moore *is* a poet, and therefore is *not* a reasoner', and Bentham declared bluntly, 'All poetry is misrepresentation.'[23] A later and subtler generation of utilitarians was to deplore this insensitivity; Mill regretfully detected in his mentors 'an undervaluing of poetry, and of Imagination generally, as an element of human nature'.[24] But this protest came too late; in the meantime the utilitarians appeared to have triumphed. English poetry went undeniably into decline. Keats, Shelley and Byron died in the space of a few years; even in their lifetimes they had felt that the age of poetry was over, and now a cruel destiny seemed resolved to give substance to their fears. True, Wordsworth was not silent, but perhaps it would have been better if he had been. And as it so happened, publishing slumped badly in the 1820s, especially the publishing of poetry.[25] The causes of this depression were complex and remain partly obscure, but a glib explanation was readily available in the triumph of science and utilitarianism. Lytton decided, 'The genius of this time is wholly anti-poetic', and suggested the reason: 'When Byron passed away, the feeling he had represented craved utterance no more . . . we awoke from the morbid, the passionate, . . . the death of a great poet invariably produces an indifference to the art itself. . . . Insensibly acted upon by the doctrine of the Utilitarians, we desired to see Utility in every branch of intellectual labour.'[26]

The personalities who seem to us quintessentially Victorian are not those whose entire lives were passed in the queen's reign— Hopkins, Pater, Wilde—but men born between 1800 and 1825: Gladstone, Dickens, Tennyson, Ruskin. (One of Strachey's Eminent Victorians, Thomas Arnold, died when Victoria had been on the throne less than five years.) The distinctive tone in English life which we call Victorian was set by men whose characters were formed at a time when it seemed that English poetry had sunk into insignificance. This feeling, or the memory of it, persisted a long time: *Aurora Leigh* was published in 1856, half a dozen years after Tennyson had taken the country by storm with *In Memoriam*, and yet the heroine complains that she was driven to write prose by the public indifference to new verse. FitzGerald had written nine years earlier, 'As I often think, it is not the poetical imagination, but bare Science that every day more and more unrolls a greater Epic than the Iliad'.[27]

Science and poetry were still eyeing one another warily in 1877, when Mallock published *The New Republic*. In this satire there are one or two scientists who are enthusiastic about their century; the other characters are all markedly weary of the world and at odds with the age in which they live. 'My own poems . . . could only have been written in evil days,' says Mr. Luke, a caricature of Matthew Arnold. 'They were simply a wail of pain; and now that I am growing braver, I keep silence. Poetry in some ages is an expression of the best strength; in an age like ours it is the disguise of the worst weakness.'[28] This is parody, but not unfair parody. No one felt more keenly than Arnold the difficulty of writing poetry amid the drab materialism of modern England; in 1853 he wrote, 'In the sincere endeavour to learn and practice, amid the bewildering confusion of our times, what is sound and true in practical art, I seemed . . . to find the only sure guidance, the only solid footing, among the ancients. They . . . knew what they wanted in art, and we do not. It is this uncertainty which is disheartening, and not hostile criticism.' These are touching words, and revealing. The present age, he explains, is 'wanting in moral grandeur'; it is 'an age of spiritual discomfort'.[29] He does not reflect that spiritual discomfort and moral uncertainty might be fertile soil for the growth of poetry. Perhaps he should have thought more deeply about those Athenians whom he so loved. The plays of Euripides, and even the *Antigone* of Sophocles and the *Prometheus* of Aeschylus, were surely produced in a time of intense spiritual discomfort, a time when the old moral certitudes were being undermined by the speculations of rationalistic philosophers. Arnold desperately wanted to be 'Greek'; if only he had been truly Greek, he would have been eager to make poetry out of his own unease, rather than aspiring to a strength and objectivity which fate had denied him.

However, there were some writers who, like Byron, found a way of turning weakness into strength, of using the contrast between epic past and prosaic present to serve the spirit of the age. George Eliot's *Middlemarch*, set in a workaday manufacturing town in the English midlands, unexpectedly opens with a discussion of St. Theresa, a woman whose 'passionate, ideal nature demanded an epic life'. But that is impossible for most women: 'Many Theresas have been born who found . . . no epic life . . . perhaps only a life of mistakes, the offspring of a certain spiritual grandeur, ill-matched with the meanness of opportunity; perhaps a tragic failure which found no sacred poet and sank unwept into oblivion.' There will be no great bards to glorify the ordinary heroisms, the commonplace tragedies of modern life; on the other hand prose is still possible, otherwise the next 900 pages would be so much waste of paper. There is even a positive advantage to prose: epic glorified exceptional men and deeds in the elevated language of poesy, but the novel could commemorate simple people and everyday events. As Aurora Leigh said, 'All men are possible heroes.'

Tennyson was another who tried to create strength out of weakness. He prefaced his *Morte d'Arthur* with a scene at a Christmas party; the host is asked why one of the guests, the poet Hall, has burnt his epic on King Arthur:[30]

> 'Oh! sir,
> He thought that nothing new was said, or else
> Something so said 'twas nothing—that a truth
> Looks freshest in the fashion of the day:
> God knows: he has a mint of reasons: ask.
> It pleased *me* well enough.' 'Nay, nay,' said Hall,
> 'Why take the style of those heroic times?
> For nature brings not back the Mastodon,
> Nor we those times; and why should any man
> Remodel models? these twelve books of mine
> Were faint Homeric echoes, nothing-worth . . .'

But it turns out that the eleventh book was rescued from the fire. Hall is persuaded to read it; and the *Morte d'Arthur* begins. The elaborate and rather flat preamble expresses Tennyson's sense that the age of heroic deeds, and therefore the age of epic poetry, is passed, vanished like the dinosaurs. Life now is cosy and jolly, like the Christmas party, but not the stuff of which epic is made; and in any case Homer has left poets with nothing to say in that line. Tennyson is often regarded, and justly, as one of the most Virgilian of English poets, but of Virgil nothing here is said; it is Homer who casts the withering shadow over modern verse.

The *Morte* is a mere fragment, and it is presented *as* a fragment; *In Memoriam* is, from one point of view, an elegy swollen to enormous length. Yet Tennyson himself described it as a sort of *Divine Comedy*,[31] and compared to Dante's epic, it looks almost as fragmentary as the *Morte d'Arthur* does when set beside the *Iliad*. Tennyson turns his lack of confidence almost into an artistic credo; he says that he is writing 'brief lays, of Sorrow born'; Sorrow takes a 'slender shade of doubt' and 'makes it vassal unto love':[32]

> And hence, indeed, she sports with words,
>   But better serves a wholesome law,
>   And holds its sin and shame to draw
> The deepest measure from the chords:
>
> Nor dare she trust a larger lay,
>   But rather loosens from the lip
>   Short swallow-flights of song, that dip
> Their wings in tears, and skim away.

The flight of a swallow is a beautiful thing, and its nervous motion, darting and flickering, is an essential part of that beauty. And likewise the hesitancy, the anxiousness of *In Memoriam* are an essential part of its quality and value.

Later Tennyson deliberately stands on its head a traditional poetic theme. Horace claimed to have built a monument more durable than bronze, loftier than the pyramids; this boast was repeated, more or less, by Ovid, and later by Shakespeare: 'Not marble, nor the gilded monuments Of princes, shall outlive this powerful rhyme'. Tennyson, however, declares that his rhyme is feeble and the monument of Hallam will outlast it:[33]

> Methinks my friend is richly shrined;
> But I shall pass; my work will fail.

'What hope is here for modern rhyme?' he asks, and contrasts his poetic weakness with the youthful strength of primitive poetry:[34]

> And if the matin songs, that woke
> The darkness of our planet, last,
> Thine own shall wither in the vast,
> Ere half the lifetime of an oak.

Dawn imagery was particularly associated with the Greeks; there is little doubt that Tennyson was thinking of them, and above all of Homer. He stresses the contrast between the vitality of the early poets and his own frailty in order to bring out the pathos of the human condition in his own time of doubts and uncertainties. Poetic inadequacy is eloquently associated with spiritual doubt:[35]

> So runs my dream: but what am I?
> An infant crying in the night:
> An infant crying for the light:
> And with no language but a cry.

Only if we see *In Memoriam* as 'a sort of *Divine Comedy*', can we understand why it ends with a long epilogue in which Tennyson abandons the subject of his dead friend and describes his sister's wedding. The main body of the poem is a hell, or purgatory, of sorrow; the marriage is an equivalent to Dante's *Paradise*, though it is, of course, no more than an earthly paradise. The bride enters 'glowing like the moon Of Eden on its bridal bower', and her eyes 'brighten like the star that shook Betwixt the palms of paradise'. But the work ends with Hallam in the heavenly paradise:[36]

> That friend of mine who lives in God,
>
> That God, which ever lives and loves,
> One God, one law, one element,
> And one far-off divine event,
> To which the whole creation moves.

The very last line of the poem is a reminiscence of the very last line of Dante's epic, where God is called 'The love that moves the sun and the other stars.' Tennyson had in mind one of Hallam's own poems containing an even closer echo of Dante: 'The Love Toward which all being solemnly doth move.'[37] So *In Memoriam* closes with a conscious memory of a greater poem and a greater poet: the echoes of a tremendous past vibrate to the very end.

Many attempts were made during Tennyson's lifetime to find modern forms for the mythology of Greece, among them William Morris's *Life and Death of Jason* and *Earthly Paradise*, and *The Epics of Hades* by his namesake Sir Lewis Morris, which enjoyed in its time an enormous popularity. When the Poet Laureate himself came to write his full-dress epic, *The Idylls of the King*, he took the opposite road; his theme was British, but he kept inserting phrases and quirks of language which recall Greek poetry. If we take his own notes on his description of Avilion—[38]

> Where falls not hail, or rain, or any snow,
> Nor ever wind blows loudly; but it lies
> Deep meadowed, happy, fair, with orchard lawns
> And bowery hollows crowned with summer sea.

—we find that on these four lines alone, he cites two passages from the *Odyssey*, one from the *Iliad*, and an ode of Pindar, as well as a celebrated imitation of the *Odyssey* by Lucretius. And apart from the many echoes of this kind, he also repeats lines in the manner of Homer, and mimics Greek idiom by beginning paragraphs with 'and' or 'for' or even 'but—for . . .'

The two poets who loom over the *Idylls of the King* are Homer and Tennyson's particular favourite Theocritus, the originator of pastoral verse. Renaissance critics had agreed that whereas epic was the loftiest of poetic forms, pastoral was the humblest and meanest; yet Tennyson blends these opposites together. There is a sort of paradox even in his title: 'Idylls' suggests the slenderness of Hellenistic art, while 'King' reverberates with the glory of heroic deeds. Tennyson's son records that the poet's brother-in-law Lushington used to refer to the 'Epylls of the King', because 'according to him they were little epics (not idylls) woven into an epical unity, but my father disliked the sound of the word epylls'.[39] As well he might.

He knew, of course, that he could not hope to rival Homer, and as with *In Memoriam* he consciously expressed his homage to a greater master. 'Idyll' is derived from the Greek *eidullion*, meaning a little picture, or a sketch; Tennyson himself pronounced it with a long 'i', as if to emphasize its etymology.[40] His *Idylls* contain 10,224 lines, more than the *Aeneid*; yet they are no more than a fragmentary epic, a collection of sketches. Byron turned epic into satire; Tennyson made it tentative, hesitant, troubled with doubts, and instinct with yearning for vanished beauties.

The *Idylls of the King* are certainly too diffuse and episodic; we shall, however, judge Tennyson's failure more sympathetically if we understand what he was trying to do. His son wrote,

> If epic unity is looked for in the 'Idylls', we find it not in the wrath of an Achilles, or in the wanderings of an Ulysses, but in the unending war of humanity in all ages—the worldwide war of sense and soul, . . . the central dominant figure being the pure, generous . . . Arthur,—so that the links . . . which bind the 'Idylls' into an artistic whole, are perhaps somewhat intricate.[41]

The defensive tone is unmistakable: Tennyson's contemporaries judged that unity was essential to an epic poem, and they doubted whether he had achieved it. Hallam Tennyson compares and contrasts his father's work with Homer; it is interesting to set his apologia beside the judgement of Gladstone, who knew Tennyson well and Homer intimately: 'We know not where to look . . . for a nobler . . . conception of man . . ., than in the Arthur of this volume. Wherever he appears, it is as the great pillar of the moral order, and the resplendent top of human excellence.'[42] These words reflect Tennyson's intention, if not his achievement. Both the Homeric epics are dominated by a single man, the *Odyssey* by Odysseus, the *Iliad* by Achilles; Tennyson designed Arthur for this central role. He tried to be in some sense Homeric; he failed because he was not Homeric enough. The *Iliad* is the poem not just of Achilles, but of Achilles' wrath; 'wrath' is its very first word. Tennyson intended to create an equivalent of this wrath; just as the anger of Achilles undermines the Greeks, bringing the Greek army to the brink of defeat and Achilles himself to the verge of moral disaster, so the cancer of adulterous passion spreads through Camelot, degrading its inhabitants and eventually bringing its society to collapse. But whereas Homer united heroic action and moral conflict in the single person of Achilles, Arthur remains apart from the plot of the *Idylls*. He seems irrelevant. Tennyson's other fundamental mistake was to make the Arthurian world too insubstantial. We first see the city of Camelot through the eyes of the young Gareth; it is magical, unreal, a symbol rather than a reality, the baseless fabric of a vision. The Homeric world is so solid. How well we know the little plain of Troy—the rivers Simois and Scamander, the walls and the fig tree, and the sea beyond with the Greek ships drawn up along the beach. It is a real battleground, and the heroes themselves are no less actual; Hector, Ajax, Odysseus, Agamemnon—we know them all. But no one *cares* for Arthur or Lancelot or Guinevere; Tennyson's poem has many beauties, but the story does not engage our emotions.

Perhaps the finest analysis of why such a work was bound to fail had already been made back in 1857, when Matthew Arnold gave his lecture *On the Modern Element in Literature*. His title was paradoxical, for he dealt mainly with the fifth century B.C., and argued, not unconvincingly, that Sophocles and Thucydides were essentially more modern than Shakespeare and Raleigh. But although he wanted Victorian poets to imitate the Greeks, and although he regarded Homer as the greatest of Greek poets, he did not believe that epic poetry had any future; even Virgil had lived too late. Epic, he said, is the art form of a primitive age; the poetic impulse of a modern age must be expressed in drama. Homer, therefore, is without peer:

> The epic form, as a form for representing . . . nearly con-temporary events, has attained, in the poems of Homer, an unmatched . . . success; the epic form as employed . . . for the reproduction . . . of a past age has attained a very considerable success. But . . . for the poetic treatment of the events of a *past* age, the epic form is a less vital form than the dramatic form. The great poets of the modern period of Greece are accordingly . . . the *dramatic* poets . . . the dramatic form exhibits, above all, *the actions of man as strictly determined by his thoughts and feelings*; it exhibits, therefore, what may be . . . always interest-ing. But the epic form . . . exhibits . . . also the forms of out-ward life, the fashion of manners, . . . that which is local or transient . . . In the *reconstruction*, by learning and antiquarian ingenuity, of the local and transient features of a past age . . . it is impossible to feel the liveliest kind of interest.[43]

What Arnold said about epic was acute, but he erred in thinking that drama was exempt from the same dangers. The error was un-fortunate; his own *Merope* was only one of a series of Hellenic dramas which diverted the energy of Victorian poets from more fruitful fields.

Merope was written under the shadow of Sophocles; he was more successful with *Sohrab and Rustum* where Homer is the presiding genius. But this is not to say that the argument of his inaugural lecture was mistaken. The trouble with *Merope* was that he stuck too close to Greek drama; unwisely, he tried to rival Sophocles. *Sohrab and Rustum*, less than 900 lines long, does not challenge comparison with the *Iliad*, although it is deeply influenced by Homer. And it enjoys another advantage over *Merope*: a tale taken from medieval Persian epic might sound just the kind of legend in which 'it is impossible to feel the liveliest kind of interest', but whether he

realized it or not, the story of a man who is destroyed by his father
held a special significance for the son of Dr. Arnold of Rugby.

Sohrab and Rustum is perhaps the most Greek poem that Arnold
wrote, not despite the oriental setting but because of it. The myths
and legends of Greece had become cluttered up with post-renaissance
associations; by taking an entirely fresh story Arnold swept this
lumber away. *Merope* is faithful to the form of Greek tragedy, but
false to its spirit, because it reads as though written in a dead
language. Mercifully, there could be no pretence that Persian legend
was a living part of English culture, and so Arnold was free to go his
own way. None the less, *Sohrab and Rustum* is stuffed full of Homeric
phrases. Many of these echoes have little point and the effect is
sometimes rather schoolmasterly; but in other places Arnold used
reminiscences of Greece to produce something new, as in the opening
lines:

> And the first grey of morning filled the east,
> And the fog rose out of the Oxus stream.
> But all the Tartar camp along the stream
> Was hushed, and still the men were plunged in sleep . . .

The Greek influence is felt in the very first word: 'and'. It is a Greek
habit to begin each sentence with a connective; at the same time the
repetitions of 'and' sound vaguely biblical; so at once Arnold sets an
archaic, epic tone. But also by starting as it were in mid-sentence,
he conjures up a picture of a sunrise over a vast plain, a huge and
steady and resistless process, yet so gradual that one can hardly see
the moment of its beginning. (We may compare another beginning
and another sunrise: the start of Strauss's *Thus Spake Zarathustra*,
where the pedal C held pianissimo for four whole bars before any
other note is sounded serves to create a sense of great space and great
quiet and great strength.) And Arnold adds to the dawn another
large force of nature: the ceaseless flow of the Oxus. He expects his
readers to know their *Iliad*, and to remember Scamander, the river of
Troy, but for once he might fairly claim to have trumped Homer.
Oxus is as real as Scamander, far vaster, and rich in exotic associations. Arnold invests it with a symbolic significance too: again and
again he reminds us of its presence in the background, and the poem
ends with a beautiful description, comparing the river's course
towards the Aral Sea with the journey of human life towards its goal
in death. Oxus pervades *Sohrab and Rustum* as Scamander does not
the *Iliad*; Arnold has taken a minor feature of the Homeric story and
enriched it by advancing it to a position of central importance.

Rustum himself, aloof and sullen in his tent, meditating on the afflictions of his old father at home, is designed to resemble Achilles. His 'slaughterous hands' recall the 'man-slaying hands' of Homer's hero; and he receives an embassy in a scene closely modelled on the ninth book of the *Iliad*.[44] Achilles is by far the greatest warrior at Troy; the plot of the *Iliad* depends on the assumption that he is always victorious. So the parallelism between Rustum and Achilles intensifies the sense of tragic inevitability. Once Rustum does decide to fight, he must win; his adversary has no chance. Sohrab for his part corresponds to Patroclus. His dying speech is imitated from the dying speech of his Homeric model,[45] and the echoes of the *Iliad* fill it with a peculiar irony. Sohrab knows that Rustum is his father but he does not know that his opponent is Rustum; Rustum knows that his victim's name is Sohrab, but he does not know that he has a son. Patroclus assures Hector that Achilles will avenge him, but in Arnold's version of the story Hector and Achilles are one and the same person. Sohrab thinks that he is speaking to Hector, as it were, but he is really speaking to Achilles. The Homeric correspondences become most poignant by ceasing to apply; Achilles and Patroclus had the satisfaction of vengeance, but Arnold's heroes are denied it.

To Arnold's contemporaries his use (or misuse) of Homer was glaringly obvious. Readers today are probably more conscious of the Victorian characteristics of the work; Arnold seems to have so much more in common with Tennyson than with any Greek. But he may have the last word himself; comparing his poem with the *Morte d'Arthur* he wrote, 'I think the likeness, where there is likeness . . ., proceeds from our both having imitated Homer.'[46]

III

SELF-CONSCIOUSNESS

'What Government do you belong to?' asked the Hazrat Sahib.
'The Government of Inglistan.' . . .
'Is Inglistan part of Hindostan?'
'Yes.'

Robert Byron, *The Road to Oxiana*, pt. 3.

'Ah, Afghanistan,' said Chichester. 'That's in India, isn't it?'

Ib., pt. 5.

Geography

F O R two thousand years and more the Mediterranean Sea was the centre of the world. Greece, the birthplace of European civilization, is a peninsula thrust out into the Mediterranean from the continental landmass. Magna Graecia extended eastwards along the Anatolian seaboards and westwards to southern Italy; Alexander's armies swept thousands of miles eastwards through Persia and descended into the plains of India; but the Greeks never crossed the mountain ranges—Alps, Carpathians and Cévennes—that divide southern Europe from the north. Italy is another promontory extending out of the hinterland, and the Roman empire was always essentially a Mediterranean rather than a European power. In the time of Augustus Gaul was the only part of northern Europe which had been effectively subjugated; Germany was never conquered, except for its western rim, nor were the regions which we now know as Hungary, Poland and Czechoslovakia. It may not be pure chance that the principal power bloc in northern Europe today, the Soviet empire, extends west even of Rome and Florence, but does not reach down to the Mediterranean coast; the Roman empire of the first century and the Russian empire of the twentieth divide between them most of Europe apart from Scandinavia, and there is remarkably little overlap. The Romans controlled the whole of the Mediterranean littoral, including Africa and Syria, long before they attempted to conquer the primitive island of Britannia; eventually southern Britain was to be a Roman province for three and a half centuries, but it was always on the rim of the empire, with nothing to the north of it but sombre wilderness and marauding tribes. A great wall was built across the fogbound desolation to keep the barbarians from the gates; even so, when the empire came under pressure early in the fifth century, Britain was one of the first areas to be abandoned.

A thousand years later the Renaissance began; its influence spread northwards and westwards, to France and the Low Countries, and thence to England. Francis I brought Italian artists to Fontainebleau and the Loire valley; Henry VII of England had his tomb designed by a Florentine. The importation of these foreign masters testified to the wealth and importance of their employers, but proved at the same time that northern Europe was in some sense provincial. Meanwhile merchants and diplomats travelled to Italy, and brought back glowing accounts of unimagined splendours. 'Farewell Monsieur Traveller,' says Rosalind to Jaques: 'Look you lisp, and wear strange suits; disable all the benefits of your own country: be out of love with your nativity . . . or I will scarce think you have swam in a gondola.'[1] The silver sea which served England in the office of a wall served also to bar it from the centre of events.

The Renaissance turned men back to Latin writers for guidance and inspiration; but Latin writers could only increase an Englishman's sense of his country's insignificance. To them Britain was a semi-fabulous land: Horace uses the epithets 'remote', 'most distant'; Catullus seems to speak of the 'horrible and most distant Britons'; the text is corrupt and English editors have been eager to emend. Virgil's Meliboeus announces with extravagant despair that exile will take him into unimaginably remote and hostile regions, to Syria, to the Sahara and to 'the Britons utterly divided from the whole world'.[2] Tennyson alluded to this passage when he saluted Virgil 'from out the Northern Island, sundered once from all the human race'; but the word 'once' is his own addition. He knew that Britain had formerly been on the edge of the known world, but he knew too that things had changed. The Atlantic Ocean, and not the Mediterranean, was now the world's central sea. The British stood astonished at the sudden importance of their small island. Introspectively they sought to see themselves through other eyes: listening to the eternal ocean on Dover beach, Arnold thought of Sophocles hearing it long ago on the Aegean, just as he now heard it 'by this distant northern sea'.[3] This attitude was not necessarily born of humility; we hear the overtones of imperial pride in Flecker's *Santorin*:

'What is your ship?' 'A British.'
'And where may Britain be?'
'Oh it lies north, dear lady;
It is a small country.'

While the Renaissance unified the culture of the west by giving all Europe a common interest in the wisdom of the ancient world, the Reformation broke up the old unity of the church. To a casual eye the result was that the north of Europe became Protestant, the south Catholic. This was bound to create the feeling that there was some fundamental difference, whether of climate, race or temperament, between the countries of the north and south—a sort of geographical self-consciousness. The shift of power northward, from Italy, Spain and Portugal to Austria, France, Prussia and England, is a fact of history. Unlike most large vague facts it was of a kind to force itself on the attention of the English ruling classes. England prospered and Italy decayed, and English noblemen used their prosperity to make the Grand Tour and see Italy for themselves. Of course the Italian cities were marvellously beautiful, and the travellers could not but be aware of Italy as a centre point from which artistic authority radiated outwards; after all, English architecture was named from the Italian Palladio, and even Handel's operas were written to Italian words. Equally, though, the Grand Tourist marked the contrast between the former might of Italy and its present decline, political, cultural and physical. A century later modern Italy struck Ruskin as still 'a wreck, and a viciously neglected one'. Clough asked satirically if the 'Northern pilgrim' must regard cleanliness as a virtue restricted to chilly climates; for him the contrast between classic past and ignoble present was epitomized by the sight of a young Roman pissing against a column of the Pantheon. The passage of time had indeed wrought great changes. Matthew Arnold inspected the Grande Chartreuse in a mood of sceptical pity; he likened himself to a Greek thinking of his own gods as he stood on a 'far northern strand' looking at a fallen Runic stone. Nordic and Greek paganism both died; Catholic and Protestant Christianity, Arnold thought, were both dying; history repeats itself, and yet is turned upside down, for the Romish superstition of southern Europe is compared to the old heathenism of Scandinavia, while it is Arnold, the northerner, who resembles the cultivated Greek.[4]

The Germans had long felt the magnetic pull of the south. They were drawn in body towards Italy, and in imagination to Greece; for Winckelmann the two experiences were already fused into one.

Goethe gave classic expression to the longing for the south—a
northerner's longing, for all that he gives the song to Mignon, an
Italian girl. 'Do you know the land where the lemon trees blossom,
where the golden oranges glow in the dark foliage, a soft wind blows
from the blue sky. . . .' That is modern Italy; but in the next verse
we seem to go back to the classical past: 'Do you know the house? Its
roof rests on columns, the hall gleams . . . and marble figures stand
and look at me.'[5] Goethe began his fifth Roman elegy with the words,
'How glad . . . I feel now on classical soil!' In Italy not only did the
northerner come to the south, but modern man returned to the
ancient world. The land of Greece seemed inaccessible, but this did
not weaken its hold upon the imagination. Quite the contrary; the
idea of Greece could retain all the brightness of the Mediterranean
world as experienced in Italy, but it was also a mould into which
visionary passions could be poured. Hölderlin exalted Greece, as he
could not have exalted any country which he had seen with his own
eyes, as a holy land, the banqueting hall of the immortals, with
mountains for tables and ocean for floor.[6]

In 1809 A. W. Schlegel delivered his lectures on the drama; six
years later they were translated into English, and their influence in
Britain was wide and lasting. Schlegel had the knack of clear exposition, together with the ability to impose large simple patterns upon
literary history; he systematized and popularized the ideas that had
been more cloudily expressed by the poets about the differences
between ancient Greece and the modern world, between south and
north. He allowed that the renaissance reaction against Gothic art
was

> pardonable in the Italians, among whom a love for ancient
> architecture, cherished by hereditary remains of classical edifices,
> and the similarity of their climate to that of the Greeks and
> Romans, might . . . be said to be innate. But we northerns are
> not so easily to be talked out of the powerful, solemn im-
> pressions which seize upon the mind at entering a Gothic
> cathedral. . . . To the application!—the Pantheon is not more
> different from Westminster Abbey . . ., than . . . a tragedy of
> Sophocles from a drama of Shakespeare.[7]

A number of ideas are combined in these pregnant sentences: the
influence of climate upon art, the emotions inspired by 'classical soil',
and the contrasts between south and north, classic and romantic,
antiquity and the Middle Ages. Schlegel had the highest admiration
for the Hellenic achievement:

The mental culture of the Greeks was a finished education in the school of Nature. Of a beautiful and noble race, endowed with . . . a cheerful spirit under a mild sky, they lived and bloomed in the full health of existence; and . . . accomplished all that the finite nature of man is capable of. The whole of their art and poetry is the expression of a consciousness of this harmony of all their faculties. They invented the poetry of joy.

Yet, as Schiller had said, the serenity of Greek culture and religion was beyond recall; in attributing to the Greeks so much harmony and joy, Schlegel was indicating that their way of art and life belonged to the past. But at the same time he also associated the Greeks' cheerfulness with the warmth of their climate; and the association between the north, the Middle Ages and Gothic architecture led him on to another more startling claim:

The character of Europe has, since the commencement of the middle ages, been chiefly influenced by the Germanic race of northern conquerors, who infused . . . vigour into a degenerated people. The stern nature of the north drives man back within himself; and what is lost in the free sportive development of the senses, must . . . be compensated by earnestness of mind. Hence the honest cordiality with which Christianity was welcomed by all the Teutonic tribes, so that among no other race of men has it penetrated more deeply . . . [or] displayed more powerful effects.

Forgetful of Assisi and Avila, Schlegel associates the south with paganism and antiquity, the north with Christianity and modernity. Moreover, the mistiness of the northern climate inspires a sense of melancholy, a consciousness of the infinite; and these are features of modern, romantic art. 'Among the Greeks human nature . . . was conscious of no defects'; but we are conscious of original sin. Hence modern poetry—or as Schlegel calls it, 'northern poetry'—is essentially melancholy. With the coming of Christianity, 'everything finite and mortal is lost in the contemplation of infinity; life has become shadow and darkness . . . hence the poetry of the ancients was the poetry of enjoyment, and ours is that of desire.' This theory gets Schlegel into predictable difficulty; the principal subject of his lectures, after all, was Greek tragedy. He concedes that there can be sorrow in Greek poetry and liveliness in modern poetry, but the traces of original joy in one and melancholy in the other are always present, 'in some indescribable way'. The special pleading is obvious, and the success of his ideas requires explanation.

In the Mediterranean world antiquity seemed to be still present. Many a northern traveller in Rome was impressed, like Clive Newcome, by the 'great silent population of marble': 'There are battered gods tumbled out of Olympus and broken in the fall . . .; there are senators namelessly, noselessly, noiselessly . . . lurking in courts and gardens.' Rome seemed to be a melancholy city, mourning for vanished glories; Byron called it 'the Niobe of nations', hardly a phrase to fit the smart, traffic-tormented metropolis of today.[8] In fact the gulf between north and south was wider in the last century than at almost any time before or since. Nowadays every country in Europe has experienced the effects of industry and technology; pylons and power stations, telephones and televisions, are very nearly as common in Mediterranean countries as they are in Britain or America. But in the nineteenth century England, and later Germany, were transformed far more rapidly and radically than the nations of the south. In its earlier stages the industrial revolution suggested to many people that however important southern Europe had been in the past, the present and future belonged to the north; and on a less abstract level, it had multiplied the visible differences between northern and southern landscape and way of life. As the Englishman journeyed south, he seemed to travel backwards in time. Wood had opined that Ionia retained the shaggy, uncultivated character that it had possessed in Homer's time. Cory wrote from Egypt, 'We invaded not as snobs, but as poets, a bit of garden. . . . There was a boy paddling quietly in a shallow opalescent stream, one of the *ochetoi* of Homer.' 'It is astonishing what a good guide old Herodotus still is in that land,' observes Disraeli's Grandison of the same country.[9] Symonds wrote,

> On the Mediterranean shores too the same occupations have been carried on for centuries. . . . The same fields are being ploughed, the same vineyards tilled . . . as those in which Theocritus played . . . how ancient is the origin of local super-stitions, who shall say? . . . Live blood in the eye is still a sign of mysterious importance (*Idyll* III. 36). . . . City and country are not yet wholly harmonised by improved means of loco-motion. Then the people of the south are perfectly unchanged . . .

Symonds is expatiating on what he calls the 'permanence of rustic manners'; the survival of the ancient world in the south is associated with the severance of city from country, the absence of improved locomotion. He was always fond of contrasting southern luminosity with the misty landscapes of the north; but in at least one place he conflates this contrast with two other contrasts, between the ancient and modern worlds and between the fresh air of the countryside and the pollution of industrial cities. After lauding the 'Genius of the Greeks', he continues,

> Of . . . this conscience whole and pure and reconciled to nature, what survives among us now? . . . The blear-eyed mechanic, stifled in a hovel of our sombre northern towns . . . could scarcely be taught even to envy the pure clear life of art . . . which was the pride of Hellas.[10]

Mme. de Stael had spoken of the *fatigue du nord*; Disraeli's *Contarini Fleming* is permeated by this emotion. The hero, bred in Scandinavia, recounts his travels in southern lands; Greece, he tells us, was an enchantment, Athens the most beautiful sight he had ever beheld, 'the bright capital of my youthful dreams'. He is by birth half Saxon, half Italian, and so although the south has for him all the charm of an exotic novelty, he is in a sense coming home; he thinks of himself as a bright 'bird of passage' escaping from a long Nordic exile.[11] Fleming's mixed parentage is symbolic; 'Some will always be found,' Symonds wrote, with Landor in mind, '. . . to whom Greece is a lost fatherland, and who, passing through youth with the *mal du pays* of that irrecoverable land upon them, may be compared to visionaries.' Macaulay cannot be called a visionary; but on classical soil he too felt the sense of being at the ancestral heart of things, at home in a landscape known in youth, and even in infancy. He said that when he saw olive trees in Italy he knew the feeling with which Washington Irving heard the nightingale 'when he came to England, after having read descriptions of her in poets from his childhood'; he thought of Virgil and Sophocles, of the Athenian veneration for the tree, and of the images drawn from the olive in the Bible.[12]

Symonds was too rhapsodical; the better poets knew that they were rooted in their native soil, and sought to touch their readers by expressing the conflict between their longing for the south and the pull of affection that drew them to the English earth. In *Beppo* Byron described his pleasure in fleeing from the smoke and rain of London to the wine and dark eyes of Italy, a land of warmth, sun, sin and soft-syllabled speech; yet this was the poem in which he, who seldom had a kind word for the country of his birth, quoted Cowper: 'England, with all thy faults, I love thee still.' 'Happy is England,' Keats began a sonnet in which he interrupted declarations that

English sights sufficed for him with sighings for a southern shore. There is a subtler and more touching uncertainty in Arnold's *Thyrsis*. Superficially this elegy for Clough seems to be full of yearnings for the south—and for the past, since once again time and geography are confused with evocative illogicality. 'Alack for Corydon no rival *now*'; but long ago when a Sicilian shepherd died, one of his mates would pipe a ditty in his memory, and Proserpine would hearken.[13]

> For she herself had trod Sicilian fields . . .
> But ah, of our poor Thames she never heard!
> Her foot the Cumner cowslips never stirred . . .

Arnold sets the sunlight and the oleanders of the south in contrast to the 'rude ground' of England with its fogs and brambles; and yet, though Sicily is the true pastoral country, the landscape of happiness that Clough has lost by his death in Florence is the landscape around Oxford. As Arnold describes the daffodils and fritillaries, the creeping mist, and the distant prospect of the university city, we realize the beauty of this unclassical place. The memories of the Greek bucolic poets so carefully worked into the elegy are used, in the end, to irradiate an English scene.

'Rome has agreed with you, I see,' says Mr. Brooke in *Middlemarch*, '—Happiness, frescoes, the antique—that sort of thing.'[14] When the Victorians went south, honeymooning, happy-go-lucky natives, art and antiquities were all blended into one confused experience. Flora Finching was ecstatic:

> In Italy is she really? With the grapes and figs growing everywhere and lava necklaces . . . that land of poetry with burning mountains picturesque beyond belief though if the organ boys come away from the neighbourhood not to be scorched nobody can wonder being so young and bringing their white mice with them most humane, and is she really in that favoured land with nothing but blue about her and dying gladiators and belvederas though Mr. F. himself did not believe for his objection when in spirits was the images could not be true there being no medium between expensive quantities of linen . . . all in creases and none whatever, which certainly does not seem probable though perhaps in consequence of the extremes of rich and poor which may account for it.[15]

In the queer poetry of Flora's extravaganza a Victorian attitude is perfectly exemplified; she is a middle-class Mrs. Gamp giving voice to middle-class folk myths about the south and the antique. She links blue skies with dying gladiators, and they were indeed linked in the Victorian imagination.

The fascination which the dichotomy between north and south held for the Victorians can be measured by its appearance in illogical places. In *Romola* George Eliot compares a midsummer morning in a northern land with the same day in Florence; later she transfers the contrast between north and south into a purely Italian context: 'There is something grim and grave . . . about Florence . . .,' Tito remarks, 'I wish we lived in southern Italy, where thought is broken, not by weariness, but by delicious langours . . . I should like to see you under that southern sun, lying among the flowers . . ., while I sang to you some . . . strain that seemed all one with the light and the warmth.'[16] These words should be spoken in a northern clime; in Florence they are out of place. Pater's Marius the Epicurean, too, possesses an essentially northern sensibility. He is brought up in sober, grey surroundings, and when he travels south, he is startled, for all the world like Dorothea Brooke or Mary Garland, by the colour and noise of Roman life. Pater, however, is aware of the paradox and savours it: 'He relished especially the grave, subdued, northern notes . . .—the charm of the French or English notes, as we might term them—in the luxuriant Italian landscape.'[17]

Mrs. Gaskell entitled one of her novels *North and South*. On the surface its subject is the dichotomy between the north and south of England, but as it proceeds she reveals that she has also a larger contrast in mind. 'Remember,' says Thornton, the northern mill owner,

> we are of a different race from the Greeks, to whom beauty was everything, and to whom Mr. Bell might speak of a life of leisure and serene enjoyment . . . I don't mean to despise them. . . . But I belong to Teutonic blood; it is little mingled in this part of England to what it is in others; we retain . . . their spirit; we do not look upon life as a time for enjoyment, but as a time for . . . exertion.[18]

Here the parallel between the division of England into north and south and the similar division of Europe is brought out; for this purpose Thornton is made to allege implausibly that the people of Lancashire are more Teutonic than other Englishmen. Mrs. Gaskell also maps out a sort of religious geography. Hale's son goes south to Portugal and becomes a Roman Catholic; conversely, when Hale himself quits the Established Church and becomes a Dissenter, he

abandons Hampshire for Manchester. In Mrs. Gaskell's depiction the
north is all gritty and industrial, while the south is a lush, pastoral
country bathed in sunlight.

Thornton's mother tells Hale, 'I have no doubt that classics are
very desirable for people who have leisure . . . classics may do very
well for men who loiter away their lives in the country or in colleges;
but Milton men ought to have their . . . powers absorbed in the work
of today.'[19] Mrs. Gaskell's contrast of south and north is a contrast
between gentry and bourgeoisie, between leisure and industry; but
it also marks the opposition between past and present, between
ancient Greece and Victorian England. There is a similar antithesis
in Dickens's novels. The education in Gradgrind's school at Coke-
town is characteristic of northern England—scientific, utilitarian,
factual—while down in Sussex Dr. Blimber offers a wholly classical
training to the children of the upper middle class. In Mrs. Gaskell's
novel Bell points out that northerners like bustle and struggle; they
lack the patience for 'sitting still and learning from the past'.
Significantly, this spokesman for southern values is an Oxford don, a
professional scholar. Thornton tells him, 'If we do not reverence the
past as you do in Oxford, it is because we want something which can
apply to the present more directly.'[20] Yet Thornton, who represents
the best sort of northerner, goes to Hale to learn Greek and to read
Homer, Plato and Thucydides. Eventually he will marry a southern
wife; in his offspring the virtues of south and north, of Greek past
and English present, will be combined.

Australians travel north to visit the South Sea Islands; Californians
agree that the Far East lies a few thousand miles to the west of them.
The way in which western man conceives the entire planet is centred
on Europe; indeed the very phrase 'western man' tells its own story.
Besides, there does seem to be a certain grand simplicity about the
physical shape of Europe. Even today, the northern traveller can
hardly cross the Alps without the sense that he has broken through a
great barrier, and descended into a magically different world. The
Alps are, undeniably, a large geographical fact; yet they come to
have a symbolic importance, whether as the meeting point of north
and south or as the barrier between them, which sometimes seems to
transcend mere geography. Mignon's song ends not beside a peaceful
southern shore but on a perilous mountain track: 'Do you know the
mountain and its cloudy path? The mule picks its way through the
mist; . . . the rock-face falls sheer. . . . It is there, there our way
leads!' In one of Pater's fables Duke Carl of Rosenmold, travelling
south in search of Hellas, realizes that 'the Alps were an apex of

natural glory, towards which, in broadening spaces of light, the whole of Europe sloped upwards. Through them . . . were the doorways to Italy . . . from yonder peak Italy's self was visible!' But at this point the duke turns back. 'These things presented themselves at last only to remind him that, in a new intellectual hope, he was already on his way home. Straight through life, . . . with one's own self-knowledge as a light thereon, not by way of the geographical Italy or Greece, lay the road to the new Hellas.'[21] Like the sensible world in the philosophy of Plato, the physical contour of Europe is to him the emblem of a greater spiritual fact. A strange notion; yet it is true that the shape of Europe has penetrated deeply into our consciousness, deeper than most of us realize. Even Tolkien, who created an entirely imaginary continent, could not shake off the spell. Middle Earth is a recreation of Europe; the Shire, as its name suggests, is 'English'; the Hobbits travel south (and east) across a great range of mountains, and then come to Ithilien. Like the traveller crossing the Alps, they seem suddenly to have entered a new world: 'The long journey . . . had brought them far south of their own land, but not until now . . . had the Hobbits felt the change of clime.' Ithilien is Italy, as the name implies; the landscape is rich with tamarisk and asphodel, with olive and bay. Although Tolkien's imagination was possessed by Celtic and Teutonic legend, he even suggests that this southern land has a classical past: 'Ithilien . . . now desolate kept still a dishevelled dryad loveliness.'[22] Even the contrast between antique glory and present decay is there.

In *The Stones of Venice* Ruskin compared an English and an Italian cathedral.[23] The former is dark, rugged, confused, with harshly cawing birds echoing about it, whereas St. Mark's as approached from the street of San Moise is 'a long low pyramid of coloured light' that seems to be made of gold and opal; its pillars are of jasper and porphyry, while high above 'the crests of the arches break into a marble foam, and toss themselves far into the blue sky in flashes . . . of sculptured spray.' Ruskin has eloquently bent the evidence; the case could be very differently presented. The typical English cathedral lies within a close; on a summer's day it basks in the sunlight, encircled by wide lawns of brilliant green and warmly coloured houses of red brick or golden stone. But the piazza of Venice is approached by dark, narrow passages, past a romantic chaos of high mouldering walls, punctured by quaint irregularities of window and balcony. The square itself is a vast expanse of grey paving, surrounded by endless colonnades of grey stone; a bleak sight on a dull day. The one gay exception to the general sternness is St. Mark's itself, but this exception does nothing to strengthen Ruskin's case. Salisbury Cathedral (for instance) is a superbly logical building, a finely controlled pyramidal construction with every proportion nicely judged—a classical composition, one might say; St. Mark's is romantically irregular, 'a confusion of delight' in Ruskin's own phrase. He speaks himself of 'unexpected rising and falling of weight and accent in its marble syllables; bearing the same relation to a rigidly chiselled and proportioned architecture that the wild lyric rhythm of Aeschylus or Pindar bears to the finished measures of Pope'.[24] It might seem natural for him to bring two Greek poets into the comparison, since he wants to stress the southern character of St. Mark's; and yet what a curious choice they make. Strangely, it is the English poet who is rigidly proportioned in the manner of a Greek temple, while Aeschylus and Pindar, the southern poets, are notoriously turbulent and romantic. In the very act of drawing out his contrast between north and south Ruskin exposes the difficulties of his view.

In another eloquent, and truer, passage he suggested how climate, geology and the visible landscape together determined the character of a nation's art. Lifting his readers thousands of feet into the air, he invited them to scan Europe from south to north, passing from 'a great peacefulness of light, Syria and Greece, Italy and Spain, laid like pieces of a golden pavement into the sea-blue' to where 'the orient colours change gradually into a vast belt of rainy green', and thence to 'mighty masses of leaden rock and heathy moor'. The same contrast is found in the fauna: on the one hand the bright colours of tigers and leopards, glistening serpents and birds of paradise; on the other, the osprey, wolf and bear. Ruskin, in fact, associates the south with the east; the very name Gothic, he says, implies a degree of sternness 'in contradistinction to the character of Southern and Eastern nations'. To Byron also the balmness of the Greek climate had seemed as much oriental as southern: the islands were 'Edens of the Eastern wave. . . . Far from the winters of the west'.[25]

Travel in the Levant taught him that even ancient Greece could look very different seen through the eyes of a modern Greek; 'Land of Albania! where Iskander rose,' he wrote.[26] The Macedonian conqueror had been known to his own people as Alexandros. In England he was called Alexander the Great, in Greece Iskander; the one name has a noble and familiar ring, while the other suggests an oriental warlord, and it was amusing to reflect that the two appellations denoted one and the same person. Flecker, who was in the British consular service at Smyrna and Beirut, grew keenly conscious of how strange the Greeks can appear from an Asian vantage point. Greece and Italy become the inscrutable occident, the mysterious west; the Pope is transformed into the Caliph of Rum. In *Hassan*, an orgy of camp orientalism, Flecker indulged himself with these ideas. 'Is not her neck a pillar of the marble of Yoonistan?' asks Selim; with a start of surprise we realize that Yoonistan is Greece. Rafi tells of the caliph's 'camels, and elephants, his statues of Yoonistan, and his wines of Ferangistan, his eunuchs of Egypt, and his carpets of Bokhara. . . .' The audience is expected to take a knowing pleasure in finding that Greece and France, curiously disguised, figure merely in passing among a host of other splendours. Strangers come to pay their respects to the caliph: a Chinese philosopher, the Rajah of the Upper Ganges, a Turkoman wrestler, and among them an 'ambassador of the infidel Empress Irene, mistress till God wills of . . . the lands of Rum'. Again, there is a piquancy in observing that the emissary of the Roman empire is just one among many ambassadors, and less regarded than an Indian princeling or a wandering dervish. Even the foundations of western rationality can sound strangely exotic in an eastern mouth. 'Who art thou?' asks Hassan; and Ishak replies, 'Who am I? Ten books were written by Aflatun and twenty by Aristu to answer that mighty question.' We know the philosophers Ibn Sina and Ibn Rushd by the Latinized names Avicenna and Averroes; Flecker reverses the usual process by orientalizing Plato and Aristotle.[27]

Aflatun and Aristu recur in his *Ballad of Iskander*:

> Sultan Iskander sat him down
> On his golden throne, in his golden crown,
> And shouted, 'Wine and flute girls three,
> And the captain, ho! of my ships at sea.'

Alexander becomes an eastern version of Old King Cole, and he is dressed like the king in a nativity play. His speech is childlike:

> 'Daroosh is dead, and I am King
> Of Everywhere and Everything.'

This sounds like A. A. Milne:

> If I were King of Timbuctoo,
> I'd think of lovely things to do.
> If I were King of Anything,
> I'd tell the soldiers, 'I'm the King!'

We, the 'grown-ups', are meant to smile indulgently at the naïveties of Flecker's ballad, but only a long tradition of historical and geographical self-awareness could produce the apparent artlessness of this nursery-rhyme style.

History

The 'spirit of the age' is . . . a novel expression. I do not believe that it is to be met with in any work exceeding fifty years in antiquity. The idea of comparing one's own age with former ages, or with . . . those which are yet to come, . . . never before was itself the dominant idea of any age.

Mill[28]

When Macaulay reviewed Ranke's *History of the Popes*, he paused to reflect upon the durability of the Roman Catholic Church: 'She may still exist in undiminished vigour when some traveller from New Zealand shall, in the midst of a vast solitude, take his stand on a broken arch of London Bridge to sketch the ruins of St. Paul's.' This passing comment became famous, for it appealed to the imagination of the age. The Victorian fancy was recurrently haunted by the ancient world; Englishmen dressed themselves in imaginary togas and sauntered up and down the Sacred Way chatting about Caesar and Cicero. The Romans, by contrast, imagined no other civilization in their stead; Rome was the Eternal City, and the poems of Virgil and Horace are instinct with a confidence that the empire would endure until the end of time. We, however, cannot forget that the civilization of Greece and Rome was to vanish utterly; and so the more an Englishman attempted to commune with the people of antiquity, the more he became aware of possessing a secret that was hidden from them, and the more insistent became the urge to buttonhole one of those old Greeks and Romans and tell him what the future had in store. It is a simple, rather childish fancy to imagine oneself explaining television to Shakespeare or the aeroplane to Leonardo, but even Cory could not resist inviting a Dorian shepherd to the Thames Valley for a picnic and some literary conversation:[29]

Oh dear divine Comatas, I would that thou and I
Beneath this broken sunlight this leisure day might lie;
Where trees from distant forests, whose names were strange to
 thee,
Should bend their amorous branches within thy reach to be . . .

Then thou shouldst calmly listen with ever changing looks
To songs of younger minstrels and plots of modern books,
And wonder at the daring of poets later born . . .

A Victorian might try to imagine himself as an ancient Greek, but the
Greek that he became tended to be one strangely obsessed with the
future; and from there it was easy to imagine other Greeks sharing
this obsession. Landor makes Pericles say, 'We are little by being
seen among men . . . we become greater by leaving the world. . . .
Humiliating truth! That nothing on earth . . . can do so much for us
as a distant day.'[30] Landor could never enter fully into the spirit of
the past because he always had one eye fixed on the present, and the
'distant day' that he has in mind is clearly his own; but we can hardly
suppose that Pericles would have cared a fig for the opinions of a
race whose character and civilization he could not possibly have
conceived. As Hazlitt said, 'We are always talking of the Greeks and
Romans;—*they* never said anything of us.'[31]

Pater put into the mind of his hero in the second century A.D.
almost the same thought that occurred to Macaulay in the nineteenth: 'Marius . . . seemed to foresee a grass-grown forum, the
broken ways of the Capitol and the Palatine hill itself in humble
occupation. This impression,' Pater adds, 'connected itself with
what he had already noted of an actual change even then coming over
Italian scenery'.[32] Was Italy really altering so very much in the age
of the Antonines, the very period singled out by Gibbon for its
happy and uneventful prosperity? But a man of the nineteenth
century, and above all an Englishman, saw his country in constant
change.

Pater describes the reflections of Marius' friend Flavian upon
three lines of the *Odyssey*: 'One might think . . . that there was but
the almost mechanical transcript of a time, naturally, intrinsically,
poetic, a time in which one could hardly have spoken at all without
ideal effect, or the sailors pulled down their boat without making a
picture in "the great style". . . . Must not the mere prose of an age,
itself thus ideal, have counted for more than half of Homer's poetry?'[33]
But surely sailors in the second century pulled down their sails much
as they had done in Homer's time; it was only with the coming of
steam that things greatly changed. Indeed, Flavian himself suspects
that his idea may be fallacious: 'Might not another, in one's prosaic
and used-up time . . . discover his ideal . . .?' And he goes on to
imagine a 'New Zealander' looking back at Rome: 'Would not a
future generation, looking back upon this, under the power of the

enchanted-distance fallacy, find the ideal to view, in contrast with its own languor—the languor that . . . seemed to haunt men always?' Well, who so languorous, who so enchanted by distance, as Pater? And what age, in his view, so prosaic and used-up as the nineteenth century? A teasing equivocation runs through the novel; Pater presents the second century both as a prosaic, matter-of-fact epoch and simultaneously as a poetic, enchanted land of lost content. Flavian's questions are answered in the very act of their utterance; it is Pater himself who has answered them by inventing Flavian and writing the book. The technique is highly artful, acutely self-conscious.

Historical self-consciousness is an experience very exquisite, very cultivated; but this sort of cultural narcissism can easily become enervating. Languor, languor—we should not be surprised to hear this word echoing in Pater's prose at this moment. In his *Imaginary Portraits* he rang melodious changes on this theme. In *Denys l'Auxerrois* he looked at Dionysus through medieval French eyes, in *Duke Carl of Rosenmold* he filtered the rapture of Hellenism through the mind of an eighteenth-century German princeling. In *Sebastian van Storck* he showed how historical self-awareness could slide into a death wish: the hero fancies 'that he himself would like to have been dead and gone as long ago, with a kind of envy of those whose deceasing was so long since over'. We may doubt whether such a refined and complex melancholy was often felt among the Dutch citizenry of the seventeenth century. Even *The Renaissance* is in large measure a search for new ways of looking at the Greeks, through the eyes of Winckelmann, or the Florentines, or even the Provençal poets of the Middle Ages. Symonds too admitted that he had been drawn to write about the renaissance because it had caught something of the Greek spirit. Seven solid volumes appeared (1875–1886); yet he confessed, 'It was very different when one used to write about Greeks! They gave everything. One had only to express . . . one's sense of the blessing.'[34]

Pater's game of looking at the Greeks through alien eyes could be played in the visual arts also. Burne-Jones designed a series of tiles depicting Greek myths—'Theseus in the Labyrinth', 'Paris and Helen'—in a gothic style. They are charmingly *faux naïf*. Helen is a sweetly innocent medieval damsel; Theseus is dressed as a young squire, while the Minotaur peers round from behind a wall like a mischievous child playing hide-and-seek. Wilde achieved a similar effect in words. In *The Critic as Artist* Gilbert explains how the *Iliad* still lives in the imagination:

Yet every day the swan-like daughter of Leda comes out on the battlements . . . in his chamber of stained ivory lies her leman. He is polishing his dainty armour. . . . With squire and page, her husband passes from tent to tent . . . behind the embroidered curtains of his pavilion sits Achilles . . ., while in harness of gilt and silver the friend of his soul arrays himself. . . . From a curiously carven chest . . . the Lord of the Myrmidons takes out that mystic chalice . . .

The emphasis on courtly love, the exquisitely decorative stage pro-perties, and the language—chalice, leman, carven,—all medievalize Homer.

Flecker addressed some verses *To a poet a thousand years hence*:

> I who am dead a thousand years,
> And wrote this sweet archaic song . . .

Flecker's is a sophisticated and paradoxical attitude, and the win-some simplicity of his style is part of the paradox and the sophistica-tion. To see ourselves as others see us is the path to self-knowledge, but Flecker develops the process to the extent of falsifying what he is; for in what sense was the Edwardian age archaic? He asks his poet of the early thirtieth century,

> But have you wine and music still,
> And statues and a bright-eyed love,
> And foolish thoughts of good and ill,
> And prayers to them who sit above?

Wine, statue, bright-eyed love—these words conjure up the lyric age of Greece more naturally than the reign of Edward VII; after all, who offered 'prayers to *them* who sit above' in Flecker's lifetime? He revels in the fantasy of picturing his own over-civilized age as an archaic period. How amusing to represent the twentieth century as— comparatively—an age of faith! At the same time he also implies that archaic Greece is 'modern' and alive in the poetic imagination. This feeling was perhaps forced upon him by the nature of the evidence. The ethos of archaic Greece is vastly remote from our experience, far more remote even than the fifth century; yet there survive from it fragmentary poems about getting drunk and making love, records of friendships and quarrels, petty griefs and small delights, as intimate as anything in Greek literature. Flecker knew that the world was old, and that poets had little to say that had not been better said already: 'Old Maeonides the blind Said it three thousand years ago.' Yet strangely enough the literature of Flecker's time will seem youthful a thousand years hence. It is young and old, archaic and decadent at one and the same time.

Henry James's Roderick Hudson, arriving in Rome in the nineteenth century, feels 'a deep relish for the element of accumulation in the human picture and for the infinite super-positions of history'. More surprisingly, Marius enjoys the same pleasure in the Rome of his day: 'Much which spoke of ages earlier than Nero lingered on, . . . immeasurably venerable, like the relics of the medieval city in the Paris of Lewis XIV; the work of Nero's own time had come to have that sort of old-world . . . interest which the work of Lewis has for ourselves; while . . . we might perhaps liken the architectural finesses of the archaic Hadrian to . . . our own Gothic revival.'[35] In literature, too, Pater is at pains to draw out the parallels between the second century and his own: '*Hellas*, in its earliest freshness, looked as distant from [Flavian] even then as it does from ourselves.' And indeed there are some strange similarities between the Roman Empire and the Victorian age; Pater noted that the younger Pliny had said, 'I am one of those who admire the Ancients, yet I do not, like some others, underrate certain instances of genius which our own times afford. For it is not true that nature, as if weary and effete, no longer produces what is admirable.'[36] Dorian Gray might have said it. Similarly, Pater likens the 'euphuism' of Antonine literature to modern French romanticism, for 'there is nothing new, but a quaint family likeness rather, between the Euphuists of successive ages'.

'I adore simple pleasures,' says Wilde's Lord Henry Wotton. 'They are the last refuge of the complex.' Marius has to disentangle a similar paradox. How is he to reconcile his love for the bold simplicity of old literature with his admiration for the exquisite refinement, the false simplicity, of modern art. His rearing 'had lent itself to an imaginative exaltation of the past'; yet he feels

> that the present had, it might be, really advanced beyond the past, and he was ready to boast in the very fact that it was modern. If, in a voluntary archaism, the polite world . . . went back to a choicer generation . . . for the purpose of a fastidious self-correction . . ., at least it improved, by a shade or two of more scrupulous finish, on the old pattern; and the new era, like the *Neu-zeit* . . . at the beginning of our own century, might perhaps be discerned.[37]

Pater speaks of the *Neu-zeit*, the new time; for him the piquancy of the second century was that it was both very old and very young. On the one hand, Flavian is oppressed by the weight of the past. 'Why not be simple and broad,' he wonders, 'like the old writers of Greece? . . . the most wonderful, the unique point, about the Greek genius . . . was the entire absence of imitation in its productions. How had the burden of precedent laid upon every artist increased since then!'[38] Marius himself is a romantic pilgrim passing through a weary world, a Harold in Italy; an 'old instinctive yearning' is stirred in him as he crosses 'the old, mysterious and visionary country of Etruria'. But he lives in an age of transition: 'The picturesque, romantic Italy of a later time—the Italy of Claude and Salvator Rosa—was already forming, to the delight of the modern romantic traveller.' Above all, there was Christianity; Marius is delighted with 'the gracious spirit of the primitive church, . . . in that first early spring-tide of her success.'[39] The seasonal metaphor is important; April breeds lilacs out of the dead land (in the words of a later writer), the new world is to be created by the death of the old. Marius witnesses the infancy of the Middle Ages; when he attends a Christian service, he detects 'the advent of some new or changed spirit into the world, mystic, inward, hardly to be satisfied with that wholly external . . . life which had been sufficient for the old classic soul'. As Pater admits, 'The reader may perhaps think that Marius . . . must have descended, by *foresight*, upon a later age than his own, and anticipated Christian poetry and art . . . under the influence of St. Francis.'[40] This strange and beautiful new birth may seem to make the age of Marius very unlike the age of Pater; however, there were Victorians who, though oppressed by the oldness and darkness of the world in which they lived, looked to the coming of a new era. Carlyle wrote, 'Deep and sad as is our feeling that we yet stand in the bodeful Night; equally deep . . . is our assurance that the Morning also will not fail.'[41] Though Arnold felt that he was observing the relics of a dead religion at the Grande Chartreuse, he too hoped that a new day would follow the night: 'Years hence, perhaps, may dawn an age, More fortunate, alas! than we.' But his assurance was not strong:

> Wandering between two worlds, one dead,
> The other powerless to be born, . . .
> Like these, on earth I wait forlorn.

And even the seer of Cheyne Walk dared not predict what time the new dawn would arise: 'The doom of the Old has long been pronounced . . . but, alas, the New appears not in its stead; the Time is still in pangs of travail with the New.' In cooler language Mill agreed: 'The present age . . . is an age of transition. Mankind have outgrown . . . old doctrines, and have not yet acquired new ones.' 'All ages are ages of transition,' Tennyson said, 'but this is an awful moment of transition.'[42] The charm of *Marius* was that it portrayed an age of transition which had an indubitably glorious future ahead; the second century is a softened version of the nineteenth.

Ruskin thought that no building reached its prime until it was a few centuries old; Pater opined that time had enhanced the beauty of the Venus de Milo by rubbing away the precision of its outline. In such attitudes the inward vision of the historical imagination some-times played as large a part as the literal vision of the eye: when Keats glorified the Elgin Marbles for mingling 'Grecian grandeur with the rude Wasting of old Time', he judged that aesthetic loss was outweighed by imaginative gain. George Eliot compared a woman's faded beauty to a Greek temple, 'which for all the loss it has suffered . . . has gained a solemn history, and fills our imagination the more because it is incomplete to the sense'.[43] The very pastness of the past could be a delight. 'In the distance everything becomes poetry,' Novalis said: 'distant mountains, distant people, distant events'; and Goethe had approved Humboldt's opinion, 'Antiquity should only appear to us from a great distance . . . as completely past and gone.'[44] It was not necessary to read Germans to have this feeling; one seemed to breathe it in with the very air of England. As a boy, Tennyson was already possessed by 'The Passion of the Past'.[45]

> A height, a broken grange, a grove, a flower
> Had murmurs 'Lost and gone and lost and gone!'
> A breath, a whisper—some divine farewell—
> Desolate sweetness—far and far away . . .

There is melancholy here, but also pleasure in melancholy, and strangely enough it was possible to combine the sense of distance with that other sense, strong in so many people, that the Greeks were modern, closer to us than our own medieval ancestors; one might even take pleasure in the paradox. Keats marvels at his Grecian urn because it is so ancient and yet so fresh; the world of Marius is the urn's analogue in prose.

Christianity was genuinely youthful, but in the realm of literature Flavian is forced to conclude that the archaism of his own time is not a genuine rebirth: 'That unconscious ease of early literature . . . could never come again. . . . Perhaps the utmost one could get by conscious effort, in the way of a . . . return to the conditions of an earlier . . . age, would be but *novitas*, artificial artlessness, naiveté.'[46] However, Pater hints, even here, at the possibility of a new freshness. One of the strangest survivals from later antiquity is the *Pervigilium Veneris*, a poem of uncertain date about love and springtime. This curious work, with its haunting refrain and hypnotic rhythms, has seemed to many readers to belong half-way between the ancient world and the Middle Ages; this quality made it peculiarly attractive to the taste of the *fin de siècle*. In 1895 J. W. Mackail devoted to it the purplest of purple passages, and concluded, 'With a sudden sob the pageant ceases . . . a second spring . . . was not to come for poetry till a thousand years later; once more then we hear the music of this strange poem, not now in the bronze utterance of a mature . . . language, but faintly and haltingly, in immature forms that yet have notes of new and piercing sweetness.' And here he quoted the quaint verses of medieval England and Provence.[47]

Pater imagines that the *Pervigilium* was written by his own Flavian. He described the second century by the metaphor of springtime, and a poem which not only seemed to blend antiquity and the Middle Ages but also depicted a festival in honour of spring had a special charm for him. There is, besides, a note of personal sadness at the end of the piece which seems to foreshadow the melancholy of more recent poets; the modern reader may think of Keats's nightingale when he reaches the last stanza: 'The swallow sings, we are silent; when is my spring coming? When shall I be like as the swallow that I may cease to be silent?' The *Pervigilium* also delighted a greater man than Pater. T. S. Eliot began as a decadent and developed into a modern; he too lived in an age of transition. It is fitting, therefore, that the *Pervigilium* should be quoted at the end of the most famous poem of the twentieth century; *The Waste Land* concludes with a formidable compilation of fragments taken from vastly divergent times and places, and a morsel of the *Pervigilium*, itself a blend of two different ages, is appropriately among them.

IV

THE
NINETEENTH-CENTURY
BACKGROUND

The Established Order

EDUCATION

W HEN Stanley wrote the life of Dr. Arnold (1844), he looked back on the 'popular outcry' against classical education as a thing safely in the past and attributed its defeat partly to the fact that 'the one Head-master, who, by his political . . . opinions, would have been supposed most likely to yield to the clamour, was the one who made the most . . . decided protest against it.'[1] Perhaps the danger had never been so very grave. Some of the utilitarians were opposed to classical education, but their opinions carried the less weight because it was noticed that their objections applied equally to all literary studies whatever. And in any case there was dissension in the ranks: James Mill, for instance, put his son through a formidable programme of Greek and Latin authors. Sydney Smith had created more of a flurry in 1809 with a review in which he castigated the classical teaching of the English universities, especially Oxford. Of the many replies to this attack, the fullest was from Edward Copleston, later to be Provost of Oriel, who discovered in classical studies not only a high practical value but a remarkable degree of moral efficacy: 'A high sense of honour, a disdain of death in a good cause, a passionate devotion to the welfare of one's country . . . are among the first sentiments, which those studies communicate to the mind.'[2]

The many arguments produced on either side of the debate are of less importance than the fact that both parties got their way. Classical education remained dominant for many years, but it was modified in the ways that the radicals wanted. Smith himself set a high value on the classics; what he disliked was the way in which they forced out other subjects, and more particularly the narrowly linguistic and literary method by which they were studied. He attributed these defects to 'the miserable . . . littleness of ecclesiastical instructors'; the timorous dons of Oxford, he supposed, were afraid to allow their pupils free inquiry into ethics, metaphysics, and political thought.[3] What he did not appreciate was that these other subjects could be pursued as part of a classical education. J. S. Mill and Grote, utilitarians of the second generation, argued that classical studies should be broadened to include the history and thought of the ancient world.[4] From his very different standpoint, Newman agreed: history and philosophy, he said, were the two essential 'enlarging studies'.[5] Ancient history was added to the syllabus at Oxford in 1830, at Cambridge in 1851;[6] in its final form the Oxford Greats course consisted of five terms spent on ancient literature, followed by seven of history and philosophy. 'It doesn't seem to me that one gains the quintessence of the University unless one reads Greats,' says the hero of Mackenzie's *Sinister Street*; this is the wistful confession of one, who, like Mackenzie himself, has read Modern History.[7]

In an essay on *The Use of the Classics*, Dr. Arnold wrote, 'A classical teacher should be fully acquainted with modern history and modern literature no less than with those of Greece and Rome . . . a mere scholar, cannot possibly communicate . . . the main advantages of a classical education.'[8] Arnold was one of the first Englishmen to appreciate the importance of Niebuhr's history of Rome, and at the end of his short life he was not only headmaster of Rugby but Regius Professor of Modern History at Oxford as well. It was for the classics a remarkable stroke of fortune which gave to such a man so great an influence upon English education. He also encouraged the move away from Latin towards Greek. Himself the historian of Rome, he believed that 'half . . . of the Roman history is, if not totally false, at least scandalously exaggerated; how far different are the . . . impartial narratives of Herodotus, Thucydides, and Xenophon'.[9] He introduced Pindar and Aristophanes into the curriculum at Rugby; Aristotle and Thucydides were his own greatest loves.[10] When Mill was asked to support an *Association pour l'encouragement des études grecques en France*, he mentioned in his reply that England had no need for a comparable society; and when Taine visited England some twenty years after Arnold's death, he observed that English schoolboys were inferior to their French counterparts in knowledge of Latin, but markedly superior in Greek. He was also struck by how religious they were.[11] Greek and godliness—Taine was seeing Arnold's ideal realized.

Ruskin denounced the error of 'mistaking erudition for education' and suggested that headmasters should 'try whether it is not as easy to make an Eton Boy's mind as sensitive to falseness in policy, as his ear is at present to falseness in prosody'.[12] Arnold believed that he could achieve this end at Rugby by teaching ancient history. Thucydides claimed to write for the instruction of future generations, so that they would know what to expect when circumstances like those he described arose once more; and Arnold took him at his word. Rugbeians admired 'his illustrations of ancient by modern, and modern by ancient history'. 'Aristotle, and Plato,' he said, 'and Thucydides, and Cicero . . . are most untruly called ancient writers; they are virtually our own countrymen and contemporaries'; and he suggested that the history of Greece from Pericles to Alexander afforded a political lesson more applicable to modern times than did any other period earlier than the eighteenth century.[13] This trust in the value of ancient history for the aspiring statesman has little in common with the habit of quoting classical authors in the House of Commons, which was a superficial and often spurious indicator of the speaker's learning. In Disraeli's *Endymion* Scrope says, 'In the last parliament we often had Latin quotations . . . I have heard Greek quoted here, but that was . . . a great mistake. The House was quite alarmed.' That account is probably true to life. Brougham, however, told Zachary Macaulay that his son should soak himself in Demosthenes if he wished to be an orator, and claimed that he had himself never spoken so well as when almost translating from the Greek.[14] But the effects of Greek history on political thinking were not all as good as Arnold thought. Lytton opposed the unification of Italy on the ground that Greece had lost its greatness when it ceased to be made up of city-states. One of Thucydides' central themes is the bitter conflict between the few and the many ('the nobles and the Commons,' Mitford misleadingly called them), and those who saw England in a Thucydidean light were liable to develop a bleak pessimism.[15] In 1819 Arnold thought daily of the sedition at Corcyra, and lamented that the message of Thucydides was not heeded; during the agitations for a reform bill, he argued that Greek and Roman history showed the danger of premature concessions to democracy. We find Newman at the same time thinking in Greek terms: 'The nation (i.e. numerically the *plēthos* [multitude]) is for revolution.' Gladstone was perhaps right to suspect that study of the ancient historians sometimes encouraged 'the cruder forms of oligarchic or democratic prejudice'.[16]

Lord Houghton noticed that his contemporaries were happy with English versions of Dante and Goethe, but affected a snobbish disdain of reading classical authors in anything but the original.[17] One of the chief reasons why statesmen and reviewers made so much use of classical quotation was social: the man who knew Latin and Greek was a gentleman. Thackeray's Colonel Newcome remarks, 'There is nothing like a knowledge of the classics to give a man good breeding.' Pendennis concentrates on the classics after trying mathematics and finding that 'one or two very vulgar young men, who did not even use straps to their trousers . . . beat him completely.' Mrs. Blimber, in *Dombey and Son*, likes to see her husband's pupils in 'the largest possible shirt collars and the stiffest possible cravats. It was so classical', she said. Even more than Latin, Greek was the stamp that authenticated culture and class; a fact which George Eliot brought out neatly in *The Mill on the Floss*. 'Does every gentleman learn Greek?' Tom Tulliver asks Philip Wakem. '. . . will Mr. Stelling make me begin with it . . .?' 'No, I should think not—very likely not,' is the reply. But every gentleman does learn Greek; Philip hesitates precisely because Tom's breeding is questionable.[18]

George Eliot saw how the classics were made to bolster another small but important snobbery. Tom boasts to Maggie, 'I should like to see you doing one of *my* lessons. Why, I learn Latin too. Girls never learn such things. They're too silly.'[19] In *Middlemarch* she again showed how the Greek language was used to shore up the self-esteem of the English male:

> 'Well, tell me [Fred Vincy says to his sister] whether it is slang or poetry to call an ox a *leg-plaiter*.'
> 'Of course you can call it poetry if you like.'
> 'Aha, Miss Rosy, you don't know Homer from slang.'

Similarly, when Dorothea asks her husband about Greek accents, she acquires 'a painful suspicion that here indeed there might be secrets not capable of explanation to a woman's reason'. And on a different level of artistic achievement there is this cry of anguish in *The Junior Dean*, a novel by Mrs. Marshall: 'Oh, Neil, you—you forget I'm only a woman, and I have done so little Greek.' As early as 1808 Smith summed up the attitude of the Tom Tullivers: 'We cannot deny the jealousy which exists . . . respecting the education of women. There is a class of pedants, who would be cut short . . . a whole cubit, if it were generally known that a young lady of eighteen could be taught to decline the middle voice.' And he gave the best of all reasons for studying Greek: 'The great use of her knowledge will be that it contributes to her private happiness.'[20] It says much for the fascination (or prestige) of Greek that there were women who strove to surmount the barriers placed in their path. In the realm of fiction there was Don Juan's acquaintance,

> That prodigy, Miss Araminta Smith
> (Who at sixteen translated *Hercules Furens*
> Into as furious English) . . .

and Trollope's Jane Crawley, who 'passed her life between her mother's work-table and her father's Greek, mending linen and learning to scan iambics'.[21] Such ladies had their counterparts in actual life, women such as Mrs. Browning or George Eliot herself. Taine heard of a guest at a country house who 'discovered that his hostess knew far more Greek than he did, . . . and confessed himself beaten: whereupon . . . she wrote his English sentence of excuses in Greek . . . this Hellenist is a woman . . . of fashion: furthermore, she has nine daughters . . . and . . . numerous house guests.'[22] Such people, however, were exceptional. C. S. Parker protested that 'the sacred precincts of the classics' had been tabooed against women, with the result that girls knew more about modern languages and literature, and sometimes more about science, than their brothers. Houghton observed that if boys had a gift for music or drawing, it was neglected, and such French and German as they possessed was probably picked up from a sister's governess.[23] The converse of the notion that some subjects were too tough for girls was a feeling that others were too lightweight for boys. In this way the classics tended to become an instrument of philistinism: the study and practice of art and music were regarded as womanish things and the Victorian ideal of the well-rounded man was badly dented on one side. ('I wish he were not so fond of music, it will interfere with his Latin and Greek,' Ernest's father reflects in *The Way of All Flesh*.)[24] Classical studies were themselves debilitated by this attitude: as Ruskin noted indignantly, Greek visual art was excluded from the Oxford curriculum.[25]

Only a tiny minority of Victorians learnt Greek, and perhaps only a minority of that minority took any serious interest in their studies. The contempt which many undergraduates felt for the keen student is revealed in Cuthbert Bede's description of 'Mr. Sloe, the reading-man', who paces his garret at night, 'at which time could be plainly heard the wretched chuckles, and crackings of knuckles (Mr. Sloe's way of expressing intense delight), with which he welcomed some miserable joke of Aristophanes . . .; or the disgustingly sonorous way in which he declaimed his Greek choruses.'[26] On the whole, it was the reading men who went on to write books, and this attitude must have been much commoner in life than in literature, where it was politely suppressed; even so robust a philistine as Bede felt the need to put in some sententious words in praise of the classics. But his real feelings are clear: Mr. Sloe is not quite a gentleman, and it seems to be an extra cause of offence that he actually enjoys his Greek.

Eventually the social and cultural exclusiveness associated with the classics was to contribute to their downfall, but for a long while it served to increase their prestige. Before elementary schooling became universal men appreciated more readily the power that education gives, and the power of knowledge was often confused with the social advantages which education, and especially a classical education, conferred. Hardy was to show the poignancy of this confusion in *Jude the Obscure*. Moreover, though the true lovers of the classics were few, they included a great many of those who gave the Victorian age its religious, moral and political tone. If the reading men felt themselves to be embattled—and Matthew Arnold's metaphors, 'barbarian' and 'philistine', suggest that perhaps they did—their ardour for learning and culture was the more increased. The best of them were zealous to spread knowledge among the working classes, an aspiration that was encouraged by the opening of Toynbee Hall in Whitechapel (1884), followed by more 'university settlements' in other cities. Marx would have approved the end if not the means: 'He would have scourged those contemptible souls out of the temple who would prevent the workers from appreciating the culture of the classic world.'[27] A perfect symbol of a Victorian ideal was provided as late as 1916 by William Temple's lectures on *Plato and Christianity* to the W.E.A.: an eminent churchman, a firm belief in the enduring beauty and moral force of Greek thought, and working men for the audience.

Mill said that one of the benefits of studying the ancient world, and especially Greece, was that 'we are taught . . . to appreciate . . . intrinsic greatness, amidst opinions, habits, and institutions most remote from ours; and are thus trained to that large and catholic toleration, which is founded on understanding, not on indifference'. Matthew Arnold agreed; those who practised a constant commerce with the ancients seemed to him to be 'more truly than others under

the empire of facts, and more independent of the language current
among those with whom they live'.[28] His father, conceding that men
often threw their Greek and Latin aside in later life, believed none
the less that they gained from their early studies, even when they did
not realize it themselves, a greater liberality of tastes and notions. It
was not knowledge, he decided, but the means of gaining knowledge
that he had to teach.[29] Cory told his pupils that they would forget
much of what they learnt, but at least the shadow of lost knowledge
would protect them from many illusions.[30] Or as the schoolmaster in
Kipling's *Regulus* puts it, 'It sticks—a little of it sticks among the
barbarians.'

Just how good a Victorian education could be at its best is suggested by Cory's witty, sensitive and serious contribution to
Farrar's *Essays on a Liberal Education*. The task of a teacher, he
argued, is to educate the curiosity, and he urged his fellow teachers
not to be too tough intellectually. He noted, for example, that boys
preferred transcendental to empirical philosophy; their masters
should indulge this taste. 'Make the young enthusiast show cause for
his judgements; if not at the time, yet hereafter, he will discover the
weakness of the pleading. Give him plenty of truth, or what you
honestly believe to be truth, and he will know that other things are
false by mere juxtaposition. . . . Nor is there anything more to be
avoided than undue pressure in attacking opinions held, or'—and
this is a most sympathetic touch—'pretended to be held by the
young. It is needless to say how unfair it would be . . . besides . . .
there is the mischief done by boring.' He warned that younger
schoolmasters tended to set too high and rigid a standard. Indeed, it
was a part of his wisdom to recognize the frailties of teachers as well
as of their pupils: 'Men of strong will do not so very often become
schoolmasters . . .: the classical teacher is generally a possible
clergyman in his strength and in his weakness.'[31]

In the latter part of Victoria's reign the possible clergymen were
to face a challenge to their authority which they were ill-equipped to
resist; but half way through the century their position seemed
secure. When Cobden tentatively suggested in 1850 that there might
be more useful information in one issue of *The Times* than in the
whole of Thucydides, the remark was greeted with a storm of
derision and hung round his neck like an albatross for the rest of his
career. His biographer, John Morley, was moved to protest at the
use of this standing joke by journalists who knew little more about
Thucydides than Cobden himself, 'but who now wrote as if that rather
troublesome author were the favourite companion of their leisure

hours'.[32] No doubt there was much hypocrisy, but that is in itself a fact of significance.

CHRISTIANITY AND THE GREEKS

> Nor can I do better . . . than impress upon you the study of Greek literature, which not only elevates above the vulgar herd, but leads not infrequently to positions of considerable emolument.
>
> Thomas Gaisford, Christmas Day Sermon.

> If it were not for Lit. Hum. I might be climbing
>   A ladder with a hod.
> And seven hundred a year
>   Will pay the rent and the gas and the 'phone
>   and the grocer . . .
>
> MacNeice, *Autumn Journal*, sect. 12

Gaisford's dictum may be apocryphal, but it has a symbolic value. As Regius Professor of Greek he was paid a mere £40 a year, but he was also Dean of Christ Church; the large emoluments to which he referred were not academic but ecclesiastical. When Jowett succeeded to Gaisford's chair, his income actually went down, since he was obliged to give up the bursarship of his college; but for nearly ten years proposals to pay him adequately were defeated by fierce clerical opposition. Pusey feared that he could not support an increase without thereby condoning the professor's heresies, and when in 1864 the university was asked to raise the stipend to £450, Keble was dubious, Denison said that principle was being sacrificed to expediency, and the Bishop of Oxford declared that the proposal aimed a 'deadly blow at the truth of God'.[33] The Established Church had indeed forged a strange alliance with the ancient Greeks. In George Eliot's novels we hear of one bishop that 'though he was not an eminent Grecian, he was the brother of a whig lord', of another that 'he's all Greek and greediness'.[34] In Trollope's *Last Chronicle of Barset* Crawley asks what Arabin has done that he should be a dean: 'I beat him at everything; almost at everything. He got the Newdigate, and that was about all.' Arabin's prize was for poetry in mere English; Crawley, as the better classical scholar, feels entitled to higher preferment in the church.[35] Copleston was rewarded for his counterblast to Sydney Smith with a Doctorate of Divinity.[36]

Smith himself said of the English clergy, 'They fancy that mental exertion must end in religious scepticism; and, to preserve the principles of their pupils, they confine them to the safe . . . imbecility of classical learning. A genuine Oxford tutor would shudder to hear his young men disputing upon moral and political truth.'[37] Without a doubt many 'ecclesiastical instructors' clung to the classics out of sheer conservatism and a fear of the unknown. Smith could not resist the observation that the 'great system of facts' which the young Englishman knew best was 'with whom Pan slept?—with whom Jupiter?—whom Apollo ravished?'—but a clergyman himself, he could hardly emphasize the incongruity of clergymen pressing this information on their charges.[38] Only the occasional gadfly—a Shelley or a Swinburne—would insist that the Greek and Christian moralities were fundamentally irreconcilable.

None the less, some of the greatest Victorians experienced, not always consciously, a conflict between their passion for ancient Greece and their Christianity.

> Why, wedded to the Lord, still yearns my heart
> Towards these scenes of ancient heathen fame?

asked Newman in a sonnet written at Messina. He was entranced by the 'voice of bard that came Fixing my restless youth with its sweet art'; tears started to his eyes at the memory of the 'mad deeds that set the world aflame', by which he apparently meant the Athenian expedition against Sicily. Finally he answers his own question, too easily perhaps, in this way:

> Nay, from no fount impure these drops arise;
> 'Tis but that sympathy with Adam's race
> Which in each brother's history reads it own.

Of no great value as poetry, the sonnet is moving as the document of a soul's struggle against the spell of Greece. Henry Alford, Dean of Canterbury, composed his religious works in the reasoned style of a cultivated divine; not so his history of Greek poetry. After arguing that the Homeric epics were stitched together from ballads in the time of Pisistratus, he wrote, 'Reader, examine as thou wilt—judge as thou canst—. . . but in thy "heart of hearts" never call in question the identity or truth of THE IDEAL HOMER!' And he ends his chapter on the *Odyssey*:

A cloud is on the king—his brow darkens—the Odyssey is ended.
READER—THIS IS THE GREATEST WORK OF HUMAN GENIUS.[39]

His Christian writings do not assume this vatic tone.

Greece could be an alarming temptation. 'It is much easier,' says the hero of *Tom Brown at Oxford*, 'to face the notion . . . of a daemon or spirit such as Socrates felt to be in him, than to face what St. Paul seems to be meaning.' His friend answers, 'Yes, much easier. The only question is whether we will be heathens or not.'[40] In Ruskin the conflict reached a painful intensity. 'Ask yourselves,' he told one audience, 'what you expect your own children to be taught . . . Is it Christian history, or the histories of Pan and Silenus? Your present education, to all intents and purposes, denies Christ.' Yet in the same lecture he seemed to be trying to turn the Greeks into honorary Christians: 'Leonidas . . . died with the most perfect faith in the gods of his country, fulfilling the accepted prophecy of his death'—'Classicalism began . . . with Pagan Faith'—'So far as we are believers indeed, we are one with the faithful of all times—one with the classical believer of Athens and Ephesus. . . .' The Greeks may even teach the Victorians to be better Christians, for 'all ancient art was *religious*, and all modern art is *profane*'.[41] The case of Gladstone is still more eloquent. A visitor to Hawarden suggested a game: each member of the company was to say on which day either past or future he would most like to live. Gladstone chose a day in ancient Greece when Athens was at the zenith of its glory. The visitor chose the day of Pentecost. Gladstone looked ashamed and withdrew his choice, substituting 'a day with the Lord'.[42]

Heine said that all men were either Jews or Greeks. Arnold, knowing that his fellow countrymen could not so easily be divided into two opposite camps, preferred to speak of Hellenism and Hebraism as the two points between which the human spirit must for ever oscillate. Perhaps all ages are divided against themselves, but the Victorian age seemed to those who lived in it to be peculiarly a divided age, and they have bequeathed this picture of themselves to posterity. 'It was the best of times, it was the worst of times . . .'— Dickens began his tale of revolutionary France with a series of antitheses, only to find himself adding that these combinations of opposites made the late eighteenth century so very like the present time. It was a time, certainly, when both faith and doubt grew in strength and fervour; and similarly progress and decline, hypocrisy and integrity, all forms of conformity and disaffection, social, moral and political, seemed to have intensified. The religious conflict was often fought out within the compass of a single human mind, and in other ways too many of those eminent men whom we or their contemporaries have chosen to regard as typically Victorian seem to have represented their age in microcosm by being pulled in different directions by contrary impulses. Arnold was a melancholy romantic who sought to be classically serene; Dickens was torn between reformism and convention, as later between Ellen Ternan and respectability; Ruskin wanted art to be untrammelled by rules and laid down strict rules for making it so. Gladstone's character was the product of an enormous impetuosity reined in by rigid self-control; indeed it was the balance of these opposing forces that made his personality so powerful. Two books dominated his life, Homer and the Bible, and it is tempting to categorize the two sides of his temperament as the Hellenic and the Hebraic; but which would be which? Are we to contrast Hellenic temperance with the fierce energy inspired by revealed religion? Certainly, there is no questioning the passionate ardour of Gladstone's faith. On the other hand, his self-control was achieved by earnest prayer, and his Homeric studies were impelled by wild and eccentric enthusiasm. His Hellenism and his Hebraism were inextricably intertwined and in this as in so many other ways he typified his age.

But it was also characteristic of the age, or of its more enquiring members, to feel that between faith in Christianity and the love of Greece there must be a tension; Arnold was being consciously heterodox when he argued that Hellenism and Hebraism could be painlessly combined. Would a priest today be disturbed by the thought that he had been too much moved by Thucydides? And surely a modern Christian who found himself caught out by a prig as Gladstone was would shrug the matter off, deprecating too much seriousness in a parlour game. The Victorians were not so easily satisfied, and with Victorian energy they set about justifying the study of a pagan culture by a Christian people. Most of the arguments in favour of classical education were not specifically Christian; however, even its opponents conceded that parsons needed Greek in order to study the New Testament. This argument could be broadened to include every English gentleman, who, according to the *Quarterly Review* of January, 1863, 'should be able to read that portion of his Bible in the language especially selected by Providence for the communication of His last revelation to man'.[43] With startling exactitude the writer calculated that there are 1,237 places in St. Matthew and 1,089 in St. Mark where the Authorised Version falls short of the original 'in perfect distinctness and precision'. Alford wrote, 'No other language will ever express the meaning of God's Spirit as it may be seen to be expressed and known by those who read the New Testament in the original Greek. . . . Is it worthy of our Protestant position . . . that while we cry "Give the Bible to all", we should suffer it, in its depth and glory and beauty, to remain a dead letter to ourselves?'[44]

Why, though, was the study of Greek in schools and universities directed almost entirely to authors so different from the New Testament in dialect, let alone belief? One answer was that culture was one of the blessings offered to man by God and it was pre-eminently by the study of Greek that culture could be acquired. Frederick Temple maintained that Rome, Greece and Asia, as well as Judaea, had each been allotted by the economy of Providence a role in the education of the world. 'To Greece was entrusted the cultivation of the reason and the taste'; we owe to her art, science and logic. Moreover, Greek ideas had an essential part to play in the creation of moral wisdom and even in the revelation of God's nature: 'Conscience, startled at the awful truths which she has to reveal, too often threatens to withdraw the soul into gloomy . . . asceticism: then is needed the beauty which Greece taught us to admire, to show us another aspect of the Divine Attributes.'[45] In Matthew Arnold's terms, Hellenism was a necessary corrective to Hebraism; and Temple, unlike Arnold, was no doubter.

Westcott, the Bishop of Durham, wrote that 'the work of Greece . . . lives for the simplest Christian in the New Testament'. His view was that in the progress of Greek thought one can detect not one but several stages in the development of divine revelation. 'It is impossible,' he wrote, 'to overlook the relation in which Aeschylus stands to the Bible. He appears as the interpreter of a divine law.' Aeschylus was a 'preparation' for Plato, and Euripides too was a 'religious teacher' in whom appears a further 'distinct stage in the preparation . . . for Christianity'. The bishop meant that word 'preparation' seriously; the Greeks, like the Jews, had advanced step by step towards an ever greater understanding of the nature of God.[46]

Westcott saw that the political and cultural conditions of the times had been essential elements in the success of Christianity: 'Without the discipline of the Persian supremacy and the quickening impulse of Greek thought, a medium could not have been prepared [for] the revelation of the Gospel.' Kingsley put the same point in simple language for children: 'Greek became the common language of educated people. . . . And therefore it was that the New Testament was written in Greek, that it might be read . . . by all the nations of the Roman empire; so that, next to the Jews . . . we owe more to these old Greeks than to any other people upon earth.'[47] Any Christian may and perhaps must accept that the divine plan was to plant the seed of Christianity in a soil especially favourable to its growth; but it is one matter to believe in divine providence and quite another to think that by a little honest research its working can be confidently explained. From a scholarly point of view enquiries such as Westcott's could only have a bad effect, since they encouraged students of Greece to impose patterns on history that may not be there and to judge literature by standards which its authors would neither have understood nor accepted. Even in theological terms Westcott was imprudent, for it was all too easy for syncretists such as W. B. Richmond to represent his position as a 'refusal to treat Pagan and Christian as antagonistic terms'.[48]

'They hardly know that Christ was a Jew,' George Eliot wrote of her contemporaries. '. . . I find men educated at Rugby supposing that Christ spoke Greek.' Her first complaint could be applied with some colour of justification to the young Newman. In his *Apologia* he summarized his early opinions:

> Pagan literature, philosophy, and mythology . . . were but a preparation for the Gospel. The Greek poets and sages were in a certain sense prophets. . . . There had been a divine dispensation granted to the Jews; but there had been in some sense a dispensation carried on in favour of the Gentiles. . . . In the fulness of time both Judaism and Paganism had come to nought.[49]

This last idea went further than Westcott was ever to go; Newman's perversely systematic mind had not only divided Hellenism sharply from Hebraism, but had separated Christianity no less firmly from both. Christ was neither Greek nor Jew; or else he was both in equal measure. Later, in *The Idea of a University* Newman reduced the dispensations of providence to an almost mathematical formula and got a satisfactorily Catholic answer out of it: Greece plus Jewry equals Rome. Jerusalem, he argued, is the fountainhead of religious knowledge as Athens of secular knowledge. Rome combines the 'gifts' of Athens and the 'grace of Jerusalem'; 'She has . . . dispensed the traditions of Moses and David in the supernatural order, and of Homer and Aristotle in the natural.'[50] It is all very neat; a little too neat.

A sense of the close alliance between Christianity and the study of the classics, strangely but eloquently blended with an awareness of tension between them, runs right through the nineteenth century. But it was not until our own century that this sense was given its boldest expression. In 1933 T. S. Eliot argued, 'It is high time that the defence of the classics should be dissociated from objects which . . .

are of only relative importance—a traditional public-school system
. . ., a decaying social order—and permanently associated where they
belong, with something permanent: the historical Christian Faith.'
And he blandly set out an astonishing paradox as though it were a
self-evident truth: 'It is only upon readers who wish to see a Christian
civilization survive . . . that I am urging the importance of the study
of Latin and Greek. If Christianity is not to survive, I shall not mind
if the texts of the Latin and Greek languages become more obscure . . .
than those of the language of the Etruscans.'[51] Without the Victorian
tradition behind him he could never have penned those words.
However, classical studies were no longer under the control of
Christian instructors; also, as MacNeice was discovering, they no
longer paid so well.

Some Victorian Attitudes

RISE AND FALL

In *Marius the Epicurean* the hero and Flavian visit the site of a Greek
colony in Etruria. 'How strong,' they reflect, 'must have been the
tide of men's existence in that little republican town, so small that
this circle of gray stones . . . had been the line of its rampart! An
epitome of all that was liveliest . . . in the old Greek people . . ., it
had enhanced the effect . . . by concentration within narrow limits.'
The Greek world was so small; it seemed a microcosm of the larger
world, a place where life and history appeared to be simpler and
bolder. Macaulay remarked that the history of Greece was the best
commentary on the history of Italy; in both cases there was a country
divided into small independent commonwealths, a brief blaze of
brilliant achievement, and a rapid decline.[52]

Symonds, with that Victorian fondness for analogies drawn from
the human lifespan, announced that there were five periods of Greek
literature, 'superb adolescence, early manhood, magnificent maturity,
robust old age, and senility'. Matthew Arnold wrote, 'The culminating age of . . . Greece I call . . . a great epoch; the life of
Athens in the fifth century . . . I call one of the most highly
developed, one of the marking periods in the life of the whole human
race. It has been said that the "Athens of Pericles was a vigorous
man, at the summit of his bodily strength and mental energy".'[53] If
the literature of Greece rose and fell in a parabola, might not the
same be true of her history? Indeed literary works, so Macaulay
claimed, have their character determined by the historical era in
which they are composed; the Peloponnesian War changed the

character of Greece, and this was why Thucydides was more scientific and less picturesque than Herodotus.[54]

The nineteenth century was an age of universal histories; sometimes with heroic enthusiasm, often with fatal superficiality, the Victorians tried to impose laws and systems upon the infinite complexity of human experience. In our own time such energy and confidence have seldom been seen, except in Arnold Toynbee, the Procrustes of Chatham House and perhaps the last of the Victorians. Euripides called Athens 'the Hellas of Hellas', the quintessence of Greece; and the English Hellenists believed him. Now if the history of Greece is seen as essentially the history of her most famous city, it does indeed seem, like her literature, to have followed a fairly straightforward pattern; Lytton wrote a book entitled *Athens, Its Rise and Fall*. To Mill the story of Athens had the sublimity, and by implication the simplicity, of the Homeric epics: reviewing Grote, he said of Greek history, 'Its characters, its situations, the very march of its incidents, are Epic. It is a heroic poem . . . Athens, as a collective personality, may be called the hero. The fate of Athens speaks to the . . . sympathies like that of the Achilles or Odysseus of an heroic poem.'[55] Grote was no poet, but Mill had rightly interpreted his message. In the period after the death of Alexander, the Greeks spread their civilization more widely than ever before and achieved their greatest feats in science and mathematics, but Grote was not interested in describing this new era. When Demosthenes died in 322, his city's last hope of liberty died with him; Athens survived, but not the Athens that Grote admired, and at this point he drew his story to a close. Frederick Temple could write casually, as though it were undisputed fact, 'Greek history hardly begins before Solon, and it hardly continues after Alexander.'[56]

Matthew Arnold could identify the pivotal moment at which the decline of Greece began; it came with Athens' failure at Syracuse and her consequent defeat by Sparta: 'That was the true catastrophe of the ancient world: it was then that the oracles . . . should have become silent . . .; for from that date the intellectual and spiritual life of Greece was left without an adequate material basis of political and practical life.' Ruskin went even further, affirming that Thucydides' subject had been 'the central tragedy of all the world, the suicide of Greece'.[57]

Hazlitt declared that the 'Theseus' from the Parthenon appeared 'a world of grace and grandeur in itself, and to say to the sculptor's art, "*Hitherto shalt thou come, and no farther!*" What went before it was rude in the comparison; what came after it was artificial.'[58] The theory of rise and fall had already been applied to Greek sculpture by Winckelmann, who introduced into the study of art the conception of historical cycles within which a civilization's creative powers, like a living organism, went through a process of growth and decay. He divided the art of antiquity into four periods, the archaic, the sublime or grand (this was the age of Pheidias), the beautiful, and the imitative. The same pattern, he maintained, could be detected in Italian painting.[59] Symonds took over this idea: 'Greek sculpture,' he wrote, '. . . passes from the austere, through the perfect, to the simply elegant.' He compared the three orders of Greek architecture, and the progress of painting from Giotto through Raphael to Correggio as instances of the same law. Schlegel had traced the operation of this law in Greek tragedy: 'Aeschylus is grand, severe, and not infrequently hard. In the style of Sophocles, we observe the most complete proportion and harmonious sweetness. The style of Euripides is soft and luxuriant.' Symonds neatly combined Schlegel and Winckelmann: 'Aeschylus rough-hewed like a Cyclops, but he could not . . . finish like Praxiteles . . . Sophocles attempted neither Cyclopean nor Praxitelean work. He attained to the perfection of Pheidias . . . like Praxiteles, [Euripides] carves single statues of eminent beauty.'[60] Sophocles and Euripides were contemporaries, while Praxiteles flourished some fifty years after both of them were dead; but Symonds did not trouble himself with awkward details. The belief in a pattern of rise and fall was so pervasive that it crops up in unexpected places: James Elmes, an admirer of the Greek Revival, was sure that British architecture was improving all the time, but he tried none the less to fit this belief into a scheme of growth and decay:

> Architecture, like poetry, like painting, . . . has its rise, its progress, its perfection, and its decline. Its rise with us, was with the Aborigines of the island; its progress with the Anglo-Saxons, the Normans, and . . . the English; but when it will arrive at its perfection . . . is not the immediate object of inquiry.[61]

In *The Stones of Venice* Ruskin produced almost a parody of the theory. There were two periods in the history of the Venetian state, he maintained, the turning-point being the 'Serrar del Consiglio', and he continued with crazy precision, 'I date the commencement of the Fall of Venice from the death of Carlo Zeno, 8th May, 1418.'[62] In *Aratra Pentelici* his passion for constructing systems was carried to bizarre extremes. The sixth, fifth and fourth centuries, he says, 'are the period of Central Greek art; the fifth, or central, century producing the finest'. The progress and decline of Greek art in the nine centuries before Christ form a perfectly symmetrical pattern, thus:[63]

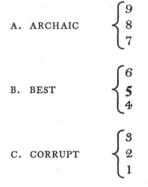

As he plunged downwards to the verge of madness, Ruskin increasingly displayed with unnatural clarity, as in a magnifying glass, the virtues and vices typical of himself and his age. The diagram in *Aratra Pentelici* is an exaggerated example of the Victorian desire to identify the 'best' period of any art and model oneself upon it. Ruskin made himself into the most influential critic of art that England has known; eloquence and energy played a large part in his success, but he owed some of it to his determination to establish rules for distinguishing good art from bad. In his last book, written in the intervals of brain fever, his lifelong concern with 'rightness' became an obsession. The palazzi of Florence are 'rightly hateful', a sketch is 'rightly felt', a concert 'rightly given'; and we even hear about 'rightly girlish directions' and 'right dancing'. Nature itself is subject to normative rules: Skiddaw and Saddleback are instances of 'the proper types of majestic form'.[64]

When Pater wrote that 'Breadth, centrality, with blitheness and repose, are the marks of Hellenic culture', he was echoing Winckelmann, but with one difference; 'centrality' was his own addition. The word 'central' occurs constantly in *The Renaissance*. He had picked up the habit from Ruskin, who spoke of 'the central character of Venetian art', of Dante as 'the central man of all the world', of the Doge's Palace as the world's central building.[65] The idea that cultures go through a process of growth and decline, and more particularly the idea that this process is symmetrical, had a profound effect upon beliefs and judgements. Ruskin believed that what was central was also right. He establishes the central character of

Venetian art by arguing from the historical and geographical situation of the city—here 'Roman, Northern, and Arabian elements' meet together[66]—but he clearly implies that the art of Venice is therefore of a special excellence; the virtues of centrality are assumed, not argued for. Pater thought that the age of Pericles was 'productive in personalities, many-sided, centralised, complete'.[67] Here is another leap of faith; because the fifth century was 'central', Pater assumes that the people of the period possessed especially well-rounded characters.

When Arnold called the fifth century a culminating epoch, he used a dangerous metaphor, for anything that is culminating is presumably higher than all else around it, and 'highest' is commonly a synonym for 'best'. When Symonds stated that in the Zeus of Olympia Pheidias 'touched the highest point of art', was he not influenced by the idea that the sculpture was produced in a culminating era? After all, the statue perished a thousand years ago; so how else was he apprised of its transcendent excellence? He also wrote that Sophocles represented Greek art 'in its most refined and exquisitely balanced perfection'.[68] Again the metaphor is treacherous. If the best art is poised perilously upon a fulcrum, then there need only be a tiny error in either direction and the balance will come crashing down on one side; so the rules come to seem enormously important. The dangers of this attitude were that the Greeks might come to seem hidebound and unimaginative. Arnold kept repeating depressingly that the great merit of Sophocles was his 'adequacy'; he was central, he measured up to the rules. But sculpture was the branch of art most dominated by Greek influence, and it was here that the effects were most pernicious. The characteristics of Greek sculpture of the best period became laws from which none might deviate. Pater turned the centrality of Greek sculpture into 'this standard of artistic orthodoxy'.[69] In Woolner's *Pygmalion* these lines recur several times:

> And this in pure immortal marble he
> Laboured to show; bound by those rules of Art
> The Wise had found inexorably fixed.

Woolner was a sculptor; the straitjacket that he ordered was for himself.

DISCIPLESHIP

The taller the statue, the louder the crash; Strachey's debunking essays would have created less sensation if the Victorians had not honoured their heroes so excessively. One of their demigods was Carlyle, and of all his lectures none were more successful than those *On Heroes, Hero-Worship, and the Heroic in History*. Kingsley's *Alton Locke*, an ardent admirer of Carlyle, takes an interest in the very way in which well-known authors drink their coffee, and on being introduced to a distinguished ambassador feels inclined to fall on his knees, and own a master of God's own making. Nor were such attitudes confined to fiction, particularly when directed towards the illustrious dead, whose technique with the coffee cup could not be tested and found wanting. Macaulay imagined 'the breathless silence in which we should listen to [Milton's] slightest word, the passionate veneration with which we should kneel to kiss his hand', and then congratulated himself on lacking the common inclination to idolize the great.[70]

The romantics had encouraged a belief in something called genius, an almost palpable quality, utterly different in kind from even the highest talent. The greatest artists and statesmen thus became enveloped by an aura almost of sanctity, while the charm and value of minor art was underestimated. Ruskin wrote, 'With poetry second-rate in *quality* no one ought to be allowed to trouble mankind. There is quite enough of the best.' Dr. Arnold refused to make any use at Rugby of such 'second-rate Latin poets' as Propertius: 'Of all useless reading, surely the reading of indifferent poets is the most useless.' Macaulay confessed that he admired no historians much except Herodotus, Thucydides and Tacitus, adding with magnificent condescension, 'There is merit, no doubt, in Hume, Robertson, Voltaire and Gibbon.' In a curious essay which is half a reaction against the Victorian style of Hellenism, half a reassertion of it, Virginia Woolf wrote, 'Greek is the impersonal literature; it is also the literature of masterpieces. There are no schools; no forerunners; no heirs. . . .' From the fifth century only the greatest writers have survived in any quantity; this circumstance, combined with a belief in the transcendent nature of genius, misled her into thinking them virtually independent of tradition and society. Thanks to the accidents of survival Greek literature of the 'best period' looks at first glance just what the Victorians thought a literature should be: a few towering peaks and no foothills. Even in the fourth century the picture seems remarkably simple; there are three giants, Plato, Demosthenes and Aristotle, and no one else who even reaches their shoulders.[71]

The writers of Augustus' reign had served as models in the

eighteenth century, but it had never been easy to idealize the age in which they lived, because they had themselves been so critical of it, so humbly conscious too of their dependence on Greece. Moreover, we know something about their personalities: Virgil was shy and tongue-tied, Horace plump and irascible, and so on. But with the doubtful exception of Socrates we have no idea what any of the fifth-century Greeks were like as people. They do not tell us themselves, and we have no other means of remedying our ignorance. It is hard enough to imagine how men thought and felt in ancient Rome, but far harder in the case of Greece, where we have no private documents comparable to Cicero's letters. Even the outward form of Hellenic society is surprisingly hard to reconstruct. From Latin writers we get partial but vivid pictures of social quirks and customs; the Athenians have been less obliging. Furthermore, they did not debunk themselves; even the plays of Aristophanes are shot through with a sense of the greatness of Athens. He makes fun of great men, but seldom in such a way as to diminish their stature. Besides, of all the great Greek writers Aristophanes had the least influence in the last century. The Victorians did not greatly value the comic muse, and in any case teachers shrank from introducing their pupils to so rich a storehouse of obscenity. Thomas Arnold did not even read Aristophanes until he was forty, and for long kept him off the Rugby curriculum. Ruskin made an honest man of him, but at the cost of taking away the fun: the jests of Aristophanes, he revealed, were 'bitter, purposeful, sorrowing'.[72] The White Queen, who could believe six impossible things before breakfast, would have recognized in Ruskin a kindred spirit.

The Last Days of Pompeii and *Marius the Epicurean*, despite being set in Italy under the empire, are concerned as much with Greek civilization as with Roman; but there are very few Victorian novels actually set in ancient Greece, and those insignificant. Lytton left *Pausanias the Spartan* unfinished, while Landor's *Pericles and Aspasia*, a collection of imaginary letters, merely illustrates why the novelists kept clear of Hellas. It is less a novel than a succession of moral reflections; Landor sees the Greeks not as real people but as the heroic figures on a bas-relief, else he could not have allowed them to compose those dead, marmoreal epistles about their own excellences. The historical novelists were usually confident of their ability to get under the skins of past generations, but subconsciously they seem to have realized that the Greeks remained aloof; even in fiction they could only be viewed from a distance.

The effect of hero-worship on historiography was notable. When

Thomas Arnold argued that Greek history from Pericles to Alexander was particularly instructive because of its modernity, he reluctantly conceded that the period of Roman history between the Gracchi and the Antonines was more completely modern, but he added that we know less about it, because the writers of the time were inferior to the Greek, and the freedom of enquiry less.[73] This was a poor argument; Arnold forgot the importance to the historian of first-hand sources—letters, documents, decrees—and these have come down to us from Rome in far greater abundance than from Greece. Nor did he consider that inferior writers may be more useful sources than their betters, because they have less capacity to select and interpret events to fit their own theories. There can be no serious doubt that we know more about Rome in the time of Cicero, when we can trace the progress of events virtually from day to day, than about any period of Greek history. Arnold went astray because he was writing about Thucydides; he seems to assume that the greatest of historians must be the most reliable, and he wants the student to submit himself to a master spirit. Grote was not so compliant, and argued that the demagogue Cleon, depreciated by his personal enemy Thucydides, was really a far-sighted statesman. The title of Richard Shilleto's riposte—*Thucydides or Grote?*—suggests that because Thucydides is the greater historian of the two his account is the more readily to be accepted.

The habit of discipleship affected education too; the pupil's attention was mostly directed to a very few writers of the highest genius. It was excellent that the student had the opportunity to know the best authors intimately; but the critical temper was often insufficiently encouraged. Cory, most subtly reflective of Victorian schoolmasters, warned of the risk of supposing that classical authors could not err: 'What was taken to be classical taste by those who did battle against useful knowledge was, to a great extent, irrational imitation and phrasemongery.' He agreed that his task was to teach taste, but he explained that taste is 'discrimination, a kind of reasoning'; we must recognize 'mere copiousness of sound' in Cicero and 'monstrous fatuities' in Aeschylus.[74] His principle was good: a breathy enthusiasm for the masterpieces of the past was no training for the mind, nor in the long run would it help to defend classical education against attack.

A posture of genuflexion induces cramp if it is kept up for long. As the century wore on, readers tended to stray more and more into hitherto neglected byways; Theocritus and Apuleius were two favourites of the aesthetes. Pater explained, 'If our modern education . . . really conveys to any of us . . . idealizing power, it does so (though dealing mainly . . . with the most select and ideal remains of ancient literature) oftenest by truant reading.' There is truth in this; to be always upon the peaks of Parnassus can leave one a little breathless. Besides, hero worship was going out of fashion; Yeats spoke for a new generation when he suggested that the classic authors were not wholly harmonious personalities but people as erratic and imperfect as ourselves:[75]

> You ask what makes me sigh, old friend,
> What makes me shudder so?
> I shudder and I sigh to think
> That even Cicero
> And many-minded Homer were
> *Mad as the mist and snow.*

BOSWELLISM

At first sight it may seem a paradox that the growth of hero-worship should be accompanied by an increase in what Macaulay called 'Boswellism': a desire to glimpse the private lives of great men, to catch them off their guard, to observe their foibles and mannerisms. However, the paradox is not hard to resolve. Boswell's *Life* scandalized Johnson's circle because they thought that it belittled their dead friend, but actually its effect is the opposite: the more care the author takes to record his subject's oddities and lightest words, the more the reader feels that he is in the presence of a great man; for why else should these trivial intimacies be of such absorbing interest? The information that Cromwell had warts does not diminish him. On the contrary, it provokes the response, 'To think that even he had this imperfection'; which only serves to strengthen the impression of greatness.

Not content with peering into the private, daily lives of great men, the Victorians boswellized the past wholesale; the more one reverenced the ancients, the more exciting it was to find that one had something in common with them. Ruskin counted among the most useful lessons of his childhood the discovery 'that the Greeks liked doves, swallows, and roses just as well as I did'. George Eliot's Dorothea is overcome by a 'sense of revelation, this surprise of a nearer introduction to Stoics and Alexandrians, as people who had ideas not totally unlike her own'. Even Landor, who carved the Greeks in laborious marble, was not immune from a desire to depict the great 'off duty': 'To-day there came to visit us a writer who is not yet an author: his name is Thucydides . . . Sophocles left me about an hour ago . . . Euripides was with us at the time.' This goes hand in hand with an attempt to bring Athenian life and customs before the reader's eye: 'Hither come the youths and maidens,' Pericles superfluously tells Sophocles, '. . . hither come citizen and soldier. . . . O what an odour of thyme . . . and from what a distance . . .' Sophocles responds by informing his friend that the celebrants are wearing white costumes.[76] There is a touch here of Lytton's insistent didacticism: ' "Yes," said the aedile's wife . . . "he is a *retiarius* or netter; he is armed only, you see, with a three-pronged spear like a trident . . .; he wears no armour. . . ." '[77] One hears the voice of Mr. Puff in *The Critic*, 'The less inducement he has to tell all this, the more . . . you ought to be obliged to him; for . . . you'd know nothing of the matter without it.'

'Who are these coming to the sacrifice?' Keats asked about the figures on his Grecian urn. 'What little town . . . is emptied of its folk . . .?' The past is dead, and yet by means of the vestiges that remain it seems almost to come alive again; almost but not quite. It is this poignant sense of being so near and yet so far with which Keats tantalizes himself. If only clay and stone could speak . . .—a vain wish, but one which in the early 1800s seemed almost to be coming true with the uncovering of Pompeii. Excavations had begun in 1748, but progress was desultory until Napoleon took an interest, and their biggest influence on English taste came with the publication of Gell's *Pompeiana* (1817–1832). The effect on the decorative arts was considerable, but far more lasting was the effect on the way people thought about the past. Never, before the discoveries at Pompeii and Herculaneum, had the public been able to view the everyday, domestic life of so remote a period; and after all, the emotion that Keats felt is the more poignant in proportion to both the antiquity and the ordinariness of the objects that inspire it.

The progress of archaeology gave birth to a new kind of history which gave special emphasis to the manners and customs of past ages, for history, like politics, is the art of the possible. And just as the development of political economy led to the theory that economic motives lie behind all human behaviour, so the growth of social history induced the belief that historical events should be explained by the nature of the societies in which they happened. This attitude could be brought to the study of literature: in a book written for the English market, K. O. Mueller aimed to show how Greek literature 'sprang from the taste and genius of the Greek races and the constitution of [their] civil and domestic society'.[78] The rise of the historical novel, and in particular the international reputation of Scott, was another powerful stimulus to social history. Conversely, social history influenced the historical novel: the aim of Thackeray's Esmond was to strip the 'mask and cothurnus' from history and make it 'familiar rather than heroick'.[79] History and the novel merge in Becker's *Charicles*, a highly didactic account of an Athenian lad's daily life, which was translated into stilted English by Frederick Metcalfe and widely used in schools. Metcalfe claimed in his preface,

> This description of the every-day pursuits . . . of the Greeks, this glimpse at their domestic scenes, and introduction . . . to the interior of their dwellings, will not only infuse additional zest to the student's survey of their life as a nation; but will also [help] in estimating the motives and springs of their public actions . . . on the same principle that we . . . contemplate the doings of public men with more curious interest, should we happen also to enjoy their private . . . acquaintance.[80]

This passage reveals how close is the connection between the boswellizing of individuals and the boswellizing of whole societies; it also suggests how easy it is to pass from enjoying boswellism to believing that it holds the clue to understanding history.

In the last century many people still felt that the novel was necessarily a trivial form of art; T. H. Green and Symonds, for example, both argued on Aristotelian grounds that reading novels is a form of self-indulgence:[81] we enjoy them because the characters are just like ourselves, but for that very reason they cannot ennoble us as a great classical play can. Thirlwall felt sure that novel-reading was a sign of decadence, since the novel's parentage could be traced back no further than a late epoch of Greek literature, when 'the powers of the national mind were miserably enfeebled'.[82] The novelists' response to such criticism tended to be ambivalent: on the one hand they affected a studied modesty, stressing how humble and inglorious their stories were; on the other, they implied that the lives of unexceptional people were in a way a nobler theme than the kings and demigods of heroic poetry. The historical novel was perfectly suited to this ambivalence: though it humanized history, it also glamourized everyday life, clothing it in history's seriousness and dignity. Lytton wrote in the preface to *The Last Days of Pompeii* (1834), 'No man who is thoroughly aware of what Prose Fiction has now become . . . can so far forget its connection with History, with Philosophy, with Politics—its . . . obedience to Truth—as to debase its nature to the level of scholastic frivolities; he raises scholarship to the creative, and does not bow the creative to the scholastic.' The modern reader may be surprised to find footnotes and citations in a novel; Lytton, by contrast, excuses himself for not including more of them.

The preface ends with the hope that the book may be 'a just representation of the human passions and the human heart, whose elements in all ages are the same'. And later we are told, 'In the tale of human passion, in past ages, there is something of interest even in the remoteness of the time. We love to feel within us the bond which unites the most distant eras—men, nations, customs perish; THE AFFECTIONS ARE IMMORTAL!'[83] Kingsley told his readers that he had shown them their own likenesses in *Hypatia*;[84] the book is subtitled, *New Foes under an Old Face*. This theme, announced in the first chapter of *Waverley*, runs persistently through the historical novels of the last century, distinguishing them sharply from the works of such modern counterparts as Mary Renault. She too may be concerned deep down to show the unity underlying the *apparently* enormous variety of human behaviour and belief in different ages, but on the surface she emphasizes our alienation from the ancient Greeks. Most of her books are narrated in the first person by a frank, confiding voice describing—as we realize with a sense of shock—the most extraordinary behaviour as though it were the most natural thing in the world. She uses the first person narrator to show how human beings, ordinary respectable human beings, can think and act so differently from ourselves. The historical novelists of the last century usually chose third person narrations; they pointed to the similarities between past and present with an omniscient objectivity.

The convenience of historical fiction was that it could mask a facile escapism behind a façade of serious purpose. Lytton glamourizes antiquity in the very act of claiming to do the opposite; indeed the historical novelist's ambivalence about the past is by him almost schematized. Were the ancients essentially like us, or were they not? Lytton has his cake and eats it: while he persistently likens the lower classes of Pompeii to modern Italians, so different from a northern people such as the English, he no less assiduously compares their superiors to the *beau monde* of London. He also notes that Pompeii was a 'half-Grecian colony . . . mingling with the manners of Italy so much of the costumes of Hellas'.[85] The minor characters are Roman, as petty and silly as ourselves; but the hero and heroine are Greek, and wondrously high-minded. The book is a celebration of Hellenic virtue and genius; but by setting it in imperial Italy, Lytton is able to look back on the great age of Greece, as the hero Glaucus does himself, with a gaze of distant adoration. The plot is a sentimental melodrama which floats like froth upon a turgid mass of archaeological pedagogy; and even the archaeology becomes a means of self-indulgence. The guests at a dinner-party stroll over the famous mosaic of the barking dog; Glaucus stretches out on one of the seats 'which the visitor . . . sees at this day in that same tepidarium'.[86] The modern tourist sees these relics with a metaphorical 'do not touch' inscribed upon them; the reader, however, is invited to put himself in the shoes of the characters in the novel and treat those celebrated objects with a casual familiarity; in fact, to indulge the tourist's furtive fantasy. Glaucus' home turns out to be the well-known House of the Dramatic Poet.[87] Antiquaries, Lytton tells us, have named the house wrongly; *we* know better. Thus the reader is lured into a bogus sense of intimacy with Pompeii, and flattered by the possession of a special knowledge denied to pedants and professors. Lytton can even use archaeology to lend his own work a spurious venerability: 'Let the traveller search . . . for the house of Ione. Its remains are yet visible; but I will not betray them to the gaze of commonplace tourists.'[88]

Despite its date, *The Last Days of Pompeii* has something of a late Victorian air; it seems of a piece with the paintings of Poynter and Tadema. This is explicable: the boswellizing tendency was to increase throughout the century, and even to affect the way in which Greek literature was read. Macaulay commented on the *Protagoras*, 'A very lively picture of Athenian manners. There is scarcely anywhere so interesting a view of the interior of a Greek house. . . .'[89] Maybe he was merely recording a useful source, as a historian should; but it would be easy to slide from this into thinking that depicting a classical interior was part of Plato's purpose, as it was Becker's and Lytton's. When Symonds writes, 'With Plato and Aristophanes for guides we can . . . reconstruct the life of the Athenians, animate the statues . . ., and see . . . the Pnyx crowded with real human beings', he may seem simply to be playing the part of the social historian; but in truth he has the sentimental impulse to interpret any work of Greek literature as a portrait of the artist set against a richly picturesque backdrop. The verses of Mimnermus, for example, 'breathe the air of sunny gardens and cool banquet-rooms, in which we picture to ourselves the poet lingering . . ., endeavouring to crowd his hours with pleasures . . . yet . . . made fretful among his roses. . . .'[90] From this it was but a short step to the idea that all literature, even drama, is a form of auto-biography; Wilde claimed that 'behind the painted masks of an Aeschylean play or through some Sicilian shepherd's . . . reeds the man and his message must have been revealed'. Pater described the Meditations of Marcus Aurelius as 'the romance of a soul', and in his last book he interpreted Plato's dialogues as precisely that. People of very different kinds shared the desire to assimilate the people of bygone ages to themselves: just as the middlebrows turned the Greeks and Romans into Victorian middlebrows, the aesthetes turned them into aesthetes. Samuel Butler wrote, 'If a person would understand . . . any . . . ancient work, he must never look at the dead without seeing the living in them, nor at the living without thinking of the dead. We are too fond of seeing the ancients as one thing and the moderns as another.' He was attacking, as people so often do, the fault into which he and his contemporaries were the least likely to fall.[91]

V

TRAGEDY

A fiat went forth that only one, or in some cases two, visits more could be made to the Greek play.

It was too exciting.

Alan St. Aubyn, *The Junior Dean*[1]

THERE is scarcely one of the Attic tragedies that does not contain passages of notably difficult Greek; and maybe this simple fact is the chief reason for their scant influence upon English literature before the last years of the eighteenth century. To be sure, *Samson Agonistes* is perhaps the most Greek in spirit of all English plays; but here as elsewhere Milton stands immensely alone, a giant set apart from all other writers of his age and nation. Homer attracted eighteenth-century translators as eminent as Pope and Cowper, but Greek tragedy, for whatever reason, was left to lesser men: the names of Francklin, Potter and Wodhull are not inscribed in the pantheon of English poetry. This may help to explain why the tragic poets were so little appreciated in England for so long; it was the Germans, in the end, who taught the English to revere them.

Winckelmann had attributed simplicity and calm grandeur to the best literature of the Greeks as well as to their sculpture. Lessing disagreed; while sharing Winckelmann's feelings about sculpture, he held that the representation of violent emotion was possible and appropriate in poetry. The Greeks had recognized the distinction: Philoctetes does not suffer with calm dignity; he shrieks and howls. These two critics had already begun between them to show the variety of interpretation that could be applied to Greek tragedy, and to the German romantics that variety was to be a powerful stimulus.

A. W. Schlegel delivered his lectures on the drama in 1808; seven years later they were translated into English. It was these, more than the genius of Goethe or Schiller, that brought Englishmen to realize the greatness of Greek tragedy. For the most part Schlegel followed Winckelmann, praising Greek drama for its statuesque perfection; 'It is only before the groupes of Niobe or Laocoön,' he wrote, 'that

we first enter into the spirit . . . of Sophocles.'[2] Paradoxically, the less
he was read, the greater his influence grew—at second hand. For the
rest of the century most English writers were to adopt his account of
Greek drama, with minor variations, and those who were sternest in
criticizing him, such as Symonds and De Quincey, were usually those
who depended upon him the most. Innumerable schoolboys and
undergraduates, many of whom may not even have known his name,
must have derived their idea of Greek tragedy indirectly from his
lectures. But though his influence outlived its usefulness, it was
valuable at the time, because he excited people sufficiently to send
them back to the original texts. And in the high summer of
romanticism it was inevitably Aeschylus who stirred their most
ardent enthusiasm. Now Aeschylus cannot easily be fitted into a
picture of Grecian serenity, and indeed Schlegel allowed a more
romantic interpretation, detecting in him a resemblance to Dante and
Shakespeare: 'All his poetry,' he decided, 'evinces a sublime . . .
mind. Terror is his element . . ., he holds up the head of Medusa . . .'[3]
He preserved the analogy with sculpture by comparing Aeschylus to
Pheidias, but Pheidias to any Englishman suggested the grand,
rugged figures from the pediment of the Parthenon, carved in a style
markedly different from the cool classicism that Winckelmann had
admired. Symonds was to vary the metaphor, saying that Aeschylus
'rough-hewed like a Cyclops' and comparing each of his plays to a
'gigantic statue'.[4] Throughout the century, in fact, Aeschylus was
usually seen as a Gothic or romantic artist. Men like Pater who
wished to portray the Greeks as calm and classical were forced to
ignore him altogether; he was too strong for them. Symonds compared him to Marlowe and Victor Hugo; conversely, Swinburne
addressed Hugo as Aeschylus. Tovey praised Weingartner for
describing the solemn fugue in Beethoven's 'Eroica' Symphony as
Aeschylean; Virginia Woolf likened Aeschylus to Shakespeare and
Dostoyevsky. Ruskin found in both Aeschylus and Shakespeare the
grotesque element that he loved in Gothic architecture but missed in
Greek buildings and 'the lower Greek writers'; and we have found
him comparing the shafts of St. Mark's to 'the wild lyric rhythm of
Aeschylus and Pindar'.[5] Pindar, indeed, was the other Greek poet
who was invariably portrayed as a turbulent romantic, and the two
were often compared. Symonds talked of 'the *Sturm und Drang* of
Pindar's style', no doubt recalling that Pindar and Aeschylus were
the two poets who had most thrilled the young Goethe, and compared
him successively to a rocky mountain, a blazing fire, an Alpine
torrent, and a thunderstorm at sunset, 'while drifting scuds of hail and

rain, tawny with sunlight, glistening with broken rainbows, clothe peak and precipice and forest in the golden veil of flame-irradiated vapour'.[6] The gimcrack grandeur of this imagery was evidently meant to share the splendiferous quality of the poetry that it purported to describe.

The picture of Pindar as an untamed child of nature derived originally from Augustan Rome. 'Like a river rushing down from the mountain,' Horace had written, 'swollen by the rains above its wonted banks, Pindar seethes . . . with deep-toned voice . . . he is borne along in a metre freed from rule. . . .'[7] Inspired by this account, English poets had been composing Pindaric odes for some two centuries, but these usually owed little to Pindar himself: a stanza of irregular form and a certain grandiosity of tone were enough to make a poem 'Pindaric'. Pindar's language is difficult and his distinctive qualities inimitable in English; so his influence was never likely to be wide. Shelley's habit of clothing abstractions in metaphors of sumptuous brilliance makes him perhaps the most truly Pindaric in spirit of all English poets, but there is little reason to suspect a direct influence. Francis Thompson, who named Blake and Aeschylus as his favourite poets, aimed for a loosely Pindaric effect in poems such as his *Ode to the Setting Sun* and *A Corymbus for Autumn*, with their asymmetrical stanzas and Grecian trimmings. *The Hound of Heaven* is not Greek in subject-matter, but here again Thompson is Pindaric or Aeschylean in his romantic metre and his use of grandiose compound adjectives: wind-walled, lucent-weeping, cypress-crowned. Pindaric too is the plush, luscious imagery: gold, banquets, chariots, milk, the spume of the sea.

The poet who learned most from Pindar was Hopkins (a professional scholar, sure enough), who wrote analyses of his metre and at the time of his death was planning a book on the 'Dorian measures' as 'an introduction on the philosophy . . . of rhythm in general';[8] he also worked on the choruses of Aeschylus. In him poetry and scholarship were a unity; the study of Greek metre inspired his sprung rhythm, and the invention of sprung rhythm stimulated his researches into Greek metre. Writing to Bridges in defence of *The Leaden Echo and the Golden Echo*, he said, 'The long lines are not rhythm run to seed. . . . No, but what it *is* like is the rhythm of Greek tragic choruses or of Pindar: which is pure sprung rhythm.' But he was less at ease about Pindar's influence on another poem: 'The Deutschland would be more generally interesting if there were more wreck and less discourse, I know, but still it is an ode and not primarily a narrative. There is some narrative in Pindar

but the principal business is lyrical.'[9] Pindar often begins by address-
ing a muse or deity, and Hopkins likewise begins with a prayer to his
God. Like Pindar again, he combines heroic narrative not only with
general reflections about man and god but with some account of his
own life and circumstances. Moreover, *The Wreck of the Deutschland*
is, like Pindar's poems, a victory ode, a celebration of the human
spirit triumphant. Hopkins probably had the *Fourth Pythian* particularly in mind as he wrote: it is by far the longest of Pindar's odes
just as *The Deutschland* is by far the longest of Hopkins's poems; in
fact, they are virtually the same in length, and in both the central
narrative is concerned with a voyage by sea. The bold, strange
language of Hopkins's ode was utterly unlike anything that he had
attempted before; it seems that Pindar pointed the way for him to
the style that he was to make so distinctively his own. None the less,
he had created an immensely original poem; indeed it is not despite
his originality but because of it that he was able to learn from Pindar,
whereas for most poets to be Pindaric meant merely to strike a
bardic attitude and beat a big drum.

Aeschylus was more easily appreciated, and especially the
Prometheus Bound, above all because the lonely, defiant Titan,
suffering for his magnanimous rebellion against the ruling power of
the universe, seemed a superhuman embodiment of the romantic
hero. Byron said that he had been passionately fond of the *Prometheus*
as a boy and could 'easily conceive its influence over all . . . that I
have written'. His ode to Prometheus was stimulated by re-reading
the play with Shelley; his *Manfred* reminded the *Edinburgh Review*
'more of the *Prometheus* . . . than of any more modern performance'.[10]
Shelley himself, atheist, republican and Old Etonian, felt for the
story of the rebellious god a special and predictable affection; no less
predictably, it was Marx's favourite among Greek plays. Swinburne
used it as a stick to beat the godly with: 'In the face of the earlier
revelation of Prometheus to a prophet of our own Aryan race, what
does it matter that in the eyes of sundry children of circumcision
Jehovah may seem to have begotten Jesus . . .?'[11]

'Prophet', 'revelation'—it was fun to steal the Christians' clothes.
Swinburne described his *Altar of Righteousness* as 'Aeschylus v.
Moses', and planned a paper 'on Athens and Jerusalem as the two
rival fountains of light and darkness . . . showing how Aeschylus, the
greatest Greek poet, would have been less if he had not been a Greek,
while Dante . . . would have been greater if he had not been a
Christian.'[12] Had he taken up Aeschylus merely *pour épater*, he would
no doubt have lavished his chiefest praise on the *Prometheus*, but he

knew and loved him too well; it was the *Oresteia* that he called 'the greatest spiritual work of man'.[13] Swinburne hated religion; milder agnostics, who wanted a substitute for their lost faith, were still more drawn to the 'spiritual' element in Greek tragedy. Matthew Arnold expected poetry to take over the role of Christianity: 'In poetry . . . our race . . . will find an ever surer and surer stay. There is not a creed which is not shaken, not an accredited dogma which is not shown to be questionable. . . . Our religion has materialized itself in the fact, in the supposed fact . . . and now the fact is failing it. But for poetry the idea is everything.' Arnold believed that in the best art and poetry of the Greeks 'religion and poetry are one' and 'the idea of beauty . . . adds to itself a religious and devout energy'.[14] In the tragedians he found the perfect, indeed the only, realization of his poetic ideal. Here was a drama sprung from sacred ritual and animated by an authentic religion. That religion had perished; but it had inspired in the tragedians an enormous moral energy which was still arresting, still modern after two and a half thousand years. And by a miracle this intense moral seriousness was expressed in a poetry that could stand comparison with anything in the literature of the world. For the Greeks, Arnold said, 'the aim of tragedy was *profound moral impression*'; Greek tragedy gives us 'a lofty sense of the mastery of the human spirit', and this in turn 'conducts us . . . to *a sentiment of sublime acquiescence in the course of fate, and in the dispensations of human life*'.[15] Sublimity, moral dignity and a sort of religious submissiveness—where else could Arnold have found all these together? He wrote of the Greek poets from Pindar to Sophocles, 'No other poets so well show to the poetry of the present the way it must take; . . . no other poets, who have so well satisfied the thinking power, have so well satisfied the religious sense.'[16] Then he quoted from the *Oedipus Tyrannus*, translating it into a kind of scriptural language: 'Oh! that my lot may lead me in the path of holy innocence of word and deed. . . . The power of God is mighty . . . and groweth not old.' And he comments, 'Let St. Francis—nay, or Luther either,—beat that!' With these words, which conclude an essay designed specifically to contrast pagan and medieval religious sentiment, he comes perilously close to retracting all that he has said in the previous pages. Even he, who was so concerned to distinguish Hellenism and Hebraism, found it hard to resist drawing comparisons between Greek tragedy and Judaeo-Christian thought.

Macaulay observed that Aeschylus 'often reminds us of the Hebrew writers' and likened his plays to the Book of Job. Apologists for religion seized every opportunity to convert the tragic poets into *animae naturaliter Christianae.* Eventually this was to lead to a reaction: Forster's Mr. Jackson observes, 'You know the Greeks aren't broad church clergymen. . . . Boys will regard Sophocles as a kind of enlightened bishop, and something tells me that they are wrong.'[17] Small blame to them, though, when real bishops agreed with them: both Westcott and Lightfoot wrote approving essays about the religious thought of the Greek tragedians. Newman turned Aeschylus and Sophocles into preachers: struck by 'the majestic lessons concerning duty and religion' in their plays, he concluded, 'Such poetry may be considered oratory also, since it has so great a power of persuasion.' Conservative Christians tended to identify themselves with the orthodox pagans of the fifth century: as early as the 1830s Keble remarked how trite was the complaint that Euripides spoke 'without due restraint of the immortal Gods'. Keble himself clearly agreed that this would be a grave objection if it were true; but Euripides, he argued, was no scoffer at the gods. In Hippolytus he depicted the purest chastity, foreshadowing Christ's promise that the pure in heart shall see God. In the *Bacchae* he tried to 'exalt the characteristic mystery, which so deeply pervades all divine things', and showed that nothing in religion is 'to be held of light account simply because its justification is not immediately apparent'.[18] A variant of this view was that Euripides had been converted from scepticism to orthodoxy in old age. Pater described the *Bacchae* as 'an *amende honorable* to the once slighted traditions of Greek belief'. Paley presented the poet as a Hellenic version of Mill or Matthew Arnold, possessed of a 'thoughtful and naturally devout mind', forced to disbelieve the 'popular theology' but finding 'no satisfaction in his unbelief'. The *Bacchae* is accordingly 'rationalistic in its tendency' but 'curiously interspersed with passages in praise of the old traditional belief'.[19] This would not be a bad description of Mill's essay on Theism.

Christians and agnostics were at one in praising the tragic poets as thinkers, and religious thinkers at that. One might have expected Arnold to discover in Euripides, allegedly a questioner of traditional belief, a spirit similar to his own, but instead he found 'an art— wonderful indeed . . .—but an art of less moral significance than the art of Sophocles and Aeschylus'. Jowett's reservation about Euripides was the same: 'The two greatest of the Greek dramatists,' he asserted, 'owe their sublimity to their ethical character.' His biographers, Abbott and Campbell, were carried rather further by enthusiasm for the piety of Sophocles. Abbott wrote an essay on 'The Theology and Ethics of Sophocles'. He conceded that Greek literature would never have quite the place of the Hebrew scriptures as a 'text-book of daily life'; it is striking that he should make this admission in a tone of mild surprise. Of the *Oedipus at Colonus* Campbell wrote, 'Oedipus is ruined in this world, but having suffered here . . ., he is accepted of the gods, and after his death becomes a spiritual power. There is even an approach to the [Hebrew] doctrine . . . of the blessedness of sorrow'.[20] This play was a particular favourite with Christian writers; it deeply impressed Newman,[21] and drew from Alford an enthusiastic sonnet, ending with praise of 'a kingly soul, Lifted to heaven by unexampled woe'. This misrepresents Sophocles: the passing of Oedipus was certainly 'wonderful if mortal's ever was', and his bones are to become a source of power to their possessors, but he is not 'lifted to heaven'; he goes down to such oblivion or shadowy existence as may be supposed to await the dead in the world below. Nor is there any indication that his sorrow is blessed, except insofar as posthumous fame is a blessing; indeed, as his end approaches, he reacts to his sufferings with increasing violence and bitterness. In the course of the century even the *Prometheus*, that favourite of the irreligious, was reclaimed for the faith. Coleridge declared that Promethus was 'the Redeemer and the Devil jumbled together'; Gladstone discerned in the play signs 'that the celestial rays had not even then "faded into the light of common day" '; Alford suggested that Aeschylus might have learnt through the mysteries 'some part of the creed of man before the flood' and asked, 'This benefactor of human kind—. . . thus crucified on high—bears he not a dim resemblance to One other whom we know? It is so—but how, we say not.'[22]

Twentieth-century scholars have reacted sharply and justifiably against the idea that the Greek tragedians were teachers or moralists. They have insisted that the proper business of the dramatist is drama; and in any case the 'messages' that can be extracted from Greek tragedy usually turn out to be distressingly banal. When Westcott discussed Euripides as a religious teacher, he did not sufficiently distinguish between the deliberate intentions of the poet and the divine purpose of which he supposed him to be the unconscious instrument; when Symonds explained Greek tragedy by saying that 'ethical philosophy is more than ever substantive in verse', he was being merely silly. None the less, the modern reaction can easily go too far. The Victorian scholar Tyrrell was not far wrong when he described Aeschylus as a great intellect who looked at the problems of life and death with an intense interest.[23] He does not treat these problems as either Plato or Isaiah would but he is very

much concerned with them. One of the glories of Greek tragedy is
that it combines the representation of men in action with the earnest
contemplation of moral, social and religious ideas. Of course
Sophocles was neither a novelist nor a philosopher; and yet we may
perhaps say that there were elements of both in him.

Was the novel the modern equivalent of Greek tragedy? Virginia
Woolf compared Aeschylus to Dostoyevsky, and Sophocles, more
unexpectedly, to Jane Austen. Coleridge classed the *Oedipus Tyrannus*
with *The Alchemist* and *Tom Jones* as one of the three most perfect
plots ever planned. Ansell, in Forster's *Longest Journey*, takes the
part of a Euripidean chorus, being both a spectator of the drama and
a participant in it: 'The irony of the situation . . . reminded him of
the Greek Drama, where the actors know so little and the spectators
so much . . . Ansell prepared himself to witness the second act of the
drama; forgetting that all this world, and not part of it, is a stage.'[24]
Hardy saw the fate of Tess Durbeyfield in Greek terms: ' "Justice"
was done, and the President of the Immortals, in Aeschylean phrase,
had ended his sport with Tess.' In making the hero and heroine of
Jude the Obscure cousins he sought to stir memories of the Aeschylean
family curse. Sue remarks, after she and Jude have heard the grim
history of a common ancestor, 'How horrid that story was. . . . It
makes me feel as if a tragic doom overhung our family, as it did the
House of Atreus.' This novel inspired Swinburne to tell Hardy that
he was *poiētōn tragikōtatos*, the most tragic of the poets.[25]

In 1939 T. S. Eliot put the Furies on to the West End stage, in a
play set in modern England. A few years earlier Yeats had written,

> What climbs the stair? . . .
> 　. . . Neither content
> Nor satisfied Conscience, but that great family
> Some ancient famous authors misrepresent,
> The Proud Furies each with her torch on high.[26]

In more prosaic language, the Furies of Greek tragedy are a
personification—a 'misrepresentation', in a sense—of an unchanging
element of man's experience. Yeats himself explained his poem by
saying, 'We have all something within ourselves to batter down and
get our power from this fighting.'[27] Some Victorians thought that
they could see the terrible message of the ancient dramatists realized
in history. Symonds wrote to a friend in 1871, 'What a fine play
Aeschylus would have written on the Crime, the Hubris, and the
Ate of France. Nemesis is a great moral fact.'[28] Carlyle described
the French Revolution as a 'natural Greek drama, with its natural

unities'. Swinburne so conceived his historical drama *Bothwell* that
to Mary Queen of Scots 'the phantom or idea of her rival is ever
present as the *protarchos ata* or first Nemesis'.[29] (The Greek phrase is
from the *Agamemnon*.)

George Eliot shared the view that Greek tragedy dealt with the
unchanging facts of human nature. A man's character is affected by
heredity, and his circumstances by the actions of his parents and
grandparents; the family curses of Greek tragedy, so she believed,
are an expression of this same reality. Similarly, the 'necessity' or
'compulsion' of which Aeschylus speaks is an unalterable fact of the
human condition: a man's evil actions can never be undone, and they
entail inevitable consequences both for himself and for other people.
She was right, or partly right: necessity in Aeschylus—on one level
at least—is psychological necessity. Agamemnon takes the decision
to sacrifice his daughter for the sake of the Greek expedition against
Troy. This sinful act produces a revulsion in his wife Clytemnestra,
tempting her to adultery and ultimately to murder. The consequence
of the murder is that Clytemnestra is killed by her son Orestes. The
consequence of matricide is that the mother's vengeful ghost incites
the Furies to torment her son. Thus one terrible deed leads inexorably to another until the final resolution, when Orestes is
vindicated and freed from persecution. Naturally there is more to the
Oresteia than this, much more; the nature of justice, the use of
suffering, the relation of human actions to fate and the will of Zeus
are further and profound questions which Aeschylus probes without,
perhaps, giving any final answer. But the moral and religious
complexity of his work gains enormously in power from being
embedded in a story which makes sense in simple—really quite
simple—human terms. The contrast with Wagner, who admired
Aeschylus deeply, is instructive. The mechanisms on which the plot
of his tetralogy depends—a ring which makes its possessor all-
powerful, a dragon's blood with miraculous properties, a Valhalla
which collapses the moment that the ring is returned to the Rhine-
maidens—are magical and arbitrary; they seem to be there to suit
the convenience of the composer. The great Greek dramas, however
strange or primitive the beliefs that they express may be, are rooted
in the real world in a way that Wagner's story is not; this is true
even of the *Prometheus*, in which every character but one is an
immortal. Hardy failed to measure up to Aeschylus in a different
way: there is no terrible inevitability about the fates of Tess or Jude;
they are merely accident-prone. There is more of the Greek spirit in
The Mayor of Casterbridge: the events which bring about Henchard's

downfall succeed one another inexorably, and almost all are linked to the guilty secret of his past. Only at the end does Hardy break the chain of necessity, making Henchard die in romantically squalid circumstances for no better reason than to round off the book in an atmosphere of satisfying gloom. He makes no explicit reference to Greek drama in this novel, but he does quote the saying of Novalis, 'Character is fate'[30]—an aphorism which had already been borrowed by George Eliot and which summed up her own interpretation of Greek tragedy. More prudent than Hardy, and more subtle, she did not challenge direct comparison with the Greek dramatists, but stressed the differences between their art and her own as much as the resemblances.

Victorian novelists could sprinkle allusions to Greek tragedy through their books without obvious artificiality because they lived in an age when there were people who found in these plays a powerful consolation for their distresses. Shattered by the news of his sister's death, Macaulay found one solace only. 'That I have not utterly sunk under this blow,' he said, 'I owe chiefly to literature . . . I have gone back to Greek literature with a passion quite astonishing to myself.'[31] Plato cheered him, but it was in the tragedies that he found the words which spoke to his condition. A few months later he copied down some bleak and famous lines from the *Oedipus at Colonus*,[32] lines that were afterwards to be recalled by Yeats at the end of *A Man Young and Old*:

> Never to have lived is best, ancient writers say;
> Never to have drawn the breath of life, never to have looked into
>   the eye of day;
> The second best's a gay goodnight and quickly turn away.

Like Macaulay, Yeats felt the undying eloquence of Greek tragedy; but indirectly. His very free translation of the *Oedipus at Colonus* was made from the French, since he was unable to read it in the original; and he confessed without remorse that the last line of *A Man Young and Old* was 'very bad Grecian, but very good Elizabethan and so it must stay'.[33] Macaulay, on the other hand, was in the habit at the time of his bereavement of reading a Greek play in the original every Sunday.[34] Yeats used the tragic poets when it suited him, Macaulay submitted himself to their influence; each was in a way typical of his time.

The imprisoned Wilde drew comfort from the same source. 'In the most wonderful of all his plays,' he wrote, 'Aeschylus tells us of the great Lord who brings up in his house a lion-cub . . . and loves it because it comes bright-eyed to his call and fawns on him for its food. . . . And the thing grows up and shows the nature of his race . . . and destroys the lord . . . and all that he possesses. I feel that I was such a one as he.'[35] Theatrical as always, Wilde saw himself as the protagonist of a Greek tragedy, a great man brought down by what Aristotle called *hamartia*, a fatal error or mistake. How neatly that metaphor from the *Agamemnon* fitted his own case: by the lion-cub Aeschylus had meant Helen, and Wilde for his part considered that he owed his ruin—not to a *femme fatale* precisely, but to Lord Alfred Douglas. The bright-eyed Bosie had fawned on him for his food, or so he chose to think: the pages of *De Profundis* are sprinkled with bitter complaints of the debts that he had incurred giving the boy luxurious little suppers at Willis's and sumptuous dinners at the Savoy. It was Lord Alfred's father who had goaded him towards catastrophe, and the son had shown the 'nature of his race' (or 'the nature of his parents', as Aeschylus actually says) by turning against Wilde in his time of need. Despite the scriptural title of *De Profundis* and its pervasive religiosity, no other work of Wilde's is so full of Greek echoes and quotations. With nostalgia he recalled 'the grace of sweet companionship, the charm of pleasant conversation, that *terpnon kakon* [pleasant evil] as the Greeks called it'. It is Phaedra, in the *Hippolytus* of Euripides, who uses these words to describe long conversations; a woman ruined, like Wilde, by a perverted passion. He turned to the same poet again when he looked forward to his release:[36] 'I . . . hope to go at once to some little seaside village abroad. . . . The sea, as Euripides says . . . washes away the stains and wounds of the world'—and here he quoted, thereby revealing how far he was in spirit from the lapidary simplicity of the Greek, for 'the world' and 'stains and wounds' are his own embellishments; Euripides says 'all the ills of men', nothing more.

Macaulay's nephew claimed that his uncle's thoughts 'were often for weeks together more in Latium and Attica than in Middlesex'.[37] Trollope was not being fantastic when he portrayed in Josiah Crawley a man who would escape into ancient Greece from the poverty and anxiety that beset him in his parsonage:

'When they have rid themselves of me they may put him here, in my church; but not yet,—not yet. Where is Jane? Tell her that I am ready to commence the Seven Against Thebes with her.' . . . The Seven Against Thebes was commenced with great energy . . . Mrs. Crawley from the kitchen would hear him reading out with sonorous, rolling voice, great passages from some chorus.

Like Wilde, he sees himself as a tragic hero: 'He read much Greek
with Jane on that afternoon, pouring into her young ears . . . his
appreciation of the glory . . . and the humanity, as also of the awful
tragedy, of the story of Oedipus. His very soul was on fire at the
idea of clutching the weak bishop . . ., and crushing him. . . .'[38] But
Trollope is using Sophocles to create a dramatic irony of his own. At
the start of the *Oedipus Tyrannus* the king puts too much confidence
in his capability; he scorns the prophet Teiresias, as Crawley scorns
his bishop. But Oedipus will be brought low and expelled from his
kingdom, while Crawley, for his part, will be driven to resign his
office. Trollope pictures him, as he prepares for this painful task,
reverting to ancient Greece once more, but in an altered mood.[39]
He reads the story of Polyphemus in the *Odyssey* and compares it to
Samson Agonistes: 'It is the same story. Great power reduced to
impotence, great glory to misery, by the hand of fate,—Necessity,
as the Greeks called her; the goddess that will not be shunned.' And
of Milton's hero he says, 'The impotency, combined with his
strength, or rather the impotency with the memory of former
strength and former aspirations, is so essentially tragic!' We may
think it disproportionate for a poor clergyman to compare himself to
the great heroes of poetry and drama; and indeed Trollope intends us
to think so. Crawley displays courage and fortitude, but these noble
qualities are flawed by pride and even a taste for self-dramatization.
He is devoted to the pastoral care of his parishioners; yet in time of
trial he turns for comfort not to the Bible but to pagan Greece. The
references to classical poetry are not only an ironic comment upon
Crawley's history; they also reveal his personality.

The Greek tragedies are concentrated; they have the formidable
compression of a coiled spring. Seeming to possess romantic
sublimity without romantic indiscipline, they held a special attraction
for the Victorians, who were half the heirs of the romantics, half in
rebellion against them. As Arnold said, 'The Greek tragic forms . . .
satisfy in the most perfect manner, some of the most urgent demands
of the human spirit. If, on the one hand, the human spirit demands
variety and . . . range, it equally demands . . . depth and concentration
in its impressions.'[40] The longest Greek tragedies contain fewer than
1,800 lines, and the *Prometheus* conjures up its world of titanic
immensity in a mere 1,100. Victorian imitators failed to match this
concision: *Merope* totals 2,024 lines, *Atalanta* 2,317. De Quincey
objected that the Greek dramas were too short for 'the contraction
and expansion, the knot and the *dénouement*, of a tragic interest,
according to our modern meaning'. More shrewdly, G. H. Lewes

noted the contrast between the serenity of Goethe's *Iphigenia* and the
ancient dramas, which dealt with the darkest passions: these are 'for
ever kept in agitation, and the alternation of pity and terror close
only with the closing of the scene . . . this drama is distinguished by
the very absence of the repose which is pronounced its characteristic.'[41] Though rebuked for this opinion by Arnold, Lewes was
essentially right: in a play such as the *Oedipus Tyrannus* each act is so
charged with emotion and suspense that when (for example) Oedipus
and the chorus greet the news from Corinth with an outburst of
brief, deluded joy, we feel that a dam has given way under the
intolerable weight of the passions pent up behind it.

Why then did so many nineteenth-century critics stress the
reposefulness of Greek tragedy? Even at a first sight the notion seems
to run counter to the evidence. In the words of Schiller's epigram,
'Oedipus tears out his eyes, Jocasta hangs herself, both guiltless; the
play has come to a harmonious conclusion.' When Arnold tried to
answer Lewes, he seemed to imply that he meant 'repose' only in a
peculiar and restricted sense: 'Sometimes the agitation becomes
overwhelming,' he admitted, 'and . . . the torrent of feeling flows for
a space without check . . . but the balance of feeling is restored before
the tragedy closes: the final sentiment in the mind must be one . . .
of acquiescence.' He went on to say that 'This sentiment of
acquiescence is, no doubt, a sentiment of *repose* . . . Sophocles does
not produce the sentiment of repose, of acquiescence . . . by avoiding
agitating circumstances: he produces it by exhibiting to us the most
agitating matter under the conditions of the severest form.'[42]
Expressed thus, Arnold's disagreement with Lewes would seem to be
slight: but it is apparent from elsewhere, not least from the style of
Merope itself, that in his heart of hearts he thought that the Greek
drama was reposeful in a much stronger sense; after all, he had
inherited his idea of it from the romantic critics, and when they had
said that it was calm, they had meant that it was calm all through.
And in any case what he wrote in the preface to *Merope* was hardly
consistent; at one moment he located the reposefulness of Greek
tragedy in the sentiment of acquiescence that the spectator feels
when the play comes to an end, at another in the severity of its
formal construction, apparently unaware that these are two quite
different things. Besides, if the reposefulness of a play is to be found
in a final restoration of the balance of feeling, the tragedies of
Shakespeare are at least as reposeful as those of the Greeks; but
Arnold wanted to think of reposefulness as a peculiarly Hellenic
quality.

At least Arnold saw that his view required defence and explanation; other English critics were prepared to assert the opinions that they had received from German writers with unreflective confidence. Hazlitt declared that the plays of Sophocles were 'hardly tragedies in our sense of the word. They do not exhibit the extremity of human passion and suffering.' The aim of ancient tragedies, he explained, was to show how the greatest calamities could be borne with the least emotion: 'Firmness of purpose, and calmness of sentiment, are their leading characteristics. . . . The mind is not shaken to its centre; the whole being is not crushed. . . . All is conducted with a fatal composure.'[43] This was not only wrong but silly; and De Quincey was even sillier: 'Struggle there is none,' he wrote, 'internal or external . . .' (What about Agamemnon and Clytemnestra? one wonders. Or Phaedra? or Orestes?) 'Medea, the most tragic figure in the Greek scene, passes through no flux and reflux of passion, through no convulsions of jealousy on the one hand, or maternal love on the other. She is tossed to and fro by no hurricanes of wrath, wrenched by no pangs of anticipation.'[44] It is hard to believe that he had read the plays.

Especially influential, and especially misleading, was Schlegel's notion that the chorus represents the 'ideal spectator'; this came of reading the plays with little or no chance of seeing them on stage. Nietzsche was eventually to demolish the theory in a couple of pages.[45] Is it characteristic of the ideal spectator, he asked, 'to rush on stage and deliver the god from his fetters'? And besides the spectator remains conscious that what he sees before him is a work of art, whereas the chorus is bound to regard the characters on the stage as veritably existing. Lastly, Schlegel had ignored the historical development of tragedy; its primitive form consisted of the chorus alone without actors, and 'a spectator without drama is an absurdity'. Nietzsche remarked that Schlegel's theory was 'dazzling because of . . . the typically German bias for anything called "ideal" '; but its appeal was equally great in England, and it encouraged the tendency to regard the tragedies more as poems than plays. Hazlitt called the *Prometheus* 'less a tragedy than an ode'. Macaulay declared in his youthful essay on Milton that 'the Greek Drama . . . sprang from the Ode', and said of Aeschylus, 'Considered as plays his works are absurd; considered as choruses they are above all praise.'

Later, however, he came to appreciate the power of Aeschylus as a dramatist, noting for example that the long silence of Hamlet upon his first appearance was 'very fine, but not equal to the silence of Prometheus and Cassandra in the Prometheus and Agamemnon of

Aeschylus'.[46] And indeed even *Prometheus*, the most static of all Greek tragedies, cries out for performance. Not only is the hero's silence in the first scene contrasted with his sudden outburst of passionate, solitary lament; his chained and motionless form is put into comparison first with the gracious, floating figures of the daughters of Oceanus and later with the darting agitated movements of the tormented Io. Nor does Aeschylus disdain the simpler, more sensational methods of creating theatrical interest: Oceanus arrives riding a winged monster, his daughters drift in upon some kind of aerial machine, and the play ends with thunder, lightning, earthquake and the titan shouting defiance amid the confusion.

'Less a tragedy than an ode'—Hazlitt's inadequate description of the *Prometheus Bound* would do admirably for *Prometheus Unbound*; but Shelley himself was well aware how greatly he differed from Aeschylus. Although he took the *Persae* as the model for his own *Hellas*, he freely admitted that the result was not a true drama but 'a series of lyric pictures'.[47] In the preface to *Prometheus Unbound* he revealed why he had not tried to follow the story told in Aeschylus' lost play: first, he shrank from a direct comparison with so great a poet, and second, he was 'averse from a catastrophe so feeble as that of reconciling the Champion with the Oppressor of mankind'. Greek writers, he observed, had not scrupled to adapt the mythology to their own purposes, and he now 'presumed to employ a similar licence'. It was characteristic of him to defend a departure from his Greek model in terms of fidelity to the true Greek spirit, and his preface is a fine account of how a keen study of antiquity might accompany and even enhance a vigorous modernity. He remarked, for instance, that his imagery was often drawn from the operations of the human mind: 'This is unusual in modern poetry. . . . But the Greek poets . . . were in the habitual use of this power; and it is the study of their works . . . to which I am willing that my readers should impute this singularity.'

In the *Agamemnon* Clytemnestra relates how the tidings of victory have been brought from Troy by a chain of beacon fires leaping from Ida to Lemnos, from Lemnos to Athos, and so onwards until the message reaches Argos. In *Hellas* Shelley took up this theme and transferred it to a more abstract plane:[48]

> Freedom's splendour burst and shone:—
> Thermopylae and Marathon
> Caught, like mountains beacon-lighted,
> The springing Fire . . .

It lived; and lit from land to land
Florence, Albion, Switzerland.

The beacon fires of Aeschylus have been transformed into the torch
of liberty, the hills and promontories of Greece into whole nations.
Shelley's poem is like a beacon itself; he does not merely echo
Aeschylus, but catching sight of the light from distant Greece, he
kindles his own new fire in response. To the reader who remembers
the *Agamemnon* this combination of homage and independence is
moving and impressive.

The first words of Aeschylus' Prometheus are a great lament, an
appeal to earth and air and the all-seeing circle of the sun to witness
his sufferings. In *Prometheus Unbound* these elements are transformed (the verb is Shelley's own) by the dawn of a new age of joy
and freedom:[49]

> Soon as the sound had ceased whose thunder filled
> The abysses of the sky and the wide earth,
> There was a change: the impalpable thin air
> And the all-circling sunlight were transformed,
> As if the sense of love dissolved in them
> Had folded itself round the sphered world.

And in a larger sense the whole poem is a transformation of
Aeschylus: it starts as something like a Greek tragedy, but then like
a butterfly cracking open its chrysalis, it breaks from this outworn
mould and escapes into rhapsody. In Aeschylus' play the Oceanides
enter amid soft music and sweet perfumes; Shelley builds upon this
theme, creating from it an ecstatic nature-worship mingled with a
romantic Platonism—the visions of John Martin put into words.
This is a magnificent conception, and only in one respect does
Shelley fail badly. His Prometheus is wholly brave and good, his
Jupiter wholly evil. Aeschylus had more feeling for the true
complexity of things.

No poet of the nineteenth century had a stronger sense than
Shelley of his debt to the Greeks. But he was unafraid; he would
learn from Aeschylus and then go his own way. With Arnold the
case was different: it was timidity that turned his thoughts to Greece.
'The tradition is a great matter to a poet,' he wrote in the preface to
Merope; 'it is an unspeakable support.' Whereas Shelley invented
boldly, Arnold nervously admitted, 'Where driven to invent . . . I
could not satisfy myself until I discovered in Pausanias a tradition
which I took for my basis. . . .' The play, in fact, was an exercise, a

means to an end: 'I have long had the strongest desire to attempt, for my own satisfaction, to come to close quarters with the form which produces such grand effects in . . . the Greek masters; to try to obtain . . . a fuller . . . feeling of that beauty, which . . . so powerfully affected me.' Indeed, he had originally thought to achieve his purpose by translating Aeschylus or Sophocles. There is something touching in the humility with which Arnold submits to following his Greek heroes, but such discipleship was not the way to make great poetry. Perhaps the best feature of *Merope* is the portrayal of the tough but not unfeeling ruler Polyphontes, a complicated mixture of personal ambition and genuine principle. But though his character is quite skilfully depicted, he is out of place in what aspires to be a Greek tragedy. Arnold excites no pity or terror; an air of sweet reasonableness pervades the play. Merope wishes Polyphontes no ill, although he has murdered her husband; she trusts that a bad conscience (a typically pallid substitute for the Furies of the Attic stage) will be punishment enough.[50] Polyphontes himself is a Tory politician who has killed the previous king as the only method of counteracting his democratic policies. He could almost belong to a Victorian novel; indeed, he bears a certain resemblance to George Eliot's Bulstrode, the devout evangelical whose prosperity and position are owed to one dishonest act committed many years ago. When Bulstrode erred, it was in the confidence that good would come of his misdeed, because he was one of God's elect; similarly, Polyphontes is 'the too bold man, who dares Elect himself Heaven's destined arm'.[51] It would be awkward in any play with a Greek subject for the characters all to be Victorians; in one so closely modelled upon Sophocles' *Electra* it is disastrous.

Goethe wisely left the chorus out of his *Iphigenia*; Arnold was not so venturesome. His chorus is indeed the ideal spectator, which only serves to demonstrate how gravely Schlegel was mistaken. Arnold gives the maidens of the chorus no function to perform whatever; indeed, they do not utter a single word for more than three hundred lines after their entrance. This would be intolerable in the theatre, but so far is he from visualizing the play in performance that he slips the chorus on to the scene between two lines of a continuous speech. Yet unless a Greek tragedy is intended for performance, and for performance under certain distinctive conditions, its conventions become merely pointless and burdensome. Obsequious to the rules of Greek drama, he is utterly false to its spirit. His references to the gods are occasional and half-hearted. How could they be otherwise? Hopkins rebuked Bridges for putting a goddess into his *Ulysses*:

'Her speech is the worst in the play: being an unreality she must talk unreal. Believe me, the Greek gods are . . . the merest frigidity, which must chill and kill every living work of art they are brought into.' His own method was different: 'I sent you a sonnet . . . in which a great deal of early Greek philosophical thought was distilled; but the liquor of the distillation did not taste very Greek, did it? The effect of studying masterpieces is to make me admire and do otherwise.'[52] Yet Hopkins himself could get caught up in the game of recreating ancient Greece. Bridges had earlier written *Prometheus the Firegiver*; Hopkins referred to it as Π.Π.* (the poem's title would be *Prometheus Purphoros* in Greek). 'What a sense of style,' he told his friend, '. . . how vigorous the thought, and how Greek.' Dixon agreed that it was 'a very good poem: particularly the choruses: extremely Greek in feeling.' Mackail thought that it came nearer to the Greek spirit and tone than any English play since Milton.[53] All these men assumed that to be Greek was to succeed; it had become an end in itself.

The success of Swinburne's *Atalanta* had made it seem that there was still life in the old Greek forms, but in reality the play owed its popularity to the lilting alliterative choruses that were its least Hellenic feature. While the world admired his innovations, the poet strangely congratulated himself on his lack of originality: 'I think it is pure Greek . . . Shelley's Prometheus is magnificent and un-Hellenic. . . . As for . . . Merope the clothes are well enough but where has the body gone?' Yet Swinburne too was eager to submit himself to the guidance of a Greek master: 'It must always be as evident that I am, in this line of work, . . . a disciple of Aeschylus as that Arnold is a pupil of Sophocles.' He told Symonds that he was learning Aeschylus by heart. His second Hellenic drama, *Erechtheus*, was designed to be more 'purely genuine in its Hellenism of form and thought' than *Atalanta*. The lyrics were to 'conform rigidly to the *musical* rule of Greek tragedy'; Jowett had provided 'hints from the . . . scholarly point of view, on which side I want to make this poem impregnable'.[54] One cannot help being impressed by the vigour with which Swinburne set about destroying his own talents, and all for love of Greece.

The choruses of *Atalanta* are even more detached from the action than in *Merope*. Worse still, Swinburne uses them as a means of sticking his tongue out at Christianity like a naughty child. The moral tensions of Aeschylus are debased into abuse of 'the supreme evil, God': 'All we are against thee . . . O God most high.' This pose of

* i.e. P.P.

cosmic defiance, surprising in a company of Greek maidens, consorts awkwardly with the calm bleak paganism expressed elsewhere in the play:

> And there is no light after, and no storm,
> But sleep and much forgetfulness of things.

Even this attitude is more Roman than Greek: in Aeschylus the dark life of the underworld has a fearsome reality; Agamemnon and his queen cry out for vengeance from beyond the grave.

'Horrid word to spell,' Cory said of Erechtheus;[55] a sharp piece of literary criticism in just four words. Swinburne's chorus assure the heroine,

> In all time
> Thy name shall blossom, and from strange new tongues
> High things be spoken of thee

—a false prophecy, since the name of Chthonia is not often upon our lips, perhaps because it is unpronounceable. For this drama Swinburne had chosen a myth of exceptional oddity and obscurity, and not surprisingly it failed to fire his imagination; what was Chthonia to him or he to Chthonia? The dullness and artificiality of such supposedly Hellenic plays as *Erechtheus* cast a blight, in the public's eyes, over the whole of Greek tragedy; in Gilbert and Sullivan's *Thespis* Jupiter pronounces a dreadful execration:

> Away to earth, contemptible comedians,
> And hear our curse, before we set you free;
> You shall all be eminent tragedians,
> Whom no one ever goes to see!

Arnold had made Sophocles, the man who 'saw life steadily and saw it whole', the patron saint of his crusade against the Philistines, but he made him sound so dull: 'The peculiar characteristic of the poetry of Sophocles is its . . . *adequacy*; that it represents the highly developed human nature of that age . . . in its completest . . . development.'[56] But who would join a crusade that had 'Adequacy' and 'Development' emblazoned upon its banners? Perhaps Pater might have; he wrote in *The Renaissance* that Greek tragedy showed how a conflict of rival claims might be treated with serenity and display the dignity of the human spirit; but he then passed quickly to another subject.[57] If he accepted Arnold's picture, this was because it enabled him to dispose tidily of the tragic poets, who did not well fit his Winckelmannish conceptions.

Other Greek writers continued to excite a lively interest right up to the end of the century, but the influence of the tragic poets declined markedly; those who were still responsive to them turned increasingly from Sophocles to Euripides. Forster was thinking of his own undergraduate days at Cambridge when he wrote in *Maurice*, 'They argued . . . about Sophocles, then in low water. Durham said it was a pose in "us undergraduates" to ignore him.' Browning wrote in praise of those

> certain few that (wisest they of all)
> Had, at first summons, oped heart, flung door wide
> At the new knocking of Euripides,
> Nor drawn the bolt with who cried 'Decadence!
> And, after Sophocles, be nature dumb!'

These words, though given to a fifth-century Greek girl, reflect his own reaction against the classicizing Hellenism of Arnold.[58]

The variety offered by three different masters had always been one of the attractions of Greek tragedy: 'When I was a boy,' Coleridge said, 'I was fondest of Aeschylus; in youth and middle age I preferred Euripides; now in my declining years I admire Sophocles.'[59] The critics, simplifying as critics inevitably do, had overstated the differences between the three poets; they exaggerated the ruggedness of Aeschylus and the sophistry of Euripides, while Sophocles was turned into an exemplar of classical perfection. This last judgment contained an element of truth, but it also owed much to the theory of symmetrical rise and fall which placed Sophocles, in defiance of chronology, midway between the other two poets at the culminating point of Greek literary history. All three are exceptionally complex writers; but it was so much easier to tag each one of them with a label. Mrs. Browning spoke of 'Aeschylus the thunderous', 'Sophocles the royal' and 'Euripides the human, With his droppings of warm tears'; the characterizations are typical.[60]

Speaking crudely, one can say that Aeschylus was the most influential of the three in the romantic period, Sophocles in the middle of the Victorian age and Euripides towards the end of the century. (Swinburne is not really an exception, for with his pose of Promethean hostility to the Deity he was a Byronist born too late.) Schlegel, Macaulay, Keble and Arnold all assumed in their essays and lectures that Euripides was the least of the three poets. It was widely agreed, though, that he was the most modern of them. He was 'like a modern Frenchman', Coleridge thought, 'never so happy as when giving a slap at the gods'. Alford thought him 'of the three great masters, unquestionably the greatest *Dramatist*, in the modern sense'. Mrs. Browning, by describing him as elevating things common, turned him into a forerunner of George Eliot. Pater found in the *Bacchae* 'touches of a curious psychology, so that we might almost seem to be reading a modern poet'.[61]

However, the Victorians tended to worship those artists who were most unlike themselves—Homer, Raphael, Bach—and perhaps the supposed modernity of Euripides did not help his reputation. Bit by bit, though, he forced himself on their attention, almost against their will. At the age of fifteen Macaulay judged him 'the vilest poet that ever put pen to paper'; ten years later he wrote that, 'Instead of correcting what was bad, he destroyed what was excellent. He substituted crutches for stilts, bad sermons for good odes.' But in India, after his more careful study of the tragic poets, he found that Euripides had 'made a complete conquest' of him, concluding that if more of Sophocles had survived, and less of Euripides, their relative reputations would be greatly altered.[62] Arnold tried hard to make *Merope* Sophoclean, but his naturalistic, unemphatic delineation of character was more in the manner of Euripides, as was the detachment of his choral odes from the action; indeed, he could not resist basing one of them on a fragment from Euripides' *Cresphontes*.[63] Swinburne purported to detest Euripides. Now a hearty dislike of some part of Greek literature is a sure sign of the really eager Hellenist (one might compare Macaulay's feelings about Xenophon of Ephesus: 'below the lowest trash of an English circulating library'),[64] and Swinburne laid into his *bête noire* with the warmth that arises from an intimate and personal enmity. 'Sophist' and 'pedant' are the mildest terms that he employed: 'I should very much like,' he said, 'to see the play of Euripides which contains 500 consecutive lines that could be set against as many of mine.'[65] In the light of this boast it is fascinating to read his *Phaedra*, a long and monotonous fragment of pseudo-Greek tragedy that attempts to improve upon Euripides' *Hippolytus*, and fails. Why did he regard Euripides as a personal rival? Surely because he felt akin to him and unconsciously projected on to him his own self-doubt and self-loathing. Gleefully inspired by Mrs. Browning's reference to the poet's 'droppings', he said that Euripides had been 'troubled with a dysentery of poetic imagination and a diarrhoea of rhetorical sophistry'; the description would apply much better to himself.

And the influence of Euripides kept seeping irresistibly into his work. Consciously or unconsciously he modelled his Atalanta, a virginal huntress devoted to the cult of Artemis, upon Hippolytus. It is almost incredible that he should have proclaimed himself a disciple of Aeschylus while he was writing *Erechtheus*. The plot is strongly reminiscent of the *Hecuba*; stranger still, he tried to follow the version of the story used in Euripides' lost play *Erechtheus* so far as it can be reconstructed—dramatic evidence of how he unconsciously identified himself with the poet whom he claimed to despise. Some fragments survive from the lost play, including a speech of 55 lines by the victim's mother. Swinburne translated nine of them and incorporated them into his play. The translation is almost literal, and yet the difference between the two passages is enormous. Euripides makes the mother's speech psychologically revealing: she is trying to justify her decision to allow her daughter's cruel death. Her unease is shown by touches of aggression—'I hate those women who prefer their children to the good'—and self-congratulation: 'O country, would that all your inhabitants loved you as I do.' In Swinburne the drama and the agony of moral choice have disappeared: the mother calmly lists the reasons why the daughter must die (in a speech of 134 lines) and the daughter as calmly accepts them. The serenity of the daughter exemplifies the difference between neoclassical calm and the authentic Greek feeling. In the *Hecuba* Polyxena, the sacrificial victim, looks forward to her death stoically indeed, but as an escape from the humiliation of slavery, and perhaps only to console her mother Hecuba with the thought that her fate is not as piteous as it appears; Hecuba herself will wreak a gruesome revenge, blinding Polymestor and murdering his sons. Swinburne's Chthonia seems to accept her death without a pang, and her mother, astonishingly, tells her how lucky she is to have the chance of being sacrificed: 'Then hast thou . . . a better part than we, A holier portion than we all.'[66]

In Browning Euripides found a champion who appreciated the dramatic function of his speeches and debates. Like Arnold and Swinburne, Browning put himself into a posture of discipleship, incorporating translations of *Alcestis* and *Heracles* into *Balaustion's Adventure* and *Aristophanes' Apology*. His version of *Alcestis* is interspersed with Balaustion's comments analysing the dramatist's stage technique and skill in drawing character. But Euripides was not always so fortunate in his admirers. Pater took the *Bacchae*, a work of violent beauty and ferocious animation, and announced that the whole play was penetrated by a 'sort of quiet wisdom'. Even when he described the ecstasy of the maenads, he made it sound like the emotion of a don taking a walk in the country: 'that giddy, intoxicating sense of spring—that tingling in the veins, sympathetic with the yearning life of the earth.' Euripides' subtle portrayal of Pentheus is severe but sympathetic—the young king is a weak man pretending to be strong, a mixture of puritanism and prurience, of honour and narrow-mindedness—but of this Pater was unaware: 'Like the exaggerated diabolical figures in some of the religious plays . . . of the Middle Age, he is an impersonation of stupid impiety.'[67]

The objections of earlier generations to Euripides had decided the criteria by which he was to be judged. The best answer to these objections would have been to point to the role of his 'sermons' in the unfolding of plot and character: in the *Medea*, for example, Jason's sententiousness is symptomatic of his smug, shallow personality, and it goads Medea into justifiable rage. Similarly, the catastrophe in the *Hippolytus* is hastened by the hero's slightly priggish reasonableness: Theseus, suspecting him of incest, sees this as the coolness of a villain and is driven to fatal fury. However, Euripides had been established as a preacher, and in the imagination of critics a preacher he remained. He had been accused of propagating atheism; clerics defended him not by denying that he propagated anything at all but by making him the advocate of an undogmatic Christianity. Then, towards the end of the century, his supposed scepticism and radicalism came to seem an advantage: suddenly he seemed to have anticipated the latest fashions in drama. Sir Richard Livingstone, who provides a fair test of the taste of his time, since he never had an idea of his own in his life, wrote that Euripides was 'an Ibsen who writes heroic drama; a Bernard Shaw who is a great poet'. 'The comparison between Euripides and Mr. Shaw has often been made,' Norwood wrote in 1911, and went on to reveal the Greek writer's hostility to 'political inequality and bureaucracy': 'He loves to inveigh against officials . . . and he is never weary of praising the middle-class.' He and Verrall turned the plays of Euripides into *romans à clef*: 'On the Euripidean stage,' Verrall decided, 'whatever is said by a divinity is to be regarded in general as *ipso facto* discredited.'[68] In short, the poet was a rationalist, who intended the miracles he depicted to be understood as elaborate fakes perpetrated by the fraudulence of priestcraft. In Verrall's time theologians were much exercised over the historicity of biblical miracles; by a curious coincidence Euripides turned out to have a similar preoccupation.

The difficulty in coming to a just estimate of the tragic poets was and is that the errors of the critics were seldom without an element of truth. Euripides was not simply a propagandist; yet he was deeply concerned with ideas, and often with controversial ideas. *Medea* is not a feminist tract, but it does castigate conventional male attitudes

towards women. Shaw was stimulated by the *Bacchae* to look for
modern equivalents of orgiastic religion, and the outcome was his
study of the Salvation Army in *Major Barbara*, a play in which the
name of Euripides recurs again and again, like a leitmotiv. Shaw may
have been Euripidean; it does not follow that Euripides was Shavian.
In any case, it is never a good method of advocacy to praise a writer
for his resemblance to another writer: his peculiar merits get
ignored, and he is made to seem merely an inferior version of
someone else. Even if Euripides was a good Shavian (which is
doubtful), Shaw was presumably a better.

By chance Euripides' reputation had begun to revive in England at
about the time that Nietzsche was launching a new assault upon him
in Germany; *The Birth of Tragedy* was written in 1870–1871.
According to Nietzsche Attic tragedy had triumphed through a
union of the Apollonian and Dionysiac impulses; Euripides shattered
this unity by replacing myth and mystery with logic and argumenta-
tion: 'Now every spectator could behold his exact counterpart on the
stage and was delighted to find him so eloquent. . . . From now on
the stock phrases to represent everyday affairs were ready to hand.'[69]
Nietzsche's influence was slow in reaching England, but when it
came, the prevalent notion that Euripides was a Shaw *avant la lettre*
made the criticisms in *The Birth of Tragedy* seem all the more
plausible. When A. R. Orage, one of Nietzsche's first English
admirers, attacked Shaw, he threw in the inevitable comparison:
'Euripides . . . was unable to put a soul into his plays. For a soul he
substituted an idea. The descent was rapid . . . Euripides in a decade
after Sophocles' death was down among the propagandists. Shaw is
there still.'[70] This was nonsense, and careless nonsense, for Sophocles
outlived his rival; but it serves to show how Euripides was judged
guilty by association.

The artistic credo of the Victorians was at once timid and foolhardy: imitate the best work of the past, and if possible improve
upon it. Architects built Decorated churches, painters made quat-
trocento pictures, composers wrote Handelian oratorios (with
Mendelssohnian modifications). The Victorians read the Greek
tragedies and saw that they were good; what more natural, then,
than to write more of them? But the old mythology was dead, and
they merely produced academic oddities. Wagner, who made the
most heroic of all attempts to originate a new form of expression
from the ashes of Greek drama, observed that it was the 'folk' who
created art; the Greek unity of author and spectator had been
shattered, and modern society had degenerated from 'national

community' into 'absolute egoism'.[71] Even for Wagner the problem
was insoluble: he could not create a new folk mythology. His music
can grip the hearts and bowels of an audience, but the drama itself
remains obstinately unaffecting. Tristan or Brünnhilde are puppets,
not puppets of fate even but of Wagner's personal concerns and
artistic convenience; no one ever suffered more from absolute egoism
than he.

A hundred years ago it was beginning to look as though modern
writers had nothing to learn from the Greek drama; and yet in our
own century it has again exercised a powerful influence. That
influence became more indirect: Eliot's *Sweeney Agonistes* was
inspired less by Aristophanes than by what Norwood said about him,
and though Yeats adapted Greek tragedies for the Abbey Theatre he
was really more stirred by Nietzsche than by Sophocles. None the
less, John Cowper Powys could say in 1938, 'The three great tragic
dramatists of Athens have come to dominate . . . the imaginative
culture of Europe . . . this same tremendous tradition . . . will still be
found, like a submerged spirit under the ship's keel of each powerful
new book.'[72] There is exaggeration here, no doubt; but of no other
branch of ancient literature could the same have been said without
absurdity. Thanks to Nietzsche, the dark, Dionysiac side of the
Greek drama had been rediscovered; thanks to Freud, moreover, the
twentieth century has acquired a new folk mythology of its own, and
a large part of that mythology was derived from a play of Sophocles.
It may have been fortuitous that two of the most influential minds
of the last hundred years should have turned their attention to Greek
drama; it may be that their interpretations were to some degree
misguided; but they could never have enabled the Greek plays to
regain their hold over the imagination of modern men if there had
not genuinely been new riches in them to be discovered. Thus the
many-sidedness of Greek tragedy, so ill appreciated in the nineteenth century, ensured its continued vitality in the twentieth. For
Sophocles saw life whole in a fuller sense than Arnold ever realized;
saw not only the light and the sweetness, but the bitterness and the
dark.

VI

GEORGE ELIOT AND THE GREEKS

T H E novel is by nature an anti-classical art form. This is not to say that the classics play no part in it, but it is perhaps not surprising that none of the major nineteenth-century novelists, except for Thackeray, went to an English university. Some of them doubtless gained by their loss (Dickens might have had much of his vitality refined away by Oxford or Cambridge); some, though, strove valiantly to compensate for what they had missed: Trollope kept up his Latin with characteristic efficiency, and late in his life, when his fame as a novelist was secure, wrote a life of Julius Caesar; Hardy dramatized his struggles with the ancient languages poignantly in *Jude the Obscure*; and there is little doubt that Dickens himself would have liked the prestige of classical accomplishments. David Copperfield, his fictional *alter ego*, was a dab hand at Latin verses, and even assisted in compiling a Greek lexicon.[1] Dickens satirized classical education in *Dombey and Son,* and utilitarian education in *Hard Times*; it is plain that Dr. Blimber's Academy is far more affectionately treated than Mr. Gradgrind's information factory. And in *David Copperfield,* for the only time, Dickens portrayed his ideal of a school; the style is old-fashioned, the curriculum classical, and the headmaster a serious scholar and lexicographer. Dickens did not confine this attitude to his fiction: he sent his sons to Eton. In the last century an admiration for the classical attainments of young gentlemen went a long way down in society; there is a touching scene in *David Copperfield* which brings this out and perhaps sums up Dickens's own attitude to the knowledge that he never acquired. David recalls his childhood visits to the pawnbroker: 'The principal gentleman . . . took a great deal of notice of me; and often got me

. . . to decline a Latin noun . . . or to conjugate a Latin verb . . . while he transacted my business.'[2] In reading the Victorian novelists one is usually aware of a classical culture as part of the background of English life. The great exception is Henry James, and by that exception one is reminded that James was not, after all, an Englishman. And indeed there is a certain hollowness in his portrayals of supposedly brilliant people. One frankly wonders, in Jamesian phrase, what his clever and discerning people are so finely, so beautifully clever *at*.

No novelist can compare with George Eliot in fervency of enthusiasm for the ancient world. Her sex barred her from what she ironically called the 'Eleusinian mysteries of a University education';[3] yet without tutors to coax or threaten her into knowledge she acquired a degree of learning which many a university man might have envied. Latin meant nothing to her; all her passion was for Greek. When she was ill she did not turn to the light literature which is the invalid's usual fare: 'She sits up in bed,' wrote G. H. Lewes, 'and buries herself in Dante or Homer.' (The illness was perhaps not grave.) A certain John Fiske described meeting her: 'I know every bit of the "Iliad" and "Odyssey" as well as I know the "Pickwick Papers",' he boasted, but confessed that when he tried to argue with her about the Homeric question she outgunned him: '[She] seems to have read all of Homer in Greek too . . . talked of Homer as simply as she would of flat-irons.'[4] Her imagination was soaked in Greece, and nothing was more natural to her than to use Greek literature as part of the small change of social intercourse.

In *Amos Barton*, the first of her *Scenes of Clerical Life*, she introduced a theme which was to recur throughout her novels: 'I wish to stir your sympathy with commonplace troubles . . . such as walks neither in rags nor in velvet, but in very ordinary decent apparel.' Barton is desperately ordinary: 'His very faults were middling—the quintessential extract of mediocrity.'[5] George Eliot's purpose is to show the tragedy of everyday unromantic suffering; but she puts this characteristically modern theme into what may be called a Greek context. Barton has an unfortunate tendency to mis-spell words. This weakness is 'unfortunate, as he was known not to be a Hebrew scholar, and not in the least suspected of being an accomplished Grecian. These lapses . . . surprised the young ladies. . . .'[6] He stands in contrast to the story's most admirable character, the Revd. Martin Cleves, good-natured, popular with the farmers, yet 'perhaps the best Grecian of the party'.[7] Barton is the man who is in every way mediocre, and he is not much good at Greek; Cleves is outstanding and this is exemplified by his accomplishment in the language.

George Eliot herself tried to rival Cleves's cultivation: the Countess Czerlaski, she wrote, 'had serious intentions of becoming *quite* pious . . . when she had once got her . . . settlement. Let us do this one sly trick, says Ulysses . . ., and we will be perfectly honest ever after—' At this point George Eliot quotes two lines of Sophocles in Greek, and continues, 'The Countess did not quote Sophocles, but she said to herself. . . .'[8] Two lines of Greek verse in a short story were rather extraordinary; indeed George Eliot herself was later to refer ruefully to 'that solitary bit of pedantry', because the *Quarterly Review* pounced on a couple of mistakes in her accents.[9] Reviewers then were made of sterner stuff. Now George Eliot was a self-conscious writer, and her bit of pedantry had a purpose. The key is in the words 'the Countess did not quote Sophocles, but . . .' George Eliot is indicating that Greek tragedy deals with gods and heroes whereas she only deals with ordinary people; but ordinary people experience joys and sufferings that are as real and important as those of the heroes of high tragedy. Greek drama is relevant to the nineteenth-century novel not because it is similar, but rather by force of contrast.

She uses the same technique in *Janet's Repentance*, the third of the *Scenes of Clerical Life*. 'Mighty is the force of motherhood! says the great tragic poet to us across the ages, finding . . . the simplest words for the sublimest fact'. (And again she quotes in Greek: the bit of pedantry in *Amos Barton* was not solitary after all.) 'It transforms all things by its vital heat. . . . Yes! if Janet had been a mother. . . .'[10] George Eliot is here using Sophocles to make two favourite points. First, the nature of human experience is unchanging; those glorious emotions which the Greek poets celebrated so sublimely are still with us. Secondly, an ordinary woman like Janet Dempster, a middle-class housewife with a weakness for the bottle, is as worthy a subject for literature as the princess Electra. In *Mr. Gilfil's Love Story*, too, there are references, some half facetious, to ancient Greece. She quotes from Sophocles' *Ajax*, and alludes to the poisoned garment in the *Trachiniae*.[11] The village of Shepperton, with its 'turnpike roads and a public opinion', is 'in a state of Attic culture compared with . . . Boeotian Knebley'. In the kitchen of a stately home there is 'an oak table, high enough surely for Homer's gods'.[12] To simple people the world of the upper classes is a realm of Olympian splendour.

The Greek references in *Scenes of Clerical Life* are somewhat

clumsy; in *Adam Bede* they are more subtle. Here George Eliot
returns to her theme of the dignity of ordinary sufferings. Indeed she
devotes a whole chapter to describing her method: she is creating a
'Dutch painting', revealing what is noble in the low and the commonplace.[13] As she has said earlier, 'The existence of insignificant people
has very important consequences. . . . It can be shown to . . . call
forth many evil tempers . . . and many heroisms . . . and . . . to play
no small part in the tragedy of life.'[14] She is not using the word
tragedy loosely; as she explains, 'Family likeness has often a deep
sadness in it. Nature, that great tragic dramatist, knits us together
by bone and muscle, and divides us by . . . our brains; blends yearning
and repulsion; and ties us by our heart-strings to the beings that jar
us. . . .'[15] Here she is thinking of the greatest and most oppressive
family drama in Greek literature, the *Oresteia*. Aeschylus brings out
the likeness of Orestes and Electra to their great father both in their
virtues and their faults; he displays with shattering power the
claustrophobia of a house at enmity with itself; he shows how with
terrifying inexorability one horror leads to another: once Agamemnon
has 'put on the yokestrap of necessity', he is doomed and so in turn
are his wife and son. Now George Eliot is only painting a Dutch
picture; but she can use the echo of Aeschylus to give a resonance to
her modest story.

The plot revolves around the seduction of Hetty Sorrel by the
squire's grandson, Arthur Donnithorne; the book portrays the
disastrous effect of the gentry meddling with the lives of their social
inferiors. The comparison between the English upper classes and the
Olympian gods, glanced at in the *Scenes of Clerical Life*, is here more
fully developed. Mrs. Irwine is likened first to a statue of Ceres, then
to 'an Olympian goddess'. Hetty is a girl 'to whom a gentleman with
a white hand was as dazzling as an Olympian god', and as for the
squire, 'he might have been earth-born, for what she knew'.[16] Even
the place where Arthur and Hetty meet belongs to a magical, pagan
world: 'It was the sort of wood most haunted by the nymphs: you
see their white sunlit limbs gleaming athwart the boughs . . . you
hear their soft liquid laughter.' Indeed when Arthur flirts with
Hetty, 'it was as if she had been wooed by a river god'.[17] If we
remember our Greek mythology, we catch the irony: the nymphs
who were pursued by gods usually met an unpleasant fate.

This theme is subtly developed in another way. The parson is
kindly, worldly-wise, and undogmatic; his strongest feelings are not
for religion but for the Greek classics: 'His mental palette . . .
found a savouriness in a quotation from Sophocles or Theocritus

that was quite absent from any text in Isaiah or Amos . . . Mr.
Irwine's recollections of young enthusiasm and ambition were all
associated with poetry and ethics that lay aloof from the Bible.'[18]
There is an intriguing anachronism here. The action of *Adam Bede*
opens in 1798. Irwine is presumably about forty-five; he would
have been up at university early in the 1770s. His enthusiasm
specifically for Greek authors, which would not have been strange in
an intelligent country parson of George Eliot's day, would have
been very abnormal in someone of his date. But whether or not she
was conscious of her anachronism, it serves an artistic purpose.
Arthur goes to visit Irwine and finds him still at breakfast with a
favourite book beside him, 'the first volume of the Foulis *Aeschylus*,
which Arthur knew well by sight'.[19] Again, a country parson of the
time would be most unlikely to be deep into such a difficult author.
(And there is another implausibility. The Foulis *Aeschylus* was a de
luxe edition, illustrated by Flaxman, something more to look at than
to read. At all events, one would hardly read it over breakfast for
fear of getting egg on its handsome pages.)

But George Eliot has a particular reason for introducing Aeschylus.
This scene is the turning point of the whole book. Arthur has come
to tell his old friend about his flirtation, which is getting out of hand.
If he can succeed in sharing his secret with a third person, he and
Hetty will be safe for the future, and tragedy will be avoided. But
Irwine's mind is full of his book: 'I dare say, now,' he remarks
humorously, 'even a man fortified with the knowledge of the
classics might be lured into an imprudent marriage, in spite of the
warning given him by the chorus in the *Prometheus*.' If we pick up
the reference, there is a powerful irony concealed in these casual
words; for what the chorus say is, 'It is by far the best to marry in
one's own rank.'[20] A few lines later they add the prayer, 'May I
never marry a god'; we may recall that Arthur seemed like a god to
Hetty. Irwine suspects that Arthur wants to make a confession and
tries to steer the conversation on to more serious ground, still with
Greek tragedy foremost in his mind. He talks about 'the inward
suffering which is the worst form of Nemesis. . . . Our deeds carry
their terrible consequences . . . consequences that are hardly ever
confined to ourselves.' But this sudden seriousness scares Arthur off.
He cannot now bring himself to tell his story; it would make a mere
flirtation sound altogether too large a matter. The admission is never
made, and the tragedy pursues its inexorable course. So Aeschylus
plays a double role in this scene. His dramas foreshadow the future
development of the plot: 'Our deeds carry their terrible consequences';

once we put on the harness of necessity it controls our future actions. And by a second irony it is Aeschylus himself, in Irwine's mouth, who has scared Arthur from revealing his secret. It is a brilliant use of ancient literature in a distinctively modern setting.

Later Hetty is compared to 'a woman spinning in young ignorance a light web of folly and vain hopes which may one day close round her . . . a rancorous poisoned garment, changing . . . her fluttering, trivial butterfly sensations into . . . anguish'.[21] This is a reference to Euripides' *Medea*, one of George Eliot's favourite works. In this play Jason deserts his wife, Medea, in order to marry the princess Glauce. In revenge Medea decides to murder her own children, but first she sends them to present a robe and crown to her rival. Glauce is a silly, harmless butterfly. Thrilled with Medea's gifts, she puts them on in front of her mirror, and trips about admiring her own beauty, just like Hetty in her room at the Poysers putting on the bangles that Arthur has given her.[22] But the robe is poisoned, and Glauce dies in agony. Now *Medea* is above all a play about child murder. Once we recognize the allusion, we have a sinister hint that Hetty will destroy the baby.

In *Daniel Deronda* this play is again directed to a finely ironic end. Vandernoodt is discussing the battle between Gwendolen and her husband's former mistress: 'It's rather a piquant picture—Grand-court between two fiery women. . . . It's a sort of Medea and Creusa business' (Creusa is an alternative name for Glauce in some versions of the story) '. . . Grandcourt is a new kind of Jason: I wonder what sort of part he'll make of it. It's a dog's part at best.'[23] Vandernoodt is thinking of an Italian play, but he says more than he realizes. If we know Euripides, we remember that Jason is as cheap a villain as any in Greek tragedy. We realize, too, that Gwendolen, like Glauce pitiably vain and innocent, will suffer horribly for her involvement with this modern Jason.

In *Adam Bede* George Eliot continues to develop her Aeschylean theme. At the party to celebrate Arthur's coming of age, the climax of his glory and success, Aeschylus reappears like a spectre at the feast. 'Ah, my boy,' Irwine remarks, 'it is not only woman's love that is *aperōtos erōs*, as old Aeschylus calls it. There is plenty of 'unloving love' . . . of a masculine kind.'[24] The remark helps to define Irwine's character—the humorous gentleman scholar—but it has also a symbolic value. Gradually Arthur comes to feel the yoke of necessity: 'His deed . . . was already governing him tyrannously and forcing him into a course that jarred with his habitual feelings.'[25] He has to face Adam, who appears to him like one of the grim avengers of Greek mythology: 'Adam . . . stood like a terrible fate before Arthur. . . .' Once again George Eliot sets before us the word Nemesis, and concludes, 'Our deeds determine us, as much as we determine our deeds.'[26]

She also uses the classics more lightheartedly, when Poyser's farm hands sing some cheerful doggerel at their harvest supper.[27] This piece of nonsense is an excuse for a broad parody of Homeric scholarship:

> As to . . . this song—whether it came from the brain of a single rhapsodist, or was gradually perfected by a school . . . of rhapsodists, I am ignorant. There is a stamp of unity, of individual genius upon it, which inclines me to the former hypothesis, though . . . this unity may rather have arisen from that consensus of many minds which was a condition of primitive thought, foreign to our modern consciousness.

But even to this burlesque there is a serious side: George Eliot means to indicate something of the unchanging dignity and vigour of peasant life and lore. Irwine calls Mrs. Poyser 'one of those untaught wits that helped to stock a country with proverbs. I told you that capital thing I heard her say about Craig—that he was like a cock, who thought the sun had risen to hear him crow. Now that's an Aesop's Fable in a sentence.' And Mrs. Bede describes her son as 'tall and upright like the poplar tree', ignorant of course that this is one of Homer's similes.[28] Similarly in *Middlemarch*, 'Hiram Ford . . . shouted a defiance which he did not know to be Homeric.—"Yo're a coward, you are. Yo git off your horse, young measter. . . . Yo daredn't come on wi'out your hoss an' whip . . ."' [29] The joke derives from *Tom Jones*, but it reaffirms George Eliot's own message.

In *The Mill on the Floss* she again used Greek tragedy as a means of comparing the great with the humble. As a child Maggie Tulliver takes a dislike to her long hair and gets her brother Tom to cut it off; but then she sits 'as helpless and despairing among her black locks as Ajax among the slaughtered sheep. Very trivial, perhaps, this anguish seems to weather-worn mortals.'[30] As George Eliot explains later, 'There were passions at war in Maggie . . . to have made a tragedy, if tragedies were made by passion only, but the essential *ti megethos* which was present in the passion was wanting to the action; the utmost Maggie could do . . . was to push . . . Lucy into the . . . mud.'[31] The phrase *ti megethos*, 'a certain largeness', is especially ironical as applied to a small child; it is taken from Aristotle, who argued that the action of a tragedy had to have a certain greatness or grandeur about it. George Eliot rejects this view, and devotes a whole chapter to discussing the downfall of the Tulliver family in terms of her artistic theory. It was a fall 'which even sorrow hardly suffices to lift above the level of the tragi-comic'; but the suffering of mankind 'is represented . . . by hundreds of obscure hearths; and we need not shrink from this comparison of small things with great'.[32] Those last six words are the essence of her artistic creed. Later, when Maggie is asked if she would like to be a tenth muse, she replies, 'Not at all . . . if I carried a harp in this climate, I must have a green baize cover. . . .'[33] Classical mythology seems absurd in modern England; and yet not altogether so. Describing Maggie and Tom's different struggles, George Eliot insists in all seriousness, 'So it has been since the days of Hecuba, and of Hector, tamer of horses: inside the gates the women . . . offering prayers . . . outside the men in fierce struggle with things divine and human. . . .'[34] Troy and St. Oggs, the Scamander and the Floss are not so very different after all. Indeed, on the next page we learn that Tom would literally like to go in for taming horses.

The references to Greek literature in *The Mill on the Floss* seem uncontrived because a part of the book is devoted to a witty account of the Tulliver children's classical schooling. Poor foolish Mr. Tulliver is anxious to give his son 'a good eddication', and for this purpose he consults his friend Riley. A clergyman is proposed, but Tulliver, who for all his folly preserves a certain shrewdness, has his doubts: 'My notion of the parsons was as they had got a sort of learning as lay mostly out of sight. And that isn't what I want for Tom. I want him to know figures, and . . . how to wrap things up in words as aren't actionable.' But Riley answers, 'The schoolmasters who are not clergymen are a very low set of men generally.'[35] Social considerations defeat utilitarian, and Tom is duly sent to the Revd. Mr. Stelling. George Eliot gives a splendid picture of the dryness of an education based on learning grammar by rote: 'Mr. Stelling was not the man to . . . emasculate his pupil's mind by . . . explaining, or to reduce the tonic effect of etymology by mixing it with smattering, extraneous information such as is given to girls.'[36] Those words are keenly ironical from the pen of such a learned lady, while her awareness that Greek culture was entwined with class snobbery gives a poignancy to her observation that 'Mr. Tulliver had a destiny as well as Oedipus, and . . . he might plead, like Oedipus, that his deed was inflicted on him rather than committed by him.'[37]

Her next book, *Silas Marner*, is the only novel of hers in which Greek literature plays no part, and indeed the only one that can be printed without the use of a Greek fount; after this she wrote *Romola*, her only historical novel. Now historical novels, by a pleasing paradox, date more easily than novels of contemporary life, revealing with greater clarity the preoccupations of the time at which they are written. We have our own notion of the Florentine Renaissance and George Eliot had hers, and the differences between the two conceptions tell us much about George Eliot's age. Significantly, it is here, more than in any other of her books, that she conveys a sense of the excitement of scholarship and the sheer thrill of the Greek language.

Tito is a young Greek, who as a child was rescued from destitution by Baldassarre, a scholar, who has educated him and shared his learning with him. When Tito comes to manhood, he disowns his benefactor; Baldassarre's mental powers begin to fail and he discovers that he has forgotten all his Greek; unable to prove his identity, he finds that his claim to be a scholar is greeted with ridicule. His single passion now is to have his revenge on Tito, but his efforts end in humiliating failure. Eventually we find him lying on straw in an outhouse, broken and destitute, gazing helplessly at a Greek book in front of him. And then something magical happens: [38]

He turned towards the book. . . . It was . . . an odd volume of Pausanias . . . he could see the large letters at the head of the page;

ΜΕΣΣΗΝΙΚΑ ΚΒ′

In old days he had known Pausanias familiarly; yet an hour or two ago . . . that page . . . had suggested no more meaning to him than if the letters had been black weather marks on a wall; but at this moment they were once more the magic signs that conjure up a world. That moonbeam falling on the letters had raised Messenia before him . . . the light was too pale for him to read further by. No matter: he knew that chapter. . . . The words arose within him, and stirred innumerable vibrations of memory. The light was come again, mother of knowledge and joy! . . . It was a nipping frosty air, but Baldassarre could feel no chill—he only felt the glow of conscious power.

This climactic moment of Baldassarre's life is the recovery not of Latin or Italian letters but Greek. Pausanias is not the most exciting of authors, and there is nothing dramatic about what they say: 'About Messenia, chapter 22'. The letters are exciting simply because they are Greek.

Fired by his new sense of mastery, Baldassarre walks through the sleeping city. 'That city . . . was material that he could subdue to his purposes now: . . . he was once more a man who knew cities, whose sense of vision was instructed with large experience.' If we pick up the allusion, this is a tremendous moment. The *Odyssey* begins, 'Tell me, muse, of the man of many ways, who wandered very far, after he had sacked the sacred citadel of Troy; he saw the cities of many men and knew their mind.' At this supreme moment Baldassarre is dignified and elevated by comparison with Odysseus, that other great shaggy wanderer, who had to come home furtively and hide in a swineherd's hut, like Baldassarre in his outhouse. It is a moment like the cry of 'Weialala leia' in *The Waste Land*, when suddenly the oily, sweating Thames is brought into a realm rich in romantic associations, the world of Wagner's Rhine. Odysseus, like Baldassarre, meditates a deadly revenge upon his enemies; once he arrives in Ithaca, their doom is sealed. By comparing Baldassarre to Odysseus, George Eliot arouses in us the expectation that his vengeance will swiftly follow. But she arouses this expectation only to cheat it. The use of Greek legend is cunning: the reader is kept in puzzled and anxious suspense.

In *Romola*, as before, she uses Greek tragedy as a way of commenting upon her story:

[Tito's] mind was destitute of . . . that awe of the Divine Nemesis which was felt by religious pagans, and . . . is still felt by the mass of mankind simply as a vague fear at . . . wrongdoing. Such terror . . . is the initial recognition of a moral law restraining desire. . . . 'It is good,' sing the old Eumenides, in Aeschylus, 'that fear should sit as the guardian of the soul . . . else, how should they learn to revere the right?'[39]

To George Eliot Nemesis is not so much an idea peculiar to the Greek mind as a dramatic realization of a perennial feature of human nature. For her the Greek tragedies were above all dramas of character; in some degree she saw them as novels and her novels as tragedies. 'Our deeds are like children that are born to us,' she writes; 'they live and act apart from our own will'; and we hear an echo of the chorus in the *Agamemnon*: 'The act of evil breeds others to follow, young sins in its own likeness. Houses clear in their right are given children in all loveliness.'[40]

Her use of Aeschylus and Homer is appropriate in a book so deeply concerned with scholarship. The three principal male characters are all professional Greek scholars, and the heroine is a zealous student of the language. George Eliot seems to have imagined that the whole of Florence was obsessed with antiquity: describing the typical Florentine of the time, she says, 'It was his pride besides, that he was duly tinctured with the learning of his age, and judged . . . in harmony with the ancients: he . . . had been eager for the most correct manuscripts, and . . . he had made haste to look at the first sheets of that fine Homer which was among the early glories of the Florentine press.'[41] Even Nello the barber discusses whether Virgil should be spelt with an 'e' or an 'i'.[42] George Eliot grossly exaggerates the Florentine passion for scholarship; indeed, *Romola* is riddled with anachronisms and implausibilities, which reveal much about the author and her age. She tells us that Baldassarre travelled to Greece, believing that it was important to record what its ancient appearance had been while the task was still possible.[43] This would be a peculiarly illogical activity for a Florentine, for whom Rome and indeed the Greek remains of southern Italy were comparatively close at hand. 'The Greek dye was subdued in me,' says Tito, 'till I had been dipped over again by . . . travel in the land of gods and heroes . . . I have rested in the groves of Helicon, and tasted of the fountain Hippocrene.'[44] This is a Byronic not a renaissance emotion. Bardo laments the present state of Greece: 'It is enough to overlay human hope . . . with an eternal frost to think that the ground which was trodden by philosophers and poets is crawled over by besotted fanatics. . . .'[45] Byronism again, mixed with the anti-Christian paganism of a Swinburne or a Shelley. Fifteenth-century Florence was surely one of the most creative and self-confident societies that has ever been; yet Bardo keeps complaining, for all the world like Matthew Arnold or Ruskin, about the decline of art, literature and philosophy. He also shares the nineteenth-century tendency to exalt Greek literature at the expense of Latin: 'No man,' he declares, 'is held worthy of the name of scholar who has acquired merely the . . . derivative literature of the Latins; . . . the Romans themselves . . . frankly replenished their urns at the fountainhead.'[46] Bardo is basically a Victorian free-thinker; his son has become a friar, and the father has disowned him for turning away from 'the clear light of reason and philosophy' to 'prostrate himself under the influences of a dim mysticism'. Once again, this hardly makes sense in its context: in the age of Ficino and Pico della Mirandola philosophy itself was very mystical and very dim.

We are told that Bardo's life has been a hard struggle, largely because his principles have forbidden him to take orders. This is puzzling; Bardo was married, and ordination would have meant, at the least, putting away his wife. George Eliot is again thinking of England, and in particular perhaps of Porson, who in 1792 was deprived of his fellowship at Trinity College, Cambridge, for refusing to be ordained. Normally, a college fellowship carried a statutory obligation to enter orders; there was no comparable obstacle for the agnostic scholar in Florence. To a man like Bardo the priesthood would have been, at most, a social advantage, something like becoming a freemason. None the less, George Eliot returns to this theme later in the book. Tornabuoni remarks to Tito, 'Why shouldn't you take orders someday? There is a cardinal's hat at the end of that road. . . . I think a scholar would always be the better off for taking orders.'[47] The advice is the odder in that Tito is newly a bridegroom. As Tornabuoni speaks we hear the cultivated accents of the English gentry: 'Why not take orders? You might get a deanery, maybe even a bishopric.' And perhaps we even catch a faint echo of Riley in *The Mill on the Floss*: 'The schoolmasters who are not clergymen are a very low set of men generally.'

In *Felix Holt the Radical*, George Eliot came back to the Midlands, and to her habit of comparing modern England with heroic Greece. On the second page she is already telling us that there are 'enough stories of English labours . . . to make episodes for a modern Odyssey'. Her description of the landscape, with 'the full-uddered cows driven from their pasture to the early milking', recalls many a Homeric passage, while the coachman's gossip is ironically compared to the words of Virgil in the *Divine Comedy*. Then she returns, inevitably, to Greek tragedy:

> And such stories often come to be fine in a sense that is not ironical. For there is seldom any wrong-doing which does not carry along with it . . . some tragic mark of kinship in the one brief life to the far stretching life that went before, and to the life that is to come after, such as raised the pity and terror of men ever since they began to discern between will and destiny. But these things are often unknown to the world . . .

She ends her proem by affirming that the poets' accounts of the underworld are a parable; in similar vein, she regards the ancestral curse of Greek tragedy as a metaphorical expression of the constraints of heredity and environment. One chapter opens with two quotations from Sophocles, both about the connection between past deeds and present expectations, and another with a quotation from the *Agamemnon*:[48]

'Tis law as steadfast as the throne of Zeus—
Our days are heritors of days gone by.

Three pages later she describes 'the most serious moment in Harold Transome's life': 'For the first time he felt the yoke of that mighty resistless destiny laid upon us by the acts of other men as well as our own.'[49] The phrase 'yoke of destiny' is again from the *Agamemnon*. To the reader acquainted with Greek tragedy these quotations are bitterly ironical because Harold has very nearly found himself in the position of an Orestes or an Oedipus; he has just threatened to kill a man who is, though he does not realize it, his parent:[50]

'Let me go, you scoundrel!' said Harold fiercely, 'or I'll be the death of you.'
'Do,' said Jermyn, in a grating voice; '*I am your father.*'

This is how Harold learns of the ancestral curse; he must accept the consequences of his parents' sin, the stigma of bastardy and the pains of disinheritance.

Many of the Greek dramas are public tragedies; a whole city shares the sufferings and downfall of its lords and masters. When Agamemnon is murdered, Argos groans under the yoke of tyranny; the sin of Oedipus brings the plague upon Thebes, and his downfall plunges it into civil war. Yet the sufferings of the multitude, though often represented by the chorus, remain in the background; kings and heroes occupy, literally, the centre of the stage. George Eliot ironically transfers this convention to modern England, for indeed it is not a convention, but a bitter truth. The theme appears first in *The Mill on the Floss*. Tulliver may seem a paltry Oedipus, but his ruin too involves others beside himself, such as the mill-hand: 'Good Luke felt, after the manner of contented hard-working men whose lives have been spent in servitude, that sense of natural fitness in rank which made his master's downfall a tragedy to him.'[51] In *Felix Holt* Denner, Mrs. Transome's maid, regards her mistress with a feeling 'of that worshipful sort paid to a goddess in ages when it was not thought necessary or likely that a goddess should be very moral'. She is sure that a 'born servant' should 'submissively accept the rigid fate which had given her born superiors'. When Mrs. Transome is in distress, Denner tells her, 'I know people have feelings according to their birth and station'; and George Eliot observes tartly, 'Her mistress's rhetoric and temper belonged to her superior rank, her grand person, and her piercing black eyes.'[52] These are not just literary jokes; the novelist wants to contrast the code of the upper classes, overlaid by a superficial adherence to Christianity but fundamentally pagan, with the moral earnestness of a humbler class represented by the dissenting minister Lyon and the radical Holt. She offers a nice analysis of Mrs. Transome's confused congeries of beliefs: 'The history of the Jews, she knew, ought to be preferred to any profane history; the pagans, of course, were vicious and their religions quite nonsensical . . .— but classical learning came from the pagans; the Greeks were famous for sculpture; the Middle Ages were dark. . . .'[53] Nowadays, however, Christianity goes 'hand in hand with civilisation, and the providential government of the world'; but Christianity in Mrs. Transome's mind turns out to be little more than a belief in Tory principles and the succession of the House of Brunswick. Lyon speaks suspiciously of 'the heathen precept, "know thyself",' but the Established Church, in the person of the Revd. Mr. Lingon, recommends Harold to brush up his Latin, and the bishop is full of Greek.[54]

In *Felix Holt* George Eliot makes her most elaborate use of the *Medea*. This play is one of the greatest feminist documents in European literature: the despicable Jason takes refuge, where argument fails him, in cheap assertions of male superiority, while Medea asserts the wretchedness of woman's lot with an eloquence which no female writer has yet equalled. Mrs. Transome endures from her son the sort of patronizing condescension which Jason inflicts upon Medea. 'Women,' says Harold, 'very properly, don't change their views . . . it doesn't signify what they think.' His mother answers, 'You will put the crown to the mortifications of my life, Harold. I don't know who would be a mother if she could foresee what a slight thing she will be to her son when she is old.'[55] Medea, too, reflects upon the uncertainties of parenthood; and in her most famous speech she says, 'So it was in vain, my children, that I brought you up, in vain that I suffered and was worn out with toils.'[56] As the book proceeds the parallels with Euripides become more and more open. Mrs. Transome yields to her son with the bitter comment, 'I must put up with all things as they are determined for me.' 'Women are frightened at everything, I know,' Harold observes in reply.[57] Again the reader may think of the scene in which Medea yields to Jason, and the masculine complacency with which Jason accepts her surrender. The relationship between Mrs. Transome and Denner is remarkably similar to that between Medea and her *trophos*, a word conventionally translated nurse, but which really implies a mixture of lady's maid and confidante. 'A woman's love is always freezing into fear,' Mrs. Transome tells her servant.

. . . what is the use of a woman's will?—if she tries, she doesn't get it, and she ceases to be loved. God was cruel when he made women.'[58] This recalls Medea's speech to the women of Corinth: 'Of all things which are living and can form a judgement we women are the most unfortunate creatures'; women are compelled to take husbands for their masters, and then they are trapped; if a man finds life at home dull, he can go and take his pleasure elsewhere, but women are dependent and helpless.[59] Denner, after saying that people have feelings according to their station, continues, 'And you always took things to heart, Madam, beyond anybody else.'[60] She is also aware, as we have seen, of her mistress's temper as a characteristic of her rank. The nurse says, '[Medea's] heart is violent. She will not tolerate ill treatment.' Again, the nurse warns of 'the wildness and bitter nature of that proud mind'; Medea is 'proud-hearted and not to be checked on her course, a soul bitten into with wrong'; and, 'The emotions of great people are terrible, always having their own way, seldom checked.'[61] A couple of pages later Mrs. Transome is compared to Euripides' other most savage heroine: she is a 'dishevelled Hecuba-like woman'.[62]

So far the parallels between Medea and Mrs. Transome may seem inexact, since it is her son, not her husband, who treats her with such insensitivity; but in the very inexactitude there lies a dramatic irony, for George Eliot has a surprise in store. Mrs. Transome has indeed been betrayed by a man; there have already been hints of something untoward in her relations with her lawyer, and in the very chapter which begins with two quotations from Sophocles, we learn that they had once been lovers. George Eliot comments, 'The fortunate Jason, as we know from Euripides, piously thanked the goddess, and saw clearly that he was not at all obliged to Medea: Jermyn was perhaps not aware of the precedent, but thought out his own freedom from obligation . . . with a native faculty not inferior to Jason's.'[63] There is irony again in Jermyn's being 'not aware of the precedent': Jason's smooth assurance was to be shattered by a terrible retribution, and George Eliot hints here that Jermyn's career, for all his bland self-confidence, will be smashed.

The sentence comparing Jermyn to Jason is followed immediately by Mrs. Transome's entry. The lawyer is inspecting a portrait of her in youth; 'Before three minutes had passed, however, as if by some sorcery, the brilliant smiling young woman above the mantel-piece seemed to be appearing at the doorway withered . . . by many winters.' With Euripides newly implanted in our minds, we remember that Medea was herself a sorceress. Jermyn, like Jason, broke off his affair in order to better himself by an alliance with another young lady, and like Jason he now wishes to sever the woman whom he once loved from her offspring. 'I would not lose the misery of being a woman,' says Mrs. Transome, 'now I see what can be the baseness of a man. One must be a man—first to tell a woman that her love had made her your debtor, and then ask her to pay you by breaking the last poor threads between her and her son.' Jason, too, makes both that statement and that request. George Eliot tells us that Jermyn's self-vindication served only to 'show that he was shame-proof'; Medea answers Jason's self-defence by telling him that it reveals 'the worst of all human diseases, shamelessness'.[64] Esther Lyon comes to feel that were she to marry Harold she would enter a life in which 'poetry was only literature, and the fine ideas had to be taken down from the shelves . . . when her husband's back was turned'.[65] The bitterness of Mrs. Transome's fate is that for her a 'literary' situation has become horribly true.

In *Middlemarch* George Eliot makes play with antique scupltures. Ladislaw catches sight of Dorothea in the Vatican galleries beside a statue of the sleeping Ariadne. 'There lies antique beauty,' he tells his friend Naumann, 'not corpse-like even in death, but arrested in the complete contentment of its sensuous perfection; and here stands beauty in its breathing life, with the consciousness of Christian centuries in its bosom.' It is not by chance that George Eliot positions Dorothea next to the statue of a woman asleep; she wishes to intensify the contrast between the repose of antique sculpture and the eager pulse of the modern world. As Naumann obligingly explains, Dorothea is 'antique form animated by Christian sentiment—a sort of Christian Antigone—sensuous force controlled by spiritual passion'.[66] George Eliot was writing not long after Pater had published his study of Winckelmann, and its influence is evident; but she has combined Pater's thesis with her own *idée fixe*. Dorothea, leading an ordinary life in the prosaic English midlands, is the modern equivalent of a Greek heroine. Antigone reappears on the last page of the novel: 'A new Theresa will hardly have the opportunity of reforming the conventual life, any more than a new Antigone will spend her heroic piety in daring all for the sake of a brother's burial: the medium in which their ardent deeds took shape is for ever gone.'[67] None the less, there remain 'unhistoric acts' performed by 'insignificant people', which are the modern equivalent.

This is of course George Eliot's favourite theme, but in *Middlemarch* it is perhaps handled more skilfully than before. Here the contrast between the sublimities of classic literature and the humdrum present is not merely a subject for George Eliot to lecture her readers upon in that rather schoolmarmish way of hers; it occupies the imaginations of her characters. Dorothea wants to discover how it might be 'possible to lead a grand life here—now—in England'.[68] As for Lydgate, he is a man who has failed to understand how the masterpieces of ancient poetry can irradiate everyday experience: his schooling has merely 'left him free to read the indecent passages in the school classics', and only the study of medicine can excite his passionate enthusiasm.[69] This is an admirable enthusiasm, but by itself it is not enough: Lydgate is 'too ill acquainted with disaster to enter into the pathos of a lot where everything is below the level of tragedy except the passionate egoism of the sufferer'.[70] Ordinary lives *are* tragic, to those with sufficient breadth of sympathy. It is Lydgate's failing that he does not appreciate this. He is to learn the hard way.

Middlemarch is almost as much concerned with scholarship as *Romola*, but its value is now more critically assessed. The portrait of Casaubon is a classic study of the perils of erudition; much learning has made him not mad but too, too sane, and his sensibilities have grown etiolated as his knowledge has expanded. But Casaubon has been much misunderstood. The scope of his studies is exceptionally wide, embracing Hebrew and biblical scholarship as well as classical antiquity, and the scheme of his proposed book is bold to the point of recklessness: to show 'that all the mythical systems . . . in the world were corruptions of a tradition originally revealed'.[71] This task had already been attempted, at least for the mythical system of Greece, by an eminent Englishman, and he, far from being a pedant in a country vicarage, was at the time that George Eliot was writing *Middlemarch* Prime Minister of Great Britain. Cool competent scholars recoiled from the extravagance of Gladstone's arguments; Pattison defined the character of his Homeric studies as 'a comprehensive general reading; an heroic industry . . . brought to bear to prove a perverse and preposterous proposition'.[72] Casaubon's project may have been foolhardy, but it was anything but small-minded or unimaginative. He is himself dimly aware that his commerce with the past has shrivelled his capacity for living in the present: 'I feed too much on the inward sources; I live too much with the dead.'[73] But his tragedy goes deeper: this man now 'lost among . . . winding stairs, and in an agitated dimness about the Cabeiri'[74] had once conceived an enterprise mighty in scale and majestic in its sweep, but character and circumstance have shrivelled him into pettiness. Before the story opens he has already suffered the fate which Lydgate is to endure as it unfolds.

Parson Irwine's enthusiasm for Aeschylus was anachronistic, but in *Middlemarch* George Eliot displays an acute perception of the changing pattern of scholarship. Old Mr. Brooke tries to interest Casaubon in the journal of his youthful travels: 'Look here—here is all about Greece, Rhamnus, the ruins of Rhamnus . . . I don't know whether you have given much study to the topography. I spent no end of time in making out these things—Helicon, now. Here, now!— "We started the next morning for Parnassus, . . ." All this volume is about Greece, you know.' This is exactly the spirit of scholarship at the turn of the century, when topography was all the rage, and gentlemen amateurs rambled over Greece amazing themselves with their own seriousness. Casaubon listens with polite boredom: his studies of comparative religion are scholarship of a newer, more demanding kind. But he too has been left behind; the younger generation, in the person of Ladislaw, confidently declares that his work is already out of date, because he is ignorant of the advances in historical scholarship made by the Germans.[75] Ladislaw never criticizes Casaubon for being a scholar; he only complains that his scholarship is incomplete. And Dorothea's heart is full of the romance of learning: 'To reconstruct a past world, doubtless with a view to the highest purposes of truth—what a work . . . to assist in, though only as a lampholder! . . . Since prayer heightened yearning but not instruction, what lamp was there but knowledge? Surely learned men kept the only oil.'[76] She is to be disillusioned in Casaubon, but there is no reason to think that she is disillusioned in the ancient world. George Eliot felt, like Mill, that in a world where religious certainties seemed to have crumbled into doubt, and the beauty and awe which they had once inspired were in danger of passing from the world, antiquity could provide new saints and new ideals for men to love and worship. In Dorothea she gave expression to this belief.

In *Daniel Deronda* she continued to view classical scholarship with sceptically lifted eyebrow. We are introduced to 'the Archdeacon's classical son . . . a hopeful young scholar, who had already suggested some "not less elegant than ingenious" emendations of Greek texts'.[77] Characteristically, he is an 'elegant Grecian'; no one got much praise from the Victorians for being a Latinist. However, he proves to be a Philistine and a bore, his chief interest in life being croquet. Daniel himself is a good classic—of course—but reluctant to jump through the usual academic hoops.[78] Despite the trouble

George Eliot has taken with him, he is a sentimental and unconvincing figure, and it is difficult to believe in the account of his mental development; more realistic is the portrait of his guardian, Sir Hugo Mallinger. 'I am glad you have done some good reading outside your classics,' he tells Daniel, '. . . unless a man can get the prestige and income of a don . . . it's hardly worth while for him to . . . be able to spin you out pages of the Greek dramatists at any verse you will give him as a cue . . . in practical life nobody does give you the cue for pages of Greek. In fact it's a nicety of conversation which I would have you attend to—much quotation of any sort, even in English, is bad.'[79] 'Even in English'—a nice parenthesis. Sir Hugo affects to depreciate the classics; today we are struck that an English gentleman should stress their value—their practical value—so much. 'A cartload of learning in the right place,' he explains, '. . . will tell in politics.' And he continues, 'My Greek has all evaporated: if I had to construe a verse . . . I should get an apoplectic fit. But it formed my taste. I dare say my English is the better for it.' This is not unlike Cory's argument that the shadow of past knowledge is a protection from many illusions; when George Eliot drew the portrait of Sir Hugo, she did not draw a fool.

In her last novel she was still keen to construct symbolic patterns out of Greek drama, and since the book deals to a large extent with radicals and visionaries, she took the favourite play of such people, *Prometheus Bound*. This play, as we have seen, is both very static and intensely dramatic, and she explores this paradox when she speaks of 'those moments of intense suffering which take the quality of action—like the cry of Prometheus, whose chained anguish seems a greater energy than the sea and sky he invokes'.[80] When she describes the visionary Mordecai, fated by illness and poverty to remain metaphorically motionless despite his ardent desire for action, she again refers to Aeschylus: 'There be who hold that the deeper tragedy were a Prometheus Bound not *after* but *before* he had well got the celestial fire . . .: thrust by the Kratos and Bia of instituted methods into a solitude of despised ideas, fastened in throbbing helplessness by the fatal pressure of poverty and disease.'[81] Mordecai belongs to circle of radical thinkers; Daniel is taken to one of their meetings, and finds them reading Shelley—*Prometheus Unbound*.[82] The symbolic pattern is now complete: in the present age the prophets and dreamers who would do great things for humanity are fettered by circumstance, but in a future time their successors, like Prometheus, will be released.

The use that George Eliot makes of the *Prometheus Bound* is artificial and even sentimental. Daniel brings to the dying Mordecai his long-lost sister; it is the sort of scene that makes an old-fashioned Hollywood weepie seem caustic. Sure enough, Greek drama is trundled on to the stage: 'In the heroic drama, great recognitions are not encumbered with these details; and certainly Deronda had as reverential an interest in Mordecai and Mirah as he could have had in the offspring of Agamemnon; but he was caring for destinies still moving in the dim streets of our earthly life. . . .'[83] And so on. In the circumstances, the pretence that this preposterous scene is so much more real than Greek tragedy seems merely cheap. Equally self-indulgent is this later account of Daniel's emotions:

> If he had read of this incident as having happened centuries ago in Rome, Greece, Asia Minor, . . . to some man young as himself . . . it would have appeared to him quite natural that the incident should have created a deep impression on that far off man, whose clothing and action would have been seen in his imagination as part of an age chiefly known to us through its more serious effects. Why should he be ashamed of his own agitated feeling merely because he dressed for dinner, wore a white tie . . . (etc.)[84]

However, this passage does introduce us to a more subtle motif which runs through the novel. Many Victorians felt, with some justice, that there was something peculiarly unpoetic about modern dress. George Eliot alludes to this notion when she writes, 'It has to be admitted that in this classical, romantic, world-historic position of his . . . [Daniel] wore—but so, one must suppose, did the most ancient heroes whether Semitic or Japhetic—the summer costume of his contemporaries.'[85] This is again sentimental, but earlier she has made ironic play with costume. Gwendolen and her friends decide to amuse themselves by dressing up and presenting a series of tableaux to an audience of suitably admiring friends. She discusses what part she should take with her mother, Mrs. Davilow.[86] St. Cecilia perhaps?—'Only, . . . I think saints' noses never in the least turn up . . . mine is only a happy nose; it would not do so well for tragedy.' But Mrs. Davilow, exuding quiet gloom as usual, tells her, 'Any nose will do to be miserable with in this world'; and she will indeed discover that it is not necessary to 'look the part'. Various costumes are constructed for her, 'Greek, Oriental and Composite.' The housekeeper is summoned to admire the results, and her native good sense discovers the absurdity to which superior eyes are blind: Gwendolen, she says, looks far more like a queen in her own dress than in 'that baggy thing with her arms all bare'.[87] It is an illusion to suppose that the costume of past ages will make us more dignified. Gwendolen argues with her mother about whether it is more tragic for a woman to have a high or a low voice and snaps impatiently, 'I am not talking about reality, mama.'[88] These are ironic words. Her voice, like her nose, may be unsuitable for a tragic role when she is play-acting, but she will have a tragic part to endure in life.

What about the choice of tableau? 'I can't have any Greek wickedness,' Mrs. Davilow warns. 'It is no worse than Christian wickedness, mama,' Gwendolen answers. 'And less scandalous,' adds Rex Gascoigne, who is in love with her. 'Besides, one thinks of it as being all gone by and done with.'[89] Rex is up at university; but he has no notion that Greek literature has anything to do with real life. 'What do you say to Briseis being led away?' he continues. 'I would be Achilles, and you would be looking round at me.' Rex's idea is prophetic; not only will he lose Gwendolen, but her marriage to Grandcourt will prove to be a leading into captivity. We are reminded of her amateur dramatics later when she is rich, married and miserable. Mirah has been invited to sing at a party in Park Lane. Her mind is 'chiefly occupied in contemplating Gwendolen. It was like a new kind of stage experience to her to be close to genuine grand ladies . . . and they impressed her vaguely as coming out of some unknown drama, in which their parts perhaps got more tragic as they went on.'[90] At the beginning of the novel we observe Gwendolen eager to act out a tragic role before an audience of enthralled spectators. She gets her wish.

VII

THE CONSEQUENCES OF
SCULPTURE

ALTHOUGH the nude has occupied a central place in European art, nakedness was peculiarly associated with the Greeks throughout the last century. In part this was because they had been used to seeing naked bodies in life as well as art, and regarded public nakedness as a sign not of primitivism but of civilization. Their attitude to nudity seemed to be a fundamental part of their Greekness: 'What an odd man . . .!' says Mallock's Lady Ambrose of the Hellenic Mr. Rose. 'He always seems to talk of everybody as if they had no clothes on.'[1] Winckelmann had suggested that the Greeks owed the whole nature of their aesthetics to their nakedness: 'The . . . places where completely naked youths . . . played . . . were schools of beauty. It was there that artists contemplated the perfect development of physique; the daily sight of the nude warmed their imagination and taught them . . . the beauty of forms.'[2] His picture of the artist as peeping tom is somewhat unattractive; we become awkwardly aware that both he and Rose are inverts. But it was not inverts only who warmed to the Greek freedom from embarrassment. Byron described Juan and Haidee's embracements forming 'a group that's quite antique, Half-naked, loving, natural, and Greek'. With the word 'antique' he implies a contrast between the openness of the old paganism and the constrictions of modern morality; but since he often stresses that Haidee is a modern Greek, there is a second contrast between southern freedom and the puritanism of the north. Swinburne had similar feelings:

> We shift and bedeck and bedrape us
> Thou art noble and nude and antique;

Libitina thy mother, Priapus
Thy father, a Tuscan and Greek.

Who are 'we'? The pronoun seem to stand both for the English as opposed to the Greeks and Italians, and for the modern as opposed to the ancient world.[3]

Samuel Butler found a cast of the Discobolus stuffed into the lumber-room of a Canadian museum; the custodian explained that the statue was vulgar, and chattered away about his connections with the Baptist preacher Spurgeon. Now if Christianity as a whole were un-Hellenic, the dissenting churches seemed especially so, and out of this incident Butler created his *Psalm of Montreal*:[4]

'The Discobolus is put here because he is vulgar—
He has neither vest nor pants with which to cover his limbs;
I, Sir, am a person of most respectable connections—
My brother-in-law is haberdasher to Mr. Spurgeon.'

Part of the irony is that the Discobolus should be accused of vulgarity by a man who is himself, in the true sense of the term, so very vulgar; Butler brings this out by devoting one verse to mocking him for saying 'pants' instead of 'trousers'. The Victorians found the names for modern clothing, particularly underclothing, irresistibly funny; Greek nudity could be comically compared with the absurdity of contemporary dress. Byron had laughed at the gods and goddesses

Who in the earlier ages raised a bustle,
But never put on pantaloons and boddices.

Many years later W. S. Gilbert became rather gruesomely coy:[5]

They wore little underclothing—scarcely anything—or no-
thing—
And their dress of Coan silk was quite transparent in design—
Well, in fact, in summer weather, something like the 'altogether'.
And it's *there*, I rather fancy, I shall have to draw the line.

The word 'gymnastics', as Bentham noted, derives from the Greek for 'naked'; 'With us,' he added dryly, 'there is less heat and more delicacy.' Ruskin himself agreed that in sunnier climates, where the body could more often be exposed, 'the nude comes to be regarded in a way more grand and pure, as necessarily awakening no ideas of the base kind (as pre-eminently with the Greeks)'. Giovanni Costa praised Leighton for his 'courageous purity': 'In his undraped figures . . . there is . . . no remote hint of any *double entendre* veiled by aesthetic refinement, any more than there is in the Bible, the Iliad, or in the sculpture of Pheidias.'[6] It is no accident that two of these analogies are with Greek art: the thought of Hellas was a tincture that purified whatever it was applied to.

George Eliot's Dorothea is troubled by her uncle's collection of casts and pictures, 'severe classical nudities and smirking Renaissance-Correggiosities . . . staring into the midst of her Puritan conceptions.'[7] Her unease stems equally from her Englishness and her evangelicalism; when she travels to Italy, her reaction will be a mixture of awe and half-shocked bewilderment. What was a churchman to think? Bishop Goodwin was disturbed by Tadema's Venus: 'In the case of . . . an Old Master much allowance can be made . . . but for a living artist to exhibit a . . . life-like . . . representation of a beautiful naked woman strikes my inartistic mind as somewhat . . . mischievous.' Dean Alford, by contrast, thought that sculpture was 'fitted for exciting pleasure . . . by the unclothed symmetry of the wonderful frame with which the Creator has endowed us'.[8]

Ruskin suggested that Greek bodies had a 'sunny elasticity very different from the silky softness of the clothed nations of the north, where every model necessarily looks as if accidentally undressed'; and S. C. Hall suggested that French nudes looked as if they had taken their clothes off, Greek ones as if they had never thought of clothes.[9] The distinction is not entirely due to the superior virtue of Hellas; much of it is owed to the difference between sculpture and painting. Hall was thinking of Greek statues but of French pictures; in *Middlemarch* the casts are severe and the paintings suggestive; nor was it mere chance that Alford was discussing sculpture, while Goodwin was talking about oils. None the less, Pater's claim that the beauty of Greek statues was sexless is at best a half-truth. Symonds's father was disturbed to discover his young son gazing longingly at a print of a Praxiteles.[10] If the beauty of the work had been entirely sexless, he would have had scant cause for anxiety; on the other hand, if it had been blatantly erotic, he would hardly have allowed it in the house.

The extreme delicacy attributed to the Victorians by modern folk-mythology was by no means general. The nude was Art and therefore permissible. For all his unease Goodwin was reluctant to go so far from the popular prejudice as to condemn it; covering his embarrassment with a defensive facetiousness, he asked bemusedly for enlightenment. Many households showed a willingness to admit the nude into the family circle that is striking even today. The walls of the billiard room were not seldom decorated in the most lurid taste, but even the drawing-room might contain a few ornaments of Parian china. This, as the name suggests, was designed to look both Grecian and marmoreal; it was therefore doubly superior. Some people who claimed to be teetotal would allow a little something to pass their lips if it were disguised as a patent medicine, like Congreve's Elixir, manufactured by a pious non-conformist, who built Baptist chapels in Hove out of the profits. Parian ware was the artistic equivalent of that little something.

The lady novelist Alan St. Aubyn imagined some girl under-graduates at a Greek play:[11]

> The men . . . looked lovely! And, oh, the way the Greek came out! There never was such a public exhibition of manly limbs as the scanty Greek draperies revealed. Such legs! such arms! such chests! . . .
> It brought tears into the girls' eyes—at least, into the eyes of the girls of higher culture.

At least . . . the girls of higher culture—those are the revealing words. Here was the paradox of Greek art: by the 1890s it had come to seem artificial and a little absurd; yet it could still serve to liberate the inhibitions. Twenty years earlier Pater had praised Greek sculpture for its 'central impassivity', its 'depth and repose', but he had added, 'To all but the highest culture, the reserved faces of the gods will ever have something of insipidity.'[12] The novelist's echo of this sentiment is probably coincidental, but the coincidence is significant. Greek art allowed one to contemplate the naked body with a good conscience, and at the same time to congratulate oneself on possessing a taste far removed from the common herd's. The admirer of Ingres or Greuze had not this consolation.

Hiram Powers's statue of 'The Greek Slave', a sensation at the Great Exhibition, drew from Mrs. Browning a sonnet praising the 'passionless perfection' of the work and the 'ideal sense' of the artist's protest against slavery.[13] Powers explained that his statue represented a Greek girl captured by the Turks. She is naked and her wrists are chained; we infer that she is destined for the harem. Today the erotic implications seem glaringly obvious, and yet Mrs. Browning was right after a fashion: the work is curiously frigid, curiously calm in a way that cannot be attributed to pusil-lanimity or technical incapacity on the sculptor's part. Writers had discovered that the public did not want to read about real women; they wanted creatures who were impossibly perfect, unnaturally pure. Victorian nudes were often the visual equivalent of Agnes Wickfield and Laura Bell; sags and bulges, moles and wrinkles were eliminated, in many cases not to make the works more arousing, but rather to make them less so. Grecian sculpture was attractive not because the Greeks were so frank about the display of the body but for the very opposite reason; the female genitals, for example, were always represented in a formalized manner. So much the better: it was not naked women that the public wanted to see but nudes—not quite the same thing. The perils of this evasiveness are summed up in the tragic fiasco of Ruskin's unconsummated marriage. Effie Ruskin explained, 'He had imagined women were quite different to what he saw I was and . . . he did not make me his Wife . . . because he was disgusted with my person the first evening.'[14] It appears that the great critic, who had seen countless sculpted and painted nudes, did not know that women had pubic hair.

At first the Elgin Marbles had seemed thrillingly romantic; Hazlitt had contrasted their fusion and motion with the 'stuck-up gods and goddesses' that had formerly been admired, and Haydon expected them to inspire a renaissance of English art.[15] In the time of Flaxman and Chantrey native English sculpture was perhaps more distinguished than it had been for centuries; yet as time went by the feeling grew that this form of art was not at home in the new age. Greek sculpture was faultlessly excellent, Hazlitt said; half a century later Pater was to add a significant qualification: 'the impeccable, within certain narrow limits'. Henry James makes the sculptor Hudson complain that there are so few subjects he can treat compared to a painter. As a Hellenist, he must not depict anything ugly, nor may be take a Hebraic theme.[16] Yet although the modern sculptor, as Ruskin observed, seemed to have become un-Christian, a moral stuffiness pressed upon him: 'Spotless marble seems to me false to itself,' says Hudson's patron, 'when it represents anything less than Conscious Temperance.' This attitude was complemented by the aesthetic insipidity of the critics, with their odd indifference to bulk and volume and solidity. Ruskin held that 'sculpture was essentially the production of a pleasant bossiness or roundness of surface'; Pater thought that 'outline' was the abiding characteristic of the antique world.[17]

In these circumstances Grecian sculpture easily became a visible symbol of social or cultural pretentiousness; the emperor, in a double sense, had no clothes. Byron wrote,

> But all was gentle and aristocratic
>   In this our party; polish'd, smooth, and cold,
> As Phidian forms cut out of marble Attic.

Dickens's Mrs. Jarley insists that her waxwork show is 'calm and classical': 'I won't go so far as to say, that . . . I've seen waxwork quite like life, but I've certainly seen some life that was exactly like waxwork.'[18] Phiz drew a large male statue looking down, naked but supercilious, at the humble figure of Little Dorrit as she calls at the house of the parvenu Merdles; and George Eliot imagined Mrs. Holt, a lady of irrepressible vulgarity, visiting Transome Court and sitting in a stone hall full of statues, 'in singular relief against the pedestal of the Apollo', while the two small boys who have accompanied her scamper about in brightly coloured clothes. The room's 'stony spaciousness' is 'made lively by human figures extremely unlike the statues'; the animation and bright hues of these common people are contrasted with the colourless coldness of the hall, the stillness and deadness of its contents. Mrs. Holt is intrigued by a statue of Silenus: ' "But it was odd he should have his likeness took without any clothes. Was he Transome by name?" (Mrs. Holt suspected that there might be a mild madness in the family.)'[19] George Eliot intends a serious side to this some-what laboured comedy: the artificiality of classic art, its remoteness from the comprehension of ordinary people, symbolize the un-natural conventions with which the upper-class Transomes are surrounded.

At the same time Greek sculpture became linked in people's imagination with museums. The Greek Revival style had never seemed entirely apt for churches: it was so painfully bare of the warm nimbus of sacred associations by which Gothic architecture was surrounded. For public buildings, however, it was just the thing, serious, dignified, and a little aloof; it was therefore favoured for museums, and as it happened, the first half of the nineteenth century was a great age of museum-building. The Elgin Marbles were eventually housed in a Grecian building, and one which, whatever its merits, is not easily lovable. In the circumstances, people easily came to associate museums with Greek sculpture, and Greek sculpture with culture at its most 'museumified'; this was a notion that especially appealed to the Edwardians. The hero of Forster's *Maurice* makes an assignation in the British Museum with the virile and uneducated game-keeper Scudder, who like another more celebrated game-keeper in English fiction talks a great deal of high-flown nonsense in a heartwarming regional accent. He is baffled by the museum: 'What's all this place?' And the public schoolboy replies, 'Old things belonging to the nation.'[20]

Others, less crudely, contrasted the academic deadness of museums with the vitality of the culture which they entombed. Virginia Woolf announced that Greek tragedy made one see 'hairy, tawny bodies . . . among the olive trees, not posed gracefully on granite plinths in the pale corridors of the British Museum'. Hardy spoke of 'the gloom Of this gaunt room' in his poem *Christmas in the Elgin Room*, in which he associated the removal of the marbles from Athens to London with the movement of civilization from paganism to Christianity and from south to north. Flecker wrote,[21]

> And there's a hall in Bloomsbury
> No more I dare to tread,
> For all the stone men shout at me
> And swear they are not dead;
> And once I touched a broken girl
> And knew that marble bled.

Rickie Elliot, the hero of *The Longest Journey*, is, as Flecker was, a delicate young man who writes rather pallid stuff about dryads flitting through the English countryside. As in *Maurice*, Forster sets a scene in the British Museum. The philosopher Ansell strolls round the sculpture galleries:

> The comfort of books deserted him among those marble . . . gods. The eye of an artist finds pleasure in texture and poise, but he could only think of the vanished incense and deserted temples. . . . He left the Parthenon to pass by the monuments of our more reticent beliefs—the Temple of the Ephesian Artemis, the statue of the Cnidian Demeter. Honest, he knew that here were powers he could not cope with . . .[22]

The vitality of the Greeks has triumphed over the unsympathetic English surroundings—or rather the Greece of the anthropologists, with its fertility rituals and multimammalian divinities, has triumphed over the Greece of Winckelmann, epitomized by the Parthenon frieze. The most brilliant exploitation of this theme was to come as late as 1952 with MacNeice's poem *The Other Wing*. Two stanzas evoke the childish garish gaiety of Greek mythology; then comes the contrast:

hence these muted
Miles of parquet, these careful lights,
This aquarium of conditioned air,
This ne plus ultra.

Carlyle shocked the painter Watts by declaring that among all
the sculpted figures of Pheidias there was 'not one clever man';
their upper lips were short, indicating lack of intellect. Watts
protested: what about Napoleon, Goethe, Byron? The historian
was unimpressed; the Greek jaw did not project far enough: 'There's
not a clever man amongst them all, and I would away with them—
into space.' Many years before Horace Walpole had cattily described
Lady Hamilton 'acting the antique statues': 'People are mad about
her wonderful expression, which I do not conceive, so few antique
statues having any expression at all, nor being designed to have
it.' The expressionlessness of Greek sculpture made it seem very
alien from the artistic concerns of the nineteenth century, when
writers and painters were minutely exploring the individual par-
ticularities of men and objects. The faces of those Greek ephebes
were generalized, and Blake had spoken for the whole of the nineteenth century against the eighteenth when he scrawled in the
margin of Reynolds's Discourses, 'To Generalise is to be an Idiot.
To Particularise is the Alone Distinction of Merit.'[23]

None the less, that very expressionlessness held an attraction for
some Victorian sensibilities. Like Homer, Greek sculpture offered
a place of repose from the turbulent subjectivity of modern culture.
Pater said that Greek statues were unaware of the soul with all its
maladies, and Wilde developed this idea in *The Picture of Dorian
Gray*. Lord Henry Wotton tells the painter Hallward, 'I really
can't see any resemblance between you . . . and this young Adonis . . .
he is a Narcissus, and you—well, of course you have an intellectual
expression, and all that. But beauty . . . ends where an intellectual
expression begins. Intellect is in itself a mode of exaggeration,
and destroys the harmony of any face.'[24] Although Hallward is a
painter, Dorian Gray is repeatedly compared to a statue; he is
likened to Antinous, immortalized after his death in countless
sculptures, and praised for his 'finely-chiselled nostrils', his half-
parted lips, his 'plastic throat'.[25] The implications emerge in
Wotton's meditations:

There was something terribly enthralling in the exercise of
influence. . . . To project one's soul into some gracious form . . .;
there was real joy in that. . . . He was a marvellous type, too,

this lad . . .; or could be fashioned into a marvellous type at any rate. Grace was his, and the white purity of boyhood, and beauty such as old Greek marbles kept for us. There was nothing that one could not do with him. He could be made a Titan or a toy.[26]

To a sexually tinged emotion the expressionlessness of the Greek statue, the absence of soul, the lack of individual character are a positive enticement. If Gray is indeed like a Greek marble, then Wotton may hope to stamp upon him the impress of his own mind. He will be the Pygmalion who can bring the statue to life.

The story of Pygmalion (which in its present form may be no older than Ovid) was a recurrent theme in Victorian art and literature; Shaw's play was only the latest of a series of works which investigated the relation between creator and creature. Forty years earlier, W. S. Gilbert had written *Pygmalion and Galatea*, a 'mythological comedy' about the embarrassments which threaten the sculptor's marriage when his statue inconveniently comes to life while his wife is away. In 1881 Woolner, himself a sculptor, composed a poem in twelve books about Pygmalion. He treats the story as an allegory of the artist's predicament: his technique may be flawless, but where can he find the inspiration which will make his creations 'live'? This was very much a Victorian problem: never had so many English artists become technically so well equipped, only to find that they then had nothing to say. Pygmalion's artistry is admirable and yet his statues refuse to 'come to life'; so he prays to Aphrodite to 'breathe life' into them. The prayer is fulfilled when a gust of wind blows up the robe of the girl he is sculpting and he glimpses the naked body beneath. He becomes conscious of his love for her, and at last his art is filled with 'living' inspiration.

Woolner was concerned not only with the relation between a creator and his creature, but with another more delicate topic also: the relation between an artist and his model. In 1868 Burne-Jones had begun to explore a similar theme in his four Pygmalion paintings. In the second, Pygmalion looks wistfully at his nude creation; in the last she is still in much the same position—still statuesque— but alive, with Pygmalion on his knees before her, kissing her hands and gazing up at her marmoreal breasts. The second picture is called 'The Hand Refrains', the last, evasively, 'The Soul Attains'. The soul, yes; but what of the body? Burne-Jones worked on these paintings at a time when he was emotionally entangled with his

model Maria Zambaco; she, like the mythical Pygmalion, was a
Greek, and her southern temperament proved too exhausting for
her admirer, who soon relapsed into married bliss. This episode
may contain the clue to the Pygmalion paintings. They depict the
realization of a sexual fantasy; and yet they seem to enclose, at
the same time, a different and partly contradictory message. The
whole thing, somehow, is anaemic and abashed. Even in the last
picture, when the statue has come to life, the texture of her skin
remains unpleasantly bloodless, unnaturally smooth; unlike living
flesh, and more like wax than marble. Much Victorian art seems to
quiver with concealed eroticism, but here the situation is apparently
reversed: the subject is overtly erotic (one would suppose), but the
treatment is terribly tame.

'The Hand Refrains'—the title indicates one advantage which
sculpture possesses over other arts. In Compton Mackenzie's
Carnival, Avery, an unsuccessful littérateur, falls in love with a
chorus-girl, and finds himself turning from poetry to sculpture:[27]

> Now I must mould you, Jenny . . . I'm thrilled by the thought
> of it . . . to mould your delicious shape with my own hands,
> to see you taking form at my compelling touch. . . . There's
> objective art. Ha! Poor old poets with their words. . . . You
> can't dig your nails into a word. By Jove, the Nereids in the
> British Museum. You remember . . .?
> Jenny looked blank.

Unlike Jenny, we can appreciate what underlies Avery's praise of
objective art; one cannot fondle a picture or a poem, but statues
seemed to invite the spectator to run a furtive imaginary hand
over their unresisting flexuosities. Goethe became acutely aware of
the connexion between sexual emotion and the enjoyment of
sculpture in Rome, where he spent his days among classical authors,
his nights with his mistress: 'Do I not instruct myself by studying
the forms of her lovely bosom, and running my hands down over
her hips? Not till then do I understand marble rightly. . . . I see
with an eye that feels and feel with a hand that sees.'[28] When this
theme appears in English literature, it is usually with a difference.
Goethe had perceived that the imagination might intertwine life
and art, each enhancing the other; the Victorians, more *angstvoll*
than the great German, treated the tactile qualities of sculpture as
a substitute for dangerous delights. 'Winckelmann fingers those
pagan marbles,' says Pater, adding hastily, 'with unsinged hands,
with no sense of shame or loss.' Landor makes Rhodope say of

Love: 'I have touched his statue; and once I stroked it down, all over: very nearly. He seemed to smile at me . . ., until I was ashamed.'[29] And here she adds, apologetically, 'I was then a very little girl.' Yeats was to return to this theme in one of his last poems:

> Pythagoras planned it. Why did the people stare?
> His numbers, though they moved or seemed to move
> In marble or in bronze, lacked character,
> But boys and girls, pale from the imagined love
> Of solitary beds, knew what they were,
> That passion could bring character enough,
> And pressed at midnight in some public place
> Live lips upon a plummet-measured face.

Here Yeats has penetrated to the heart of the paradox: how is it that Greek sculpture is at once mathematical, expressionless, 'soulless', and yet instinct with sexuality? The question fascinated him in the final months of his life; in an essay he argued, 'When the Doric studios sent out those broad-backed marble statues against the multiform, vague, expressive Asiatic sea, they gave to the sexual instinct of Europe its goal, its fixed type.' In the poem the point is made with gnomic concision: 'Phidias Gave women dreams and dreams their looking-glass.'[30] Within these Delphic utterances lies the key to the mystery. On the one hand Greek sculpture 'put down All Asiatic vague immensities'; it is fixed, solid, definite. On the other hand, blank, characterless expressions provided a vacant space for men and women to project their dreams and fantasies upon. Passion could bring character enough.

The Victorian male's ideal of womanhood tended to be at once oppressive and fantastic. She was to be the angel in the house, with an angel's passionless insubstantiality, conforming painlessly to the shape of her husband's character and wishes; at the same time she must offer the more substantial delights of solid, compliant flesh. Angel and mistress, vision and reality—surely only a statue come to life could perform all these functions. Consciously or unconsciously, many Victorians realized this. Watts's painting, 'The Wife of Pygmalion', moved Swinburne to raptures: 'The soft severity of perfect beauty might serve alike for woman or statue, flesh or marble, but the eyes have opened already upon love . . .: her curving ripples of hair seem just warm from . . . the breath of the goddess. . . . Her shapeliness and state, her sweet majesty and amorous chastity, recall the supreme Venus of Melos.' Soft but severe, amorous and yet chaste; such should be the Victorian wife, and such would be a Greek statue come to life. The Venus of Melos inspired similar emotions in Clive Newcome:[31]

> Give me a calm woman, a slow woman. . . . When I saw the great Venus of the Louvre, I thought, Wert thou alive, O goddess, thou shouldst never open those lovely lips but to speak lowly, slowly: thou shouldst never descend from that pedestal but to walk stately to some near couch, and assume another attitude of beautiful calm.

The living statue is both worshipful and pliable, both deity and drawing-room ornament; Gray 'could be made a Titan or a toy'. Avery's new-found enthusiasm for sculpture symbolizes his desire to 'mould' an uneducated girl in mind as well as body. 'Jenny looked blank'; on that blank page her lover can inscribe whatever he wills. Similarly, Shaw's *Pygmalion* is the story of an intellectual who 'creates' a lady from a Cockney girl. Hazlitt fell in love with a very young girl who was much his social inferior; he compared her to a marble statue, declared that he would worship her as a goddess, and called his account of his infatuation *Liber Amoris, or The New Pygmalion*. Byron had described Pygmalion's statue as 'The mortal and the marble still at strife, And timidly expanding into life.' It was the combination of mortal and marble, demureness and expansion together that was so enthralling. Pater praised the Greeks for their 'passionate coldness'; the noun and the epithet are equally important. Gilbert summed up a Victorian ideal:[32]

> She may neither dance nor sing,
> But, demure in everything,
> Hang her head in modest way,
> With pouting lips that seem to say
> 'Kiss me, kiss me, kiss me, kiss me,
> Though I die of shame-a!'
> Please you that's the kind of maid
> Sets my heart a flame-a!'

You could have your cake and eat it; the ravisher's enjoyment and the charms of honourable love were united in one experience. Many Victorians who might have winced at Gilbert's vulgarity would have agreed, in their hearts, with his sentiment.

Maria Zambaco hardly fitted this pattern; but on canvas Burne-Jones could create a Maria Zambaco from whom the sharp awkward corners had been smoothed away. There was a part of him which really preferred the statue-woman; almost all his realizations of his feminine ideal, his demure beggar-maids and captive Andromedas, are in some way passive or defenceless. But they are also to be adored: King Cophetua kneels at the beggar-girl's feet. Burne-Jones's inner feelings emerge from his drawings of the Masque of Cupid from *The Faerie Queene*. Spenser's grim pageant of the ravaging power of lust is transformed into a listless procession of vacant, androgynous nudes; Britomart, the virgin heroine who watches the fearsome spectacle, is as languid as the rest. However Burne-Jones depicts sexual passion, whether in its ennobling or degrading forms, he sees it as wistful and yearning. The passivity and marmoreality of Pygmalion's statue are in themselves an incitement to desire.

Hamlin in Vernon Lee's *Miss Brown* is a painter, partly based on Burne-Jones, who educates a servant-girl and plans to marry her to gratify his vanity and adorn his drawing-room. His design is to grace his life by 'awakening the love of this beautiful Galatea whose soul he had moulded, even as Pygmalion had moulded the limbs of the image'. Sure enough, the girl's beauty is such that she seemed to be 'no living creature, but some sort of strange statue . . . of Parian marble'. Hamlin himself agrees that she is like a statue, and incapable of what most people call passion: 'But just for that reason has she got a capacity for passion . . . such as no other woman ever had.' He intends this passion to take the form of a slavish worship of the man who has 'created' her, and yet like Cophetua he is pleased for a while to 'play that comedy of respectful distant adoration'. The combination of authority and abasement is to be found again in Davidson's *Earl Lavender*. Here the setting is explicitly sado-masochistic: the Veiled Lady is both cruel and passive, both mistress and slave; she has flogged the hero and been flogged by him in her turn. And almost inevitably the story of Pygmalion crops up once more: 'Her stillness was like that of a statue—of Galatea wakening into life.'[33]

Heine remarked that Englishwomen reminded him of statues: they were so white—and so cold. Leighton too felt this resemblance, but he expressed it in more complimentary terms: 'In the Art of the Periclean Age we find a new ideal of balanced form, wholly Aryan and of which the only parallel I know is sometimes found in the women of another Aryan race—your own.' Certainly, the statuesque style of beauty was more valued in the last century than in our own. Marius the Epicurean admires Cecilia not least because she reminds him of sculpture, indeed of sculpture animated like Pygmalion's with stirrings of a new inner life: 'Her temperate beauty brought reminiscences of . . . the best female statuary of Greece. Quite foreign however to any Greek statuary was the expression of pathetic care. . . .' When Kingsley's Alton Locke first glimpses the lovely Lillian, she appears to him 'as if fresh from the chisel of Praxiteles . . . a skin of alabaster . . . stained with the faintest flush'. Pygmalion's statue again, *just* waking into life. Disraeli praises his Theodora's Hellenic face, 'perfectly Attic in outline, with the short upper lip and the round chin, and . . . hair bound by a Grecian fillet.'[34] A short upper lip, said Carlyle, meant lack of intellect, but no matter: it was better for a woman not to look too clever, and a pouting, coquettish expression was prized.

The whiteness of sculpture was a further attraction; 'brown' is an epithet of dispraise in the Victorian vocabulary. In Trollope's *Framley Parsonage* Lady Lufton's objections to Lucy Robarts as a daughter-in-law are crystallized in two adjectives, 'brown' and 'insignificant'. Mary Garth in *Middlemarch*, although she has won the love of two very different men, is agreed to be plain. It is never made clear why, except that she is 'brown'. She admits it herself: 'What a brown patch I am by the side of you,' she tells Rosamond Vincy, who is blond, cool and unanimated, 'a sculptured Psyche'.[35] Nowadays millions of people every summer endure expense and discomfort in order to darken their skins, but before the industrial revolution, when most of the population had to work outdoors to gain a living, sunburn was not prized. A white skin was a badge of status, proving that its possessor belonged to the leisured class; and the Victorians were close enough to the pre-industrial age to have retained many of its values. Whiteness was not only beautiful, it was upper class, and by a fortunate coincidence the faces of Greek statues were held to exemplify a peculiarly aristocratic type of beauty; to this day 'chiselled' is a favourite epithet for lords and ladies in popular fiction. Brownness and insignificance go together in Lucy Robarts; Lady Lufton feels that the girl is unworthy of her son's noble lineage. Equally, the brown Mary Garth lives a simple country life, while the blond, sculptured Rosamond is a social climber. When the tailor Locke compares Lillian to a statue by Praxiteles, we know at once that she belongs to a class to which he cannot hope to aspire.

Whiteness suggested simplicity, limpidity, lucidity; it was often mentioned in connection with the Greeks even when sculpture was not in question. Besides, to a super-sophisticated mind white can appear the most sensuously enjoyable of all colours, because it is not a colour. ('Red and yellow! Primary colours!' cries the disgusted Lady Jane in *Patience*.) In *Marius* Pater quoted a 'quaint German mystic' who speaks of 'the mystery of so-called *white* things'; in *The Renaissance* he had contrasted the clarity of Hellenism with the richer but murkier coloration of the modern world: 'Hellenism, which is the principle . . . of intellectual light (our modern culture may have more colour . . ., but Hellenism is pre-eminent for light), has always been most effectively conceived by those who have crept into it out of an intellectual world in which the sombre elements predominate.'[36] Matthew Arnold talked constantly of light when he discussed the Greeks, and to the extent that he visualized his metaphor, he seems to have seen Hellenism as a *source* of illumination, radiating outwards; but Pater fixed his attention less on the origin of the light than on the way it fell upon objects. He called Winckelmann's *History of Art* a 'shrine of grave and mellow light for the mute Olympian family'; we imagine the gods frozen into sculpture and bathed in the radiance of a southern sun. As he proceeds, he gradually reveals that he associates light and whiteness and sculpture together in a complex pattern of imagery. The Greek genius in art, he explains, was primarily sculptural: 'Painting, music, and poetry, with their endless power of complexity, are the special arts of the romantic and modern ages.' We may feel that a civilization that produced Homer and Sophocles was not less poetic than the nineteenth century, while an age that gave birth to Aeschylus and Pindar yields nothing to it in complexity; and yet Pater was echoing a commonplace. The theory had been popularized in England by Schlegel, who quoted the observation 'that the ancient painters were perhaps too much of sculptors, and the modern sculptors too much of painters', and concluded that 'the spirit of ancient art and poetry is *plastic*, but that of the moderns *picturesque*'. Lepidus makes the same point in *The Last Days of Pompeii*. 'Those old poets all fell into the mistake of copying sculpture instead of painting. Simplicity and repose—that was their notion; but we moderns have fire, and passion . . ., we imitate the colours of painting, its life, and its action.'[37] Simplicity and repose are Winckelmann's terms; it is disconcerting to hear them on the lips of an ancient Roman. And indeed they are wildly inappropriate: Virgil and Horace are not in the least 'sculptural', as Lepidus claims; Lytton is thinking of his own time, when the greatest age of English painting coincided, by a historical accident, with the revolt of the romantic poets against the marmoreal cor-rectitudes of Pope and his successors. It is not by chance that Lepidus is made to single out the two 'poets laureate' who glorified the reign of Augustus; the English Augustans are the 'old poets' that Lytton really has in mind.

Pater suggests, implies, alludes; he shrinks from precision like an aesthete from an aspidistra. He admires the 'intense outlines' of the 'antique world', the 'sharp, bright edge of high Hellenic culture', but he suggests that it is best viewed from out of a more shadowy region. Perhaps it was because music is so richly emotive and yet so comfortingly indefinite that he felt it to be the modern art *par excellence*, the condition to which all other arts aspire. Certainly we must keep an ear cocked for the overtones of his melodious prose, as when he says of sculpture, 'Its white light, purged from the angry, bloodlike stains of action and passion, reveals, not what is accidental in man, but the god in him, as opposed to man's restless movement.' Here we glimpse a clue to the labyrinth of his imagery, as we pick up a few revealing words: purges, stains, passion, god, movement. He associates colour with blood, and blood with passion; those 'stains' link blood and passion together, and slip into the sentence a suggestion of guilt and unease that is never made explicit. He again contrasts Greek whiteness with the spiritual unease of the modern world in his famous account of the Mona Lisa: 'Set it . . . beside one of those white Greek goddesses or beautiful women of antiquity, and how they would be troubled by this beauty, into which the soul with all its maladies has passed.'[38] As in *Marius* whiteness is associated with religion; it is holy as well as pure, symbolizing stillness and peace, in contrast to the action and movement of the modern, coloured world. Henry James caught up the half-religious connotations of Greek whiteness:[39]

> He left her . . . among the shining antique marbles. She sat down in the circle of these presences . . ., resting her eyes on their beautiful blank faces; listening . . . to their eternal silence. It is impossible . . . to look long at a great company of Greek sculptures without feeling the effect of their noble quietude; which, as with a high door closed for the ceremony, slowly drops on the spirit the large white mantle of peace.

No single word refers overtly to religion; James is content to let the words 'eternal silence' and 'presence' evoke a numinous atmosphere, and to use the 'circle' and the 'high door closed' to suggest a solemn ritual. He finds in Greek statuary an embodiment of the sense of peace induced by a grave ceremonial; this he associates with whiteness, and here surely is the key to Pater's use of the same idea. White raiment has an honoured place in the ceremonies of the church. White is worn by the bride at the chancel step, by the priest before the altar; white is the colour of the altar-frontal itself on the greatest feast days of the Christian year. When Pater contrasted the whiteness of peace with the soul's maladies and the stains of passion, was he not thinking more than half-consciously of the peace that passeth all understanding? In the chapter of *Marius* called 'White-Nights' he says that 'the whole of life seemed full of sacred presences' to his hero as a child. Whiteness stands for the calm austerity of Marius' boyhood religion, 'the severe and archaic religion of the villa', symbolized by his father's funeral urn, a 'marble house, still white and fair, in the family chapel, wreathed always with the richest flowers from the garden'. The eternal whiteness and stillness of religion abide as a point of calm and repose in the midst of a coloured and perishable world. Pater doubtless recalled Shelley's imagery of sixty years before: 'Life, like a dome of many-coloured glass, Stains the white radiance of eternity.'[40]

Pater's use of whiteness wonderfully illustrates the power of words to comfort and cajole. He associates it with a moral as well as an aesthetic purity, and yet the metaphor is curiously slippery, forever eluding our grasp and slithering away on to new ground. When the words 'Greek' and 'white' are put side by side we inevitably think, first and foremost, of sculpture. Lepidus' outburst implies an association between whiteness and Greek statuary; and when Mrs. Browning wanted a phrase for the still pathos of Powers's 'Greek Slave', she hit upon 'thunders of white silence'. We are not surprised, therefore, to find the word 'white' slipping into Pater's prose whenever he begins to talk about sculpture. And yet we keep hearing those quietly troubling overtones; as he slides around within his cluster of metaphors, a soft insinuating voice seems to whisper some message that it dares not speak aloud. He praises the Greek conception of deity in terms which echo Shelley: 'the supreme and colourless abstraction of those divine forms'.[41] The religious tone combines with the commendation of Hellenism for 'its transparency, its rationality, its desire of beauty'. 'Transparency' connects the images of light and whiteness; here Pater associates whiteness (or colourlessness) with the ideals of Greek art and life, or at least to those ideals as interpreted by Matthew Arnold. It is almost a symbol for classicism and intellectual clarity, and yet all the while Pater is using it to evoke those naked statues and youths exercising by the banks of the Ilissus, where Socrates expounded to Phaedrus the mysteries of a passionate yet passionless love. His

shifting, slippery metaphors, clustering around the idea of whiteness, blur the distinction between different kinds of purity and
enable him to associate his sentimental Hellenism with the high-
minded Hellenism of Arnold; he implies that emotions which his
contemporaries reprehended could seem innocent in a Greek context. Naturally he does not say this aloud, and probably he never
admitted it even to himself, and yet the implication is inescapable.
In his preface he says that the early phases of the Renaissance 'have
the freshness which belong to all periods of growth in art, the
charm of *ascêsis*, of the austere and serious girding of the loins in
youth'. Pater was acutely sensitive to the penumbra of associations
surrounding words; by the mere presence of a word like 'loins'
an undercurrent of subdued sexual imagery glides into the sentence.
The word *'askēsis'*, too, is reassuringly ambivalent. It means
'exercise' or 'practice', and placed beside 'youth' and 'girding of the
loins' it cannot fail to suggest the naked gymnasts of Greece. But
it can also mean the practice of spiritual exercises: it is the word
from which 'ascetic' is derived. The reader is being coaxed into
believing that the Greek worship of beautiful youths is acceptable,
since it is enveloped in a halo of quasi-religious association.

Pater quietly conflates two different themes, the Greeks' cult of
handsome young men and the idea that in Greece mankind experienced its youth or childhood. After contrasting the white purity
of Greek sculpture with the maladies of the Mona Lisa's soul he
goes on to speak in the very next sentence of 'the animalism of
Greece'. Is he suggesting that Greek 'animalism' (whatever that
may mean) is automatically free from soul-malady? The theme
recurs in the essay on Winckelmann, in whom he detects an affinity
with the side of Plato represented by the 'brilliant youths in the
Lysis, still uninfected by any spiritual sickness'. He is of course
referring to Platonic homosexuality, though naturally he cannot
say so. He moves on to talk about Winckelmann's own emotions:
'That his affinity with Hellenism was not merely intellectual, that
the subtler threads of temperament were inwoven in it, is proved
by his romantic, fervent friendships with young men. . . . These
friendships, bringing him in contact with the pride of human form,
and staining his thoughts with its bloom, perfected his reconciliation
with the spirit of Greek sculpture.' The meaning of this seems clear
enough today; to many of Pater's early readers, and perhaps to
Pater himself, it was more opaque. None the less, he had ventured
to connect Winckelmann's worship of Greek sculpture with an
admiration for the human flesh which it represents: and besides,

does not the word 'staining', according to his allusive manner, exude a faint, very faint odour of moral unease? He no sooner puts the hint forward than he withdraws it and retreats with discreet haste from the precipice. He does not return specifically to the subject of sculpture for several pages, and when he does, his tone has altered. It is now that he describes the whiteness of sculpture, purged from the stains of passion, and the persuasive appeal of this metaphor enables him to rescue Winckelmann (and himself) from the taint of impropriety. True, we can hear the suppressed excitement in his voice when he describes the youths on the Panathenaic frieze, 'with their level glances, their proud, patient lips . . ., their whole bodies in exquisite service'; but even these ecstatic words can be rescued with the aid of the metaphor of colourlessness: 'This colourless, unclassified purity of life, with its blending . . . of intellectual, spiritual, and physical elements . . . is the highest expression of that indifference which lies beyond all that is relative or partial. Everywhere there is the effect . . . of a child's sleep just disturbed.' The absence of colour in the bas-relief is confused with the colourlessness of the Platonic forms, that other sphere of existence which transcends the relative and partial. Shelley's metaphor is at work again; and purity, spirituality, indifference and the innocence of childhood are all thrown in to acquit Greek sculpture of the unvoiced suspicion of exciting lust. Three pages later Pater makes his bland announcement that 'the beauty of the Greek statues was a sexless beauty'. In consequence there is 'a serenity . . . which characterises Winckelmann's handling of the sensuous side of Greek art. This serenity . . . is the absence of any sense of want, or corruption, or shame.' A radically ambiguous sentence, it may be observed. The colour metaphor returns in an oracular passage of baffling inconsequentiality (with the word 'therefore' patching over a gaping hole in the argument):

> The spiritualist is satisfied in seeing the sensuous elements escape from his conceptions; his interest grows, as the dyed garment bleaches in the upper air. But the artist steeps his thought again and again into the fire of colour. To the Greek this immersion in the sensuous was indifferent. Greek sensuousness, therefore, does not fever the blood; it is shameless and childlike.

And so Winckelmann, being spiritually a Greek, can finger the marbles with unsinged hands, with no sense of shame or loss: 'That is to deal with the sensuous side of art in the pagan manner.' The sleight of hand is accomplished.

Yet even here the metaphor of Winckelmann's fingers is instinct with sexual feeling. And when Pater talked of the 'transparency' of the Greek spirit, is there not perhaps, even here, a hint of the cool waters of the Ilissus with the athletes beside it? 'Poetry,' said Tennyson, 'is like shot-silk with many glancing colours. Every reader must find his own interpretation . . . according to his sympathy with the poet.'[42] Pater's prose has something of the quality of Tennysonian verse: its haunting, allusive melancholy troubles the reader but fascinates him, like the eye of a snake. But indirectly though he expressed himself, the implications did not escape his admirers. In Mackenzie's *Sinister Street* the schoolboy hero meets a stranger, who asks, 'Are you indeed like one of those wonderful white statues of antiquity, unaware of the soul with all its maladies?' Simply from the parroting of Pater and the use of the word 'white' we know at once that the speaker is homosexual. Among Dorian Gray's Hellenic charms is 'the white purity of boyhood'. Once again words are being used to assuage the conscience: since boyhood is white and pure, Wotton can reflect that to project his soul into Gray's form would be 'the most satisfying joy left . . . in an age . . . grossly carnal in its pleasures'.[43] Wilde assures himself that Wotton's (or rather his own) desires are not of a carnal kind; but falsely.

Symonds, another homosexual, composed ingenious variations on the colour theme. In his *Sketches in Italy and Greece* he combined several contrasts in a single paragraph; between Christianity and paganism, north and south, painting and sculpture, the dark anguish of romantic art and the Greeks' Apolline clarity. Light and colour are the concepts that bind these ideas together: 'Christianity . . . decked her shrines with colour. Not so the Paganism of Hellas. With the Greeks, colour . . . was severely subordinated to sculpture; toned . . . to a calculated harmony with actual nature. . . . Light falling upon carved forms . . . was enough for the Phoebean rites of Hellas.' Symonds also sought to moralize the mountains of Greece: 'Austerely beautiful, not wild with an Italian luxuriance . . ., they seem the proper home of a race which sought its ideal of beauty in distinction of shape and not in multiplicity of detail, in light and not in richness of colouring, in form and not in size.'[44] Evidently Symonds means to compare the austere, colourless landscape of the Greeks with their sculpture, and like Pater, he will use the idea of austerity to redeem Greek statues from the taint of sin. In his *Studies of the Greek Poets* he glories in the rocky bareness of the south: 'Nature is naked

and beautiful beneath the sun-like Aphrodite, whose raiment falls
waist-downward to . . . the sea, but whose pure breasts and forehead are unveiled.' He insists that Theocritus can only be understood when read in those 'sacred spots, which seem to be the
garden of perpetual spring. Like the . . . idyllist they inspire an . . .
indescribable *pothos* (yearning desire, *Sehnsucht*) . . . soothing our
spirits with the majesty of classical repose.' The mountains, he
adds, are 'carved of naked rock. We must accept their beauty as it
is, nude . . . and unadorned, nor look in vain for the . . . picturesque-
ness of the Alps.'[45] There is a contradiction in these words. The
naked landscape of the south is soothing, classical, restful—but no,
it excites a yearning desire. *Pothos*, a longing for something absent,
is indeed one of the more 'romantic' of Greek concepts—it was a
pothos, said the historians, that drove Alexander the Great onward—
but even so Symonds must give it a modern gloss by identifying it
with *Sehnsucht*. We associate this word with the German romantics;
like Goethe, he is in love with a land where the lemon-trees bloom,
but like Goethe again he views it from the distant vantage-point of
the north. 'Do you *know* that land . . .? *There* would I like to go,'
sings Mignon, whose longings, we are told, take hold only of what
seems unreachable and infinitely distant.[46] Symonds, too, invites his
readers to see the south as an unattainable land of lost content; and
yet it was easy for an Englishman with a little money to settle in
Italy, as Symonds did himself. Only by pursuing his hints about
the clarity, sanctity and nakedness of southern scenery can we
disentangle his paradox. While he is talking about landscape, his
thoughts are with Greek sculpture and the Greek way of life, which
seemed to the later Victorians to have the capacity to soothe and
disturb simultaneously. The sculptured nudes of the fifth century
are, undeniably, calm, but they forced upon the spectator's remembrance features of Greek society which might well agitate him.
The Greek experience suggested to Symonds that fleshly passions
had once been untroubling and free of guilt. But this would never
be possible again: one could only gaze upon the innocence of the
Greeks from afar, with *Sehnsucht* in fact, like a northern sojourner
in a southern land.

But perhaps the very distance of the Greeks might be reassuring
as well as melancholy. Pater, who like Symonds himself preferred
the hard edge of sculpture to have been softened by the slow action
of time, seems to have associated whiteness with remoteness, the
pale hazy light of the far horizon perhaps. White is the colour of
clarity; it is also the colour of mist. 'White nights, I suppose,' he

meditates in *Marius*, '. . . should be nights not of quite blank forget-
fulness, but passed in continuous dreaming, only half veiled by
sleep.'[47] Perhaps it would be safer after all to keep the Greeks at a
distance, in a dreamy haze, than to view them face to face. 'Here
Shelley dreamed his white Platonic dreams,' Lionel Johnson wrote
in his poem on Oxford. But Shelley did not want to dream about
the Greek experience; he wanted to possess it and devour it. It
seems a sad thing that this passionate hunger should dwindle to a
self-indulgent yearning which shrinks even from the objects of its
own desire, that the white radiance of truth should be transmuted
into the obnubilating whiteness of a mist or a dream. Yet Pater
did succeed, after all, in expressing a peculiar and complicated state
of mind in haunting and pregnant language; for surely his misfortune was that evasion sat not only on his lips but occupied the
very citadel of his heart.

VIII

THE INTERPRETATION
OF GREECE

The Greek Language

F ROM Coleridge to Kingsley, from Sydney Smith to Wilde, writers loved to declare that the very language of Greece was an enchantment, and far superior even to the Latin tongue. 'You have come to hear my ode!' says a Roman poet in Lytton's *Last Days of Pompeii*. 'That is indeed an honour; you, a Greek—to whom the very language of common life is poetry.' Macaulay decided, 'The Latin language is principally valuable as an introduction to the Greek. . . . We cannot refuse our admiration to that . . . perfect machine of human thought, to the flexibility, the harmony, the gigantic power, the exquisite delicacy, the infinite wealth of words.'[1]

As a boy Winckelmann was thrilled by the mere sight of Greek lettering;[2] the enticement of those symbols drew him on to the studies that were to govern his life. Children love runes and codes and cabbalistic signs; even in adult life there is perhaps a childlike pleasure, as Tolkien discovered to his profit, to be derived from the exploration of unfamiliar letter-forms, the sense of initiation into a secret or a mystery. Now of all the languages that a western European in the last century might expect to use only Greek was not written in the Roman script. In *Romola* Baldassarre's recovery of power is symbolized by his recovery of Greek letters, 'magic signs', and George Eliot stresses her point by writing them in big black capitals on their own. Hardy is still more typographically emphatic: in a single chapter of *Jude the Obscure* H KAINH ΔΙΑΘΗΚΗ is written three times, and every time in capital letters.[3] These words, Greek for 'The New Testament', unite Jude's religious emotions and his classical studies; they represent to him his Christian duty and, at the same time, the worldly ambitions that he hopes to realize through an education in the ancient tongues. He stares at the letters; then, conquered by the lusts of the flesh, rushes off to the voluptuous Arabella. When he returns,

> There lay his book . . ., and the capital letters . . . regarded him with fixed reproach . . ., like the unclosed eyes of a dead man:
>
> ### Η ΚΑΙΝΗ ΔΙΑΘΗΚΗ

The sheer sound of Greek is also a delight to Jude:[4]

> The policemen and belated citizens passing along under his window might have heard . . . strange syllables mumbled with fervour within—words that had for Jude an indescribable enchantment: . . .
> 'All hemin heis Theos ho Pater, ex hou ta panta, kai hemeis eis auton.'

We can hardly doubt that the enchantment was as strong upon Hardy as upon his Jude Fawley. It was even stronger upon Schliemann, whose story might seem to belong more to hagiography than to real life. He was fourteen years old and a grocer's apprentice when he heard a man reciting Homer and prayed to have the happiness of learning Greek. Later he made his fortune in the indigo trade, but threw it up at the age of thirty-six in order to devote the rest of his life to archaeology. He had been learning Greek for two years, not daring to begin earlier for fear of falling under the spell of Homer and neglecting his livelihood.[5] No doubt the words that he heard in the grocer's shop were wrongly pronounced; none the less, the beauty that he found there need not have been the product of self-deception. Greek is exceptionally abundant in short, light syllables; its fluidity and grace are qualities that hardly any pronunciation can destroy. It is equally fluid as a medium of expression; MacNeice explained,

> There are things you can do in Greek you never could do in English. The two negatives for instance—*ou* and *mē*—and even more the exquisite subtlety of the double negative *mē ou*. And the wealth of particles. . . . And that wonderful Greek word *an* which you can even tack on to a participle . . . the same with hockey; we learnt the economy of the wrist-flick, began to aspire in all things to a grace that was apparently effortless.

Virginia Woolf attempted to analyse the special quality of Greek:

> Every ounce of fat has been pared off. . . . Then, spare and bare
> as it is, no language can move more quickly. . . . Then there
> are the words themselves which . . . we have made expressive
> to us of our own emotions, *thalassa, thanatos, anthos** . . . so clear,
> so hard, so intense, that to speak plainly yet fittingly without
> blurring the outline . . ., Greek is the only expression. It is
> useless, then, [she added with crushing certitude] to read
> Greek in translation.[6]

She brought out the taut simplicity of the Greek by attacking a
recent translation: 'Professor Mackail says "wan", and the age of
Burne-Jones and Morris is at once evoked.' No doubt she was right;
but did she manage any better herself? Her metaphors of clear
waters, bright sunlight, sharp outlines, and naked athletic bodies
evoke the age of Arnold and Pater, overlaid with the fastidiousness of an upper-class Englishwoman: 'Greek is the only expression'
—'Liberty's is the only shop'. Perhaps she gives a fair impression
of the language of Sophocles, but her account is hopelessly inapplicable to Aeschylus or Thucydides or almost any other Greek writer.
It is probably impossible to define in words the distinctive
character of any language, not least because one of the qualities
of any good language is the capacity to be used in very different
ways. A lady is alleged to have said, 'It's a funny thing. The
French call it a couteau and the Germans call it a Messer, but we
call it a knife, which after all is what it really *is*.' She had a
point; somehow we feel that *thalassa* is not quite the same thing
as sea. Perhaps this is a sentimental feeling; at least it can easily
become so. 'Oh, Chronos, Chronos, this is too bad of you!' exclaims
Bunthorne in Gilbert's *Patience*. *Chronos* simply means 'time'; the
aesthete uses a Greek word to disguise the banality of what he says.
Beerbohm lists the works of Enoch Soames: 'Next, a dialogue
between Pan and St. Ursula—lacking, I rather felt, in "snap".
Next, some aphorisms (entitled ἀφορίσματα†).'[7] Again, the Greek
word, and still more the Greek script, add a touch of spurious
distinction.

Gilbert and Beerbohm were plainly satirical, but when Wilde
wrote *The Critic as Artist*, he may not have known himself whether
he was in jest or in earnest. Pater had discovered how a foreign
word or two could be used to season the dish: 'It has been said that

* sea, death, flower
† aphorismata

all the great Florentines were preoccupied with death. *Outre-tombe! Outre-tombe!*—is the burden of their thoughts.'[8] A tart, paradoxical savour comes from the application of words so richly redolent of French romanticism to the fresh world of an earlier Italy. Wilde goes a step further, blending Greece with both France and Germany: speaking of the overture to *Tannhäuser* (a work which itself puts pagan Venus into northern, Christian Europe), his Gilbert says, 'To-night it may fill one with that *erōs tōn adunatōn*, that Amour de l'Impossible . . .' Pater is again in Wilde's mind when Gilbert lights a cigarette. Marius took 'for his philosophic ideal the *monochronos hēdonē* of Aristippus—the pleasure . . . of the mystic *now*.' Gilbert remarks, 'There is nothing left for me now but the divine *monochronos hēdonē* of another cigarette.' There is a piquancy about using a Greek expression to describe a uniquely modern pleasure. Brooke found a piquancy of a different but kindred kind when he wrote from Berlin,[9]

> *eithe genoimēn* . . . would I were
> In Grantchester, in Grantchester!

The Greek words are simply the equivalent of the English 'would I were'; but the mere sound of those lucid syllables is enough to intensify the poet's yearning. He contrasts them with the ponderous words, oppressive both in sound and meaning, that he hears and sees about him, words such as *temperamentvoll* and *verboten*. He feels confined and constricted, but his longing to escape from his Teutonic surroundings, though expressed in Greek words, is directed not towards Greece itself, as it would have been in Pater, but rather—and here is the tang of paradox—to his native England. That is his land of lost content; familiar, undramatic countryside, though there glows upon its surface the bloom of a Hellenic loveliness:

> Is dawn a secret shy and cold
> Anadyomene, silver-gold?

anaduomenē, 'arising'—the epithet of Aphrodite, born from the sea to be goddess of love and beauty.

Confined at Reading in no merely metaphorical sense, Wilde revelled in reading his Greek Testament, deriving a special pleasure from the erroneous belief that the Galilean peasants were bilingual and that Christ spoke Greek:

It is a delight to me to think that . . . Charmides might have
listened to him, and Socrates reasoned with him . . .: that he
really said *egō eimi ho poimēn ho kalos** . . . and that his last word
when he cried out 'My life has been completed, has reached its
fulfilment, has been perfected' was exactly as St. John tells us
it was: *tetelestai*: no more.'[10]

Wilde points to the pregnant concision of Greek: the single word
tetelestai contains all that is in his English paraphrase. Overcome
by the charm of the language, he could not resist slipping in simple
Greek words as he wrote: 'the Greek woman—the *gunē Hellēnis*',
' "God's Kingdom"—*hē basileia tou theou*'. The game that he played
in *The Critic as Artist* had grown serious.

A taste for Greek vocabulary was a conspicuous feature of decadent
sensibility, and words such as 'sardonyx' and 'asphodel' were freely
employed by aesthetic individuals, who sometimes, one suspects,
had very vague ideas about what the stone or the flower looked
like. A less elevated but no less sincere tribute to the attraction of
the Greek language was paid by the banausic world that the aesthetes
so despised. The slang of the educated classes included words like
nous, kudos and hoi polloi; lawn tennis was first introduced as
Sphairistike; a new board game was named Halma; galoshes were
called antigropelos, an expression allegedly derived from the Greek
words for 'against wet mud'. These are but distant echoes from the
heights of Parnassus, where a single word might be a talisman.
Byron wrote of the day 'When Marathon became a magic *word*';
Cory, bitterly grieved by his dismissal from Eton, planned by way
of consolation 'to write a little book of Greek Iambics and call it
Iophon. Nothing but the name would carry me through.'[11]

Euphony plays only a small part in such emotions. Most obviously,
Marathon became a magic word because the Persians were defeated
there. Wilde is pleased to think that Jesus spoke Greek partly
because he associates the language with Athens, with Socrates and
the fair Charmides. No doubt Cory's feelings were similar, while
Brooke in his Berlin café was probably remembering those odes of
tragedy in which the chorus yearn to escape from the sorrows
around them to a land of bliss and quietude. We cannot entirely
separate the way a word sounds to us from the associations that it
suggests; perhaps that is part of what Virginia Woolf meant when
she said that we have made Greek words 'expressive to us of our
own emotions'. The word 'sardonyx', for instance, appeals to a

* 'I am the good shepherd.'

certain cast of mind because it is exotic; the exoticism derives partly
from the spelling of the word, partly from its Greek etymology,
partly from the nature of what it denotes (a jewel), partly from the
contexts in which it has been used in modern literature. This does
not mean that no word is intrinsically more euphonious than any
other. MacNeice described his first sight of the Atlantic from the
hills of Connemara: 'Something rose inside me and shouted "The
sea!" Thalassa! Thalassa! to hell with all the bivouacs in the desert;
. . . the endless parasangs have ended.'[12] But why does every schoolboy know that Xenophon's soldiers cried 'Thalassa, thalassa' when
they saw the sea? Because of the unforgettable sound of the words,
the sound of the sea itself.

Leafing through any anthology of Victorian verse, one finds
numbers of Greek names—Apollo, Hermione, Naiads and Dryads—
starting from the pages. This is a tribute to their magic, but a
limited tribute. We see Greek mythology hazily, through the veils
successively laid over it by the Romans, the Renaissance and the
classicism of the eighteenth century. 'Now lies the earth all Danaë
to the stars,' says Tennyson in a line that conjures up the hushed
expectancy of a wide, quiet land and marvellously suggests the
night's strange mingling of peace with ecstacy; and we think not
of ancient Greece but of the Italian Renaissance, of Titian's great
evocations of voluptuous calm.[13] Earnest efforts were made to strip
Greek names and stories of associative accretions. People had
been accustomed to call the gods by their Roman names, even
when they were talking about Greek history and literature; but in
the course of the century this custom gradually died out. As Arnold
said, 'Hera and Juno are actually, to every scholar's imagination,
two different people.' Even the spelling of words could make a
difference. 'When we employ our C to designate the Greek K,'
Grote declared, '. . . we mar the unrivalled euphony of the Greek
language.' But Macaulay 'never could reconcile himself to seeing
the friends of his boyhood figure as Kleon, and Alkibiadês, and
Poseidôn'; and Matthew Arnold felt that the reformed spelling led
into 'a wilderness of pedantry'.[14] Even Grote allowed a few names
to retain their familiar form; Browning was more ruthless:

> Aischulos' bronze-throat eagle-bark at blood
> Has somehow spoilt my taste for twitterings.[15]

The difficulty is that the reformed spelling carries with it as many
overtones as the old. We are scarcely surprised that the radical,
utilitarian Grote adopts a 'rational' orthography, while the whig

historian clings to 'the friends of his boyhood'. Equally Arnold's
aspirations to a calm classicism lead him naturally to choose the
time-honoured forms, whereas the new spelling seems to suit
Browning's picture of Aeschylus' rugged genius. The eye plays a
part in our perceptions of euphony, and the syllables that sound
melodious when we read them in the original lettering can come to
seem rough and barbarous if they are transliterated into our own
script. The objection to Latinate spellings is that they blur the
edges of Greek names, so that they resemble those statues which
Pater valued the more because time had softened their outlines;
the objection to the reformed spelling is that it makes the Greeks
seem outlandish. Arnold put his case well: 'The real question is
this: whether our living apprehension of the Greek world is more
checked by meeting . . . names not spelt letter for letter as in the
original Greek, or by meeting names which make us rub our eyes
and call out, "How exceedingly odd!" ' Even now the scholars
who examine the Greeks from an anthropological or psychoanalytical
standpoint tend to eschew Latinized spellings and the literary critics
to retain them.

Greek names were often contrasted with dull, unromantic English
names. Byron takes leave to praise Don Juan's friend Johnson,

> though his name, than Ajax or Achilles
> Sounds less harmonious.

And Thackeray declares, 'One would fancy fate was of an aristocratic
turn, and took especial delight in combats with princely houses—
the Atridae, the Borbonidae, the Ivrys; the Browns and Joneses
being of no account.' Place-names could be used as well (to this day
the English find the mention of Wigan or Neasden irresistibly
comic): Mallock's Mr. Rose contrasts the Hellenic elegance of his
ideal society with 'abominable advertisements of excursion trains to
Brighton, or of Horniman's cheap tea'.[16] He concedes that even in
his utopia there will be 'the necessary *kapēloi*', but they will be 'out
of the way, in a sort of Piraeus'. *Kapēloi* simply means 'retailers';
the Greek word purifies the sordidness of trade, while 'Piraeus'
sounds better than 'Surrey Docks'.

Mr. Rose is fictional; but Arnold could be a great deal more
extraordinary in real life. 'The Function of Criticism at the Present
Time' was written under sore provocation; one gentleman had
asserted that the Anglo-Saxon race were 'the best breed in the whole
world', another that they had achieved a degree of happiness unrivalled in the world's history. Arnold ventured to dissent, quoting

a recent newspaper report: 'A shocking child murder has just been committed at Northampton. A girl named Wragg left the workhouse . . . with her young illegitimate child. The child was . . . found dead on Mapperley Hills . . . Wragg is in custody.' This was a bitter and effective riposte; but almost immediately Arnold's eloquence veered in a startling direction: 'Wragg! . . . Has anyone reflected what a touch of grossness in our race . . . is shown by the natural growth amongst us of such hideous names. Higginbottom, Stiggins, Bugg! In Ionia and Attica they were luckier . . .; by the Ilissus there was no Wragg, poor thing!'[17]

Arnold's sense of euphony was affected by his eye. Surely he would not have found 'rag' so objectionable a word as 'Wragg', though the pronunciation is identical; the w looks harsh because it suggests wringing and twisting. Besides, there is something both homely and Anglo-Saxon, it appears, about names with a g and especially a double g in them. By inventing Mr. Baggins of Bag End, Tolkien brought out the humble Englishness of his Shire. What would happen to a tragedy in blank verse, G. H. Lewes asked, if the hero's name were Wiggins?[18] Lady Glenmire in Mrs. Gaskell's *Cranford* loses status by her second marriage: 'Mrs. Hoggins! Had she . . . cut the aristocracy to become a Hoggins!'[19] The termination -ins would seem to be an extra cause of offence; the lady would have done a little better to marry a Mr. Hogg. The English feel that surnames can be a badge of class. Scots names are different; a Campbell may be a peasant or a peer.

These analogies suggest that Arnold was unconsciously affected by social feelings. No doubt the names Wragg and Stiggins do sound less melodious than Ilissus, but part of their offence is that they are plebeian. Likewise, when Byron said that Johnson was a less harmonious name than Ajax, he really meant that it was less noble. And Arnold was evidently influenced by yet other associations, for after mentioning the Ilissus, he continues, ' "Our unrivalled happiness";—what an element of grimness, bareness, and hideousness mixes with it . . .; the workhouse, the dismal Mapperley Hills, . . . the gloom, the smoke, the cold, the strangled illegitimate child!' He connects the sound of the name Wragg with both the grimness of a northern climate and the ugliness of an industrial landscape; correspondingly, the mere mention of the Ilissus conjures up the brightness and beauty of an idealized Athens. This stream stirred fewer romantic sentiments in the Athenians themselves; their poets never praised it, reserving their eulogies for the more ample river Cephisus. Early travellers in Greece noted ironically that the banks of the Ilissus were bare and its bed dry as a bone in summer. There is, in fact, a touch of sentimentality in Arnold's too easy contrast between the horrors of the present and the perfection of the past.

In *Culture and Anarchy* he replied to his critics with admirable humour, picturing their caricature of himself as 'me, in the midst of the general tribulation, handing out my pouncet-box'.[20] But this would not be a bad description of his earlier essay. Arnold was a decent and kindly man, who had no wish to mock the sufferings of the wretched Wragg; yet the moment is sad at which he turns from excoriating the complacency of his contemporaries to lamenting the inelegance of English appellations. There is no better testimony than Arnold's to the power of Greek words over the Victorian imagination; but that very power contained the seeds of its own destruction. The magic of Greek names was like one of those legendary enchantments that sap a man's acuity and vigour, and there was a danger that Hellenism itself would come to seem merely limp and querulous. When David Jones came to write his epic of the First World War, he threw commonplace English names into his Homeric catalogue of warriors:[21]

> from Islington and Hackney
> and the purlieus of Walworth
> flashers from Surbiton . . .
> Bates and Coldpepper . . .
> Fowler from Harrow and the House . . .

By this time the intrusion of Greek into a passage of English could only seem precious. In *Mr. Eliot's Sunday Morning Service* it indicates the churchgoer's etiolated refinement:

> In the beginning was the Word.
> Superfetation of *to hen*.

√

The witticism is thin, donnish. And the subsequent history of the poem has added a further irony that its author never intended: in every collected edition of his poetry the Greek has been misprinted.

The Victorian Vision of Greece

The eighteenth century saw the beginnings of a great change in the way history was written; historians, once concerned almost entirely with political and military events, began to investigate such things

as commerce, religion and social habits. In a sense they were returning to the infancy of their art; the word history originally meant
nothing more than 'inquiry', and the early Greek historians had
mixed topography, ethnography and travellers' tales with cheerful
insouciance. Herodotus began the disciplining of history by directing
these diverse elements towards the service of a unified and dramatic
narrative; a process completed by the immensely tough intellect
of Thucydides, who ruthlessly excised the decorative features of
history and concentrated upon an account of events, chronologically
arranged and keenly analysed. He stamped upon historiography the
pattern that it was to bear throughout antiquity; indeed history is
still in the popular mind the story of what happened in the past, and
it is essentially to Thucydides that we owe this conception of it.
His reputation stood very high in the last century; yet in a way
there had never been a time when historiography was less Thucydidean: Macaulay, who adored him, felt none the less that his work
afforded 'less knowledge of the most important particulars relating
to Athens than Plato or Aristophanes', and urged the future historians
of Greece to turn from war and politics to a province that had so
far been left to the 'negligent administration of writers of fiction'.[22]

Buckle considered the human race to be chiefly influenced by four
physical agents, 'Climate, Food, Soil, and the General Aspect of
Nature'; the history of Greece provided a testing ground for most
of these. The topographical work of Leake and Gell had given the
historian a new instrument, and it is a part of human nature to
claim for any new instrument an exaggerated importance. Thirlwall
began his history, 'The character of every people is more or less
closely connected with that of its land.' George Eliot let a revealing
anachronism into *Romola* when she made Bardo maintain that a
'new . . . era would open for learning when men should . . . look
for their commentaries on the ancient writers . . . in the paths of
the rivers and on the face of the valleys and mountains';[23] such
opinions do not belong in the fifteenth century. In Wordsworth's
sonnet liberty has two voices: 'One is of the sea, One of the
mountains; each a mighty Voice'—a theory gratifying to the sea-girt
British.[24] Greece had both sea and mountain, and so Greece was
again the test. Grote remarked that the Greeks' position 'made
them at once mountaineers and mariners, thus supplying them
with great variety of objects . . . and adventures'; their cities,
separated from each other by the rocky terrain, but not so far as to
destroy a sense of Hellenic identity, gave the Greeks 'access to a
larger mass of social and political experience' than any other race.

Henry Tozer, agreeing that the Greeks owed much of their adventurous and democratic temper to the combination of sea and mountain, added to Grote's arguments others less easy to assess: the sea teaches courage and hardiness, but also by its extent and changeful motion 'expands the thoughts and inspires the feeling of restless activity'; mountainous terrain is easy to defend, but equally it 'elevates the mind and inspires it with a sense of independence'. Such views had a powerful hold upon the literary imagination; in an age when the beauty of natural scenery was more highly prized than ever before, it was agreeable to think that it might have shaped the destinies of nations. Symonds held that Athens was predestined to be the mother of reason 'by virtue of scenery and situation'; the radiance of the Athenian landscape had 'all the clearness . . . of the Attic intellect'.[25] When Ruskin suggested that the Greeks had no taste for picturesque landscape, he started an agitated controversy, in which even Gladstone joined.

Gillies cited Isocrates and Aristotle to show how the Greeks themselves believed that they owed the character of their civilization to their climate. Aristotle said that those who lived in the cold of northern Europe were full of spirit, but short of intelligence; they were free, therefore, but without political organization. The natives of Asia were intelligent but wanting in spirit, and therefore always in subjection. 'But the Hellenic race, which is situated between them, is likewise intermediate in character, being high-spirited and also intelligent. Hence it continues free, and is the best governed of any nation, and, if it could be formed into one state, would be able to rule the world.'[26] These opinions were much quoted in the last century, and for an understandable reason: they could be adapted to apply neatly to Britain. The British stood amazed at their own achievements. What was the source of their energy? Perhaps the climate gave the answer. Charles Adderley declared that 'the absence of a too enervating climate, too unclouded skies' had made the Anglo-Saxon race superior to all the world.[27] In fact the argument was more plausible in the nineteenth century than it had been in Aristotle's time: the climate of Asia is not so very different from that of Attica, but the English could look to the lazy Latins to the south of them and the sluggish Scandinavians to the north, and attribute their own good fortune to the laws of nature. Others, less sanguine, accounted for English philistinism on the same grounds. Religions could be similarly explained; 'They brighten under a bright sky,' Pater said. Disraeli's evangelical Mrs. Giles hopes that the Gulf Stream will change course: 'Severe winters at Rome might put an end to Romanism.' And surely the climate affected morals too. 'We will bless God for our English homes,' said the Rev. F. W. Robertson, thanking the Almighty for the climate with which He has been pleased to afflict us: 'Its gloom . . . making life more necessarily spent within doors than it is among continental nations, our life is domestic and theirs is social. When England shall learn domestic maxims from strangers, as Rome from Greece, her ruin is accomplished.'[28] (The Romans were granted the status of honorary northerners.) Such arguments were common—in those days France and Italy, not Scandinavia, were the 'wicked' countries *par excellence* —and they had already been satirized by Byron:[29]

> What men call gallantry, and gods adultery,
> Is much more common where the climate's sultry.
>
> Happy the nations of the moral North!
>   Where all is virtue, and the winter season
> Sends sin, without a rag on, shivering forth . . .

But Byron himself claimed to find in Attica and Ionia an excellence of climate strikingly different from the rest of the Mediterranean; a claim echoed by Symonds later.[30] Both men had travelled in Greece; and yet they let fantasy overcome experience. That compelling sense of the polarity between north and south fed a belief in the importance of climate and was fed by it in turn.

Many Victorians liked also to explain history in racial terms. All over Europe nationalism was waxing strong; while in imperial England it was hard to resist the sense of a special Anglo-Saxon destiny. Thomas Arnold used his inaugural lecture from the Regius chair at Oxford to argue that civilization progressed by being transmitted from one race to another: Greece fed the intellect, Rome established the rule of law, Christianity gave the perfection of spiritual truth. The changes of the last eighteen hundred years had been wrought by 'the reception of these elements by new races', principally the German peoples, of whom the English were one. Arnold was typical of his age, both in his sense of a Germanic distinctness and in his desire to claim a kinship with the old Mediterranean world. The English were not descended from the Greek or Jewish races, he admitted, and hardly at all from the Roman, but 'morally how much do we derive from all three'. The 'element of our English race' was the distinctively modern element in English history, and yet 'here . . . we have . . . the ancient world still existing'.[31]

And racial arguments gave a quasi-scientific backing to what might otherwise seem mere speculation. Lecturing at the Royal Academy, Leighton contrasted Assyria and Egypt with the Aryan spirit of fifth-century Greece—and then went on to talk a great deal of nonsense about Pelasgians and Autochthons. Disraeli made fun of Leighton's Aryanism, but he was no less addicted to racial arguments himself. Scott had drawn attention to the existence of two races, Saxon and Norman, in medieval England, and Disraeli used this idea, despite fantastic inconsistencies, to account for the 'two nations' into which modern England was divided;[32] and he was particularly interested in the destiny of the Jews. Greece was once again the place where the significance of racial differences seemed most sharply visible, for in Greece there had been two main races, Ionians and Dorians, whose contrasting characters were symbolized by Athens and Sparta. Such ideas were further stimulated by the success of Mueller's *Dorians*, first translated in 1839, a book whose effect, through its influence on Ruskin and Pater, was still felt in the late Victorian age.

The subject was particularly interesting to the British, who could not rid themselves of the idea that the Dorians were the Scotsmen of the south. In translations Doric dialect was represented by Scotticisms; thus in Rogers's version of the *Lysistrata*:[33]

> Our hizzies, a'
> Risin' like rinners at ane signal word,
> Loupit, an' jibbed, an' dang the men awa'.

More than one reader has turned gratefully to the Greek to find out what the translation means. The use of 'Doric' as a synonym for Scottish began as a jibe at the uncouthness of North Britain, but the Scots themselves started to take a pride in the epithet. Meanwhile, Edinburgh was being filled with solemn Doric-columned buildings. To Taine's Gallic eye they seemed ludicrously out of place in the cold, windy north; but had not Mueller said that the Doric character created the Doric architecture?[34] And was not the Doric character known to have been dour and phlegmatic? The analogy between Scots and Dorians was not openly argued for, but its insidious influence betrays itself from time to time. Matthew Arnold speaks of 'Dorian highlanders', contrasting the 'mobile Ionians' with the 'steadfast mountaineers of northern Greece'. Pater, too, contrasts the Dorian 'spirit of the highlands' with 'the mobile, the marine, and fluid temper' of the Ionians, whose tendency is 'Asiatic' and 'irresponsible'; and there is a flavour of Protestantism when he praises 'the saving Dorian soul'.[35] The old dichotomy of north and south has been transferred into a Greek setting, with the Dorians as stalwart northerners and the Ionians as feckless but artistic Latins. But in reality Sparta was not, as Pater claimed, a 'little mountain town'; it lies low in a wide sleepy valley in the southernmost part of Greece. And in attributing the Ionian character to the fact that they were coastal people with the 'roaming thoughts of sailors', Pater forgot that Dorian Corinth was for centuries the greatest port in Greece, and the home of its finest art.[36]

Mill protested unavailingly against the vulgar fondness for 'attributing the diversities of conduct and character to inherent natural differences between races'.[37] The opposite view is given by Disraeli's Contarini Fleming, who contrasts the naturally artistic Greeks with the 'flat-nosed Franks': 'They . . . invent theories to account for their own incompetence. Now it is the climate, now the religion . . . everything but the truth, . . . the mortifying suspicion that their organization may be different.' Tozer compromised; the Hellenes would not have achieved greatness on the plains of Hungary, he suggested, but then nor would the Mongols in the land of Greece.[38] Usually the issue was less plainly put, and the effects of landscape, climate and race were not clearly distinguished; all three were already jumbled up in Schlegel's lectures. What did Adderley mean when he claimed that the Anglo-Saxons were 'the best breed in the world' because of their cloudy skies? Or Pater when he said that the landscape around Sparta was a type of the Dorian purpose in life?[39] Did he know himself? A sense of the distinct identity of the breed (a favourite Victorian word) was emotional rather than logical. After all, the Victorians were not to know the perils of what they were doing. They toyed with racial ideas casually and uncomprehendingly, like children playing by the power lines.

The Victorians, and especially the later Victorians, thickened the fog of vagueness surrounding the Greeks by the persistent use of themes which easily degenerated into clichés: light, youth, calm. The idea of Greek serenity derived from Winckelmann; so too perhaps did the metaphor of youth, for it was he who developed the theory that the fine arts wax and decay like a living organism: 'Arts have their infancy as well as men.'[40] But to trace these ideas back to their German origins is to give a false impression, for the secret of their power over the Victorian mind was that those origins were unappreciated. Calm, radiance and childlikeness seemed to be qualities inherent in the Greek genius, plainly perceived across a distance of two thousand years; if the Victorians had distinctly told themselves that these ideas were merely the products of an outdated scholarship, they would not have accepted them so tamely.

'O Solon, Solon, you Greeks are always children,' said the Egyptian priest, contrasting the adventurous newness of Hellenic thought with the mysterious and immemorial depths of his native religion.[41] The passage was often cited, but in such a way that its meaning was changed. Pater's recurrent theme, repeated endlessly by his disciples, was that the Greeks had a child's unreflecting superficiality: 'This unperplexed youth of humanity . . . passed, at the due moment, into a mournful maturity.' The cult of athletics was 'such worship as Greece, still in its superficial youth, found itself best capable of'. This idea was made the more enticing by the belief that sculpture was the ruling art-form of the ancient world, as music of the modern; for sculpture deals necessarily with surfaces. 'Our art,' Symonds wrote, 'appeals . . . to the emotions, disclosing . . . spiritual reality . . . Greek art remains upon the surface, and translates into marble . . . the external world.'[42]

Many of the aesthetes liked the metaphor of youth because it allowed them to slip into talking about the cult of handsome young men. At the same time, it could be put to the service of a sentimental paganism which blamed the cold breath of the Galilean for blasting a world of joyous innocence. This idea underlies Pater's picture of Greece, but he was himself too subtle to take it over wholesale. Instead, he hints at a delicate, uncertain balance of loss and gain. To be sure, the Greeks had not known the maladies of the soul; and yet Marius finds in the Christians a mystic charm which makes him 'doubt whether that famed Greek "blitheness" . . . had been, after all, an unrivalled success'.[43] In *Denys l'Auxerrois*, a fable about the return of the god Dionysus in the Middle Ages, Pater contrasts a happy but too simple paganism with the Christian world, in which people have a 'larger spiritual capacity and . . . a larger capacity for melancholy'; in fact, the pains and privileges of adulthood. We may have been better or happier in our infancy, but do we wish to return to that state? Or as Pater puts it, 'Since we are no longer children, we might well question the advantage of the return to us of a condition of life in which . . . the value of things would . . . lie wholly on their surfaces, unless we could regain also the childish consciousness, or rather unconsciousness, in ourselves.'

As a literary conception these ideas have their charm, but with the Greeks themselves they have nothing to do. None the less, the metaphor of youth has great power; it was connected with a seductively simple theory of history, which has persisted into our own century in the works of Spengler and Toynbee, and a hundred years ago it overcame not only agnostics but even a future Archbishop of Canterbury. Frederick Temple maintained that 'We may . . . rightly speak of a childhood, a youth, and a manhood of the world. The men of the earliest ages were . . . still children as compared with ourselves, with all the blessings and . . . disadvantages that belong to childhood.'[44] The argument is muddled: at one time we are told that the Greeks were children being educated in preparation for the coming of Jesus, whose time on earth represented the world's adolescence; at another that the Greeks themselves had 'the grace of the prime of manhood . . . the pervading sense of youthful beauty'.[45] Today Temple's piece seems very dated, very 'Victorian', jarring against the liberal, commonsense tone of the other contributions to *Essays and Reviews*. But the impression is mistaken, for another Victorian who delighted to see the Greeks as sweet simple children was that 'cultured Anglo-German gentleman', Karl Marx.[46] How far, we may speculate, was Marx's naïve vision of the future founded upon his naïve picture of the ancient world? And with consequences for our own times, how great?

Quietly, almost imperceptibly, the metaphors of youth and light merged into one. We catch murmurs: 'the Hellenic genius, radiant, adolescent' (Symonds), 'radiance of fresh life' (Temple), 'the first glow of a youth which has proved immortal' (Jebb); and from Pater, more suggestively, 'They are at play . . . in the sun; but a little cloud passes over it now and then.'[47] Hazlitt contrasted early Italian paintings 'covered with the marks of . . . antiquity', with the far more ancient Greek statues which still 'shine in glossy, undiminished splendour, and flourish in immortal youth and beauty'.[48] This is emotion, not logic, for he bases his idea of Greece on the physical properties of stone and varnish. It was fatally easy to confuse symbolism with geographical fact; the brilliance of the Greek climate seemed to prove that Hellenism stood for the principle of intellectual light. Pater describes Winckelmann passing from 'the tarnished intellectual world of Germany' into the 'happy light of the antique'; that is a metaphor, but in the very next sentence Pater speaks literally of 'the dusky precincts of a Germany school'.[49] In *Duke Carl* we are told, 'The god of light, coming to Germany . . . over leagues of rainy hill . . . had ever been the dream of the . . . German soul.' The duke desires to bring 'the daylight, the Apolline aurora . . . to his candle-lit people', but he abandons his journey to Greece on deciding that the true light is to be found in Germany itself, 'the real need being that of an interpreter—Apollo, illuminant rather as the revealer than as the bringer of light'. Thus Pater's fictional creature escapes from the confusion between physical and metaphorical light; but we may doubt, strange as it seems, whether Pater himself ever did so.

Youth, light and clear southern skies were blent together to represent the Greek genius as a kind of lithe, buoyant athleticism. In the age of muscular Christianity the Greeks became muscular pagans; clean fresh air became a symbol of the Hellenic spirit. Pater spoke of Greece winning 'liberty, political standing-ground and a really social air to breathe in'. 'On the high places . . . of Greek . . . art,' Jebb said, 'those who are worn with . . . modern civilisation can breathe an atmosphere which, like that of Greece itself, has the freshness of the mountains and the sea.' Henry Jenkyns argued that the classics increased men's moral excellence and invigorated their nature; especially, he added, since no land 'can be visited with greater advantage than that of classical antiquity. By an abode in its clear and bracing climate the mind becomes more healthy . . . it acquires an elasticity, a gracefulness . . .'[50]

As northerners, the Victorians felt themselves inferior to the south; as moderns, to the past. When they contemplated the glories of Hellas, these two feelings fused into one. Greece was perfect, the past was perfect; must not the Greek climate have been perfect too? According to Symonds the Greeks lived amid 'perpetual sunshine and perpetual ease—no work . . . that might degrade the body . . . no dread of hell, no yearning after heaven.' As for the Greeks' modern descendants, 'Their labours are lighter than in northern climes and their food more plentiful. . . . Summer leaves them not. . . . There is surely some difference between hoeing turnips and trimming olive boughs; between tending turkeys on a Norfolk common and leading goats to browse on cytisus beside the shore.' He need only have read Hesiod to learn that labour can be heavy in Mediterranean lands, winters bitter, and food scarce; but he preferred to view the southern landscape with the impercipience of the milord for whom the peasants are picturesque objects in the middle distance: 'The poetry of rustic life is more evident upon Mediterranean shores than in England.'[51]

Pater had been less crude, but hardly less fanciful: 'That delicate air . . . the finer aspects of nature, the finer . . . clay of the human form, and modelling . . . of the human countenance—these are the good luck of the Greek.' As the Greeks exercised in the clear sunlight their forms and features seemed to become as perfect as their climate. Hazlitt had already wondered, paraphrasing Schlegel, whether the Greeks, 'born of a beautiful . . . race . . . and placed under a mild heaven', might not have had 'a natural organization . . . more perfect . . . than ours, who have not the same advantages of climate and constitution'. Symonds contrasted the vast interior gloom of Milan Cathedral with the open air and 'perfect human forms' of the Panathenaic procession. Pater could even tell that the Spartans were 'visibly . . . the most beautiful of all people, in Greece, in the world'. Visibly! How did he know?[52]

Justification might sometimes be found for associating the character of Greek art with the climate. Virginia Woolf claimed that the nature of Attic tragedy was determined by its performance in the open on a hot day. Or as Symonds said, 'If the hero of a modern play . . . calls the sun to witness, he must point to a tissue-paper transparency. . . . But Ajax or Electra could raise their hands to the actual sun . . . nearly all the scenes of the Greek tragedies are laid in daytime and in the open air.'[53] But what is remarkable is that there should be any impressive scenes—the opening of *Antigone*, the opening of *Agamemnon*—laid in the night at all. The furtive meeting in the darkness before dawn, the loneliness of the watchman under the stars—these are important parts of the theatrical effect. 'Put out the light,' says Othello; the candle is quenched, and the Globe Theatre is not a whit darker. Aeschylus, like Shakespeare, had to lure his audience by the power of poetry into resisting the plain evidence of their senses. It is ironic that the self-taught Hardy should appreciate 'the triumphs of the Hellenic and Elizabethan theatre in exhibiting scenes laid "far in the Unapparent" ' at a time when his highly educated contemporaries did not.[54] Even their notion of the climate was wrong: the greatest theatrical festival was held in late March or thereabouts, when the Attic weather is uncertain; on one occasion the procession had to be cancelled because of snow.[55] But from Victorian Hellenists one sometimes gets the impression that not only were there no Higginbottoms by the Ilissus, but no rain ever fell there either.

'When we read their poems,' Symonds wrote, 'we seem to have the perfumes . . . and lights of that luxurious land distilled in verse. . . . In reading Aristophanes we seem to have the serene skies of Attica above our heads'—such sentiments are the staple of aesthetic criticism. They are symptoms of a process by which the Greek character was flattened out into a clear dull uniformity, ever sunny and simple and calm. Naturally enough, the Greeks themselves often failed to fit this picture; in which case the Victorians were liable to decide that they were no longer truly Greek. 'In the best

Greek work,' Ruskin said, 'you will find some things that are still false, or fanciful; but whatever in it is false, or fanciful, is not the Greek part of it. . . . The essential Hellenic stamp is veracity.' Pater blandly observed that Botticelli's Venus offered 'a more direct inlet into the Greek temper than the works of the Greeks themselves even of the finest period'. Mallock parodied him—'Ah, they are sweet verses; a little too ascetic, perhaps, to be quite Greek. They are from Euripides, I see . . .'—but the parody is barely distinguishable from its model.[56] 'Greek' and 'Hellenic' could henceforth be applied as labels to things that had no connection with the historic Greece. Tovey detected 'Greek simplicities' in Beethoven's later music and protested against the nickname of the Jupiter Symphony on the grounds that Mozart was 'as Greek as Keats. He might have written a Zeus symphony. He never did. . . .'[57] This is not meaningless talk, indeed it is all too suggestive; the usefulness of Hellenism as a metaphor reveals its decline as a living and complex force.

In the heyday of Arnold and Pater there was, as it so happened, no classical scholar in England of genuine originality of mind. The literary men set the tone, and the professional scholars followed tamely behind them. Jebb insisted that there was no conflict between 'true Hellenism' and Hebraism: 'The best Greek work . . . is essentially pure; to conceive it as necessarily entangled with the baser elements of paganism is to confound the accidents with the essence; the accidents have passed away; the essence is imperishable.'[58] The Hellenic spirit seems to be a sort of 100 % pure alcohol, to be distilled, by some unexplained process, out of what the Greeks actually said and did. The depth and variety of Greek art and belief were being forgotten, and thus at the very moment that Nietzsche was revealing to Germany the fierce, Dionysiac side of the Greek soul the English were marching boldly backwards towards Winckelmann and Goethe. Pater himself did once write, in a moment of insight, that the view of Greek religion as a religion of art and beauty was only a partial one: 'The eye is fixed on the sharp, bright edge of high Hellenic culture, but loses sight of the sombre world across which it strikes.' But one glance into the dizzy depths is enough for him, for he goes on immediately to say that religions brighten under a bright sky, and concludes that the Greeks' achievement was to brush the dark side of their beliefs under the carpet: 'The Dorian worship of Apollo . . . with his unbroken daylight, always opposed to the sad Chthonian divinities, is the aspiring element, by force . . . of which Greek religion sublimes itself. . . .

It was the privilege of Greek religion to be able to transform itself into an artistic ideal.'[59] Such, certainly, was the transformation which Hellenism underwent at Pater's hands. Yet even where Nietzsche's influence has been strong, the feeling has persisted that the distinguishing characteristic of Greek art is a calm, balanced lucidity. Music again provides the test. Stravinsky liked to talk about the Apolline and Dionysian elements of art; there is nothing Greek about his most Dionysiac ballet, *The Rite of Spring*, whereas *Apollon Musagète* is consciously Hellenic in the lucid texture of its string orchestra and the austere purity of its clean, astringent discords. And when Sibelius described his plan for a symphony as 'Joy of life and vitality. . . . In three movements—the last an Hellenic rondo',[60] we can guess what he had in mind: a fresh healthy animalism, vigorous but spare.

Despite its great influence on England Hellenism oddly refused to blend easily with the other influences acting upon art and thought. As Pater said, 'The spiritual forces of the past, which have . . . informed the culture of a succeeding age, live indeed, within that culture, but with an absorbed, underground life. The Hellenic element alone has not been so absorbed . . . Hellenism is not merely an absorbed element in our intellectual life; it is a conscious tradition in it.'[61] In Pater's time Hellenism was beginning to seem highbrow and alien. Once its independence had been a source of strength to it; now, in an age of eclecticism, it was becoming a weakness.

The Gods

> Where are they, the half-deceivers,
> Statue-forms and young men's fancies,
> Gods of Greece?
> > Flecker, *Donde Estan?*

One of the rarest events in history is the death of a religion. Once any new system of belief has commended itself to a considerable body of people it is seldom altogether eradicated; Zoroastrianism, founded more than two and a half thousand years ago, has survived for the past millennium or so with less than 150,000 adherents. Even the small, eccentric sects that spin off the edges of the great religions have great powers of endurance, unless they are extirpated by persecutions of the utmost savagery and efficiency; even the half-religions—spiritualism, occultism, astrology, neoplatonism—seldom perish entirely: they are merely forgotten for a while, to be revived again whenever traditional means of comfort and edification seem to have lost their efficacy. Religions do not die; they become cataleptic.

To this general rule there is one enormous exception. The growth of Christianity completely destroyed the great Indo-European pantheons, Norse, German and Greco-Roman. Some time in about the sixth century A.D. the last man died who believed in the existence of Juno and Venus and Apollo, and in the succeeding centuries Asgard and Niflheim went the way 'of Olympus. The old gods faded quietly away and their disappearance was virtually unregretted until the later part of the eighteenth century, when the German Hellenists, eager to revive every aspect of Greek culture, were brought up against the impossibility of summoning the old religion back to life. Their disappointment was summed up by Schiller in *The Gods of Greece*, perhaps the most influential single poem ever written by a German. This was a lament for the disappearance of a mythology which portrayed the gods as serene, happy beings, and at the same time invested everyday sights with a portion of the divine: 'Where now, so our wise men say, there is only a soulless ball of fire revolving, once Helios used to drive his golden chariot in calm majesty. Oreads thronged these heights, a Dryad perished with that tree . . .'

The Gods of Greece appeared in 1788. Its evocative power is shown by Mrs. Browning's attempt, more than fifty years later, to combat it in *The Dead Pan*. Teutonic melancholy was not for her:

> O ye vain false gods of Hellas,
> Ye are silent evermore! . . .
>
> Get to dust, as common mortals,
> By a common doom and track!
> Let no Schiller from the portals
> Of that Hades, call you back . . .
>
> O brave poets, keep back nothing;
> Nor mix falsehood with the whole!
> Look up Godward! speak the truth in
> Worthy song from earnest soul!

Despite the pious sentiments and the hearty, blustery tone, the poem has the ring of insincerity. Schiller does not mention Pan, but Mrs. Browning seems to have had a weakness for him. One of her most popular poems begins, 'What was he doing, the great god

Pan . . .?'[62] Another describes how she was woken from sleep by her dog; for a moment she thought that he was Faunus, and started, 'as some Arcadian, Amazed by goatly god in twilight grove'. A pleasing fancy, it would appear; but the poetess has to overcome her 'surprise and sadness' at losing the vision before ending very properly by thanking Christ, 'the true PAN, Who, by low creatures, leads to heights of love.'[63] With these other poems in mind we may find it hard to believe her when she writes in *The Dead Pan*,

> Earth outgrows the mythic fancies
> Sung beside her in her youth:
> And those debonair romances
> Sound but dull beside the truth.

Do they? Even Mrs. Browning seems to feel in her own despite the sadness of the old deities' defeat:

> Have ye left the mountain places,
> Oreads wild, for other tryst?
> Shall we see no sudden faces
> Strike a glory through the mist?
> Not a sound the silence thrills,
> On the everlasting hills.
>   Pan, Pan is dead.

When *The Gods of Greece* was first published, it was taken to be an attack on Christianity, but Schiller blames the spiritual deadness of his age at least as much upon science; the 'wise men' who have told us that the sun is merely a ball of fire are the physicists and astronomers. This aspect of Schiller's ideas was appreciated in England where the Industrial Revolution was making the destructive effects of science more obvious than they could possibly have been in Weimar. And the English romantics added the further idea that the loss of gods and nymphs had made the writing of poetry difficult or impossible. Mrs. Browning herself thought Schiller's doctrine 'still more dishonouring to poetry than to Christianity'.[64] But such thoughts were far from the doctrine's originator, who was writing at a time when German poetry was rising to heights that it had never reached before.

Compared to Schiller Wordsworth relied more on feeling, less on thought. Whereas the German regretted the loss of the Greek gods because it impoverished the life of the mind and removed an incentive to nobility of thought and action, the English poet mourned it because it diminished the pleasure and consolation to be got from nature:[65]

> Great God! I'd rather be
> A Pagan suckled in a creed outworn;
> So might I, standing on this pleasant lea,
> Have glimpses that would make me less forlorn;
> Have sight of Proteus rising from the sea;
> Or hear old Triton blow his wreathed horn.

'Little we see in Nature that is ours,' Wordsworth says; even the sea 'moves us not'. And this is the fault not of Christianity or the Enlightenment but of the modern money-grubbing world in which 'getting and spending we lay waste our powers'.

Wordsworth's influence was great; still greater was Byron's. Childe Harold grieved for the vanished Olympians:

> Oh! where, Dodona! is thine aged grove,
> Prophetic fount and oracle divine? . . .
> All, all forgotten . . .

Byron enraptured the public with his picture of a 'land of lost gods'; and yet, illogically but evocatively, he portrayed Greece as a place filled with divine presences: 'Where'er we tread, 'tis haunted, holy ground.' The very phrase 'land of lost gods' is resplendently ambivalent: have the gods disappeared altogether, or does the poet imply that Greece is still haunted by melancholy divinities, bewildered survivors of a classical Götterdämmerung? Byron seems unable to decide whether the gods have gone or no: in a single stanza he tells us that the olive is still 'ripe as when Minerva smiled' and that Apollo still gilds the long, long Grecian summer.[66] But the very equivocation adds to the poetic charm; the evanescence of the Grecian gods—no sooner are they espied than they seem never to have been present at all—is wistfully suggestive. Schiller, too, had celebrated the springlike beauty of Greece: 'Lovely world, where art thou?—return again, gracious blossom time of nature! . . . All these blossoms have fallen at the wintry blast of the north.' But his love for Greece was purely cerebral; those blossoms are the burgeonings of art and thought. Byron gave actuality to Schiller's 'lovely world'.

The chorus in Shelley's *Hellas* lament for Apollo, Pan and Jove, routed by the 'killing truth' of Christianity:

> Our hill and seas and streams,
> Dispeopled of their dreams . . .
> Wailed for the golden years.

These sentiments come incongruously from Greek women captured by the Turks; they are the poet's own. 'I am glad to hear that you do not neglect the rites of the true religion,' he wrote to Hogg from Italy. 'Your letter awakened my sleeping devotion, and . . . I . . . suspended a garland, & raised a small turf altar to the mountain-walking Pan'—and here Shelley added in brackets, with an endearing touch of pedantry, the title of the mountain-walking Pan in Greek. Pan, indeed, was something of a favourite in Shelley's circle. Peacock signed a letter 'in the name of Pan', and Leigh Hunt wrote to Hogg at Marlow, 'I hope you paid your devotions as usual to the Religio Loci, and hung up an evergreen. If you go on so, there will be a hope . . . that a voice will be heard along the water saying "The great God Pan is alive again"—upon which the villagers will leave off starving, and singing profane hymns, and fall to dancing again.'[67]

How serious were Shelley and his friends about these devotions? Surely not at all, we tell ourselves; these rites were an amusing way of cocking a snook at the orthodox, and of satisfying, if only in play, the atavistic appetite of humankind for the performance of ritual acts. Surely it was only a game, we say, a pleasing flight of fancy: at best the gods of Greece are, in Flecker's phrase, but 'half-deceivers'. This answer may be right and yet a little facile; men do not always know themselves whether they are joking or in earnest. Edward Calvert, one of that group of painters nicknamed 'the Ancients' because of their adoration of antiquity, erected in his little back garden an altar to Pan. W. B. Richmond, who used to receive from him 'many a picturesque vision in words of the relationship of the ancient gods with the modern world', did not doubt that he was serious. Dickens imagined many fantastic eccentricities flourishing in and around the metropolis—Wemmick in his castle, Venus in his shop—but he never pictured anything so extraordinary as the worship of a Peloponnesian goat god in a London suburb.

No doubt Calvert was exceptional, but the question remains: why did Pan in particular have such a hold upon the romantic imagination? Pan was not one of the Olympian gods, who had already been frozen by Goethe and Winckelmann into poses of statuesque calm. He had a dual character, both parts of which were attractive to a generation born at about the time of the French

Plate I

Greece in England. James Stuart adapted the Arch of Hadrian in Athens to decorate the park at Shugborough, Staffordshire. Built in 1764, the style may be Athenian but the materials and setting are northern. (*See page 6f*)

Plate II

Another example of Greece in England. In 'Hylas and the Nymphs' J. W. Waterhouse surrounds figures taken from Greek mythology with northern vegetation on a sunless summer day. (*See page 190*)

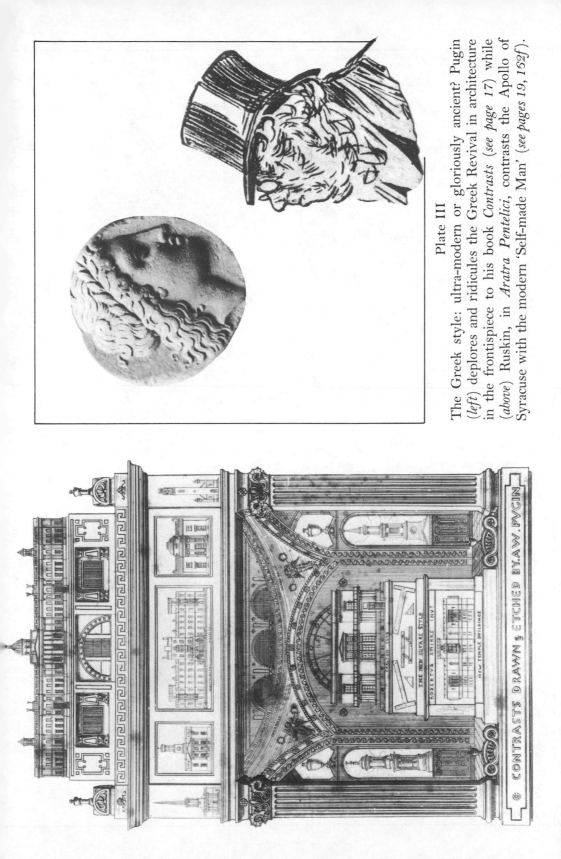

Plate III

The Greek style: ultra-modern or gloriously ancient? Pugin (*left*) deplores and ridicules the Greek Revival in architecture in the frontispiece to his book *Contrasts* (*see page 17*) while (*above*) Ruskin, in *Aratra Pentelici*, contrasts the Apollo of Syracuse with the modern 'Self-made Man' (*see pages 19, 152f*).

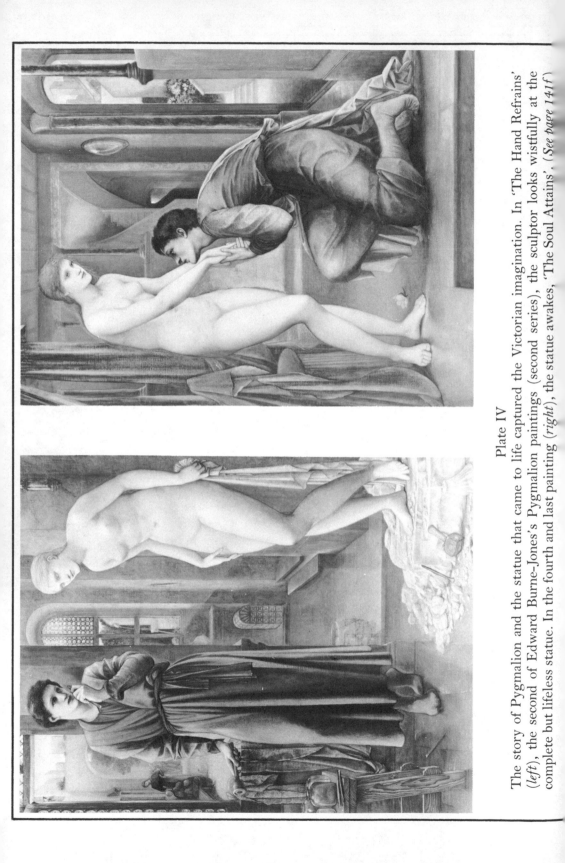

Plate IV

The story of Pygmalion and the statue that came to life captured the Victorian imagination. In 'The Hand Refrains' (*left*), the second of Edward Burne-Jones's Pygmalion paintings (second series), the sculptor looks wistfully at the complete but lifeless statue. In the fourth and last painting (*right*), the statue awakes, 'The Soul Attains'. (*See page 141f*)

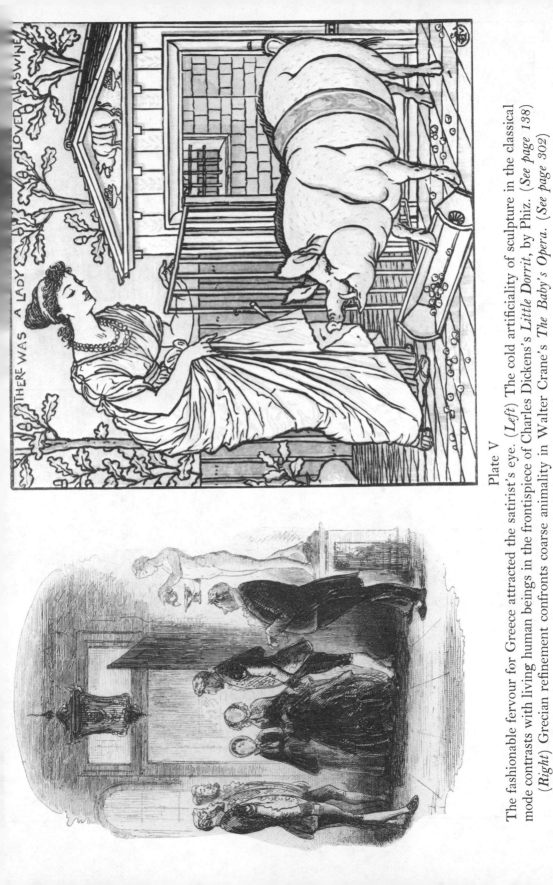

Plate V

The fashionable fervour for Greece attracted the satirist's eye. (*Left*) The cold artificiality of sculpture in the classical mode contrasts with living human beings in the frontispiece of Charles Dickens's *Little Dorrit*, by Phiz. (*See page 138*) (*Right*) Grecian refinement confronts coarse animality in Walter Crane's *The Baby's Opera*. (*See page 302*)

Plate VI

Variations on a frieze composition. (*Above*) Albert Moore's 'A Summer Night' is tinctured with hints of japonaiserie and aesthetic languor. (*See page 325*) (*Below*) 'Greek Girls Playing at Ball' by Lord Leighton typifies academic High Art, with laboriously executed, improbable drapery. (*See pages 307, 311 and Plate VII*)

Plate VII
In the early studies for his pictures, Leighton drew his figures nude and then laid on the drapery as if encasing their bodies in plaster. An under-painted version (*above*) and the final version (*below*) of 'Captive Andromache' demonstrate the technique. (*See page 311*)

Plate VIII

The Victorian love of dressing up. In Lawrence Alma-Tadema's 'A Reading from Homer' the listeners sprawl as if on comfortable hearthrugs and sofas rather than hard marble. (*See page 318*)

Revolution. On the one hand, he was a naughty, goatish creature, gloriously free from the restraints imposed by civilization or Christian morality; on the other, he became in late Greek theology the god of universal nature. The Greeks themselves accepted the false etymology which connected the name of Pan with the Greek word for 'all', and Pan became the god of the pantheists. The romantics wanted to get back to nature, but 'nature' is a word with many meanings. In part they wanted to escape from cities, from the artificiality of society, from the cycle of 'getting and spending'; Pan god of the countryside was a symbol of their nostalgia and their hopes. But at the same time they wanted to study the natural world more deeply, to understand its quiddity, to penetrate to its essence, to make a primrose more than just a yellow primrose. Wordsworth accordingly adopted a form of pantheism. Richmond accounted for Calvert's religion by saying, 'Pantheism . . . had gripped the intelligence . . . of a very highly-strung, poetical nature.' Naturally Pan was his god.

Hunt spoke to Hogg of the 'Religio Loci'. He too was drawn to the old paganism not by abstract cogitation but by a feeling for nature and, more especially, for the particular quality of particular landscapes. It was landscape, again, that led Ruskin to discuss the nature of the Greek gods and their place in modern literature; and his chapters on this subject in *Modern Painters* are still illuminating after more than a hundred years. He once wrote that no day passed 'without convincing every honest student of antiquity of some partial error, and showing him better how to think';[68] he did not approach the ancient Greeks armoured in the hard shell of self-confidence with which he came to art and architecture, and he was all the better for this lack.

He took as an example two lines from a poem by Kingsley:

> They rowed her in across the rolling foam—
> The cruel, crawling foam.

He comments, 'The foam is not cruel, neither does it crawl. The state of mind which attributes to it these characters of a living creature is one in which the reason is unhinged by grief. All violent feelings . . . produce in us a falseness in all our impressions of external things.' To this 'falseness' Ruskin gave a name that has since become famous: the 'pathetic fallacy'. This fallacy, he claims, is 'eminently characteristic of the modern mind' and he skilfully argues the point with the help of a comparison between Keats and Homer. He quotes Keats's description of a wave breaking out at sea:

> Down whose green back the short-lived foam, all hoar,
> Bursts gradual, with a wayward indolence.

'That,' he says, 'is quite perfect, as an example of the modern manner. . . . But Homer would never have written such words. He could not have lost sight of the great fact that salt water could not be either wayward or indolent. He will call the waves "over-roofed", "full-charged", "monstrous", "compact-black" . . . But every one of these epithets is descriptive of pure physical nature . . .'[69] This was very acute. Ruskin implied, it is true, that the Greeks never used the pathetic fallacy, which is an exaggeration; but in general his contrast between Greek and modern attitudes was both original and just.

Does the absence of the pathetic fallacy in Homer mean that Keats is the greater writer?

> Stay a moment. Homer *had* some feeling about the sea; a faith in the animation of it much stronger than Keats's. But all this sense of something living in it, he separates in his mind into a great abstract image of a Sea Power. He never says the waves rage, or the waves are idle. But he says there is somewhat in, and greater than, the waves, which rages, and is idle, and *that* he calls a god.

'What is Apollo,' asked Symonds rhetorically and foolishly, 'but the magic of the sun whose soul is light? . . . What is Pan but the mystery of nature . . .?' He was trying to turn the Greeks into a whole nation of Wordsworths, a race for whom nature was 'the secret of their sympathies, the wellspring of their deepest thoughts'.[70] But precisely because they lived closer to nature than Symonds they were less eager to commune with it. As Ruskin had already shown, their preferred scenery consisted of gardens and cultivated land, where nature was safely under control.[71] If Symonds had read *Modern Painters*, he would have found his feeble question rebuked:

> I do not think we ever enough endeavour to enter into what a Greek's real notion of a god was. We are so accustomed to the modern mockeries of the classical religion . . . that we seem to have infected the Greek ages themselves with the breath . . . of our hypocrisy; and are apt to think that Homer, as we know that Pope, was merely an ingenious fabulist.[72]

These sentences are a fascinating mixture of good sense and eccentricity. Ruskin realized that Greek religion was utterly unlike romantic pantheism and that it is hard to imagine the beliefs and emotions associated with it; on the other hand, there is a certain absurdity in his picture of Homer as the representative of an age of faith, rebuking modern Europe for its infidelity. On the same page we find him anxiously exonerating the Greeks from the charge of idolatry, which was, he says, 'neither the whole, nor the principal part, of Pagan worship. Pallas was not, in the pure Greek mind, merely a powerful piece of ivory in a temple at Athens.'[73] The Greeks were not Romanists, so to speak, but good sound Protestants.

Ruskin was led into this earnest defence of Greek beliefs because like Wordsworth and his followers he passionately desired to invest nature with religious associations. 'You have despised . . . all the deep and sacred sensations of natural scenery,' he told his public,

> . . . You have made racecourses of the cathedrals of the earth. Your *one* conception of pleasure is to drive in railway carriages round their aisles, and eat off their altars . . . the beautiful places of the world . . . are, indeed, the truest cathedrals— places . . . to worship in; and . . . we only care . . . to eat and drink at their most sacred places.[74]

But unfortunately talk about nature's cathedrals and the sacred emotions inspired by mountain scenery was commonplace among gushing tourists who had dipped into the lake poets. How was Ruskin to convince these enthusiastic people of the sacrilegiousness of picnics? A remark in *Sesame and Lilies* suggests that he perceived an answer: modern Christians could be taught a proper reverence by the Greeks. Speaking of North Wales he declares, 'These are the hills, and these the bays . . ., which, among the Greeks, would have been . . . faithful in influence on the national mind. That Snowdon is your Parnassus; but where are its Muses? that Holyhead mountain is your Island of Aegina; but where is its Temple to Minerva?'[75] This is unreasonable: Victorian Welshmen can hardly be blamed for failing to worship a set of pagan goddesses. Did Ruskin seriously regret the passing of Greek religion? Strange as it may seem, a part of him did.

The construction of a railway through Monsal Dale in Derbyshire provoked him to a protest which among even his writings is outstanding for mingled vigour and delicacy:

> There was a rocky valley between Buxton and Bakewell, once upon a time, divine as the vale of Tempe; you might have seen the gods there morning and evening—Apollo and all the sweet

Muses of Light, walking in fair procession on the lawns of it. . . . You cared neither for gods nor grass, but for cash . . . You enterprised a railroad through the valley. . . . The valley is gone, and the gods with it; and now, every fool in Buxton can be at Bakewell in half-an-hour, and every fool in Bakewell at Buxton.[76]

Ironically, when the railway line was closed some years back, the viaduct over the River Wye, now much admired, was carefully preserved.

This talk of gods and muses was charmingly poetic, no doubt, but Ruskin wanted it to be something more. In the final chapter of *Praeterita*, the last of all his writings, he announced,

I must here once for all explain distinctly . . . the sense in which throughout all my earnest writing of the last twenty years I use the plural word 'gods'. I mean by it, the totality of spiritual powers, delegated by the Lord of the universe to do . . . parts of His will . . . in meekness accepting the testimony and belief of all ages, to the presence, in heaven and earth, of angels and the like,—with genii, fairies, or spirits. . . . For all these, I take the general word 'gods' as the best understood in all languages.

Finally he quotes, with understandable pride, his denunciation of the Buxton and Bakewell railway, introducing the passage with these astounding words:

No true happiness exists, nor is any good work ever done . . ., but in the sense or imagination of such presences. The following passage . . . gives example of the sense in which I most literally and earnestly refer to them.[77]

In other words, he *literally* believes in Apollo and the Muses. We react with incredulity; yet that is what Ruskin emphatically and explicitly declares. More than thirty years earlier he had counted among the uses of the imagination its power to refresh the weary mind

with such innocent play as shall be most in harmony with the suggestive voices of natural things, permitting it to possess living companionship . . . and to create for itself fairies in the grass and naiads in the wave.[78]

Now, in his old age, he could no longer distinguish fact from fantasy.

Greek mythology fascinated him throughout his life, but only once did he devote an entire book to it, and this, *The Queen of the Air*, is one of his maddest works. It is eloquent, however, because he was trying to reconcile in it the conflict between the view expressed in *Modern Painters*—that nowadays the Greek deities can be no more than an imaginative decoration of nature—and the feeling ultimately to be summed up in *Praeterita* by the plain statement that the gods actually exist. On the one hand, he insists that Greek mythology is 'literal belief', 'deeply rooted' in the mind of the general people and 'vitally religious';[79] and there are one or two moments of startling insight that seem almost to anticipate Frazer or Freud. On the other hand, much of the book is devoted to the rationalization of Greek myth. Athena, for example, is the goddess of fresh air, and so when Homer says that she laid Penelope into deep sleep, 'and made her taller, and made her smoother, . . . and breathed ambrosial brightness over her face', he means that the lady went to bed early and left the window open. To us such allegorical interpretations seem to be not only wrong but prosaic, robbing the *Odyssey* of its magic, but Ruskin would have viewed the matter the other way round: he was bringing magic back to the experiences of everyday life. 'Whenever you throw your window wide open . . .,' he wrote, 'you let in Athena, as wisdom and fresh air at the same instant; and whenever you draw a . . . full breath . . ., you take Athena into your heart, through your blood; and with the blood, into the thoughts of your brain.'[80] One would normally assume that such language is figurative, but with Ruskin one can never be quite sure; throughout this book he is striving to reconcile Greek myth with modern science. In later life he moralized the natural world as he had earlier moralized art. On his last visit to Venice he was 'impressed with the sadness and even weakness of the Mediterranean coasts' and in *The Queen of the Air* not even vegetables escape moral scrutiny: beans are commended as 'the most entirely serviceable and human'—human!—'of all orders of plants', and the hapless potato is denounced as 'the scarcely innocent underground stem of one of a tribe set aside for evil'.[81]

Such bizarre assertions are the extreme consequence of his attempt to do under modern conditions what the Greeks, as he thought, did spontaneously, by the very nature of their beliefs. In *Modern Painters* he had not been so foolhardy; he envied the Greeks, but he did not think to imitate them. His achievement there was to recognize how difficult it was to enter imaginatively into the spirit of Greek religion, and to perceive how greatly the Greek attitude to nature differed from the superficially similar pantheism of the romantic age. He saw that Greek beliefs were complex, and he expounded these complexities with both subtlety and lucidity. After offering allegorical interpretations of parts of the *Iliad*, he added, 'But I do not believe that the idea ever weakens itself down to mere allegory. When Pallas is said to . . . strike down Mars, it does not mean merely that Wisdom . . . prevailed against Wrath. It means that there are, indeed, two great spirits, one entrusted to guide the human soul to wisdom and chastity, the other to kindle wrath and prompt to battle.'[82] In other words, the allegorical element is only one part of Greek religion; and stressing the vitality of that religion, Ruskin rejected the simple schematism that opposed Hellenism and Hebraism:

> There is not the smallest . . . unspirituality in this conception. If there was, it would attach equally to the appearance of the angels to Jacob . . . or Manoah . . . the highest authority which governs our own faith requires us to conceive divine power clothed with a human form . . ., and retaining, nevertheless, sovereignty and omnipresence in all the world. This is . . . the heathen idea of a God; and it is impossible to comprehend . . . the Greek mind until we grasp this faithfully.[83]

Ruskin believed the Greek gods to be both abstract and actual; and he was thus able to give a more convincing account than could his contemporaries of how the Greeks conceived the relation between their deities and the natural world. 'With us,' he concluded, '. . . the idea of the Divinity is apt to get separated from the life of nature; and imagining our God . . . far above the earth, and not in the flowers or waters, we approach those visible things with a theory that they are dead; governed by physical laws, and so forth. But coming to them, we find the theory fail.' We cannot, he says, resist the feeling that the fountain sings and the flowers rejoice, and so we fall 'into the curious web of hesitating sentiment, pathetic fallacy, and wandering fancy, which form a great part of our modern view of nature.' The Greek felt otherwise: ' "The tree *is* glad," said he, "I know it is; I can cut it down: no matter, there was a nymph in it".'[84] In this way Ruskin could explain, what most Victorian scholars could but weakly deny, how the Greeks could believe that the visible world was filled with divine presences and yet have little or none of the modern feeling of love for nature. This much was shrewd; the strange feature of Ruskin's exposition is the apparent implication that Greek beliefs were in some respects truer than those of the nineteenth century. The theories of the scientists 'fail'; Christian beliefs in transcendence and monotheism seem inadequate. Though Ruskin's passionate adherence to Christianity was at times shaken to its foundations, his love and admiration for Greek beliefs never wavered.

His temperament led him to give a strongly moralistic tone to his account of Greek religion: Athene is the spirit of Wisdom, Ares of Wrath. But it was his interest in classical and modern landscape that drew him to investigate Greek beliefs in the first place, and throughout his life he loved Greek mythology above all because it enabled him to invest the British landscape with a numinous splendour, and, at the same time, to express his feeling for the *genius loci*. He liked to distinguish 'the fishermen and ocean Gods of Solway' from 'the marchmen and mountain Gods of Cheviot': he liked to 'think of the Tay as a goddess river, as Greta a nymph one'.[85] Symonds too enjoyed imagining that the landscape was charged with numinous presences; unlike Ruskin, though, he could not manage this in Derbyshire or Northumberland, but only in southern landscapes, where, he said, 'The oread dwellers of the hills, and dryads . . . seem possible . . . men themselves are more a part of nature here than in the North, more fit for companionship with deities of stream and hill.'[86]

The south was an unsullied region where antiquity survived; even, perhaps, in the people's religious practices. Wilde felt it 'always a source of pleasure . . . to remember that the ultimate survival of the Greek Chorus is to be found in the servitor answering the priest at Mass'. Baron Corvo, fantastical, Catholic, and decadent, imagined in *Stories Toto Told Me* an Italian peasant boy relating tales in which Christian tradition and pagan legend were curiously intermingled. So charming, the ignorance of these simple folk! Symonds might well have entered into this spirit, had not his agnosticism led him in a different direction. In one of his essays he describes a Sunday walk near Menton:

Everything fits in to complete the reproduction of Greek pastoral life. The goats eat cytisus. . . . Pan sleeps in noontide heat. . . . Nothing is changed—except ourselves. I expect to find a statue of Priapus or pastoral Pan. . . . Surely, in some far-off glade . . . there must still be a pagan remnant of glad

Nature worship. . . . So I dream until I come upon a Calvary. . . . There is the iron cross . . . the nails, the crown of thorns. . . . Nothing can take us back to Phoebus or Pan. Nothing can identify us with the simple natural earth.[87]

These are again second-hand sentiments, but this time the influence is Heine's. As a German and a Jew, Heine felt the contrast between the ancient and modern worlds acutely, seeing it also as a contrast between Hellenism and Hebraism. In his *Pictures of Travel* he quoted one of Homer's descriptions of the gods feasting. Then he continued, 'Suddenly there came gasping towards them a pale Jew . . . bearing a great cross of wood . . . and he cast the cross on the high table of the gods . . . and the gods . . . melted in utter mist.'[88] In a poem called *The Gods of Greece* he combated Schiller's appeal to the ancient deities to come back: 'I have never loved you, ye gods! For the Greeks are repugnant to me.' Zeus is now white-haired and miserable, Apollo's lyre is silent; younger gods have driven out the old, who are now exiled and defeated. He reverted to this theme in some of his last prose writings. Part of *The Goddess Diana* describes how Diana, Apollo and Dionysus invade a gothic castle. In *The Gods in Exile* he discusses the fates of the pagan deities in the Middle Ages; Mercury set himself up as a merchant; Apollo became a shepherd in Austria, but was executed by the church authorities because his singing shocked them. Bacchus became Father Superior of a monastery in the Tyrol, with Silenus and Pan for cook and cellarer, and once a year they would throw off their monkish robes and hold a Dionysiac revel.

Thespis; or, the Gods Grown Old was the first collaboration between Gilbert and Sullivan; so far had Heine's theme penetrated the English consciousness. Arnold had popularized the dichotomy between Hellenism and Hebraism; and Pater developed Heine's witty fictions, composing two stories about the return of pagan gods in the Middle Ages, both of them set in France: *Denys l'Auxerrois*, in which the hero proves to be an avatar of Dionysus, and *Apollo in Picardy*.[89] But Heine has suffered a sea-change in the course of crossing the Channel. In the first place, Pater does not draw a sharp dividing line between antiquity and the Middle Ages; his eclectic temper sought for strange similarities in dissimilar things, and he brings out the resemblances, as well as the conflict, between ancient Greece and the Christian centuries. Secondly, whereas Heine is interested only in the great abstract question of the change that came over culture and civilization with the victory of Christianity,

Pater's concern, like that of the English romantics before him, is more concrete and visual, being largely with art and landscape. When Dionysus comes, the ancient and medieval worlds are blended together; therefore the miracle must happen in the distinctive scenery of 'midland France', a 'happy mean between northern earnestness and the luxury of the south'. Under the god's influence the sculptors working on the cathedral develop a new style, combining the seriousness of the Middle Ages with the greater technical assurance of the Greeks. When Apollo comes to Picardy, it is the architecture that he affects: a barn is being built, and though gothic, it acquires a 'classical harmony'; the stone has the texture of antique marble, and the gable is 'almost a classic pediment'.

In the middle of the last century there was a vogue for paintings of elves and fairies. Often these were mildly titillating (fairies do not wear clothes), but they were popular also because they offered a British equivalent to the nymphs and sylvans of antiquity. Wishing to invest their native landscape with an atmosphere of numinous wonder, the Victorians liked to pretend that there were fairies (or rather faeries) at the bottom of their gardens. Pater had many imitators because he (and Ruskin) showed that there was a more sophisticated way of indulging this fancy, by setting Greek gods among English scenery. Flecker carried this theme off with some verve in *The Ballad of Hampstead Heath*, which relates how Bacchus descended upon London:

> He spake in Greek, which Britons speak
> 　　Seldom, and circumspectly;
> But Mr. Judd, that man of mud,
> 　　Translated it correctly.

> And when they heard that happy word,
> 　　Policemen leapt and ambled:
> The busmen pranced, the maidens danced,
> 　　The men in bowlers gambolled.

But in *Oak and Olive* he was flimsily whimsical:

> When I go down the Gloucester lanes
> 　　My friends are deaf and blind:
> Fast as they turn their foolish eyes
> 　　The Maenads leap behind . . .

Have I not chased the fluting Pan
Through Cranham's sober trees?
Have I not sat on Painswick Hill
With a nymph upon my knees . . .?

This theme is markedly Edwardian; even the sardonic Saki composed a story about Pan-worship in the English countryside. Sometimes the tone is hushed and reverent. In Grahame's *Wind in the
Willows* the Rat and the Mole come to a 'holy place' where they
behold Pan: 'The Mole felt a great Awe fall upon him . . . some
august Presence was very, very near . . . he . . . saw the backward
sweep of the curved horns . . . saw . . . the long supple hand still
holding the pan-pipes. . . .' Most adults today are unimpressed by
this sort of holy whimsy; but it still holds many children spellbound.

Most of the littérateurs who practised this genre have been
forgotten; but Beerbohm's skit upon them survives.[90] The pro-
tagonists of *Hilary Maltby and Stephen Braxton* are rivals; each has
produced a first novel which is competing with the other to be the
most successful book of 1895. Maltby's *Ariel in Mayfair* is described
as delicate and fanciful; it tells how 'Ariel re-embodied himself . . .,
leased a small house in Chesterfield Street, was presented at a
Levée . . ., and worked meanwhile all manner of amusing changes
among the aristocracy.' Braxton's novel is called *A Faun on the
Cotswolds*; Beerbohm comments, 'From the time of Nathaniel
Hawthorne to the outbreak of the War, current literature did not
suffer from any lack of fauns. But when Braxton's first book appeared
fauns had still an air of novelty about them. We had not yet tired
of them and their hoofs and their slanting eyes and their way of
coming suddenly out of woods to wean quiet English villages from
respectability. We did tire later.'

Beerbohm's satire is exceedingly acute; he appreciated that the
advent of gods (or fairies) was a theme that had been used for
different ends. Maltby exploits it for the purpose of comic fantasy;
so in real life did Flecker, and Beerbohm himself. Indeed, is not
Maltby, small, dapper, an exile in Italy, a fastidious stylist, in part
a parody of his own creator? Towards the end of the nineteenth
century the supernatural suddenly became respectable in literature:
Wilde and even Henry James were prepared to use it to express
symbolic truths about society and its members. Braxton, however,
is somewhat different. A city-dweller like Saki was pleased to think
that the countryside was seething with dark superstitions and
volcanic passions; some recent films have shown that this fantasy

still appeals to the urban mind. Beerbohm delicately insinuates that Braxton's rustics are preposterously earthy. 'There remains deep down within our souls,' said Symonds in his usual refined tones, 'some primal sympathies with nature, some instincts of the Faun, or Satyr, or Sylvan, which education has not quite eradicated.'[91]

In his *Four Quartets* Eliot describes a visit to Little Gidding in midwinter. It is not a beautiful spot: the road is rough, and the dull façade of the church is hidden behind a pigsty. Yet this is a holy place; God is present in the flat, sodden countryside of Huntingdon-shire, 'Now and in England'.[92] It may seem inept to compare Eliot with Flecker and Grahame, and yet they have much in common; in all three there is a concern with landscape and its supernatural associations. Beerbohm was shrewd to make Braxton's faun appear in the Cotswolds: Gloucestershire was a favoured setting for such Hellenic intrusions, because it was felt to be so quintessentially English; this is where Flecker saw the Maenads. The poet enjoys the piquant contrast between exotic Greece and the everyday English scene, between goatish Pan and the 'sober' trees. The proper nouns, Cranham and Painswick, are important: sturdy, solid English names. And yet they evoke one of the more romantic regions of the country. Flecker's attitude is complex: at the very moment that he stresses the ordinariness of the English landscape, he is asserting with Ruskin that 'you might have seen the gods there morning and evening'. The same complexity is to be found in Eliot: on one level 'Now and in England' means 'in our familiar, commonplace circumstances', and yet as he repeats the word 'England' we realize that it reverberates with heroic associations, recalling the history of which the community at Little Gidding was a small but glorious part. We sense the throb of patriotism, the sudden catch at the heart. Unlike Flecker, Eliot does not find his Deity in a conventionally picturesque setting; but like him, he extols the magical beauty of the ordinary English countryside:

> If you came this way in may time, you would find the hedges
> White again, in May, with voluptuary sweetness.

Grahame, for his part, uses the names of flowers to stress the Englishry of the place where Pan is seen. 'The rich meadow-grass seemed . . . of a freshness and greenness unsurpassable. Never had they noticed the roses so vivid, the willow-herb so riotous . . . they stood on a little lawn of marvellous green, set round with . . . crab-apple, wild cherry, and sloe.' This is not a Grecian scene.

No more Greek is the watery landscape in J. W. Waterhouse's picture of 'Hylas and the Nymphs'. Here is a good old English pond with muddy, sludgy banks and greeny-brown waters; just the sort of place where Tom Brown might be angling or Jeremy Fisher propelling his punt. (On another canvas Waterhouse set the indubitably northern Ophelia in much the same marshy world of reeds and weeds and squashy vegetation.) It is a sunless summer day. We can even determine the time of year within quite narrow limits: it is late June or July, since there are water-lilies and the yellow flags are in flower. The nymphs are rising from the waters, pubertal, unmistakably English, and naked. And they have shed their inhibitions with their clothes; despite their shy, wistful expressions, there is a gleam of invitation in their eyes, and two of them reach out their arms to the young man. Here Greece and England are blended pictorially, as elsewhere in verse and prose.

It was best for the gods to go by their Greek names, which sounded grand and elemental, whereas the Roman names merely brought to mind the tame classicism of the eighteenth century. Besides, had the Romans themselves really believed in their gods? 'No passing beggar or fiddler . . .,' said Yeats, 'has ever . . . been awe-struck by nymph-haunted or Fury-haunted wood described in Roman poetry. Roman poetry is founded upon documents, not upon belief.' But Greek poetry could be genuinely spooky: 'When I prepared *Oedipus at Colonus* for the Abbey stage I saw that the wood of the Furies . . . was any Irish haunted wood.'[93] It is Eros, not Cupid, who stands in the middle of Piccadilly Circus; a period piece, since only perhaps in the 1890s would anyone have thought to commemorate the evangelical Lord Shaftesbury with a statue of a pagan god of sexual desire. However, Londoners quickly took their revenge on this intrusion of an alien culture by pronouncing him Eeross.

For Pan *was* dead, and all the preciosities and poetasteries of the *fin de siècle* could not make the old gods live. Forster made the point in *The Longest Journey*. 'I had a great idea,' says Rickie Elliot, 'of getting into touch with Nature, just as the Greeks were in touch; and seeing England so beautiful, I used to pretend that her trees and coppices and summer fields of parsley were alive.'. . . I got in such a state that I believed, actually believed, that Fauns lived in a certain double hedgerow near the Gog Magogs.' In consequence, he takes to writing short stories of the whimsically numinous kind. One of them, as he tells Agnes Pembroke, is about a girl who rebels against her fiancé's vulgar materialism and rushes into the woods, where she turns into a dryad; or so the story implies, for the word 'dryad' is never used. Agnes objects: 'You ought to put that part plainly. Otherwise, with such an original story, people might miss the point.' Forster portrays her as silly and shallow throughout the novel, but we are meant to feel in this case that her commonsense philistinism has exposed the artificiality of Rickie's Hellenism. There is an irony too in her belief that this hackneyed theme is so original. Forster returns to this motif later, when Rickie is dead and Mr. Pembroke is proposing to issue his stories posthumously under the title *Pan Pipes*. Wonham asks, more shrewdly perhaps than he realizes, 'Are you sure "Pan Pipes" haven't been used up already?'[94] And here there is a further irony still: Pan's pipes are 'used up' because Greek religion is used up. Eliot is immeasurably superior to Flecker not least because his God is or has been authentically a part of English belief.

Wilde addressed a villanelle to Pan:[95]

> No nymph or Faun indeed have we,
> For Faun and nymph are old and grey, . . .
>
> Ah, leave the hills of Arcady!
> This modern world hath need of thee!

In one of his earliest poems, written at about the same date, Yeats uttered a conventional lament over the greyness of the modern world, beginning, 'The woods of Arcady are dead.'[96] But now it has changed its meaning: standing first among his collected poems, it seems to rebuke Wilde's appeal with the stern voice of the new century.

IX

HOMER AND THE
HOMERIC IDEAL

Homer

Ever since it was erected, the Albert Memorial has seemed to embody the quintessence of the Victorian age. It was meant to. Shaped like a gigantic reliquary, it was intended not only as a monument to the dead prince whose statue was enshrined, like the bones of a medieval saint, beneath its lavishly encrusted canopy, but also as an expression of the nation's pride in its achievements and faith in its destiny to come. Four great heaps of statuary at the corners of the monument symbolize the four continents, all of which had witnessed the splendour and energy of imperial Britain. Higher up, four more groups represent Manufactures, Commerce, Engineering, Agriculture; a still more obvious tribute to the genius of the island race. Below the columns that uphold the canopy runs a frieze depicting the world's great poets, sculptors, architects and composers. On the whole the British are rather over-represented— Lawes and Bishop consort with Mozart and Beethoven; Bird and Bushnell rub shoulders with Bernini and Michelangelo—but the prejudice is unsurprising. The front side of the frieze is devoted to poetry, probably the art in which the British have most excelled. The centre of this section, directly beneath the feet of Albert himself, is the most conspicuous place in the whole frieze. Surely we shall find Shakespeare in this supreme position? But no: Shakespeare and Dante recline modestly, like attendant angels, at the foot of the central throne, while Virgil and Milton lurk still more diffidently behind them. Enthroned in the place of highest honour is Homer. This is an astonishing tribute to Homer's sway over the Victorian imagination. Apart from the founders and heroes of the great religions, and with the possible exception of Alexander the Great,

Shakespeare is the most famous man who has ever lived. He was and is the most admired writer in the world; and he is English. Yet Homer is preferred before him. Plucking a Grecian lyre, his left foot planted upon a Grecian stool, he strikes a note of silent dissonance with the Gothic extravaganza above him.

Some fifty years later a no less astounding obeisance was made to Homer's pre-eminence. The tercentenary of Shakespeare's death fell in 1916, in the midst of war and at a time of shrill nationalism. As Poet Laureate, Bridges commemorated the anniversary with a big Pindaric ode, praising the glories of Great Britain in adequately soul-stirring language and ending with a paean of gratitude to the nation's valiant soldiery. This is much what we should expect to read in an official poem; it is the more remarkable, therefore, to find Shakespeare first introduced as one

> Whom when she bore the Muses lov'd
> Above the best of eldest honour
> — Yea, save one without peer—
> And by great Homer set,
> Not to impugn his undisputed throne,
> The myriad-hearted by the mighty-hearted one.

It is hardly possible to exaggerate the extraordinariness of these lines. This grand patriotic ode was composed with the specific purpose of praising Shakespeare; yet he is no sooner mentioned than Bridges goes out of his way to emphasize his inferiority to another man.

'With the single exception of Homer,' Shaw declared, 'there is no eminent writer, not even Sir Walter Scott, whom I can despise so entirely as I despise Shakespeare when I measure my mind against his.' Shaw's intention was to provoke, and in singling out Homer and Shakespeare he was acknowledging that these were the two poets who had been most reverenced in recent times. Gladstone's judgement of Homer was a verbal equivalent of the Albert Memorial frieze: 'The consent of mankind has irrevocably assigned to him a supremacy among poets, without real competitors or partners, except Dante and Shakespeare.' Shelley thought that Shakespeare was perhaps the greatest individual mind known to us, but that as a poet Homer exceeded him in the truth and grandeur of his images. 'Is Homer or Shakespeare the greater genius?' Carlyle asked himself, and answered, 'It were hard to say.' Froude wrote, 'Whether one or two, the authors of the Iliad and the Odyssey stand alone with Shakespeare far away above mankind.'[1]

The Victorians encountered Homer even in the nursery. 'Tom will play at Homer!' the infant Macaulay's playmates complained to his mother. As a child Thomas Arnold loved 'acting the battles of Homeric heroes as he learned them from Pope's translation of the Iliad'. Kinglake's mother taught him 'in earliest childhood . . . to find a home in his saddle, and to love old Homer, and all that Homer sung'. Ruskin recollected having Scott's novels and Pope's *Iliad* for constant reading as a child. On Sundays these books were forbidden, and the boy had to make do with Bunyan and Defoe; which no doubt had the effect of making Homer seem all the more fun. The *Iliad* with its blood and battles and the *Odyssey* with its giants and shipwrecks had a simple, direct appeal which none of the poetic classics could rival. George Eliot's Tom Tulliver is not much good at his books, but even he is excited by Philip Wakem's account of the *Odyssey*. Mackenzie catches the atmosphere of upper-class English boyhood at the end of the century: 'Michael was for the Trojans against the Greeks, partly on account of the Greek verbs, but principally because he once had a straw hat inscribed H.M.S. Hector. He was also for the Lancastrians against the Yorkists, and . . . for the Jacobites against the Hanoverians.'[2] Many schoolboys must have noticed, too, that the locomotives of the Firefly class on the Great Western Railway were named from the heroes of the *Iliad*. 'Our first boy's feeling with the Iliad,' Froude said, 'is, that Homer is pre-eminently a poet of war; that battles were his own passion. . . . This is our boyish impression, and, like other such, it is very different from the truth.'[3] Here was another of Homer's glories: the companion of childhood still spoke to the adult, but in a new and deeper tone.

While the young Ruskin and the young Thomas Arnold were poring over Pope's translation, the grown-ups were turning against it. Leigh Hunt declared, 'Pope, in that elegant mistake of his . . . called *Homer's Iliad*, turns the Dodonaean oak of his original into . . . smooth little toys.' And Lamb observed, 'What certainly everybody misses in Pope, is a certain savage-like plainness of speaking in Achilles—a sort of indelicacy—the heroes in Homer . . . utter all the cruel, . . . all the *mean thoughts* even of their nature, which it is the fashion of our great men to keep in.'[4] When Keats first looked into Chapman's Homer—that is, when he first got away from Pope— he felt that he was breathing the pure Homeric air as never before. In Hunt's words, 'Chapman . . . blows as rough a blast as Achilles could have desired to hear . . . Keats's epithets of "loud and bold" showed that he understood him perfectly.'[5] Pope remained in disgrace throughout the century. Matthew Arnold conceded that he was powerful in elevated passages, but thought him tasteless and ineffective in plain narrative. Ruskin was more outspoken: a brilliant page of *Modern Painters* exposed how Pope's periphrases had destroyed the 'bitter and terrified lightness' in the 'simple, startled words' of Odysseus to Elpenor.[6]

These attacks were part of a general reaction against Augustanism. Pope had been held up as a model of correctitude, but Macaulay argued that in the best sense Scott and Wordsworth were more correct than he; and Homer, similarly, was far more correct than Virgil, because his narrative was more skilful, his descriptions truer, and his characters better drawn. Gladstone remarked, 'Homer walks in the open day, Virgil by lamplight. . . . From Virgil back to Homer is a greater distance, than from Homer back to life.'[7] It might be thought that the nineteenth century had more in common with the reign of Augustus than with archaic Greece, that the art of Keats and Tennyson was closer to Virgil's than Homer's. Precisely so; the Victorians felt, as Virgil and his contemporaries had felt, that they were living in a secondary age, and for this very reason they looked back to Homer, as Virgil had looked back, with a distant and admiring gaze. Virgil had taken Homer as a point of reference, a standard of comparison; and the Victorians did the same.

In a famous sonnet Keats declared how sweet it was for one who had been long in city pent to 'look into the fair and open face of heaven'. It was with something of the same spirit that he escaped from his own time and place into the Homeric world, that 'wide expanse' of 'pure serene'.[8] Just as the Victorians fled to the countryside from the urban ugliness around them, so they went to Homer as a refuge from the spiritual ills of their time; and like Keats, they often used metaphors of open air and physical well-being when they talked about him. Symonds saw in Achilles 'the type of the Hellenic genius . . . as it still dazzles us in its . . . unrivalled physical energy.' 'Homer *animates*,' Arnold thought, '—Shakespeare *animates*—. . . the Gipsy Scholar at best awakens a pleasing melancholy. But this is not what we want.' And in a lecture he named 'out-of-doors freshness, life, naturalness' as Homeric qualities.[9] Alford conceived the Homeric epics as a kind of natural force; in a sonnet he imagined the young Homer lingering by running waters and storing his soul with the sounds that he would one day pour forth in melody. To some people Homer's healthiness was a moral quality. From the Oxford chair of poetry the Scotsman

J. C. Shairp attacked the decadence of modern literature, 'so weakening, so morbidly self-conscious, so unhealthily introspective'; 'What
more effective antidote,' he asked, 'than the bracing atmosphere of
Homer, and Shakespeare, and Scott?'[10] Andrew Lang, another
Scot, made the same point, turning against the aesthetes their
favourite imagery of wine and music and the heavy scents of flowers:

> As one that for a weary space has lain
>   Lulled by the song of Circe and her wine
>   In gardens near the pale of Proserpine,
> Where that Aeaean isle forgets the main,
> And only the low lutes of love complain,
>   And only shadows of wan lovers pine,
>   As such an one were glad to know the brine
> Salt on his lips, and the large air again,
> So gladly, from the songs of modern speech
>   Men turn, and see the stars, and feel the free
>   Shrill wind beyond the close of heavy flowers
>   And through the music of the languid hours
>   They hear like ocean on a western beach
>   The surge and thunder of the Odyssey.

The last line quickly became famous, because it corresponded to
what everyone believed or wanted to believe. Swinburne said that
Homer and the sea kept time together in his mind's ear;[11] F. W.
Newman had called Homer's beauty a wild beauty, smelling of
the mountain and the sea; and Landor had made his Cleone remon-
strate with a friend who preferred the *Prometheus* to Homer by
saying, 'But the Iliad is not a region; it is a continent; and you
might as well compare this prodigy to it as the cataract of the Nile
to the Ocean.'[12] It was not just his invigorating tone or the sound
of his verse that made Homer seem like the sea. He is immense—
Goethe started to study Homer because he wanted to undertake
something infinite—and not only immense, but immensely uniform.
Shakespeare is endlessly varied; 'myriad-minded', Coleridge called
him.[13] Bridges borrowed the epithet in order to contrast Shakespeare
with the 'mighty-minded' Homer, who is endlessly the same.
Such, too, was the impression of Homer that Carlyle jotted down:
'. . . The singleness and massive repose as of an ancient picture. . . .
Simplicity (not multiplicity), almost vacuity, yet sincerity, and the
richest toned artless music.' The sea is primeval, it is the oldest
thing that we know, and by a natural association of ideas Carlyle,

impressed by the sheer antiquity of Homer, turned his thoughts to a scene by the sea shore: 'The whole is very *old*. "Achilles sitting weeping by the hoary beach looking out into the dark-coloured sea;" still, *einfach*, with a kind of greatness.'[14]

And Homer's success seemed so effortless; Arnold claimed that Homer never lost his 'lovely ease and sweetness', and Cleone says, 'We are carried over an immensity of space, bounding the earth, not bounded by her, and having nothing above but the heavens.' In *Marius* Pater quoted three lines of the *Iliad* and described their effect upon Flavian: 'How poetic the simple incident seemed, told just like that! Homer was always telling things after this manner. And one might think there had been no effort in it.'[15] Here was another aspect of his uniformity; as Arnold said, 'Homer has not Shakespeare's variations: Homer always composes as Shakespeare composes at his best.'[16] But despite his objectivity and absence of effort—what Carlyle called his 'massive repose'—he was in ceaseless, energetic motion (in this too like the sea); Arnold named rapidity as the first of Homer's qualities, and Bagehot, a touch sardonically, agreed:[17] 'Homer is the briskest of men. The Germans have denied that there was any such person; but they have never questioned his extreme activity.'

By its latent savagery the sea holds a particular appeal for civilized men; how pleasant from a position of comfort and security to contemplate something so grand, archaic and untamed. F. W. Newman delighted in the very wildness of Homer's beauty; Lamb rejoiced in the savagery of his heroes because it was unlike the 'fashion of our great men'. Wolf's theories were at first greeted with enthusiasm in England; the romantics enjoyed the notion that the Homeric epics were the rude, virile utterances of a barbarous people, like those old English and Scottish ballads which so fascinated them. They saw Homer as they saw Shakespeare, spontaneous, natural, gloriously imperfect and unpredictable. Newman argued that Homer resembled Shakespeare in mixing grandeur with 'coarse wrangling', 'buffoonery' and 'mean superstition': 'As in earlier England, so in Homeric Greece, even high poetry partook of the coarseness of society. This was probably inevitable, precisely because Greek epic poetry was so natural.'[18] However, the Victorians became increasingly dissatisfied with the picture of Homer the balladist. The appearance in 1838 of Maginn's *Homeric Ballads*, lively renderings of passages from the *Odyssey* in a rollicking metre, marked a turn in the tide; people were entertained, but they could not help seeing that Maginn had produced a travesty. When

Newman published his queer, archaic translation of the *Iliad* in 1856, he was not so much idiosyncratic as out of date; and by bringing down upon his head the cultivated wrath of Matthew Arnold, he was to earn for himself a kind of immortality. Newman said that 'Homer rises and sinks with his subject', and Arnold retorted that Homer's manner invests his subject with nobleness. Newman claimed that Homer's style was 'quaint, flowing, garrulous', and Arnold replied that it was essentially grand. Like Keats and Landor, Arnold found himself comparing Homer to the spacious heavens: 'Homer's grandeur is not the mixed and turbid grandeur of the great poets of the north . . .; it is a perfect . . . grandeur. Certainly his poetry has all the energy and power of the poetry of our ruder climates; but it has, besides, the pure lines of an Ionian horizon, the liquid clearness of an Ionian sky.' He contrasted Homer, who composed with his eye on the object, with Pope, who composed with his eye on the style. It is almost as though Homer's grand style were no style at all, but a transparent medium through which one gazed, unimpeded, at the reality beyond. 'Liquid clearness', 'clearest-souled', 'limpidness'—such were the expressions that Arnold used, and they join with his emphasis on Homer's 'swift-flowing movement' (virtually his only point of agreement with Newman) to conjure up a picture of pure running water.[19] Homer was a source of refreshment, and an inexhaustible source.

Arnold distinguished between the grand style simple and the grand style severe. The former, exemplified by Homer himself, is characterized by grace, lucidity and 'a want of salient points to seize . . ., which makes imitation impossible'. The grand style severe is exemplified by Milton; here we are made aware of the poet's mind and the pressure of personal emotion behind his work. 'Both these styles,' Arnold said, '. . . are truly grand; . . . but the simple is no doubt to be preferred. It is the more *magical*.'[20] Schiller had distinguished between naïve and sentimental poetry, Landor between the vast expansiveness of Homer and the 'burst and compression' of Aeschylus, Arnold himself between the northern and southern types of grandeur. The highly charged, northern type of grandeur was the modern type, rugged, individual and sometimes strained; it could be found in *Faust* or the music of Beethoven. In the other type there was no sign of struggle or difficulty, and the author's personality was invisible. For this kind of grandeur the Victorians felt a special affection; they worshipped Homer and they discovered Bach. Schiller had said that the naïve poet was like nature itself, and the Victorians were passionate for nature. Arnold

regretted that there was 'something intellectual' in the grand style
severe; it was 'much more imitable, and this a little spoils its
charm'.[21] Nature was not imitable and it was not intellectual. Nor
was Homer, and that was his glory.

The Victorians admired Homer for being so un-Victorian; yet
some of them thought that his poetry was of practical use in the
conduct of modern life. 'Did not the recollection of the heroic
simplicity of the Homeric life nerve you up?' asks Hale in Mrs.
Gaskell's *North and South*; the Christian minister sees nothing
strange in drawing moral strength from the pagan epics.[22] The
last words of Gladstone's *Studies on Homer* read almost like an
advertisement for a patent medicine: 'The spells in which this
enchanter deals have no affinity with that drug . . . which drowns the
spirit in effeminate indifference; rather they are like . . . the remedial
specific, which, freshening the understanding by contact with the . . .
strength of nature, should . . . increase its vigour and resolution
for the discharge of duty.'[23] It is striking how many public men
engaged in Homeric studies. Lord John Russell passed the time at
Geneva in translating a book of the *Odyssey*. Lord Derby translated
the entire *Iliad* into blank verse, with considerable success; at the
time of publication he had twice been Prime Minister and was to be
Prime Minister again. When Charles Trevelyan, the future governor
of Madras, was first in India, he asked Macaulay, to whose sister
he was engaged, whether he should keep up his Greek. 'I gave him
Homer,' Macaulay reported, '. . . He read with perfect rapture,
and has marched off . . ., declaring that he shall never be content
till he has finished the whole. This . . . is not a bad brother-in-law
for a man to pick up in 22 degrees of North latitude, and 100 degrees
of East longitude.' Years later, Macaulay re-read the *Iliad* during
a visit to Worcestershire.[24] Unable to tear himself away, he read
the last five books at a stretch in the course of his daily walk. Finally
he was forced to turn into a by-path for fear that passers-by should
see him weeping for Priam and Achilles. Though he was on the
Malvern Hills, it was not Langland who filled his imagination but
a poet vastly more distant in time and place and belief, and yet
somehow so much closer to his own age.

Homer's deepest admirer was the most eminent of all Victorian
statesmen. Gladstone wrote in 1886 that he was reading the *Iliad*
'for the twenty-fifth or thirtieth time, and every time richer and
more glorious than before'.[25] Over a period of forty-five years, in
the midst of immense political, theological and philanthropic
activities, he found time to write a series of articles on Homer and

five books, one of them consisting of three volumes and containing more than 1,700 pages. His diaries show how his favourite poet was knit into the fabric of his life and thought. 'Jan. 1, 1874.—a little *Iliad* and *Odyssey*. 2.—Tree-cutting.' Again in 1887: 'Worked on Homer, Apollo, etc. Then turned to the Irish business and revolved much.'[26] A year later, in a twilit room in Oxford, he fixed Mrs. Humphry Ward with the gleam of his eagle eyes and told her, 'There are still two things left for me to do! One is to carry Home Rule—the other is to prove the intimate connection between the Hebrew and Olympian revelations!'[27] This, as we shall see, meant the study of Homer. When in 1875 he resigned the leadership of the Liberal Party, he consoled himself for the end (as he supposed) of his political career with the prospect of Homeric study, 'bearing much on high and sacred ends'.[28] Schliemann's excavations at Troy in the previous year had seemed to confirm all that he had always believed; his decision to withdraw from the leadership was perhaps influenced in part by the importance of these new discoveries.

His published writings, too, show how in his mind Homer and politics were intertwined. He was strenuously opposing the Divorce Bill at the time of writing the *Studies on Homer*; accordingly, he stressed the complete absence of divorce in Homeric society and noted with satisfaction that there was no mention of marriage to a deceased husband's brother among Homer's Greeks. The minister of Queen Victoria observed with pleasure that to Homer the exercise of sovereignty by a woman was 'neither unknown nor wholly unfamiliar'. The rescuer of fallen women emphasized that 'the society of that period did not avail itself of . . . the professional corruption of a part of womankind in order to relieve the virtue of the residue from assault'. The great orator claimed that Homer had a particular interest in the varied styles of public speaking.[29] And just as he brought politics into his books on Homer, so he applied Homer in politics. The future Lord Shaftesbury was startled to hear him tell the House of Commons that Greek mythology had served a necessary purpose in foreshadowing some of Christ's teachings; this, characteristically, was in a speech on Church Rates. It was the *Studies on Homer* that induced Lytton to ask him to undertake his mission to the Ionian islands, and it was his passion for Homer that led him to accept. *The Times* mocked him for accepting such an insignificant appointment, but the temptation to learn more about Homer's geography had been too great. Besides, he was glad, as Lytton had suggested, to 'reconcile a race that speaks the

Greek language to the science of practical liberty'.[30] Years afterwards, in *The Hellenic Factor in the Eastern Problem*, he mixed discussion of current affairs with an historical analysis of the Greek character, attributing its decline since ancient times to the corrosive effect of Turkish domination. Gladstone's policy was always sympathetic to the modern Greeks; they may have owed more to Homer than they knew.

To Gladstone the study of Homer was not only a passion but a duty, indeed a double duty: to education and to religion. In 1850 the Oxford classical syllabus was divided into 'Mods' and 'Greats': five terms of the poets and orators, followed by seven terms of history and philosophy. Undergraduates were now required to offer twelve books of Homer, but this was insufficient for Gladstone, to whom the two epics were a complete course of Mods and Greats in themselves, containing a 'world of religion and ethics, of civil policy, of history and ethnology, of manners and arts' which could 'hardly be . . . understood, by those, who are taught to approach Homer as a poet only'. (Nor was this view unique; F. W. Newman said, 'He is alternately Poet, Orator, Historian, Theologian, Geographer, Traveller.')[31] Gladstone wanted Homer to be studied throughout the full four years of the Oxford course, and the *Studies on Homer* were written to further this end. By reading Homer the youth of England could learn the arts of government, for here 'an admirable school of polity' was to be found. Gladstone was struck by the 'intense political spirit' pervading the poems; a spirit, moreover, that was uniquely accessible to the English among modern nations, since it still lived and breathed 'in our institutions, and . . . even in the peculiarities of those institutions'. He sanguinely saw the Homeric constitution as containing political freedom within a framework which included vestiges of the old patriarchal monarchy: 'It is the very picture before our own eyes in our own time and country, where visible traces of the old patriarchal mould still coexist . . . with political liberties of more recent fashion, because they retain their hold on the general affections.' Comparing the relative condition of slaves and hired labourers in Homeric society, he observed, 'The position . . . of the slaves was probably analogous to that of domestic servants among ourselves, who practically forfeit the active exercise of political privileges, but are in many respects better off than the mass of those who depend on bodily labour.'[32] Gladstone drew the conclusion that slavery in Homer's time was not so bad; we may draw another.

No matter was too large or too small for his attention. On the

grand scale, he detected in Homer the 'essential germ' of the form
of constitution enjoyed in Britain and America: 'I mean the government by a threefold legislative body, having for one of its members
. . . a single person, in whose hands the executive power . . . is
lodged.' But he also took space to note Agamemnon's opening words
to the Greek assembly—'Friends, Danaan heroes, satellites of
Mars'—and compared them to the English custom, 'according to
which the word 'Gentlemen' would be commonly used, though the
audience should be composed in great part of the humbler class . . .
these words are so many proofs of that political freedom . . ., which
exacts this kind of homage from the great and wealthy. . . .'
Gladstone's friend Doyle was another who brought memories of
the epics to the political battleground: he regretted that English
statesmen did not pay enough attention to Homer, and claimed
that Sarpedon had refuted Bright's speeches against the Crimean
War three thousand years before Bright was born. And Gladstone's
arch-rival Disraeli gave an epic dignity to his account of Peel's
overthrow by describing the protectionists passing through the
lobby in language designed to recall the catalogues of Homer
and Virgil:[33] 'They trooped on: . . . Mr. Bankes, with a parlia-
mentary name of two centuries, and Mr. Christopher from that
broad Lincolnshire which protection had created. . . . Devon had
sent there the stout heart of Mr. Buck—and Wiltshire, the pleasant
presence of Walter Long.' Gladstone told Ruskin that he was 'a
firm believer in the aristocratic principle—the rule of the best'.[34]
We cannot say how greatly he was inspired or fortified in this
belief by Homer, but we do know the tenacity with which he fastened
on to his favourite authors and sucked every drop of moral juice
out of them. (Ruskin, for his part, claimed that Homer had influenced
his own public activities; the St. George's Guild was founded to
realize his ideal of 'kinghood', and this ideal was derived from
Homer.)[35] It is of interest that the greatest statesman of his day
saw England as a Homeric society; and he was not alone in this
view, as we shall see. Here as elsewhere he was, in a hugely
magnified and perhaps distorted form, the type and representative of
his age.

The religious import of Homer was a subject even dearer to his
heart. The doctrine of economy held that the development of Greek
thought and civilization had a necessary role to play in preparing
for the gospel. Gladstone accepted this view, especially commending
Plato and Aristotle as 'earnest, manful seekers after truth',[36] but
combined it, oddly though not illogically, with an insistence that

Homer was superior in both ethics and theology to all later Greek
writers. The Homeric world, he said, 'stands between Paradise
and the vices of later heathenism', and he meant it literally: Homer
was far closer to the Garden of Eden than the classical Greeks, and
Homeric religion contained memories of God's revelation to
primitive man.[37] Besides, since the patriarchs were immensely
long-lived (see *Genesis*, chapter 5), we must suppose that traditions
were better preserved in the earliest times;[38] Gladstone does not
consider the possible unreliability of a 965-year-old memory.
(Somehow he reconciled these ideas with the belief that the poet
was a profound religious thinker, whose theological system was
largely developed by himself: Homer must be prophet as well as
historian.)[39] It was evident, he thought, that Jupiter, Neptune and
Pluto (he used the Roman names) were a memory of the Trinity.
Apollo was a relic of belief in a Messiah, as can be seen from his
double character as Saviour and Destroyer (a page is allotted to
demonstrating that Apollo's rape of Marpessa was 'not of a sensual
character'). Was Minerva the Logos or the Holy Spirit? Did Latona
represent Eve or the Virgin Mary? How curious that the poems
contained no mention of the sabbath! Gladstone's perversely ingenious mind was able to turn even the most awkward features of
Homeric religion to advantage. The poet's conception of the gods
is blatantly anthropomorphic, but doubtless 'it was an old and
pure tradition that first gave to men the idea of God in human
form; the idea which . . . became that of Emmanuel, God with us.'
Homer's gods often behave deplorably, and appear to excel men
only in that they are immortal. Gladstone was not abashed: here
was 'testimony to the truth of the representation conveyed in Holy
Writ, that death has been the specific punishment ordained for sin:
and that therefore in passing beyond the human order we . . . pass
beyond its range.'[40]

These were eccentric opinions; but once again the eccentricity
consisted in pushing certain Victorian tendencies to extreme limits.
Kingsley had already congratulated the early Greeks on the superior
purity and truth of their religion and even Matthew Arnold offered
an allegorized interpretation of Apollo which made him sound
distinctly like Christ.[41] Athens, he suggested, owed her achievements
to the 'Delphic discipline'; 'For Apollo was . . . the author of every
higher moral effort; he was the prophet of his father Zeus, in the
highest view of Zeus, as the source of . . . moral order.' Gladstone
may have lacked a sense of the dark, irrational side of Greek religion,
but then so did almost all Victorians, Christians and pagans alike.

However, he offered a refreshing contrast to the pagans' sentimental notion that sexual guilt and embarrassment were Christian inventions. He pointed out, in the convoluted language of the time, that there is no trace of homosexuality in the poems, that nakedness is regarded as deeply shameful, that the status of women was higher in the Homeric age than in classical Greece; and he was delighted by the poet's almost contemptuous handling of Mars, 'the god of violence', and Venus, 'the goddess of lust'.[42] In fact, he was remarkably successful in what sounds the almost impossible task of demonstrating Homer's moral excellence according to conventional Victorian standards; perhaps because the Homeric and Victorian ages did, in a strange way, have something in common. But he went too far. For instance, Homer's women often wash and anoint male guests, but to Gladstone such immodesty was unacceptable, and he insisted, in defiance of the plain meaning of the Greek, that washing or anointing someone meant giving them the means to wash or anoint themselves.[43] In effect, the ladies merely laid out soap and towels. He alleged, too, that Helen's self-reproaches in the third book of the *Iliad* come closer to the penitential tone of Christianity than anything else in pagan literature; yet the scene ends with her and Paris retiring to bed together.[44] To him Homer was, quite literally, a sacred book, and thus he felt himself forced to defend not just the general tendency but every small detail of the epic.

That Homer had been the Bible of the Greeks was a Victorian cliché. Where Gladstone was unusual was in his desire that the poet should become the Bible of the English too; he urged his countrymen not to underestimate Homer's moral value and rebuked them for their 'somewhat narrow jealousies concerning the function of Holy Scripture'.[45] In one respect Homer did resemble the Bible; his words and phrases had sunk deep into the minds of educated men, so that a passing reference to them would be recognized and understood. He was a constant victim of waggish parody; a trivial but revealing indication of his pervasive influence. Thackeray describes Pendennis 'biting his nails by the shore of the much-sounding sea' and a footman 'with his ambrosial hair powdered . . . in his hand his cane, gold-headed, *dolichoskion*';[46] Macaulay wrote to a friend, 'I have a well-polished *asaminthos* for you, into which going you may wash, and out of which you may come, looking like a god.'[47] Lord Byron and Dean Farrar had little in common, but they both made the same Homeric joke, Farrar referring to 'the Little-Go, so called in the language of men, but known to the gods as the Previous Examination',[48] and Byron to 'what men call

gallantry, and gods adultery'.[49] George Eliot was particularly fond
of heavy jocosity at Homer's expense.[50] In his facetious novel of
university life, *The Adventures of Mr. Verdant Green*, Cuthbert
Bede liked to refer to oaths or abuse as *epea pteroenta* ('winged
words'), an expression that may reflect undergraduate usage;
equally, the dreadful Homeric drolleries of the schoolboys in Farrar's
St. Winifred's are probably taken from life.

The poets made use of the common stock of Homeric memories.
When Swinburne mentioned 'the young Gerenian Nestor' in
Atalanta, he knew that his readers would recall the elderly Gerenian
Nestor of the Homeric epics and be amused at the thought of the
old raconteur as a young man. In a poem called *Narcissus* Flecker
wrote,

> Amid the reeds I lingered
> Between desire and pain
> Till evening, rosy-fingered,
> Beckoned to night again.

In Homer it is the dawn that is rosy-fingered; Flecker's variant
brings out the perversity of the youth's passion, which turns everything topsy-turvy. Most lovers meet at night and part at dawn,
but since Narcissus loves his own reflection, he depends upon the
daylight, and the evening is to him what the dawn is to others.
Many times Homer must have inspired poets in a way that we cannot
now recover. A section of *In Memoriam* begins,[51]

> Old Yew, which graspest at the stones
> That name the under-lying dead,
> Thy fibres net the dreamless head . . .

Tennyson himself compared a phrase from the *Odyssey*, 'the strengthless heads of the dead', where the Greek for 'strengthless' is an
epithet commonly applied to dreams. Here we could not have
asserted that the poet had been influenced by Homer if he had not
told us so. But often the influence was meant to be obvious: Macaulay
modelled his *Battle of Lake Regillus* on the fight over the body of
Patroclus, and John Wilson declared in an enthusiastic review of
his *Lays*, 'The Young Poets steal from all and sundry, and deny
their thefts; he robs in the face of day. Whom? Homer.'[52] There
was no sense that open 'theft' was wrong; the task was to use Homer,
as Virgil had done, to create something fresh. This was not easy;

Virgil had remarked, when accused of plagiarism, that it was easier to steal the club of Hercules than a line of Homer;[53] a remark which recalls Brahms's reply to the critics who pointed out a resemblance between his first symphony and Beethoven's last. 'Any fool can see that,' he said, implying that a more perceptive critic would have looked for the differences in things apparently similar. The first century and the nineteenth were both secondary ages, conscious of a tremendous past. Virgil's epic is, to some degree, poetry about poetry; Brahms, in a sense, composed music about music, while Brahms's English contemporaries followed in Virgil's footsteps with works like *The Epic of Hades* and the *Idylls of the King*.

Sometimes, though, the imitations of Homeric passages in Victorian poetry seem almost pointless; it is as if copying Homer had become an end in itself. And the same can be said of the Victorian passion for translating him. Dr. Arnold had an idiosyncratic belief in the value of making schoolboys translate classical authors into period English; Herodotus should be rendered in the style of the chroniclers, Thucydides in that of Bacon, while in Homer's case 'hardly any words should be employed except Saxon'.[54] But for this paternal influence, Matthew Arnold might never have considered putting the question of how to translate Homer in the forefront of debate. In the fifteen years following his lectures five versions of the *Iliad* appeared in the hexameter metre that he recommended;[55] but the influence of the Arnold family is not in itself enough to account for the interest in the topic. Back in 1831 Macaulay had dined out and spent the evening discussing whether *pithoi* in *Iliad* 24 should be translated 'urns', 'casks', or 'vases'.[56] In the middle of the century twelve complete verse renderings of the *Iliad*, a poem of more than 15,000 lines, were published over a period of about twenty years.[57] Gladstone, Tennyson and Arnold all tried their hand at turning passages into English verse; William Morris translated the entire *Odyssey*. It was somehow assumed that translating Homer was a worthwhile activity, like doing charitable works; Trollope was improving very little on life when he described John Eames's scheme to cure his love-sickness:[58] 'He would go deep into Greek and do a translation. . . . He had a mutton chop . . ., and spent his time in endeavouring to read . . . passages from the Iliad. . . . On the next day he was cooler. . . . Greek was not the thing for him, but he would take up the sanitary condition of the poor in London.'

Most of Homer's translators will have resembled the ancient Greeks at least in this, that they regarded the Homeric poems as

by far the greatest achievement of Greek literature. And maybe
the spate of translations was in the nature of a costly and useless
tribute to Homer's deified genius; the hero must be honoured with
hecatombs of English verse. Certainly the Victorians' habit of
hero-worship was evident in their attitude towards the Homeric
question. Matthew Arnold said, 'The grand argument—or rather
not argument, for the matter affords no data for arguing, but the
grand source from which conviction . . . keeps pressing in upon
us, that there is . . . one Homer—is precisely this nobleness of the
poet, this grand manner.'[59] The unity of Homer was a matter of
faith, of believing what one could not prove. The resourcefulness
(and wrongheadedness) with which Gladstone opposed the smallest
concession to the Wolfian heresy recall the desperate ingenuity
with which Wilberforce and Philip Gosse tried to combat the
menace of Darwinism. The few Wolfians tended to be agnostics
and radicals, and they found themselves up against a distrust of
extremism that one might almost call Anglican; English, certainly,
for it was conventional for the unitarians to throw in a few remarks
about the dismal pedantry of the Germans. Grote, the leading
English Wolfian, found that even the favourable reviewers of his
History considered his opinions about Homer unacceptable. George
Eliot, another Wolfian, complained, 'How enviable it is to be a
classic. When a verse in the Iliad bears six different meanings and
nobody knows which is the right, a commentator finds this equivocal-
ness in itself admirable.'[60] Macaulay decided that the *Iliad* was a
mosaic made long after Homer's time out of several of his lays,
with bits here and there of the compositions of inferior minstrels;
this curious compromise suggests that Wolfian convictions were
struggling in his mind with an urgent desire to believe in a single
great genius called Homer.[61]

While many of Homer's admirers pictured him as an elemental
force, others sought for the stamp of a great and distinctive personality; the love of boswellism was not easily damped down.
Keble analysed Homer's character at length: he was 'deeply moved
with loving care for the heroes of old', his political sympathies were
aristocratic, he was content with his own lot, and so on. To Ruskin
Homer was one of the 'great Tory writers'; believing that 'the
greatness of a poet depends upon the two faculties, acuteness of
feeling, and command of it', he interpreted Homer's objectivity as a
triumph of intellect over the utmost efforts of the passions. Gladstone's views required that Homer be a personality of unusual
strength, energy and moral earnestness; much like Gladstone, in

fact. William Mure, whose history of Greek literature was
something of a standard work, declared that Homer excelled all
other poets in the excellence of his 'general design and composition'.
Froude claimed, 'His poems have but to be disintegrated to unite
again, so strong are they in the individuality of their genius'; adding
that the unity of their design and the distinctness of drawing in the
character had overcome the worst onslaught of the Wolfians.[62]
Homer's skill in the delineation of character was a favourite topic of
Victorian critics. Gladstone said, 'To one only . . . has it been given
to draw characters, by the strength of his own individual hand, in
lines of such force and vigour, that they have become . . . the common
inheritance of civilized man. That one is Homer.' Mure analysed
Homer's principal characters one by one; the character of Achilles,
he concluded, was 'the highest effort of the poet's genius'. Symonds
agreed: 'The centralisation of interest in the character of Achilles,
constitutes the grandeur of the *Iliad*. It is also by this that the
Iliad is distinguished from all the narrative epics of the world. . . .
In none else are the passions of the hero made the main points of the
movement.'[63]

Homer's design *is* impressive, his characters *are* very vivid; to
a large extent the Victorians were simply describing what they
found. But naturally such descriptions, which seemed to confirm
the presence of Homer's 'own individual hand', brought comfort
to the unitarians; and besides, critics, whether right or wrong,
have a way of bringing out those elements in an author that are
closest to the art of their own day. A number of recent scholars,
especially in America, have searched for symbolic patterns in
Homer, because symbolic patterns have been highly valued in
our own century; in the Victorian age the novel was the most
lively art-form, and the Victorians, consciously and unconsciously,
tended to turn Homer into a kind of novelist. One of the surprising
glories of Homer was that in spite of his grandeur his poems were
full of ordinary, everyday activities. 'No object is too homely to be
noticed,' said Shairp, 'or too simple to furnish an apt simile.' Froude
was pleased to see that Ulysses built his own house, and carved his
own bed, while Nausicaa 'drove the clothes-cart and washed linen
with her own beautiful hands'. It was Ruskin who best explained
how Homer combined intimism with epic magnificence: 'The
naturalist ideal has always in it, to the full, the power expressed by
these two words. It is naturalist, because studied from nature, and
ideal, because it is mentally arranged in a certain manner. Achilles
must be represented as cutting pork chops, because that was one

of the things which the nature of Achilles involved his doing: he could not be shown wholly as Achilles, if he were not shown doing that. But he shall do it at such time and place as Homer chooses.'[64]

Naturalism of such a kind was the aim, more or less, of Trollope and George Eliot; and even the structure of the Homeric poems seemed to have something in common with the nineteenth-century novel. Maybe it is true, as Mure and Symonds suggested, that the *Iliad* is unique among epics in being dominated by a single central personality around whom cluster a large number of lesser characters, vividly drawn; but certainly such a description makes it sound unexpectedly like *David Copperfield* or *Madame Bovary*. Froude thought that Homer's vignettes of Odysseus' boyhood showed that the hero 'was once, then, such a little creature as we remember ourselves, and Laertes a calm, kind father of the nineteenth century'. At moments he seems to attribute to Homer the sentimentality of a Dickens or a Thackeray: 'Then, as now, the little tired maiden would cling to her mother's skirt, and . . . plead with moist eyes to be carried.' Gladstone, shrewd in his assessment of Homer's male characters, lapsed into fantasy when he dealt with the women: 'The Homeric man . . . is sometimes the subject of hasty . . . passions; the woman never. She finds her power in gentleness; . . . she is eminent for the uniformity of her self-command. . . .' We are reminded of David Copperfield and his angelic Agnes, for ever pointing him upwards to higher things. He claimed that Homer's pictures of women are perfect: 'But they are pictures of mothers, matrons, sisters, daughters, maidens, wives.'[65] He did not appreciate the range of female portraiture that is so impressive in the *Odyssey*: the passionate, unscrupulous Calypso, and that tough, humorous *demi-mondaine*, Circe, bring out by force of contrast the dutiful Penelope and the maidenly charm of Nausicaa.

Farrar declared that the *Odyssey* was the best novel ever written.[66] Butler compared Telemachus to Nicholas Nickleby, and translated one of Mrs. Gamp's monologues into Homeric hexameters. His theory that the *Odyssey* was written by a middle-class lady from Sicily seems to turn the author into a Greek Brontë or Jane Austen.[67] It was commonplace to compare Homer with both the poems and novels of Scott. Doyle, who succeeded Arnold in the Oxford chair of poetry, and Shairp, who succeeded Doyle, both devoted lectures to this topic; it recurs in the writings of F. W. Newman, Gladstone and (most frequently) Ruskin. Such comparisons may seem a strange kind of compliment to Homer, particularly at a time when many people were reluctant to treat the novel as a serious form of literature, but they were a way of trying to explain the continuing life and vigour that Victorian readers found in him; Homer, they felt, was a perpetual presence in the background of modern life. 'Like the sun,' Gladstone wrote, 'which furnishes with its light the close courts . . . of London, while himself unseen by their inhabitants, Homer has supplied with the illumination of his ideas millions of minds that were never brought into direct contact with his work, and even millions more, that have hardly been aware of his existence. . . . And this universality is his alone.'[68]

Athletics

The *Iliad* is about aristocrats; no common soldier is so much as named in it, with the solitary and significant exception of Thersites in the second book. Bald, bandy-legged and hunchbacked, he can hardly be typical of the Greek army. He criticizes Agamemnon in the assembly; why, he asks, should the Greeks go on suffering merely for their king to win more booty.[69] For this he is swiftly punished. Odysseus denounces him, and then 'with his staff smote his back and shoulders: and he bowed down and a big tear fell from him, and a bloody weal stood up from his back'. The common people laugh, saying: 'Odysseus hath wrought good deeds without number ere now . . . but now is this thing the best by far that he hath wrought . . .'[70]

Bodily harm inflicted on the physically disadvantaged by the socio-economically privileged—modern sentiment recoils with distaste. Gladstone himself seems to have felt some embarrassment in defending the treatment of Thersites: 'It is railing, and not reasoning, that he represents. . . . We are not to take the ill-success of a foul-mouthed scoundrel, detested by the whole army, as a sample of what would have happened to the people, or even a party of them, when differing in judgement from their king.'[71] The defence is ingenious, but not quite convincing. Why is the only common soldier ever to speak so exceptionally ill-favoured? He speaks on behalf of the common people; yet the common people are lavish in praise of Odysseus. Surely Homer protests too much.

Tennyson seems to have thought so. In *Guinevere* he describes how Lancelot catches a spy and throws him to the ground; but then, recognizing him as the deformed Modred, he apologizes,[72]

> for in those days
> No knight of Arthur's noblest dealt in scorn;
> But if a man were halt or hunch'd, in him . . .
> Scorn was allow'd as part of his defect,
> And he was answer'd softly . . .

The *Idylls* were composed under the shadow of Homer; we are meant to remember Thersites. The Arthurian court, Tennyson suggests, is a purified version of the Achaean camp: the Christian knights know what constitutes true nobility better than the Greeks. Like Virgil, he leaves the reader to pick up the Homeric parallels for himself; the message is the more telling if it is merely implied.

Tennyson may not have been typical. 'When a scoundrel is whipped,' says Warrington in *The Newcomes*, 'I am pleased, and say, serve him right. If any gentleman will horsewhip Sir Barnes Newcome, Baronet, I shall . . . order an extra mutton-chop for dinner.'[73] In the pages of Dickens, Thackeray, Trollope, Kipling, and in countless other Victorian novels, upstarts are knocked down and cads horse-whipped. What is more, these villains are weak, ugly specimens, and this, like Thersites' deformities, is held against them as an extra fault. The chastisers, by contrast, are handsome, manly and young. Nicholas Nickleby flogs the one-eyed Squeers; John Harmon beats the one-legged Wegg;[74] Barnes Newcome, too, is a poor, puny creature. There is often a latent sadism, or at least vengefulness, in these accounts. Warrington is supposed to be a generous, noble-hearted fellow who expresses himself vigorously, but in fact his utterances seem to be bitterly vindictive; it is as though Thackeray uses him as a mouthpiece for his frustrations. The story of Thersites answers to an eternal demand of human nature, the desire to see retribution. Dickens found that the flogging of Squeers was the most popular of all his readings; the audiences cheered till they were hoarse.

In the *Iliad* the main function of the ordinary folk is to be killed by their superiors: it is unthinkable for a hero to be slain except by another hero. In *Tom Brown At Oxford* someone says in tones of incredulity, 'Jervis, Brown says you don't believe a gentleman can lick a cad, unless he is the biggest and strongest of the two.' Tom himself had been jolted by Jervis's heresy: 'The vision of terrific single combats, in which the descendant of a hundred earls polishes off the huge representative of the masses . . ., without a scratch on his own aristocratic features, had faded from his mind.'[75] Of course Hughes is poking fun at Tom, but he does suggest none the less that some of the young bloods who fought in the battles between Town and Gown saw themselves in fancy as modern versions of the epic heroes. But if violent combat was a feature of the early Victorian university, it was still more so of the Victorian public school. School stories are full of blows, bruises and black eyes; even Jowett told his nephew that if he heard his schoolfellows using profanities, he should 'give a boy a cuff in the eye who uses such language'.[76] In his preface to *The Heroes* Kingsley said of the Greeks, 'They were but grown-up children, though they were right noble children too; and it was with them as it is now at school— the strongest and the cleverest boy, though he be poor, leads all the rest.' For him the Homeric world was a sort of Rugby writ large.

The school story is, like the landscape garden, an art form of English invention, but unlike the landscape garden it has remained, for obvious reasons, exclusively English. Two of these school stories (unless one regards the shapeless saga of Billy Bunter as a story) have had a far greater influence than any others: *Tom Brown's Schooldays* and *Eric, or Little by Little*. And it is a remarkable fact that both are full of Homer. Two chapters of *Eric* are headed by quotations from the *Iliad*, and one scene describes a lesson in which Homer is being read; less expectedly, we keep coming upon re-enactments of the story of Thersites. Early in the book Mr. Williams sees his son Eric and the virtuous Edwin Russell being bullied by Barker.[77] (Most of the villains in Farrar's books—Brigson, Brogten, Bruce, Barker, Ball—begin with a B; even their names condemn them.) He lays savagely into the bully with his riding whip. Odysseus warned Thersites that if his offences were repeated his humiliation would be more severe; so does Mr. Williams: 'He flung the boy from him with . . . disgust, and said, ". . . If ever you do bully in this way again, your present punishment shall be a trifle to that which I shall then administer".' Like Thersites, Barker is humiliated in public, and the common folk applaud: 'He hears numbers of fellows, even little boys, say openly, "I'm so glad; serves you right".' The second scene is still closer to Homer.[78] The victim is Brigson, a Thersites in appearance: 'The awkward, big, ungainly boy, with his repulsive countenance, shambled out of his place.' Again retribution is summary, and humiliation public. The flogger is the saintly Mr. Rose, who beats him to the ground and canes him till he rolls on the floor. Then he repeats the warning of Odysseus and Mr. Williams: 'That flogging shall be repeated with interest on your next offence.' And again the multitude applaud:

'Three times three for Mr. Rose,' sang out
Wildney.

Never did a more hearty or spontaneous cheer
burst from . . . fifty boys than that.

There is yet a third incident, in which the parallel with Thersites
is explicit.[79] Rose has caught two boys smoking. One of them,
Booking (begins with a B—clearly a hopeless case) lies about his
offence and is fiercely punished. The other, Pietrie, owns up. Rose
canes him, but then forgives him and argues with him, until he
looks 'unusually crestfallen'. Russell later describes the scene:
' "Silly fellow," he said, pulling Pietrie's ear, ". . . remember
next time you're caught, I shall have you punished." So off went
Pietrie, *achreion idōn*, as our friend Homer says . . .' *achreion idōn*,
'looking about foolishly', is Homer's description of Thersites after
his punishment.[80]

Evidently Farrar was fascinated by this episode in the *Iliad*,
and for a particular reason. Swinburne's sharp clever nose sniffed
something odd about the 'Rev. Mr. Thwackum of Marlborough',
and when Farrar criticized him from the pulpit, he wrote: 'I have . . .
been . . . verbally swished by a pedagogue parson (the Rev. F.
(lunkey) W.(horeson) Farrar—qu. Fellator?) in public before a
numerous congregation of both sexes, in the principal church of
Glasgow.'[81] Swinburne's instinct was right. *St. Winifred's*, Farrar's
other school story, is equally rich in accounts of corporal chastisement; and in *Eric* itself the hero dies after being brutally flogged by
sailors. Even Brigson's sufferings are described in juicy detail:
he writhes and yells, twists like a serpent, and blubbers like a baby,
finally clasping his tormentor's arm and begging, unavailingly, for
mercy. It is plain, too, that the flogger, the wise and benevolent
Mr. Rose, is Farrar's idealized vision of himself.

Tom Brown's Schooldays is blessedly free from the dark overtones of *Eric*, but Hughes too saw adolescence in a Homeric light. It
is no accident that the climax of the book, Tom's fight with Slogger
Williams, is preceded by a scene which shows the boys reading the
Iliad in class.[82] They are studying Helen's lament over Hector,
and Arthur is put on to construe; but he is so moved by two particular lines that he bursts into tears[83]—Homeric tears, we are
bound to feel, when we remember how often Homer's heroes weep.
Williams jeers at Arthur; Tom rushes to his defence, and the stage
is set for an epic combat.

What is Tom's ideal? 'I want to be A1 at cricket and football, and all the other games, and to make my hands keep my head against any fellow, lout or gentleman. I want to get into the sixth before I leave, and to please the Doctor: and I want to carry away just as much Latin and Greek as will take me through Oxford respectably.'[84] Essentially this is a Homeric ideal, with an ad-mixture of medieval chivalry, and Tom's statement of his simple ambitions becomes oddly touching once we hear the Homeric words that underlie it. 'Always to be the champion and to excel over others'—Peleus' instructions to his son Achilles sum up the goal of the Homeric hero in a single line. And that excellence was not restricted to military prowess: Achilles was taught 'to be both a speaker of words and a doer of deeds'.[85] But Tom Brown is to learn that he has not achieved the ideal because he has concentrated upon deeds at the expense of words. On his last day at Rugby, a master tells him that he cannot fully appreciate Greek literature unless he is prepared to learn the nuances of the language; as with cricket, 'the delicate play is the true thing'.[86]

> 'Yes, sir,' answered Tom, looking up roguishly. 'I see; only the question remains whether I should have got most good from understanding Greek particles or cricket thoroughly. I'm such a thick, I should never have had time for both.'
> 'I see you are incorrigible,' said the master with a chuckle, 'but I refute you by an example. Arthur there has taken in Greek and cricket too.'

There is the ideal of Arnold's Rugby in a nutshell: Greek *and* cricket. It is a Homeric ideal, and Arthur, the lover of Homer, proves unexpectedly to be the modern Achilles.

Peleus' advice is quoted with overwhelming effect by Josiah Crawley in Trollope's *Last Chronicle of Barset*. From his bed of sickness he urges his daughter to keep working at her Greek:[87]

> 'If you don't take care, my dear,' he said, 'Jane will beat you yet. She understands . . . the verbs better than you do.'
> 'I am very glad that she is doing so well . . . I shall not begrudge her her superiority.'
> 'Ah, but you should begrudge it her! . . . Always to be best;—always to be in advance of others. That should be your motto.'

For the reader who recognizes the source of the motto, the reverbera-tions are tremendous. Long forgotten and bitterly disappointed, falsely accused of theft and now struck down by sickness, Crawley is yet sustained by a huge Homeric pride. He has been represented as a man whose imaginative life is passed mostly among the Greek tragedians, but now, at his lowest ebb, it is the epic poetry of a still earlier epoch that gives him the will to keep fighting. His pride is an indissoluble fusion of good and bad qualities: the defiance of misfortune and passion for Greek poetry are magnificent; but his feeling that as the superior scholar he deserves higher preferment than his old friend Arabin is unworthy. No passage in Victorian literature so eloquently displays the Victorian ideals of scholarship and competitive achievement in their grandeur—and in their narrowness.

It was characteristic of Samuel Butler, that enemy of Victorian conventions, to utter a facetious protest against the Homeric ideal: 'Homer tells us about someone who made it his business . . . always to excel and to stand higher than other people. What an uncompanionable disagreeable person he must have been! Homer's heroes generally came to a bad end, and I doubt not that this gentleman . . . did so. . . .' But to Newman Homer was 'the first Apostle of Civilization', 'invested with the office of forming the young mind of Greece to noble thoughts and bold deeds. To be read in Homer soon became the education of a gentleman.' Gladstone wrote, 'The Homeric king . . . should be emphatically a gentleman, and that in a sense not far from the one familiar to the Christian civilization of Europe.'[88]

'Always to excel over others.' The Victorian age was intensely competitive; the industrial revolution had broken down the exclusive predominance of the old landed aristocracy, and enabled men as never before to fight their way from comparative obscurity to positions of wealth and power. The spirit of competition spilled over into the schools and universities, where foreign observers were struck by the English passion for competitive sports. Taine described with amazement the importance of games in public schools, adding,

> There are . . . gentlemen in this country whose ambition and regimen are those of a Greek athlete; they adopt a special diet . . . and follow a careful system of training. As soon as they are ready they set out to obtain the prize for rowing or cricket at all the principal athletic games meetings in England. . . . I have been told of a team of eleven cricketers who actually went to play in Australia, as formerly athletes went from Punt or from Marseilles, to Olympia.[89]

Today the Graeco–Britannic ideal has spread across the entire globe; it is hard to recapture how eccentric it seemed to Taine, and how Hellenic.

'Reader!' Hughes asks in *Tom Brown at Oxford*, 'had you not ever a friend . . ., whose good opinion you were anxious to keep? A fellow . . . who could do everything better than you, from Plato and tennis down to singing a comic song and playing quoits?'[90] The university hero was an all-rounder; and the superiority was preferably effortless, like that of Achilles, who withdraws from the chariot race with the observation that he would be sure to win if he took part. At Cambridge Farrar's Julian Home 'read, and rowed, and went to lectures, and worked at classics, mathematics and philosophy, and dropped in sometimes to a debate . . . at the Union, and played racquets, fives and football, and talked eagerly . . . over the exciting topics of the day.'[91] The Union and football; a speaker of words and a doer of deeds. Gladstone, a past president of the Oxford Union, asked the students of Edinburgh University to note the Homeric heroes' unique 'union . . . of corporal with mental excellence'. 'Homer,' he added, 'shared the privilege of his most glorious epithet (*kudianeira*) between battle and debate.'[92] The 'reading men' at the universities spent so much of their lives communing with the Greeks that they were liable to imagine their own environment in Greek terms; 'The modern Athens,' Charles Reade said of Oxford, 'like the ancient, cultivates muscle as well as mind.' Even the averagely idle undergraduate might catch something of the spell. Herodotus observes that young Persians were taught to ride, shoot and speak the truth. 'It's worth learning how to play tennis, and how to speak the truth,' remarks Tom Brown. 'Alcibiades,' he muses on another occasion, '. . . must have been very like some of our gentlemen-commoners, with the addition of brains.'[93]

The university novel is another distinctively English art form; the Victorian examples specialized in heroes who combined dazzling feats of athletic prowess with brilliant scholarship. These improbable paragons were burlesqued by Beerbohm in *Zuleika Dobson*: 'The Duke had already taken (besides a particularly brilliant First in Mods) the Stanhope, the Newdigate, the Lothian, and the Gaisford Prize for Greek Verse. And these things he had achieved *currente calamo*, "wielding his pen," as Scott said of Byron, "with the easy negligence of a nobleman." He was now in his third year of residence, and was reading, a little, for Literae Humaniores. There is no doubt that but for his untimely death he would have taken a particularly brilliant First in that school also.'[94] The parenthetic words 'a little' are a nice touch: effortless ease is the thing. Absurd though they are, these nonpareils are the fictional reflection of a real educational ideal. Jowett himself offered 'some good advice' to his nephew: 'It is only this—to make yourself a good cricketer, football player, etc., and not to sit "sapping" too much while the other boys are at play. . . . The boys are not far wrong in respecting a boy who is "good at games" and I would advise you to try and gain their respect in this way as well as in books.'[95] Arnold's attitude was similar; according to Stanley, 'The Greek union of the *aretē gumnastikē* [athletic excellence] with the *aretē mousikē* [literary excellence], he thought invaluable in education, and held that the freedom of the sports of public schools was particularly favourable to it; and wherever he saw that boys were reading too much, he always remonstrated with them.'[96]

Rowing was the university sport *par excellence*, and inevitably many of the participants were reminded of the Athenian navy, manned entirely by citizens. Jervis in *Tom Brown at Oxford* addresses the fellow members of his eight as 'Old companions, *thranitai* . . .', using the Greek word for oarsmen.[97] Warre, headmaster of Eton, the most successful rowing school in England, devoted his scholarly energies to studying the Greek trireme, and would invade his assistant masters' classrooms to lecture the boys on the techniques of Athenian oarsmanship.[98] Now the Athenians of the fifth century were essentially amateurs, perhaps the most brilliant amateurs that the world has seen: Socrates was an amateur philosopher, Sophocles an amateur playwright, Thucydides an amateur historian. Here was a quality which appealed to the English temperament. 'One hates an author that's *all author*,' Byron wrote; the better writers, he claimed, 'think of something else besides the pen.'[99] Symonds was moved to raptures by the many-sidedness of Sophocles (who not only wrote the *Antigone* but was made a general allegedly on the strength of it): 'The artist and the man were one in Sophocles. . . . We cannot but think of him as specially created to represent Greek art in its most . . . exquisitely balanced perfection.' This would be little more than an echo of Matthew Arnold, if Symonds did not dwell so upon the poet's adolescence. He was 'exceedingly beautiful and well-formed . . . accomplished in music and gymnastics', and 'gained public prizes in both these branches of a Greek boy's education. His physical grace and skill in dancing caused him to be chosen, in his sixteenth year, to lead the choir in celebration of the victory at Salamis. According to Athenian custom, he appeared

on this occasion naked, crowned, and holding in his hand a lyre.'
He was perfectly *euphuēs*, a term 'which denotes physical, as well
as moral and intellectual, distinction'.[100] Sophocles, in fact, is
represented as the public school paragon (with a soupçon of pederastic
flavouring added): handsome, debonair, equally accomplished at
work and games, the star of the sports day and the prize-giving.

Even those who did not entirely admire the English method of
educating the upper classes appreciated its Greekness. Disraeli
mockingly represents Mr. Phoebus as declaring that the English
aristocracy 'most resemble the old Hellenic race' because they
excel in athletic sports, speak no language but their own, and never
read: 'This is not a complete education, but it is the highest education since the Greek.'[101] Forster neatly brought out the likeness and
unlikeness between the athletic ideals of Greece and England.
Rickie Elliot, in *The Longest Journey*, idolises Gerald Dawes, stupid,
unimaginative, a god upon the rugby pitch, with 'the figure of a
Greek athlete and the face of an English one'.[102] Dawes is engaged
to Agnes Pembroke, whose brother discusses him with Rickie:[103]

> 'If a man shoots straight and hits straight . . ., if he has the
> instincts of a Christian and a gentleman—then I . . . ask no
> better husband for my sister.'
> 'How could you get a better?' he cried. 'Do you remember
> the thing in "The Clouds"?' And he quoted . . . the description
> of the young Athenian, perfect in body, placid in mind, who
> neglects his work at the Bar and trains all day . . . with a
> garland on his head and a friend to set the pace: the scent of new
> leaves is upon them; they rejoice in the freshness of spring . . .—
> perhaps the most glorious invitation to the brainless life that
> has ever been given.

Rickie assumes that the Athenian conception of excellence and the
English ideal of the Christian gentleman are one and the same.
But he is wrong: 'For Mr. Dawes would not have bothered over
the garland or noticed the spring, and would have complained that
the friend ran too slowly or too fast.'

No one, Matthew Arnold thought, cared about British freedom
and British muscularity; but Greek freedom and Greek gymnastics
had won the admiration of mankind. 'And what can be the reason
of this difference? Surely because the Greeks pursued freedom and
pursued gymnastics not mechanically, but with constant reference
to some ideal of complete human perfection.'[104] Arnold was modifying

some incautious remarks that he had made earlier. He had said that culture, such as we find it among the Greeks, was a condition that all classes of English society had failed to achieve, not least the aristocracy, whom he nicknamed the Barbarians. Now the Greeks divided the world into Hellenes and barbarians; Arnold was implying, therefore, that the ideal of the upper classes was antithetical to the Greek idea. But what was the ideal of the upper classes? According to Arnold, it was a care for good looks and bodily exercises.[105] Too selective in those aspects of Greek life that he chose to see, he had forgotten for a moment that this was an ideal that the Greeks had advocated more eloquently than any other people. In the middle of an essay written with the express purpose of demonstrating how different the modern spirit was from the Hellenic spirit, he had stumbled, in his own despite, upon an apparent point of resemblance.

Arnold admitted that bodily health and vigour were very well in their way; but, he added, 'Does not a subtle criticism lead us to make . . . the one qualifying remark, that in these charming gifts there should perhaps be, for ideal perfection, a shade more soul?'[106] But absence of soul was precisely the quality which Pater was soon to single out as the distinguishing characteristic of Hellenic art. Later he developed this idea in his essay 'The Age of Athletic Prizemen'; but to develop an idea, for Pater, meant to add ever more subtle but elusive qualifications. In this essay we can seldom be entirely sure whether he is speaking of Greek art or the nature of the Greeks themselves; moreover, the language which he uses to describe mental experience is both complex and obscure. He introduces the word 'soul' without any attempt at definition, but later makes a distinction between the bodily soul or *anima* and the reasonable soul or *animus*. He also uses the word 'mind', which appears to be a synonym for the reasonable soul; what he means by bodily soul is never explained.

Before analysing the sculpture of the fifth century he says a few words about the Greek games, 'a gymnastic which . . . was already surely what Plato pleads for, already one half music, *mousikē*, a matter, partly, of character and of the soul, of the fair proportion between soul and body, of the soul with itself. Who can doubt it who sees . . . the still irresistible grace . . . of the *Discobolus*, the *Diadumenus*, and a few other precious survivals . . .?' On the next page he reveals, for the first time, the close connection between his appreciation of Greek sculpture and his admiration of English youth: the artist, he says, had to compete with the beauty of nature itself 'in any passable representation of the Greek *discobolus*, as in any passable representation of an English cricketer'. Pater comes close to agreeing with Mr. Phoebus that the flannelled fool was the Greek ideal of youthful excellence; Pliny said that the sculptor Myron 'did not express the sensations of the mind', and this, Pater explains, was his especial merit: 'It is of the essence of the athletic prizeman, involved in the very ideal of the quoit-player, the cricketer, not to give expression to mind, in any antagonism to . . . the body; to mind as anything more than a function of the body, whose health-ful balance of functions it may so easily perturb;—to disavow that insidious enemy of the fairness of the bodily soul as such.'

But Pater also claims to detect in Myron's Discobolus a more surprising quality: 'The face of the young man, as you see him in the British Museum for instance, with fittingly inexpressive expression, (look into, look at the curves of, the blossom-like cavity of the opened mouth) is beautiful, but not altogether virile.' 'Look . . . look . . . the opened mouth'—this so seductive parenthesis is, for Pater, strangely unreserved. And Myron did not forget, we are told, that his subjects were 'animals, young animals, delighting . . . in free course through the yielding air.' The unwary reader would hardly guess that we know Myron's work only from stiff copies of a much later date. How does Pater know what Myron did or did not forget? He speaks of Myron's statues almost as though they represented schoolboys; but in fact the face of the Discobolus, so far as we can judge it from the copies, does not look particularly young. However, Pater is so drawn to these Greek youths that he wants to give them lives and personalities. The so-called Spinario may be one of the 'alert younger brethren' of the Discobolus; we are to admire his agility, his 'perfect *naïveté*'; and Pater can even tell us his age: he is in 'his sixteenth year, to which the somewhat lengthy or attenuated structure of the limbs is conformable'.

Arnold had said that the old pagan world never shows itself to us as sick or sorry.[107] Though Pater seemed to assent to this in his *Renaissance*, by the time he came to write 'The Age of Athletic Prizemen' he was no longer satisfied with so simple or so absolute a view. When we study the statues of Greek athletes, he concluded,

A certain melancholy (a *pagan* melancholy, it may be rightly called, even when we detect it in our English youth) is blent with the final impression we retain of them. . . . Assuredly they have no maladies of the soul any more than of the body. . . . But if they are not yet thinking, there is the capacity of thought, of painful thought, in them, as they seem to be aware wistfully.

He detects this quality above all in the Diadumenus of Polycleitus. Once again, this is a work known only through uninspired copies; Pater sees the ambiguous sensitivity of the original with the eye of faith. His description makes these sculpted youths sound oddly like the blank, melancholy women of Burne-Jones, and surely the resemblance is no accident. In the sentiments that went, as he thought, to the making of these statues he felt the attraction that others found in the story of Pygmalion. And here we can see a reason for the charm that the equivocal use of the word soul had for him: it creates a delightful appearance of paradox. These athletes are passive and pliable, they are soulless; and yet they are also full of life, of bodily soul. The sculptor holds them, he observed, in a marvellous balance between rest and motion.

Pygmalion's story had a happy ending; but from Pater the theme received a subtle and melancholy twist. Two themes, indeed, are blended: the statue just waking into life and the youth just waking into manhood. Like the lover on Keats's Grecian urn, caught at the fleeting instant that he moves his lips towards his beloved and held there forever, the Greek athlete is caught at a moment of transition, not yet thinking and feeling but soon to wake to the life of thought and emotion. But this life will not be for him, as for Pygmalion's statue, a joyous fulfilment, and the reason is surely that Pater makes the Greek sculptor look upon his subject with the same eye with which he looked himself upon English youth. The beauty of a child's ignorance of the soul's maladies, as of an adolescent's 'not altogether virile' face and figure, was intensified for Pater by its very evanescence. All around him in Oxford were young athletes turning into men, a transformation in which Pater could take no pleasure but which made the brief years preceding it the more precious.

Richard Livingstone was confident that an ancient Athenian would feel at home in Oxford or Cambridge, among 'a population mainly young, active, well-developed in body and mind'; he would appreciate the 'athletic grace' and 'easy condescension' of the upper-class undergraduates. 'Surely of Oxford and Cambridge,' Livingstone added, 'most of the Funeral Speech of Pericles is still *mutatis mutandis* true.' Taine had drawn a comparison less gratifying to English vanity: 'Education, on these terms, is not unlike that of the Spartans: it hardens the body and it tempers the character. But . . . it often produces (merely) sportsmen and louts.' Which was the truer comparison, Athens or Sparta? The hero of *Sinister Street* found in the young bloods of his school elements of both:

> Michael now became one of that group of happy immortals . . .
> whose attitudes of noble ease graced the hot-water pipes. . . .
> As a whole composition it was immutable, as permanent, as
> decorative . . . as the frieze of the Parthenon. . . . Michael
> idealized the heedless stupidity of these immortals into a
> Lacedaemonian rigour. . . . He accepted their unimaginative
> standards, their coarseness, their brutality as virtues, and in
> them he found the consummation of all that England should
> cherish.

Michael himself is neither coarse nor unimaginative: it takes a
clever man to idealize the Spartans. By the time he reaches Oxford
he can detect nice distinctions between the gods of different schools.

> Michael always admired the photographs of Pop [the Eton
> prefects], for they seemed to him to epitomise all the traditions
> of all the public-schools of England . . . with something of
> that immortality of captured action expressed by great Athenian
> sculpture. In comparison with Pop the Harrow Philathletic
> Society was a barbarous group, with all the self-consciousness
> of a deliberate archaism.[108]

Such distinctions were not wholly inept; the various public schools
differed considerably in outlook, and there was no single, monolithic
'public-school ideal'.

Pater elaborated the comparison between Sparta and the English
public school in his essay 'Lacedaemon', reprinted as the eighth
chapter of *Plato and Platonism*. Sparta was perhaps the most
gerontocratic of all Greek societies, and the members of its senate
were required to be over sixty years old. Pater was blithely unaware
of these awkward facts: 'In speaking of Lacedaemon,' he wrote,

> . . . it comes naturally to speak out of proportion, it might
> seem, of its youth, and of the education of its youth. . . .
> Lacedaemon was in truth before all things an organised place
> of discipline, an organised opportunity also, for youth, for the
> sort of youth that knew how to command by serving—a
> constant exhibition of youthful courage, youthful self-respect,
> yet above all of true youthful docility.

The adult Spartiate was as reserved as an upper-class Englishman,
and for the same reason:

> A young Lacedaemonian . . . of the privileged class left his
> home, his tender nurses in those large quiet old suburban

houses early, for a public school. . . . If a certain love of reserve
. . . characterised the Spartan citizen as such, it was perhaps
the cicatrice of that wrench from a soft home into the imperative,
inevitable gaze of his fellows.

The Spartans had fags and prefects: their education involved 'as
with ourselves, the government of youth by itself; an implicit
subordination of the younger to the older'. The boys were graded
by seniority into different ranks, marked by names which 'remain
as part of what we might call their "public-school slang" '. They
were toughened in a traditionally English way: 'No warm baths
allowed; a daily plunge in their river required.' Team spirit was
essential: youth committed itself 'absolutely, soul and body, to a
corporate sentiment in its very sports'. The mention of organized
games gave Pater an opportunity to compare these ancient Englishmen with those ancient Frenchmen, the Athenians; he described
'the "playing-fields", where Lacedaemonian youth . . . delighted
others rather than itself (no "shirking" was allowed) with a sort
of football . . ., rougher even than our own, *et même très dangereux*,
as our Attic neighbours, the French, say of the English game'. He
also added a more sinister touch, while still emphasizing the English
parallel: 'Whips and rods used in a kind of monitorial system by
themselves had a great part in the education of these young aristocrats, and, as pain must surely do, pain . . . as it were by dignified
rules of art, seem to have refined them.' Another French expression,
to which Pater does not refer, is 'le vice anglais'.

   Even the Helots, the Spartans' savagely oppressed serfs, were
brought by Pater into comparison with English life, or so it appears.
These wretched people, in his belief, 'enjoyed certainly that kind of
well-being which does come of organisation. . . . The very genius
of conservatism . . . secured, we may be sure, to this old-fashioned
country life something of the personal dignity, of the enjoyments
also, natural to it.' For example, they held 'somewhat livelier
religious feasts . . . than their lords allowed themselves', when
they broke out into 'boisterous plebeian mirth'. In other words,
they were like those admirable but gratifyingly deferential peasants
and workmen who throng the pages of Victorian novels, warming
the heart with their inarticulate enthusiasm and picturesque
servility. Maybe England was not really like this, but she ought
to have been, and had been before the conservative genius of country
life had begun to be weakened by the industrial revolution. Pater's
Sparta is an England idealized.

He noted that there were stories concerning the Helots 'full of a touching spirit of natural service . . . of an instinctively loyal admiration for the brilliant qualities of one trained perhaps to despise him, by which the servitor must have become, in his measure, actually a sharer in them.' This relationship between the young master and the loyal, admiring retainer takes us, again, into the world of the Victorian novel: Pater is describing Littimer and Steerforth, or Mark Tapley and Martin Chuzzlewit. And no doubt such relationships were common enough in Victorian life. We may question, though, whether they were a feature of ancient Sparta, where the ruling aristocracy lived in perpetual fear that the Helots would revolt, and used to murder the liveliest of them from time to time for the sake of security. In Pater's opinion, however, 'Just here . . . we see that slavish *ēthos*, the servile range of sentiment, which ought to accompany the condition of slavery, if it be indeed, as Aristotle supposes, one of the natural relationships between man and man idealized, or aesthetically right, pleasant and proper; the *aretē*, or "best possible condition", of the young servitor as such.' This judgement fails to be repellent only because Pater is so manifestly incapable of imagining what the condition of slavery is like; he cannot think except in aesthetic terms. What was the purpose of the Spartan method of education? According to Pater, 'An intelligent young Spartan might have replied, "To the end that I myself may be a perfect work of art, issuing thus into the eyes of all Greece".' Yeats was wiser: 'If you had asked an ancient Spartan what made Sparta Sparta, he would have answered, the Laws of Lycurgus.'[109] In reality the Spartan system was designed to stamp out all aesthetic inclinations, in this respect, perhaps, bearing some slight resemblance to the Victorian public school at its worst. Their education had a military purpose of the most ruthlessly practical kind; there is no modern society to compare with it, but if we must have an analogy, we should look to West Point rather than the elegant academy of Pater's imagining.

Cyril Connolly was to maintain that the glamour of the public schools cast such a spell over many boys that they never entirely grew up and remained throughout life in a state of permanent adolescence.[110] Pater would seem to be in unconscious agreement. 'If you enter into the spirit of Lacedaemonian youth,' he writes, 'you may conceive Lacedaemonian manhood for yourselves'; and in the last sentence of the essay he turns the whole of Sparta, adults as well, into an enormous public school: 'Like some of our old English places of education, though we might not care to live always

at school there, it is good to visit them on occasion.' His quiet
spirit, happy, too happy at the King's School, Canterbury, could
not conceive of the brutality and thuggery built into the Spartan
system. In this respect he is very different from the German
militarists and racial purists of our own century: they did see
Sparta in her true colours, and they liked what they saw. The Nazis
wanted to bend modern society into the shape of ancient Sparta,
whereas Pater only wanted to bend Sparta into the shape of an
idealized England.

'Another day-dream, you may say'—thus he begins his final
paragraph on Lacedaemon. Pater's Sparta is a fantasy, a picture
merely, or as he puts it himself, 'a spectacle, aesthetically, at least,
very interesting, like some perfect instrument shaping to what
they visibly were, the most beautiful of all people . . .' So keen
is his nostalgia for his own schooldays, passed in the shadow of a
great cathedral, that he even pictures his young Spartans in chapel,
more or less, dissolving them into a haze coloured by Judaeo-
Christian sentiment:

> We catch a glimpse, an echo, of their boys in school chanting;
> one of the things in old Greece one would have liked best to
> see and hear . . . a manifestation of the true . . . Hellenism, though
> it may make one think of the novices at school in some Gothic
> cloister, of our own old English schools, nay, of the young
> Lacedaemonian's cousins at Sion, singing there the law and its
> praises.

Pater does not want to be a Spartan; he only wants to observe
from a distance, to 'visit on occasion'. His portrait of the writer as,
in effect, a middle-aged gentleman loitering wistfully at the edge
of the playing fields is not altogether pleasing. Essentially it is a
less crude version of the literary voyeurism practised by Symonds,
in whose writings 'visit' is again the revelatory word. Symonds
says of Plato, for instance, 'With the *Lysis* and the *Charmides* . . .
we may revisit the haunts of the wrestlers and the runners . . .
fresh from the bath and crowned with violets, chaste, vigorous,
inured to rhythmic movements of the passions and the soul.' And
after describing the statues of athletes he writes, 'If we in England
seek some living echo of this melody of curving lines, we must
visit the water-meadows where boys bathe . . . or the playgrounds
of our public schools in summer, or the banks of the Isis when the
eights are on the water.' In fact, Symonds turns all Greece into a
fantasy of compliant, innocent youth, submitting itself passively to

the writer's salacious gaze: 'Like a young man come from the wrestling-ground, anointed, chapleted, and very calm'—and naked, of course—'the Genius of the Greeks appears before us. Upon his soul there is no burden of the world's pain . . . nor has he yet felt sin. The pride and strength of adolescence are his—audacity and endurance, . . . the alternations of sublime repose and boyish noise, grace, pliancy, . . . the frank enjoyment of the open air, free merriment, and melancholy well beloved.'[111] Words such as 'frank' and 'merry', so much a part of the Victorian school story, show us that we are not really in ancient Greece. The jolly, athletic boys at the schools in the *Gem* and the *Magnet* included Tom Merry and Frank Nugent.

The test of the discipline and team spirit supposedly inculcated by English schools came in the First World War. Comparison with the Spartans seemed inevitable to Private Stephen Graham, and though his rhetoric is a debased version of Pater's manner, a certain sincerity may perhaps be glimpsed through the fog of literary artifice:

> The Spartans were not vulgar. We, alas, were excessively vulgar. In much, however, we were like the Spartans, and we were like them . . . in battle, where we did not yield. But in much also we were unlike. We did not run in our nakedness, and our eyes were not pure for women. We had not those beautiful Greek bodies, but bodies made ugly with clothes and care. And we had sins, sins, sins upon our brains. . . . All manner of things could be said . . . against us, but one positive thing redeems the rest . . . it was seen that we knew how to die, and that it was ever the same humanity that went down in the evening in France and Belgium as went down in the morning at Thermopylae.

The War turned the thoughts of Proust's sodomitical Baron de Charlus in the same direction: 'Those English soldiers whom at the beginning I . . . dismissed as mere players of football . . . well, . . . they are quite simply Greek athletes . . . they are the young men of Plato, or rather they are Spartiates.'[112] Like Taine, he associates English sportiness with Sparta, but without Taine's reservations. The compliment comes from a peculiar source, but it is a compliment none the less.

X

PLATO

For the past thirty years Karl Popper has dominated the approach to Plato. He took the final decision to write *The Open Society and Its Enemies* upon hearing that Hitler had invaded his native Austria,[1] and conceived it with the zeal of an evangelist, as a blow in the struggle against the totalitarianisms of both left and right; the second volume dealt with Hegel and Marx, but the first was wholly devoted to Plato, for here, Popper believed, was the fountainhead from which all ideologies of oppression flowed. Popper's attack stung Plato's apologists into anxious activity, but whether right or wrong, he has established the terms in which the debate is conducted. Since the war Plato's liberal friends (a diminished band) have been kept so busy trying to show that he was neither a fascist hyena nor a bolshevik beast that they have remained on the defensive. Yet a hundred years before Plato had been triumphant, a master to whom poets, churchmen, philosophers and statesmen all acknowledged their debt.

'Every man,' Coleridge remarked, 'is born an Aristotelian, or a Platonist. . . . They are the two classes of men, beside which it is next to impossible to conceive a third.'[2] This observation seems to emanate from a too simple world in which men supposed

> That every boy and every gal
> That's born into the world alive
> Is either a little Liberal
> Or else a little Conservative!

Although Plato and Aristotle might more accurately be ranged in the same camp against the materialist philosophy of Epicurus, their names have become symbols for opposite tendencies between which men, ideas, even periods of history are believed to oscillate; and in the nineteenth century many people felt that a vast vague web of Platonism encompassed them. Pater described the 'rude countryman' as 'an unconscious Platonist'; Emerson recalled lending a volume of Plato to a farmer, who returned it with the comment, 'That man has a good many of my idees.'[3] The poetry of the Romantics trails big, misty clouds of Platonic glory. 'Beauty is truth, truth beauty,' Keats wrote, distantly echoing the *Symposium*. Wordsworth's *Immortality Ode* is bathed in more or less Platonist sentiment, though Mill indignantly insisted that it was 'falsely called Platonic'.[4] The last scene of *Faust*, that sacred text, concludes with a Mystic Chorus chanting in resplendently oracular language the Platonist doctrine that all transient things are merely appearances. Inevitably, though, Goethe bends Plato in a less abstract direction: it is not dialectic that leads us on but the Eternal Feminine. But Plato's influence was far more than an airy diffusion of poetical sentiment. After two centuries of neglect, he was rediscovered in the late eighteenth century. At this time Thomas Taylor began translating him, indefatigably and inaccurately, but Shelley and his friends were perhaps the first for whom Plato once more became an inspiration and a passion. They found that their enthusiasm was not shared by scholars. Plato began exciting interest at Cambridge in the 1820s. He did not appear on the syllabus at Oxford until 1847; twenty years later he dominated it.

We are all Greeks—but above all in philosophy. The Romans gave us the basis of our legal systems, the Jews our religion; and though our literature owes so huge a debt to the Greeks, there would have been poetry and plays of a kind in Europe, and perhaps even history, if they had never existed. But all the speculative thought of the West is dependent on a revolution which began in a few towns on the coast of Asia Minor towards the end of the seventh century B.C. and culminated in Athens some two or three hundred years later. As Mill said, 'Few will doubt, that had there been no Socrates, no Plato, and no Aristotle, there would have been no philosophy for the next two thousand years, nor in all probability then.'[5] Of the three it is Aristotle who in most ages has been held to be the 'master of them that know'; but in the later eighteenth century he was beginning to fall into disfavour. He was in disgrace with the Romantics for establishing (as they believed) the rules of the French classical drama. And in general he was too down to earth; the spirit of the age craved something more transcendental. Coleridge preferred Plato for reasons which, some may think, reflect the more credit upon Aristotle: 'Plato . . . leads you to see that propositions involving . . . contradictory conceptions are nevertheless true; and which, therefore, must belong to a higher logic—that of ideas. They are contradictory only in the Aristotelian logic, which is the instrument of the understanding.'[6] However, Coleridge still regarded Aristotle with deep admiration; later in the century he was to be treated with scanter respect.

'Aristotle is dead,' said Jowett, 'but Plato is alive.'[7] This was an exaggeration: there will always be those to whose temper Aristotle is more congenial, and he is not likely to be altogether neglected as long as men care about rational thought at all. Thomas Arnold loved him, and 'spoke of him as of one intimately and affectionately known by him'.[8] But in this as in other ways Arnold was essentially not a Victorian but a man of the Regency. Newman, too, had a great respect for the Stagyrite. *The Idea of a University* is Platonist by intention and even by title; yet Newman wrote in it, 'While the world lasts, will Aristotle's doctrine on these matters last, for he is the oracle of . . . truth. . . . In many subject-matters, to think correctly, is to think like Aristotle.'[9] But even as he spoke them, his words had a dated ring.

Aristotle had to compete not only with a rival philosopher but with a hero. Who was Socrates? asked an Italian peasant; Symonds answered that he was the Jesus Christ of Greece.[10] Here was an analogy which all could understand; yet such great men as Rousseau and Shelley had sanctioned it.[11] The comparison was one which even a Christian might in a manner accept, for as Coleridge explained, the profound effect of Socrates' death drew Plato and others to reflections that 'excited an anticipation of some clearer knowledge which doubtless prepared greatly for the reception of Christianity'.[12] Bishop Thirlwall refused to meet the distinguished archaeologist Forchhammer, saying, 'No! I will never receive . . . the man who justified the death of Socrates.'[13] But Socrates' greatest merit was to be a martyr whom agnostics could claim for their own. Byron called him 'The earth's perfection of all mental beauty, And personification of all virtue.' He also compared the 'title of Blasphemer' with those of Radical, Jacobin and Reformer, adding, 'Socrates and Jesus Christ were put to death publicly as *blasphemers*, and so . . . may be any who dare to oppose . . . abuses of the name of God and the mind of man.'[14] This picture of Socrates descends from the Enlightenment: Condorcet had called his execution the first crime in the war between philosophy and superstition; Hume praised him not only for his serenity and contempt of riches but also for 'his magnanimous care of preserving liberty'.[15] These accounts made him into an eighteenth-century rationalist, progressive in politics and sceptical in religion, and prepared the way for the next century to see Plato as a liberal reformer. In fact he was a devout, even superstitious man, who prayed to Pan and listened to the promptings of his guardian spirit. Moreover, his circle was noted for its aristocratic tendencies and admiration of Sparta; it was a democracy that put him to death.

But through his death he could command the heart's allegiance. When Cory learned of the Emperor Maximilian's execution, his thoughts turned naturally to another martyr who had refused to escape from his prison: 'Socrates was lifted up against the fear of death when he thought of Achilles. . . . And Prince Max . . . would not take his life when he might have got away, for his faithful followers were to die.'[16] Matthew Arnold made the inspiration of Socrates' personality into a kind of Holy Spirit: 'Socrates . . . is dead; but in his own breast does not every man carry . . . a possible Socrates, in [the] power of disinterested play of consciousness upon his stock notions. . . .'[17] The men of the Enlightenment had taken to Socrates because they found in him a combination of personal sanctity with the temper that delights to question received ideas. Something of this feeling survives in Arnold. He was appalled to think that Faraday could be 'a great natural philosopher with one side of his being and a Sandemanian with the other'; to Archimedes, he said, this would have been impossible.[18] In fact, we know nothing about the religious beliefs of Archimedes, but Arnold tended to the blithe assumption that an agnostic reasonableness was common to all the best Greeks. Herein lay the charm of Socrates to the doubter: contemplating his life, one could have religious emotion without the religion, whereas with Christianity the flow of noble sentiment was clogged by stubborn lumps of dogma and the unyielding claims of revelation.

Mill affords the most moving example of devotion to Socrates. To his contemporaries he often seemed a desiccated and joyless person, but his writings suggest that by nature he had rich capacities for enthusiasm and affection. These were grievously bruised by his father's grim system of education, which made huge demands upon the child's mental energies and left no space for romance or fantasy. There were no soldiers or explorers for him to feed his imagination upon; but the boy still longed for heroes. Admirably and pathetically he developed a reverence for the 'heroes of philosophy': 'The same inspiring effect which so many of the benefactors of mankind . . .

experienced from Plutarch's *Lives* was produced on me by Plato's pictures of Socrates.'[19] Mill never outgrew this early hero-worship; throughout his life, whenever he wrote of Socrates, his cool prose was suffused with feeling. In the course of a dry review of Grote he suddenly described Socrates as a sort of saviour, 'a man unique in history, of a kind at all times needful, and seldom more needed than now';[20] and in his essay *On Liberty* he paid his hero an eloquent tribute: 'Mankind can hardly be too often reminded, that there was once a man named Socrates. . . . This acknowledged master of all the eminent thinkers who have since lived—whose fame . . . all but outweighs the whole remainder of the names which make his native city illustrious—was put to death . . . for impiety and immorality . . . the tribunal . . . found him guilty, and condemned the man who probably of all then born had deserved the best of mankind to be put to death as a criminal. Mill then passes to the crucifixion, 'the only other instance of judicial iniquity, the mention of which . . . would not be an anti-climax'. A few pages later he returns to Socrates, again in association with Christianity: 'Socrates was put to death, but Socratic philosophy rose like the sun in heaven, and spread its illumination over the whole intellectual firmament. Christians were cast to the lions, but the Christian church grew up a stately . . . tree.' James Mill had persuaded his son that Christianity was false, but he could not entirely stifle in him the religious emotions; these sought an outlet, and found it in Socrates.

The first utilitarians were hostile to Plato, but their criticisms did him a service by making him seem important and rousing his admirers to defend him. Bentham wrote, 'While Xenophon was writing history, and Euclid giving instruction in geometry, Socrates and Plato were talking nonsense under pretence of teaching wisdom and morality. This morality of theirs consisted in words; this wisdom of theirs was the denial of matters known to every man's experience.'[21] Bentham had a serious point, by no means easy to answer, but his baldly self-confident manner of putting it might almost have been calculated to provoke itchy disagreement. 'From the moment of reading that,' wrote Matthew Arnold, 'I am delivered from the bondage of Bentham! . . . I feel the inadequacy of his mind and ideas for supplying the rule of human society.' Mill observed sadly that Bentham had spoken of Socrates and Plato 'in terms distressing to his greatest admirers'.[22]

Bentham's criticism was broadened by Macaulay to include the whole of Greek philosophy.[23] 'Assuredly,' he wrote, 'if the tree which Socrates planted and Plato watered is to be judged by its

flowers and leaves, it is the noblest of trees.' But it bore no fruit.
To stress the contrast between ancient thought and the useful
philosophy of Bacon, Macaulay chose Plato, because he did more
than anyone 'towards giving to the minds of speculative men that
bent which they retained till they received from Bacon a new
impulse'. Did Plato approve of the invention of writing? No.
Astronomy? Yes, but merely to aid the contemplative process of the
pure intellect. Medicine? Yes again, but only 'to cure the occasional
distemper of men whose constitutions are good. As to those who
have bad constitutions, let them die.' Thanks to these attitudes,
Macaulay argued, the schools of Athens achieved nothing in a
thousand years, whereas the followers of Bacon had lengthened life,
extinguished diseases, and so on: Plato's aim was to exalt man
into a god, Bacon's to provide him 'with what he requires while he
continues to be man . . . the former aim was noble; but the latter
was attainable. Plato drew a good bow; but . . . he aimed at the
stars. . . . His arrow was indeed followed by a track of dazzling
radiance, but it struck nothing.' The essay dates from 1837 and
the tone is different from Bentham's. Ignoring Aristotle, Macaulay
is at pains to stress his admiration for Plato, taking him for the
type and pattern of a Greek thinker, the master of all other
philosophers for nearly two thousand years. Yet despite this,
nothing that he wrote earned him more lasting distrust, and it led
Matthew Arnold to regard him as the paradigm of a Philistine.

In criticizing Plato according to the principle of utility the Whig
Macaulay was borrowing the clothes of the philosophic radicals.
But by this time the radicals themselves were already abandoning
the attack on Plato, and the most eminent of the utilitarians was to
declare himself Plato's disciple. Naturally Mill could not silence the
'hard fact' men for ever; at the end of the century Spencer returned
to the attack. In his autobiography he expressed irritation at the
feebleness of Plato's mind: 'Time after time I have attempted to
read, now this dialogue and now that, and have put it down in a
state of impatience with the indefiniteness of the thinking and the
mistaking of words for things: being repelled also by the rambling
form of the argument.'[24] Having dismissed their philosophical
content, he had tried to contemplate them as works of art, 'and put
them aside in greater exasperation than before . . . there is more
dramatic propriety in the conversations of a third-rate novelist; . . .
Rameau's Nephew has more strokes of dramatic truth than all the
Platonic dialogues put together.' However, he would not wish to
exaggerate: 'Still, quotations . . . lead me to think that there are

in Plato detached thoughts from which I might benefit had I the
patience to seek them out.' And he adds broad-mindedly, 'The like
is probably true of other ancient writings.' Carlyle called him 'the
most immeasurable ass in Christendom'; on this occasion he justified
the title. In fact the significance of Spencer's attack lies precisely in
its weakness: at this time the only criticisms of Plato were coming
from those who had not seriously tried to understand him; not
until he was assailed by an opponent who really admired and feared
him would he be toppled from his throne.

James Mill was a radical, but this did not lead him to reject the
lessons of Greece. Quite the contrary; it was his very radicalism
that turned him back to antiquity, for as his son explained, he
'regarded as an aberration of the moral standard of modern times,
compared with that of the ancients, the great stress laid upon
feeling';[25] the Greek philosophers were actually better guides than
any contemporary. In his approval of repression James Mill
anticipated a notoriously Victorian characteristic; if this were the
lesson the Greeks taught, the passage of time could only increase
their importance. He was reacting against those other Hellenists,
the Romantics with their Byronic exaltation of the emotions; it was
the achievement of the Greeks, and above all of Plato, to captivate
two such different classes of men.

'Must I care about Aristotle?' Shelley demanded of his Oxford
tutor, 'What if I do not mind Aristotle?'[26] The dons of University
College saw that the young man was a trouble maker, and when he
wrote *The Necessity of Atheism*, they sent him down. Part of Plato's
appeal to the new generation was no doubt simply that of novelty;
Oxford was the citadel of Toryism, and Aristotle was her philosopher.
But Shelley's devotion had little to do with fashion; it was both
idiosyncratic and profound. He had first come across Plato in his
schooldays, when a physician from Windsor introduced him to the
Symposium.[27] This was the turning point of his life; he tried to
become Plato's disciple, even adopting the strange doctrine of
anamnesis, according to which every human being retains memories
of a previous existence before his birth. T. J. Hogg described how
Shelley would pace about the room, shaking his long locks and
discoursing in solemn tones about man's previous condition; 'Every
true Platonist, he used to say, must be a lover of children, for they
are our . . . instructors in philosophy.' Hogg also relates how he
once saw Shelley snatch a baby from its mother on Magdalen Bridge
and demand that it inform him about pre-existence: 'Surely the
babe can speak if he will, for he is only a few weeks old . . . he

cannot have forgotten entirely the use of speech in so short a time.'
The story would be of profound significance, if there were the least
likelihood of its being true.[28]

Shelley first encountered Plato in translation; to read the original,
he had to work hard at his Greek. But the effort was worth while,
and excitement reverberates through his letters: 'Plato and Calderon
have been my gods'—'I read . . . Plato perpetually'—'I read Plato
for ever.'[29] Not even the glories of Italy could distract him; at
Bagni di Lucca he spent his time translating the *Symposium* and
reading the other dialogues. At Lerici he relaxed by boating, but
Plato came boating with him. He held the tiller in one hand and a
volume of his favourite author in the other, and became so absorbed
in the book that the mainsheet jammed and the boat went out of
control.[30] Two months later he was dead, drowned in a squall off
the Italian coast. When Disraeli portrayed him as 'Marmion
Herbert' in *Venetia*, he toyed with the idea that Plato had killed
him: 'The sea had washed upon the beach another corpse . . . he
had made no struggle to save himself, for his hand was locked in
his waistcoat, where . . . he had thrust the *Phaedo*, showing that
he had been reading to the last, and was meditating on immortality
when he died.'[31] Fiction is tidier than life: Disraeli has Lord Cadurcis
(evidently Byron) drowned in the same storm. Yet the truth is
hardly less romantic, for Byron did perish for the love of Greece.
Moreover, the two poets were together at Pisa in the last year of
Shelley's life; Byron never left his bed before midday, while Shelley
rose at six or seven to read Plato and Sophocles.[32] These two regimes
symbolize the difference between the Hellenism of the two men:
Byron's passion was for the land of Greece, not its literature; Shelley
had never seen Greece with his eyes, but he dwelt there in his
imagination.

At first sight it may seem strange that Plato has so often been a
source of artistic inspiration: the material upon which most writers
work is the world as perceived by the senses, but Plato regarded
this world as illusion, the pale imitation of a reality which transcends
anything that the senses can apprehend; and he expelled the poets
from his ideal state. However, this expulsion was a profound
compliment. Shelley said that poets are the unacknowledged legis-
lators of the world, and Plato is one of the few philosophers who
might have agreed; he at least believed that poetry was important
and dangerous, and poets, like most men, would rather be feared
than ignored. And besides, those who have most intensely enjoyed
the sensuous beauties of the world have often taken a paradoxical

delight in the belief that these beauties are nothing but appearance, and mere shadow of a higher reality. As F. H. Bradley explained,

> That the glory of this world . . . is appearance leaves the world more glorious, if we feel it is a show of some fuller splendour; but the sensuous certain is . . . a cheat, if it hides some colourless movement of atoms, some spectral woof of impalpable abstractions. . . . Though dragged to such conclusions, we can not embrace them. Our principles may be true, but they are not reality. They no more *make* that Whole which commands our devotion, than some shredded dissection of human tatters *is* that warm and breathing beauty of flesh which our hearts found delightful.[33]

Or as Shelley put it, 'I always seek in what I see the manifestation of something beyond the . . . tangible object.'[34] The beauties of nature could come to seem all the more evocative by reason of their very unreality:[35]

> the Earth and Ocean seem
> To sleep in one another's arms, and dream
> Of waves, flowers, clouds, woods, rocks, and all that we
> Read in their smiles, and call reality.

To Wordsworth's benighted Peter Bell a primrose by the river's brim was a yellow primrose, and nothing more. What more could it be? Perhaps Plato had the answer.

Shelley had the gift of borrowing Plato's metaphors and yet adapting them to produce something personal and distinctive. In *Mont Blanc* he addresses the River Arve, heard at the bottom of its ravine but not seen, thus symbolizing that reality of which the sensible world offers only an echo or reflection. The mind finds its way to the 'cave of the witch Poesy',[36]

> Seeking among the shadows that pass by
> Ghosts of all things that are, some shade of thee,
> Some phantom, some faint image . . .

The metaphor of river and ravine is Shelley's own, but the rest of the imagery derives from his master. Plato compares those whose apprehensions of the world are derived from the opinions of others (and he includes poetry among such 'opinions') to prisoners chained in a cave.[37] There is a fire behind them, and a sort of marionette show; they see the shadows of the marionettes on the wall outlined against the firelight, and these in their ignorance they take to be reality. This complex parable forms part of Plato's attack upon art, but Shelley makes it the material for art; he seems to accept Plato's verdict, but in the very limitations of poetry he finds something poetic. Poetry is dim and shadowy, but therefore mysterious, magical, faintly sinister perhaps—a witch. Maybe poetry can do no more than present ghostly images of the real world; but if its beauties are just phantoms, how much more glorious must the reality be. Thus Plato's dismissal of poetry enables Shelley to use poetry to celebrate the physical world, to praise by comparison with his own weak verse the majesty of the Alps.

In the Myth of Er the universe is described as a series of concentric whorls, resembling vessels that fit into one another and coloured in various hues.[38] Out of Plato's strange cosmology Shelley created this:[39]

> The One remains, the many change and pass;
> Heaven's light for ever shines, Earth's shadows fly;
> Life, like a dome of many-coloured glass,
> Stains the white radiance of Eternity,
> Until Death tramples it to fragments.

Plato did not deny all merit to the beauties perceived by our senses, but he insisted that they were nothing compared to the beauty of the true reality. Shelley's imagery superbly preserves this conception: the rich diversity of the world is marvellously beautiful, and yet it stains the simplicity and dims the radiance of the One.

The resurrection of the dead shepherd is a feature of many pastoral elegies; in *Adonais* Shelley brilliantly perceived that Plato's doctrine that the body is a tomb or prison, an encumbrance by which the soul is obstructed until released by death, could take the place of this theme. He combines it first with an idea that is more truly Stoic than Platonic:[40]

> Dust to the dust! but the pure spirit shall flow
> Back to the burning fountain whence it came,
> A portion of the Eternal, which must glow
> Through time and change, unquenchably the same.

Then he recalls the doctrine that the sensible world is only an imitation of the world of Forms:[41]

Peace, peace! He is not dead, he doth not sleep—
He hath awakened from the dream of life—
'Tis we, who lost in stormy visions, keep
With phantoms and unprofitable strife . . .
We decay
Like corpses in a charnel . . .

Shelley had no belief in a personal immortality, but with Plato's aid he could represent the death of Keats as a kind of triumph:[42]

He has outsoared the shadow of our night . . .
He lives, he wakes—'tis Death is dead, not he . . .
He is a portion of the loveliness
Which once he made more lovely . . .

He also translated two of the epigrams attributed to Plato himself, including the most famous:

Thou wert the morning star among the living,
Ere thy fair light had fled;—
Now, having died, thou art as Hesperus, giving
New splendour to the dead.

By echoing these verses in the last two lines of *Adonais* he reminds himself that Plato, like Keats, had been a poet:

The soul of Adonais, like a star,
Beacons from the abode where the Eternal are.

Plato has attracted many poets, and with reason; but it was chance that one of the great Romantics should have had such a particular devotion to him. This chance had important consequences: Shelley had remarkable success in putting Platonic conceptions into verse; later in the century this encouraged men like Pater and Wilde, knowing that Plato had been a poet before turning to philosophy, to believe that his doctrines were naturally 'poetic'; they came to think of Plato as the Shelley of the ancient world. But this was a misleading notion. Swinburne's comment—'His scholarship was that of a clever but idle boy in the upper forms of a public school'[43]—was more a compliment to the Victorian public school than a condemnation of Shelley, but the fact remains that Shelley's understanding of his idol was very imperfect. When he explored Plato, he was venturing across uncharted seas; it was largely his enthusiasm and that of his contemporaries that encouraged the more exact study which enabled Swinburne's generation to belittle them. But in any case, a poet was a taste for grand philosophical ideas is a very different creature from a philosopher with a capacity for poetic expression. Shelley knew Plato well enough to realize how far he fell short of his master's ideal: using the conception of the soul imprisoned in the body, he wrote, 'I think one is always in love with something or other; the error, and I confess it is not easy for spirits cased in flesh and blood to avoid it, consists in seeking in a mortal image the likeness of what is perhaps eternal.'[44] He indulged this error in *Epipsychidion*, which he wrote with the somewhat ignoble aim of persuading himself that he could properly love Emilia Viviani and his wife at the same time. In the *Symposium* Plato had described how the erotic impulses could be directed to the perception of truth: a man should begin by loving one beautiful youth, then instead of loving one beautiful body he should love many, then he should love beautiful minds, then the beauty of laws and of sciences, and so on, ever generalizing his emotions until he attains to a vision of the supreme beauty and truth. Shelley takes the first stage of this process, forgets the rest, and presents Plato's scheme as a defence of free love:[45]

> I never was attached to that great sect,
> Whose doctrine is, that each one should select
> Out of the crowd a mistress or friend,
> And all the rest, though fair and wise, commend
> To cold oblivion, though it is in the code
> Of modern morals . . .

We can hear the scorn in that word 'modern': how much better they ordered things in Greece. But in reality Plato's teaching is not at all an invitation to promiscuity; on the contrary, physical desire is a crude emotion from which the philosopher must free himself. Shelley recalls Plato's account of the relation between body and soul again and again in this poem. His beloved is

> An image of some bright Eternity;
> A shadow of some golden dream . . .

>   the brightness
> Of her divinest presence trembles through
> Her limbs . . .[46]

He declares that his Emilia's form is only the mortal case of an immortal spirit, but uses this doctrine to make her physical loveliness appear the more lovely; he has used Platonism to produce almost the antithesis of Plato's original theory.

The nature of the dialogues is such that it is always hard to be sure of having grasped Plato's considered view. They depict Socrates as a master of irony; and we know too that Plato's own beliefs altered considerably in the course of his life. However, the very fact that he was so hard to pin down helped his popularity: whereas Aristotle restricted his appeal by an unyielding directness, there was something for everyone in Plato. Besides, even if one were bored by philosophy, there was such literary charm in the dialogues; when Spencer called them inferior to a third-rate English novel, he was reacting with irritation to a commonplace. Macaulay thought Plato excelled even Cervantes in the art of solemn ridicule; Jowett discerned in the Myth of Er 'touches of nature such as Defoe might have introduced'; Cory considered the *Phaedo* to be 'the one ancient book that gives one sweet pains as a fine novel or poem of our times does', and added, 'I have now been through it twice with high-minded women.'[47] Plato had made philosophy humane and even entertaining; indeed, there seems to be a touch of him even in *Alice Through the Looking-Glass*. The fluent but dubious etymologies of that notable linguistic philosopher Humpty-Dumpty (' "*Slithy*" means "lithe and slimy" . . . it's like a portmanteau—there are two meanings packed up into one word.') appears to derive from the satirical philosophy of Socrates in the *Cratylus*: 'Apollo may rightly be called *Apolouōn* (purifier); or . . . he may most fitly be called *Haplos*, from *haplous* (sincere) . . .; also he is *aei ballōn* (always shooting), because he is a master archer. . . .'[48] Socrates is more modest than Humpty-Dumpty; otherwise the two have much in common.

In 1853 Macaulay determined to read through Plato again. With formidable energy he devoured dialogue after dialogue; it comes as a relief to discover that when he had finished all but three, he was diverted by the novels of Eugène Sue.[49] He was as thrilled by Plato at Tunbridge Wells as he had been by the Attic dramatists in India. He followed the debate in the *Gorgias* with the vociferous partisanship of a spectator at a football match, scrawling on his text, 'Polus is much in the right—You have made a blunder, Socrates will have you. . . .—There you are in the Sophist's net.' To Macaulay Plato was above all an artist: 'The childish quibbling of Socrates provokes me . . . I am . . . convinced that the merit of Plato lies in his talent for narrative . . . in his humour, and in his exquisite Greek.'[50] These remarks betray a limitation. In Plato's earlier dialogues the method of Socrates is eristic: he begins by asking about an abstract quality— what is courage? or holiness?—, knocks down other people's definitions, and offers none himself. Now these dialogues are not just displays of debating technique: Socrates and Plato believed that men must truly understand the meaning of moral concepts before they can act rightly; they also knew how hard such understanding is to come by. Socrates wanted to expose the tangle of vagueness and contradiction surrounding most people's moral beliefs; only when this had been cleared away could one hope to advance to a better comprehension. Macaulay might reasonably have argued that the eristic method was an inefficient way of presenting philosophical ideas; but in fact he failed to realize that the eristic method has a philosophical purpose at all. Mill suspected him of lacking 'perception of truth' and 'a genuine love of the True and the Beautiful'.[51] Characteristically, the terms in which he expressed his suspicion were Platonist.

Macaulay attributed to Socrates 'a meek maliciousness' and a command of temper which was 'more provoking than noisy triumph'. Perhaps he revealed the source of his annoyance when he complained that Socrates 'had an ill-natured pleasure in making men,— particularly men famed for wisdom and eloquence,—look like fools'.[52] Surely he was thinking subconsciously of himself: at that time what man was more famed for eloquence than Macaulay? So his testiness was a tribute to Plato's art: his imagination was transported back to Athens with such vividness that he felt himself to be Socrates' victim. 'I think,' he wrote, 'that, if I had been in the place of Polus, Socrates would hardly have had so easy a job of it.'[53] In the *Euthydemus* Socrates mockingly describes the 'amphibious' men who divide their time between philosophy and politics; such people think themselves the wisest of men, though they are in truth inferior to both philosophers and politicians. When Macaulay read the dialogue in India, he protested in the margin that Socrates was deriding the pleasantest and noblest way of life. A page later this student of Plato reminds himself that he is a politician as well, writing beneath the last line of the dialogue, 'Yesterday the London News . . . arrived by steamer from Bombay. Peel beaten in two divisions.'[54] But in the end Socrates won him over: it was impossible, he decided, to read the *Apology* without feeling strengthened in mind, or the end of the *Phaedo* without tears. And below the last words of the *Crito* he wrote, 'When we

consider . . . the revolution which he produced in men's notions
of good and evil, we must pronounce him one of the greatest men
that ever lived.'[55]

Mill pronounced Plato 'the greatest moralist of Antiquity', and
went on to draw a comparison which Macaulay did not venture:
'Christ did not argue about virtue, but commanded it; Plato, when
he argues about it, argues for the most part inconclusively, but he
resembles Christ in the love which he inspires for it, and in the
stern resolution never to swerve from it.'[56] The analogy was not
new; for instance, Shelley had represented Christ appealing to his
Father 'by Plato's sacred light, Of which my spirit was a burning
morrow'.[57] Shelley was hostile to Christianity in every form known
to him; but many agnostics in the nineteenth century, far from
despising religion, envied the Christians their faith and sought a
secular substitute. Explaining the zeal of his youthful Benthamism,
Mill wrote, 'I now had opinions; a creed, a doctrine, a philosophy;
in one among the best senses of the word, a religion.'[58] And in his
autobiography he still maintained that the best unbelievers 'are
more genuinely religious, in the best sense of the word religion,
than those who exclusively arrogate to themselves the title'.[59] This
woolly nonsense is remarkable in so clear-sighted a man, and revealing: so eager was he to claim for himself a share in 'religion' that
he was prepared to reduce the word to meaninglessness. He even
claimed that unbelievers had a sort of deity: 'They have that which
constitutes the principal worth of all religions whatever, an ideal
conception of a Perfect Being,'—note the capital letters—'to which
they habitually refer as the guide of their conscience.' For an agnostic
of such a kind Greek philosophy held an especial attraction: Plato
undoubtedly believed in a single supreme deity, but one who seems
to be an impersonal, abstract being about whom there is curiously
little to say. A modern Platonist might plausibly claim that he
possessed some such 'ideal conception'.

In this part of his autobiography Mill certainly had the Greeks
in mind, for he began his next paragraph, 'My father's moral
convictions, wholly dissevered from religion, were very much of
the character of those of the Greek philosophers.' The son believed
that Greek ideas could still help Englishmen to learn how to live:
' "Pagan self-assertion" is one of the elements of human worth,
as well as "Christian self-denial". There is a Greek ideal of self-
development, which the Platonic and Christian ideal of self-govern-
ment blends with, but does not supersede. It may be better to be a
John Knox than an Alcibiades, but it is better to be a Pericles than

either; nor would a Pericles, if we had one in these days, be without anything good which belonged to John Knox.'[60]

Plato, on this account, did not advocate 'self-assertion'; so the reason for Mill's feeling towards him must be sought elsewhere. 'I have ever felt,' he wrote, '. . . that the title of Platonist belongs by far better right to those who have been nourished in, and have endeavoured to practice Plato's mode of investigation, than to those who are distinguished only by the adoption of certain dogmatical conclusions, drawn mostly from the less intelligible of his works.'[61] This is the sort of language with which the man in the street claims to be 'more Christian' than many regular churchgoers; the language in which Mill himself asserted that the best unbelievers are more 'religious' than their Christian counterparts. Since Socrates was his saviour, Plato's dialogues were his scriptures; Socrates and Plato even appear, incongruously enough, in the very first paragraph of his *Utilitarianism*. Though he differed from Plato in his beliefs on almost everything from ontology to political systems (his theory of number, in particular, is the most anti-Platonist ever devised), he could nevertheless write, 'I have ever felt myself, beyond any modern that I know of . . ., a pupil of Plato, and cast in the mould of his dialectics.'[62] This is the expression less of reason than of faith.

'I used to pray so much,' says Dorothea Brooke in *Middlemarch* '—now I hardly ever pray.'[63] To a former evangelical like Dorothea such a change could only mean that she had lost her faith, but George Eliot will not allow this to be so. Even in earlier days Dorothea's aim had been vaguely Platonist: 'The reaching forward of the whole consciousness towards the fullest truth, the least partial good.' Now she asks Ladislaw, 'What of your religion? I mean—not what you know about religion, but the belief that helps you most?' And he replies, 'To love what is good and beautiful when I see it.'[64] Once again the Platonist language helps to paper over the virtual meaninglessness to which the word 'religion' is reduced. Like Mill, Dorothea—or rather George Eliot—can reject Christianity but not the aura that accompanies it. Beatrice Webb was to bear some slight resemblance to Dorothea. Her autobiography describes how she lapsed from childhood Christianity into a 'dreary materialism'; but after a year studying Plato she developed a kind of religious agnosticism, and even took Holy Communion in a spirit of rationalist piety.[65]

Christians were often eager to join with unbelievers in revering Plato, and sometimes they attributed to him a place in the divine scheme not unlike that of Isaiah or Ezekiel. Such views were not restricted to suspected heretics like Jowett; the saintly and orthodox Westcott argued, 'Plato is an unconscious prophet of the Gospel. The Life of Christ is . . . the Divine reality of which the Myths were an instructive foreshadowing.'[66] Since many of the Hebrew prophets were similarly 'unconscious', as Westcott well knew, this is a substantial claim. Theologians appreciated that Plato had influenced the Fathers and recognized the Platonist element in St. John's account of the incarnation; these verses form the gospel for Christmas Day, and some Tractarians introduced the custom of reading them every Sunday at the end of mass. In the chapel of Mansfield College, a Congregational foundation in Oxford, a stained-glass window depicts two bearded figures, similar in feature; one is Amos, the other Plato.

A medieval legend told that St. Paul had wept at the tomb of Virgil, saying, 'How great a Christian I would have made you, had I found you alive'; Cory ended an undergraduate prize poem on Plato in the same vein:

> Then what a gain were thine to take that yoke,
> To learn the words a Christian weakling spoke,
> To weep for sin, and sue for grace, and bring
> To God thy reason, as an offering.

Some years earlier Thomas Arnold had declared, 'Not the wildest extravagance of atheistic wickedness in modern times can go further than the sophists of Greece went . . .: whatever audacity can dare . . . to make the words "good" and "evil" change their meaning, has been already tried in the days of Plato, and by his eloquence . . . and faith unshaken, has been put to shame.' The word 'faith' is characteristic. Christianity, he continued, was 'a treasure of wisdom and of comfort which to Plato was denied'.[67] To Arnold as to Cory, Plato was *anima naturaliter Christiana*.

Religion played a great part in Victorian politics, and both Christians and agnostics imagined Plato joining the debate. In a review of Grote's *History* Mill compared the opposition to the sophists with the modern outcry against 'godless colleges'.[68] Grote himself, though, held the sophists to have been respectable educators, esteemed by the conventional people of their day; as Stanley, a future Dean of Westminister, explained in his own review, 'According to the common view, Plato and his followers were . . . the established clergy . . ., and the Sophists the dissenters. According to Mr. Grote, the Sophists were the established clergy, and Plato was the dissenter—the Socialist who attacked the Sophists . . . as one of the existing orders of society.'[69] Grote accepted this account of his intentions. He and Dr. Arnold both read Plato with a feeling of urgency, a sense that the issues in which he had engaged were still alive. This was why they were so willing to accept an analogy which, however inappropriate, enabled them to translate ancient controversy into modern terms.

Thomas Arnold's picture of Plato endured throughout the century. His pupil Hughes imagined Tom Brown at Oxford being inspired and challenged by the *Apology* picked up by chance at a time of mental conflict;[70] there is no reason to doubt that such things happened in real life. Ruskin quoted Arnold's description of Plato with enthusiasm in *Praeterita*. In 1877, sick and depressed, he turned to Plato daily as though to a devotional work: 'Must do my Plato; I'm never well without that.'[71] Years before he had written '[Plato is] capacious in all his views, and embraces the small systems of Aristotle and Cicero as the solar system does the Earth. He seems to me especially remarkable for the sense of the great Christian virtue of Holiness . . .; and for the sense of the presence of the Deity in all things, great or small, which always runs in a solemn undercurrent beneath his exquisite playfulness and irony; while all the merely moral virtues may be found in his writings defined in the most noble manner, as a great painter defines his figures, *without outlines*.'[72] Ruskin portrays Plato as the Shakespeare of philosophers, a myriad-minded man, at once sublime, playful, ironic, noble—a Gothic philosopher, attractive to the enthusiastic, exuberant spirit of the Victorian age. Aristotle could not compete on these terms.

In politics as in religion Plato was regarded as an ally by opposite camps. Radicals tended to suppose that since he had questioned received opinions he must be one of themselves. Besides, the very title *Republic* suggested radicalism to modern readers. 'I can fancy a republic the most perfect form of government,' says Thornton in *North and South*, and Hale answers, 'We will read Plato's Republic as soon as we have finished Homer.'[73] The republican Shelley thought this work was 'the greatest repository of important truths in all the works of Plato'; but he allowed that it contained considerable error.[74] No one could agree with all that Plato said, but this became one of his strengths, because everyone agreed that he had to be reinterpreted before his principles could be applied to modern conditions. 'Many of the latest thoughts of modern . . statesmen,' wrote Jowett, 'such as . . . the reign of law, and the equality of the sexes, have been anticipated in a dream by Plato.'[75] The words 'in a dream' give the reader licence to discount whatever he finds uncongenial.

The 'reign of law' may seem to us too bland a label for Plato's formidably despotic system; but the Victorians did not have our knowledge of totalitarianism. However, the extent to which they underestimated Plato's hatred of democracy is remarkable. None of his more prominent Victorian disciples, with the weird exception of Pater, shared his enthusiasm for Sparta, but they all knew of it. Athens was admired, almost worshipped; and yet Plato's attacks were not resented. This tolerance is curious, but perhaps explicable. A good many prominent Victorians—Dickens, Ruskin and Matthew Arnold among them—were savagely critical of the materialism, brashness and philistinism of their age and nation. Yet these criticisms seem to come from an overflowing self-confidence; most of the breast-beaters had no shadow of a doubt that Britain with all its faults was the best country in the world. Who would exchange it for the degenerate and turbulent nations of the continent, or the still louder vulgarity of America? No one scourged the follies of modern England more fiercely than Ruskin; yet he could still demand, 'Where are men ever to be happy, if not in England? . . . Are we not of a race the first among the strong ones of the earth . . .? Have we not a history of which we can hardly think without becoming insolent in our just pride of it?'[76] The Victorians seem to have felt that Plato's criticisms of Athens were like their own criticisms of England, severe but fundamentally loyal.

In Mallock's *New Republic* Otho Laurence tries to explain Plato's system:[77] 'Wisdom is specially embodied in the theoretical politicians and religious speculators . . .; courage is embodied in the practical men who . . . execute the regulations and orders of the philosophers; and temperance is embodied in the commercial and industrial classes, who loyally submit themselves to their betters.' It sounds so Victorian: 'trade' is a worthy but lowly occupation, not quite suitable for a gentleman; superior to trade is the civil service; and superior to the civil service are the philosopher kings, who are represented as a sort of combination of church, state and universities. Such attitudes to Plato were not restricted to satire. Gladstone described Plato's guardians in terms which suggest the best kind of Victorian public servant: 'energetic', 'diligent', 'ready and keen in study'.[78] Like so many of his contemporaries, Gladstone saw Plato more as a moralist than a political theorist and took greater interest in the character of the guardians than in what they did. Macaulay viewed the *Republic*, so his nephew said, 'with the eyes of a Whig and an Englishman'. Like Gladstone he was blind to Plato's despotic tendency, and his own notes show that he regarded him rather as a practical reformer whose various proposals could be accepted or rejected one by one.[79]

Although the class structure of Plato's state was based on merit and not upon inherited wealth or rank, it was none the less rigid for that. In his republic each class would know its place; an arrangement sympathetic to Conservatives and to the 'Adullamite' wing of the Liberal party. Robert Lowe, who led the Adullamite opposition to the Second Reform Bill of 1867, declared in that year, 'The question of education naturally divides itself into two branches— the education of the poor . . ., and the education of the middle or upper classes.' He then tackled this question of the hour by going back to ancient Greece; a discussion of Plato's educational system led him to the conclusion that the philosopher had been largely right.[80] Few Victorians, indeed, were democrats in either the modern or the Athenian sense. Gladstone maintained that he was an out-and-out inegalitarian; Macaulay said that the eighth book of the *Republic*, which contains Plato's bitterest attack upon democracy, was unsurpassed in Greek philosophy for profundity, ingenuity, and eloquence.[81] Equally, there was an authoritarian strain in the radical thought of the nineteenth century. Few Englishmen, it is true, were much attracted by the Platonic extremism of Auguste Comte— Mill called his last work 'the completest system of . . . despotism, which ever yet emanated from a human brain'—but Mill himself, though a passionate libertarian, was hardly a democrat. No man, he held, should be enfranchised unless he had been educated, and the best educated should be entitled to more than one vote;[82] in Plato's state, similarly, a man's place and power in society depended on the degree of his wisdom and education. Plato's striking feminism, too, must have encouraged Mill, and perhaps guided him, when he wrote *The Subjection of Women*; he failed to criticize in Plato what he castigated in Comte not least because he saw him as an innovative reformer. Even Grote, the very man who had vindicated the sophists against Plato's attack, was surprisingly mild in his criticisms of the *Republic*; he admired the radical features of Plato's political theory more than he disliked its authoritarianism.

Whitehead said that the European philosophical tradition could most safely be characterized as a series of footnotes to Plato.[83]

This is a remark which could only have been made in the later nineteenth or earlier twentieth century. Even with Aristotle's name joined to Plato's, it would still have sounded odd at the beginning of the last century. 'In this matter,' Bentham wrote, 'we want no refinement, no metaphysics. It is not necessary to consult Plato, nor Aristotle. *Pain* and *pleasure* are what everybody feels to be such.'[84] Aristotle was Plato's pupil, and for all their disagreements they gave similar answers to certain questions, where a radically different kind of answer is possible. So in some periods philosophers have been gratefully indebted to these two giants, and in others they have tried to escape from their shadow. During the last century there was a reaction against empiricism and utilitarianism; in consequence the attention of philosophers was directed from modern thinkers back to the Greeks, and at the same time from Aristotle to Plato. German idealism suddenly became the vogue; a landmark was *The Secret of Hegel* (1865) by J. H. Stirling (though there were critics who muttered, 'The secret has been well kept').[85] Jowett, who gave so much of his life to Plato, was also active in introducing Hegel to English readers; the study of Plato encouraged an interest in the German idealists, and *vice versa*. Among Jowett's pupils was T. H. Green, during his short life the most influential philosophical voice in Oxford, whose idealism was firmly rooted in the Platonist tradition, and whose moral theory owed much to the Greeks, with its emphasis on self-fulfilment. The activities of professional philosophers seldom have much impact upon their fellow countrymen, but the Idealist movement is perhaps an exception. Looking back in 1939, Collingwood felt that between 1880 and 1910 the influence of Green's school had penetrated every part of the national life; 'politicians so diverse . . . as Asquith and Milner, churchmen like Gore and Scott Holland, social reformers like Arnold Toynbee' carried the conviction that the philosophy they had learnt at Oxford was important, and that their vocation was to put it into practice.[86] And in Plato they found an ancient author who seemed to be joining in debate with the newest, most stimulating thinkers of their time.

The idea had long been current that the ancient universities offered the only modern equivalent to the way of life depicted in Plato's dialogues. Cory's prize poem on Plato acclaimed the Hellenic character of Cambridge:

> O Granta! thou that hast the heart of youth
> Pulsing with genial heat of ancient truth, . . .

Whose shadowy rites and fame-lit cemeteries
Still bear high witness to the wealth and pride
Of Grecian reason's glowing summer-tide . . .

Matthew Arnold felt similarly; viewing Plato through a Keatsian
haze, he said that the Greeks were 'the great exponents of humanity's
bent for sweetness and light united, of its perception that the truth
of things must be at the same time beauty', and he believed that
this Hellenic ideal was still realized in his old university: 'We in
Oxford, brought up amidst [its] beauty and sweetness . . ., have
not failed to seize one truth,—. . . that beauty and sweetness are
essential characters of . . . human perfection.'[87] Wilde also shared
the feeling that the Isis was the modern Ilissus: in *The Critic as
Artist* Gilbert speaks of 'that lovely passage in which Plato describes
how a young Greek should be educated, and with what insistence
he dwells upon the importance of surroundings, telling us how the
lad is to be brought up in the midst of fair sights and sounds.' He
then likens this ideal to an education in Oxford, where 'one can
loiter in the grey cloisters at Magdalen, and listen to some flute-
like voice singing in Waynfleete's chapel, or lie in the green meadow,
among the strange snake-spotted fritillaries. . . .' In due course
Pater was to expand this theme.

Mackenzie gave it an ironical turn in *Sinister Street*:[88] an undergraduate writes a magazine article on 'Socrates at Balliol', provoking
from another the comment, 'And just about where he ought to have
been'. Balliol was a notoriously disputatious place. Jowett had been
dead eight years when Mackenzie came up to Oxford; in his lifetime he had seemed to be Socrates reincarnate. Socrates gathered
around him a group of adoring young admirers; Jowett too possessed,
in the words of Lewis Campbell, a 'singular personal charm which
made him irresistible to younger men'.[89] His favourite pupils were
nicknamed the 'Jowett-worshippers', and like the Socratic circle
they were intensely resented by outsiders. Both groups included
many of the most intelligent and serious young men of their day,
and both, more remarkably, contained a raffish element: Socrates
had Alcidiades among his admirers, while Jowett had Symonds and
Swinburne.

Jowett's circle felt that even his way of teaching was Socratic.
Matthew Knight, one of his pupils, wrote, 'He treated us in the
Socratic manner . . . he would argue a question contrary to his own
convictions, either in a dialectical spirit or in order to put our
opinions to the test.' George Brodrick, a future Warden of Merton

College, agreed: 'His greatest skill consisted, like that of Socrates, in helping us to learn and think for ourselves . . . no other tutor, within my experience, has ever approached him in the depth . . . of his pastoral supervision . . . of young thinkers.'[90] Socrates was no respecter of class distinctions, and the members of his circle came from differing backgrounds: Plato and Critias were aristocrats, while Phaedo was a slave, but as searchers for truth they were all equal. Likewise, the members of Jowett's reading-parties were treated as equals; the undergraduates were 'young gentlemen', but Knight was the son of Jowett's butler. Another of the Master's protégés was Frank Fletcher; Jowett discovered him when he was eleven years old, educated him and got him to Balliol, where in true Hellenic fashion he not only won the Gaisford Prize for Greek Verse but also played cricket and football for Oxfordshire; later he taught at a school in Mile End and finally became a professor at Exeter University.[91] Phaedo was freed, probably through the influence of Socrates, and founded the philosophical school of Elis in western Greece.

Cory, too, was often compared to Socrates in his influence over the young and his 'maieutic' gift of helping them to clarify their own conceptions.[92] He taught many future men of affairs, including Esher, Balfour and not least Rosebery, whose brilliance, wayward-ness and ambition perhaps made him closer to Alcibiades than any other man of his time. Nothing could have given Cory more pleasure than to be called a modern Socrates: 'Item,' he confided to his diary, 'my favourite bit of Plato, where Theodorus introduces . . . the teachable . . . Theaetetus, the ideal listener, telling Socrates that the boy is like him in having a snub nose . . ., but speaking with motherly joy of his sweet nature.' There speaks the eager, indeed the sentimental, schoolmaster. The Eton tutor was supposed to develop not only the intellect of his pupils but also their moral faculties; it was, with modifications, the educational ideal of the Greeks. Cory wrote, 'The candid . . . lads of the Platonic dialogues are with us still; we are not to worry them like Socrates, but we are frequently to remind them of the inadequacy of the grounds on which in practical talk we are obliged . . . to rest . . . exposure of error will do no harm if accompanied by open avowals of one's own knowledge and ignorance.'[93] Socrates, of course, was famous for such avowals. Dr. Arnold himself made use of the Socratic method: Stanley remarked on his 'practice of teaching by questioning'. Pupils were struck 'by his never concealing difficulties and always confessing ignorance'; his questions were designed to show the boys 'the exact bounds of their knowledge and their ignorance', and he taught them 'by gradually helping them on to the true answer'.[94]

'Plato is alive,' said Jowett. Four pages on 'Control of the Passions' in a private notebook show him learning from Plato and thinking in a Platonic way: 'It has been imagined by Sceptics that all the more intense forms of religion are really bastard . . . results of the relations of the sexes.' (This is a derivation from Plato's theory that human creativity is a 'sublimation' of sexual drives.) 'It is plain that there is a close connection between them . . . Hence, an important question, how to kill the sense or lust and leave the ideal or aspiration? How to direct . . . the heart to the eternal and invisible? (*erōs* of Plato in the Symposium).'[95] Plato could genuinely act as a guide, even for a Christian; he was performing a function now taken over by the psychologists.

So keen was Jowett's love of Greek philosophy that he was suspected of infidelity. H. H. Almond wrote, 'As to Jowett's "religion". I used to wonder what he believed. I came to the conclusion that he never put a clear . . . issue to himself . . . on any speculative subject. He was a Platonist all over.'[96] Such doubts formed the basis for the most savage portrait in *The New Republic*: Dr. Jenkinson (Jowett unmistakably) preaches a sermon; taking his text from the psalms, he launches abruptly into a disquisition on Plato, stressing the 'Christian' elements in his philosophy. Jenkinson uses the Greeks to water down the essential doctrines of Christianity, and even begins one sentence, 'Putting together, then, the ideas of these two good men, St. John and Aristotle. . . .' Finally, having reduced the gospel to a sort of vague idealism, he asks his congregation to conclude 'by doing what I trust I have shown that all here may sincerely . . . do. I mean, I will ask you to recite after me the Apostles' Creed.'[97] Mallock was grossly unfair; yet one can understand his mistrust. (Swinburne hardly helped matters by rushing to defend his old tutor against the 'offensive little Christian creature'). Jowett wrote of the *Phaedo*, 'There is nothing in all tragedians . . . nothing in poetry or history (with one exception), like the last hours of Socrates in Plato.'[98] The parenthesis has an anxious air, as though Jowett felt (or thought he felt) the death of Socrates more intensely than that of his Saviour. His private notebooks reveal him as a devout man, worried that his devotion was too weak. His profession of faith was honest, but like Newman and Gladstone he found that Greece had a strong and perilous allure. Again and again he likened Plato's teaching to Christ's; in setting out the arguments of the *Gorgias*, for example, he began thus:

> First Thesis:
> It is a greater evil to do than to suffer injustice.
> Compare the New Testament—
> 'It is better to suffer for well doing than for evil doing.' . . .
> And the Sermon on the Mount—
> 'Blessed are they that are persecuted for righteousness'
>   sake.'

But the word 'compare' is ambiguous.[99]

As he came to the end of the *Gorgias*, he became still bolder: 'The myth which terminates the Dialogue is not the revelation, but rather, like all similar descriptions, whether in the Bible or Plato, the veil of another life. For no visible thing can reveal the invisible. Of this Plato, unlike some commentators on Scripture, is fully aware. Neither will he dogmatise about the manner in which we are "born again".' Jowett comes perilously near to saying that Plato is a better Christian than certain modern divines. When he analysed the *Republic* he was yet more rash: 'The principles on which religion is to be based are two only: first that God is true; secondly, that he is good. Modern and Christian writers have often fallen short of these; they can hardly be said to have got beyond them.'[100] Here he is close to Matthew Arnold's feeling that the Greeks are more akin to us than our own ancestors, and that the Elizabethans are barbarous by comparison with the Athenians. There is much justice in this view; yet it is but a short step away from saying that the paganism of the Greeks was 'better' than the Christianity of the sixteenth century.

'Like the Scriptures,' Jowett wrote, 'Plato admits of endless applications . . .; and we lose the better half of him when we regard his Dialogues merely as literary compositions. Any ancient work which is worth reading has a practical . . . as well as a literary interest. And in Plato . . . the local and transitory is inextricably blended with what is spiritual and eternal.'[101] This is a splendid credo, spoken by a great teacher; and yet it is not altogether wise. This profession of faith in Plato comes in Jowett's introduction to the *Phaedrus*, where he tried to reduce the Platonic theory of love to Victorian terms; a heroically misguided effort, which got him into painful difficulty. He observed himself that Plato's republic presents two faces, 'one an Hellenic state, the other a kingdom of philosophers'. But the interpreter of Plato is also faced with a further paradox, uniquely difficult: on the one hand, Plato's system seems to be the most rigid and uncompromising of all philosophies; on the other, to be so elusive that men of diametrically opposed views have claimed Plato's support. Jowett was partly aware of the paradox: 'It has been said that Plato flies as well as walks, but this hardly expresses the whole truth, for he flies and walks at the same time.'[102] But though he saw the oddity, he missed the pitfalls.

The danger was essentially this. Jowett's mind was supple (his enemies called him slippery); Plato is both rigid and flexible; the gospel is uncompromisingly direct. The uncompromising aspect of Plato could well be compared to the teachings of Jesus, and yet such comparisons also required a certain flexibility or imprecision, so that it was hard for Jowett to avoid the impression that he was watering down Christ's doctrines, and perhaps Plato's as well, since he was also trying to adapt the philosopher to fit modern life. It was certainly his tendency to explain away the hard sayings of Plato a little too fluently; many readers, therefore, were bound to fear that he had become an unwitting ally of the infidels.

Such fears were to be realized, if not in Jowett, then in others. Pater spoke of 'the mystic and dreamy philosophy of Plato'. This sounds like Jowett, who insisted that 'mystic enthusiasm' and 'rapturous contemplation' were at the heart of Plato, but there is a subtle difference: the Master of Balliol might have written 'dreaming', scarcely 'dreamy'; already the edge of Plato's thought is being blunted.[103] Pater was to develop his personal version of Platonism further when he described Marius visiting a temple of Aesculapius.[104] He sees the priests pass gravely by, conversing in Greek, and hears from one of them a discourse based upon 'a theory Marius found afterwards in Plato's *Phaedrus*, which supposes men's spirits susceptible to certain influences, diffused . . . by fair things or persons'. From the priest Marius acquires a new ideal, one that we more readily associate with the name of Wilde:

> To keep the eye clear by a sort of exquisite personal alacrity and cleanliness . . .; to discriminate . . . more fastidiously, select form and colour in things from what was less select; to meditate much on beautiful objects, on objects more especially, con-
> nected with the period of youth . . . when Marius read the *Charmides*—. . . into which [Plato] seems to have expressed the very genius of old Greek temperance—the image of this speaker came back vividly to him.

The significance of this passage lies not merely in the aesthetic cast that it gives to Plato's thought but more particularly in the context in which this transformation of Plato is effected. Marius' visit to the temple is his introduction to Greek thought, which is presented as a grave, sacerdotal Platonism; the aesthetic philosophy that Marius adopts is given a religious tone. Indeed Pater designs that aesthetics should usurp the functions of religion: Marius's plan is that 'the study of music in that wider Platonic sense . . . would conduct one to an exquisite appreciation of all the finer traits of nature and of man . . . such a manner of life might come even to seem a kind of religion . . . the true aesthetic culture would be . . . a new form of the contemplative life, founding its claim on the intrinsic "blessedness" of "vision"—the vision of perfect men and things.'[105]

Mallock had imagined Jenkinson combining Aristotle and St. John; in *Marius* Pater does just that. *theōria*, contemplation or vision, is the subject of the last book of Aristotle's *Ethics*; Pater describes it as a 'vision of a wholly reasonable world', and adds, 'In the Gospel of Saint John, perhaps, some of [the Greeks] might have found the kind of vision they were seeking for.'[106] It is difficult to believe that *The New Republic* antedates *Marius* by eight years; parody anticipated actuality, and life modelled itself upon satire. And there was worse to come.

Pater's Plato and Platonism

One of the invigorating characteristics of the Victorians is their ability to write spectacularly bad books. Ruskin sometimes went astray with the alarming majesty of an express train coming off the rails at sixty miles per hour; Pater, who succeeded to Ruskin's office as the nation's *arbiter elegantiae*, could never be so formidable, but he proved with *Plato and Platonism* that his capacity for confident perversity was hardly less. Not long before his death he was asked which of his books he thought best; was it *Marius* or *The Renaissance*? Neither, he replied; if any of his works endured, he thought it would be his *Plato*.[107] We need not bow to this judgement; writers and artists tend to prefer the works upon which they are engaged at the time, and also to acquire a special affection for those of them that their contemporaries neglect. The mannered muted style of *Plato and Platonism* is indeed evidence of a laborious carefulness; but about Plato it tells us next to nothing.

Certain philosophers have a special appeal for unphilosophic minds;

in our own time the oracular utterances of Wittgenstein have enjoyed this kind of popularity. The sayings of Heracleitus have exercised a similar fascination—so mysterious, yet so terse and memorable. When MacNeice came up to Oxford, he noticed in a lavatory the graffito *Panta rhei, ouden menei*, 'All things flow, nothing remains'. T. S. Eliot headed *Burnt Norton* with two fragments of Heracleitus; and Pater too was drawn to him: 'His philosophy,' he said, 'was no matter of . . . system, but of harsh, protesting cries— . . . All things give way: nothing remaineth.' Pater turns him from a physicist into an Old Testament prophet, an Ecclesiastes proclaiming that all is vanity; the archaic 'remaineth' sets the tone.[108]

Likewise, Pater was attracted to Plato less as a philosopher than as an artist and a personality. 'It is hardly an exaggeration,' he wrote, 'to say that in Plato, in spite of his . . . literary freshness, there is nothing absolutely new . . . the *form* is new. But then, in the creation of philosophical literature, as in all . . . art, *form* . . . is everything, and the mere matter is nothing.' Habitually we think of Pater as timid and hesitant, but only a reckless man, one might suppose, would dare to dismiss so lightly the 'mere matter' of works which many of his contemporaries ranked as the highest achievement of human thought. Yet perhaps he was not so bold after all, for he appears to have been unable to believe that anyone could think or feel very differently from himself—a curious supposition for an aesthete in Brasenose College. Strange though it may seem, he was surprised and hurt to discover that the conclusion of his *Renaissance* had caused offence, and he probably had not the slightest desire to startle when he wrote, 'The business of the young scholar therefore, in reading Plato, is not . . . to adopt or refute Plato's opinions . . . his duty is rather to follow intelligently, but with strict indifference, the mental process there, as he might witness a game of skill; better still, as in reading *Hamlet* or *The Divine Comedy*, . . . to watch, for its dramatic interest, the spectacle . . . of a sovereign intellect, translating itself . . . into a great literary monument.'[109] Dante and Plato would have been equally appalled; Pater's words warn us how short is the step from art for art's sake to philosophy and even religion for art's sake.

Religion, indeed, is emphasized in his account of Plato. He compares his ideal state to the Kingdom of Heaven, and alleges that 'Hell, Purgatory, Paradise' are depicted at the end of the *Republic*.[110] Discussing a hymn by the stoic Cleanthes, in whom he claims to find Plato's influence, he concludes, 'You might even fancy what he says an echo from Israel's devout response to the announcement:

"The Lord thy God is one Lord." The Greek certainly is come very near to . . . Sion in what follows. . . .'[111] What follows, in fact, is a long quotation:

> Thou O Zeus art praised above all gods: many are
> Thy names and Thine is all power for ever.
> The beginning of the world was from Thee: and
> with law Thou rulest over all things . . .

The original Greek is written in hexameters, and neither looks nor sounds at all biblical, but Pater has arranged his English version to resemble the psalms in the Book of Common Prayer, splitting it into short sentences each divided by a colon which is not determined by the sense but simply put in to give a churchy impression. He was not trying to destroy Matthew Arnold's sharp distinction between Hellenic and Hebraic impulses, but teasing at it. Just as in *Marius* he played with the paradox of an age at once very modern and very alien, so now he toys with the concepts of Hellenism and Hebraism, bringing them close together at one moment, at another drawing them apart. In one sentence he likens Plato's state to Doric architecture, the most Greek of all Greek styles, in the next to Gothic churches.[112] He calls Aristotle 'the first of the Schoolmen', turning him into a medieval philosopher and thus opening up a great void between him and Plato, who is presented by contrast as a pure Hellene; but a few pages later he writes, 'Plato thus qualifying the . . . Puritan element in Socrates by his own capacity for the world of sense, Platonism has contributed largely . . . [to] the redemption . . . of the world of sense, by art . . ., by the creeds and worship of the Christian Church—towards the vindication of the dignity of the body.'[113] This ingenious sentence portrays Plato as supremely anti-Hebraic in his admiration for the body and the senses, and simultaneously as a great influence upon the development of Christianity.

Above all, Pater sees Plato as a poet, comparing him to Dante and even finding in him the capacities 'of a poet after the order of Sappho or Catullus'.[114] These are poets of personal feeling and indeed Pater treats Plato's works as an expression of his individuality:

> A personality, we may notice . . ., of a certain complication . . .
> the author of this philosophy of the unseen was one, for whom,
> as was said of a very different French writer, 'The *visible*
> world really existed.' . . . [His] austerity, aesthetically so

winning, is attained only by the chastisement . . . of . . . a richly
sensuous nature. Yes, the visible world . . . really existed for
him: exists still . . . when he seems to have turned . . . to
invisible things.

The 'lost spirit of Alcibiades', we are told, infuses Book 6 of the
Republic: here 'Plato is dealing with the inmost elements of personality'; he might almost be a novelist. Then the Victorian passion
for boswellism completely invades Pater's imagination and he is
launched out upon the wide waters of biographical speculation:

Plato is . . . unalterably a lover. In that, precisely, lies the
secret of the . . . diligent eye, the so sensitive ear. The central
interest . . . of his profoundly impressible youth . . . gives law
and pattern to all that succeeds it . . . the experience, the discipline, of love, had been that for Plato; and, as love must . . .
deal above all with visible persons, this discipline involved an
exquisite cultivation of the senses. It is 'as lovers use', that he
is ever on the watch for those dainty messages . . . to eye and
ear.

For one moment Pater trembles on the verge of explicitness:

He . . . knew all that we may be sure—*ta erōtika*—all the ways
of lovers in the literal sense. . . . Plato himself had not been
always a mere Platonic lover; was rather . . . subject to the
influence of fair persons. A certain penitential colour amid that
glow of fancy and expression, hints that the final harmony of
his nature had been but gradually beaten out.[115]

Plato is portrayed as a sort of Goethe, a philosophic but passionate
sage, maintaining a fine but precarious balance between strong
opposing forces. Or is Goethe the wrong comparison? A page
earlier Pater has described Plato as 'a great lover, somewhat after
the manner of Dante', continuing, 'It is of the amorous temper . . .
you must think in connection with Plato's youth.' How ambiguous
that word 'lover' is in a Platonic context, especially when Dante
is brought in to blur the picture still further. The mention of Sappho
and Catullus suggested one interpretation, while Dante seems to
imply another. The cause of this equivocation is not far to seek:
the Plato depicted here does not so much resemble Dante or Catullus
as Pater himself. It was Pater the aesthete who strove for 'an

exquisite cultivation of the senses', Pater the invert who was
'subject to the influence of fair persons', Pater the agnostic, half
drawn to Christianity, half delighted by a sense of sin, who
infused a 'penitential colour' into his flow of expression. Indeed
anyone whom Pater ever described turned, sooner or later, into
Pater himself; after a few pages even Michelangelo grows melancholy
and begins to yearn.[116]

Plato undergoes the same metamorphosis. He is the advocate of
a 'precisely regulated, a very exclusive community, which shall
be a refuge for elect souls from an ill-made world'.[117] His state has
become an ivory tower, a home of lost causes, where a few fortunate
and superior persons are blissfully sequestered from the grossness
of modern life. Pater forgets the large sacrifices which Plato requires
his philosopher kings to make for the community; indeed, he
ignores the community altogether. But Plato did not offer his rulers
a refuge from the world; on the contrary, he demanded that they
govern a whole society containing every class and condition of
men. He also forbade them so much as to enter a house in which
vessels of gold or silver were to be found. This rather disturbs
Pater's idea of the Platonic state as an idealized Oxford college,
but he finds a way round the difficulty: 'We are not to suppose in
Platonic Greece—how could we indeed anywhere within the range
of Greek conceptions?—anything rude, uncomely or unadorned . . .
if kings and knights never drink from vessels of silver or gold, their
earthen cups and plates, we may be sure, would be what we can
still see. . . .'[118] The notion of Plato's guardians as precursors of the
arts-and-crafts movement, cultivating a tasteful simplicity in their
clothing and crockery, has a certain charm; but it has little to do
with Plato.

Pater declines to believe in Plato's hostility to art. In his last
chapter, 'Plato's Aesthetics', he discusses 'the poetry and music,
the arts and crafts, of the City of the Perfect': 'Liken its music,'
he demands, 'to Gregorian music and call to mind the kind of
architecture, military or monastic again, that must be built to such
music, and then the kind of colouring . . . upon the walls.'[119] Plato
advocated a temperance entirely freed from the tyranny of the
senses; Pater transmutes this into an aesthetic cult of sensuous
austerity. We are to compare Plato's state 'to the Cistercian
Gothic . . ., when St. Bernard had purged it of a still barbaric
superfluity of ornament. It seems a long way from the Parthenon
to St. Ouen . . . or *Notre-Dame de Bourges*; yet they illustrate . . .
the direction of the Platonic aesthetics. Those churches . . . have . . .

their loveliness, yet of a stern sort.' And once again a vision of
Oxford seems to hover: in Pater's mind Gothic architecture is
associated with the education of the young, and he images the
Platonist calling to Youth, 'Stay then . . . Abide in these places.'
Meanwhile St. Bernard, like Plato, is transformed from a moral
puritan into an aesthetic purist. This perversion of history shows
the dangers of Pater's eclecticism: all too easily it rubs away the
distinctive characteristics of different periods, and reduces all men
and all ages to dreary uniformity. Philosophy is peculiarly unsuitable
for such treatment, since its task is to see the object as it really is;
and though it may be amusing to present Plato as a Greek Dante
or Gautier, in the end it is uninformative.

Pater had no comprehension of abstract thought; he needed to
reduce it to the language of sense experience. In the Myth of Er
he found a 'quite Dantesque sensibility to coloured light—physical
light or spiritual, you can hardly tell which'. Better still, this contrast between colour and colourlessness made a foundation for
biographical fantasy about the tensions in Plato's personality:

> Plato's richly coloured genius will find a compromise between
> the One which alone really is, yet is so empty a thought for
> finite minds; and the Many, which most properly is not, yet
> presses so closely on eye and ear and fancy and will. . . . Prefer
> as he may in theory that blank white light of the One . . .
> the world . . . will be for him, as he is by no means colour-blind,
> by no means a colourless place.[120]

Is this talk of colour a metaphor? Not entirely, for Plato is presented
as an Athenian Whistler, the possessor of a refined taste for subdued
coloration: 'Plato, with a kind of unimpassioned passion, was a
lover . . . of temperance . . ., as it may be *seen* . . .—seen in Charmides,
say! in that subdued and grey-eyed loveliness . . .; or in those youthful
athletes which, in ancient marble, reproduce him . . . with sound,
firm outlines, such as temperance secures.' Heracleitus turns out
to be a connoisseur with similar predilections: the very last sentences
of the book are these: 'Heracleitus had preferred the "dry soul",
or the "dry light" in it. . . . And the dry beauty, let Plato teach
us, to love that also, duly.'[121] But is there any evidence that Plato
or Heracleitus felt in this way? As it happens, Pater misrepresented
even Gautier, who spoke of the 'external' not the 'visible' world.
The two words are not synonymous.

He was not only averse to abstract thought himself but incapable

of recognizing it in others. Plato's philosophy, he declares, 'is not
a formal theory or body of theories, but a tendency, a group of
tendencies—a tendency to think or feel . . . in a particular way'.[122]
These words can scarcely be read without amazement and indignation. The theory of forms, whatever we may think of it, is the
boldest attempt in the history of western thought to create a
philosophy combining within one unified system metaphysics,
epistemology, ethics, political theory and religion. Perhaps this is
more than any philosophy can achieve; Plato may have failed, but
his is one of the grandest failures that there has ever been. In
denying that Plato produced a formal theory, Pater revealed that
his so subtle, so sensitive spirit could be crudely insusceptible of
such ideas as lay outside its restricted range.

'There have been Platonists without Plato, and a kind of traditional
Platonism in the world.'[123] Pater views Platonism as a cast of
mind; Plato is simply the Platonist *par excellence*. There exists a
'Platonic quality' which can be traced 'at all times, as the very
conscience of art, its saving salt'; it may be found in poets, historians,
even in sculpture. And what is this 'Platonism'? Not a thirst for
knowledge, not an intense conviction that the sensible world is
unreal, but a certain fastidiousness in matters of art. How characteristic that in his final paragraph he should be talking of Plato's
prose as a practical illustration of the 'intellectual astringency,
which he demands of the poet also'. How ironical too; for it is
precisely the absence of intellectual astringency, the sheer self-
indulgence, that ruins the book.

On his title page he places a motto from the *Phaedo*: 'philosophy
being the greatest *mousikē*'. This last word is untranslatable. It
is more than 'music', more even than 'art'; it stands for a complete
education in the things of the mind. Pater seized on the phrase
because he liked the idea of philosophy as an art form, and this
idea involves no great perversion of Plato's meaning; yet there is
a vast gulf between the Greek and his interpreter, for Plato demanded that art should serve philosophy and Pater desired that
philosophy should serve art. His very choice of language is revealing:
the favourite epithets 'dainty' and 'winning', the parenthetic phrase
'we may be sure', which serves well in default of evidence. The
words 'true' and 'truth' are not a conspicuous part of his vocabulary.
Yet although he diminishes the greatness of his subject, in a bizarre
way he pays Plato high tribute. It is remarkable not that he should
misunderstand Plato, but that he should want to devote a whole
book to him in the first place. Jowett and Pater had next to nothing

in common; yet both of them devoted to Plato what they believed to be their highest efforts. And in either case their work was in the best sense partisan: the Broad Churchman and the aesthete both wanted to claim him for a friend. There could hardly be a better testimony to Plato's power over the Victorian spirit; one bowed down before the unknown god, and only then did one ask what god one was worshipping. Besides, Plato is a chameleon, and Pater, precisely because he was so little of a philosopher, saw him, or almost saw him, in some of his less familiar aspects. If he exaggerated Plato's kinship to the New Testament, he was not wholly wrong to speak of 'an unworldliness which . . . will ever be the very essence of Platonism.—"Many are called, but few chosen".'[124] His stress on the aesthetic charm of Platonic doctrines is so Paterian that at times it reads almost as self-parody, and yet here too he was right in a way: Plato believed fervently that truth was beautiful, and was eager that it should appear so.

Pater's picture is essentially a fuzzier version of Jowett's; though the two dons were so different, Pater's account of Plato was more Victorian, more English, more 'Oxford' even, than either of them would have recognized. Jowett declared, truly, that the *Republic* had served as a model for the *City of God* and many Utopian writings: he also pointed to Plato's influence on Christian theology. Pater writes: 'If he sometimes surprises us with paradox or hazardous theory, [Plato] will sometimes also give us to understand that he is after all not quite serious. So about this vision of the City of the Perfect, *The Republic, Kallipolis, Uranopolis, Utopia, Civitas Dei, The Kingdom of Heaven.* . . .' He seems barely aware that these are not synonyms or that any of them represents a deeply serious ideal; Jowett's point is taken over but trivialized. Again, Jowett had insisted that Plato must be seen in his historical context, and not be judged by the standards of modern England. Pater tries to make the same point, but it comes out differently: 'As the strangely twisted pine-tree which would be a freak of nature on an English lawn, is seen . . . amid the contending forces of the Alpine torrent that actually shaped its growth, to have been the creature of necessity . . .; so, beliefs the most fantastic, the "communism" of Plato for instance, have their natural propriety when duly correlated with . . . those conditions around them, of which they are in truth a part.'[125] Whereas Jowett was eager to defend, understand and explain, Pater's words are not really a defence: they merely assume, without argument, that Plato's communism is 'fantastic'. Pater would have been horrified to be accused of slovenliness, but that, in truth, is the vice that pervades his book; the fastidiousness upon which he prided himself embraces only its form, and not at all its substance. Here is no hard gem-like flame; rather, he flickers like a candle in a wide dark room, shedding a romantic glow but providing scant illumination.

Gosse alleged that there was an estrangement between Jowett and Pater; 'But this was removed in the last year of the life of each, and the Master of Balliol was among those who congratulated Pater most cordially on his *Plato and Platonism.*'[126] Though widely believed, the story is of doubtful authenticity, but its very currency is revealing. Jowett was the representative of one Victorian ideal, dedication to public service; Pater was the prophet of another, an Epicurean withdrawal in search of a refined hedonism. The two ideals were antithetical; yet both were inspired, to some extent, by Greece. It seemed symbolically appropriate that the two adversaries should die within a year of each other, and that as they drew near to death the means of their reconciliation should be the Greek thinker whose spirit brooded over the entire age.

Plato's Decline

Wilde aestheticized Plato still further. In *De Profundis* he recalled telling Gide that 'there was nothing that . . . Plato . . . had said that could not be transferred immediately into the sphere of Art, and there find its complete fulfilment'. In *The Critic as Artist* Gilbert says, 'It may be that it is as a critic of Beauty that Plato is destined to live'; and he even suggests, 'To do nothing at all is the most difficult thing in the world, . . . and the most intellectual. To Plato, with his passion for wisdom, this was the noblest form of energy. To Aristotle . . . this was the noblest form of energy also.' Plato has become a dilettante, Aristotle a flâneur.

Aestheticism as a way of life went rapidly out of fashion around 1930; so did idealism as a philosophy. It was not a mere accident of history that the idealists were in their heyday at a time when many people wanted to cling to some vestiges of the Christianity that seemed to be failing them. As C. S. Lewis was to recall, writing of Oxford shortly after the Great War, 'The emotion that went with all this was certainly religious. . . . We could talk religiously about the Absolute.'[127] Two of his undergraduate friends were converted from atheism to anthroposophy; the search for alternative religions was still on, and even Madame Blavatsky and Colonel Olcott were still names to conjure with. Plato could be represented as their ally; for example, the Plato whom we meet in the works of Yeats is not one of the founders of rational thought but the author of the Myth of Er and the *Timaeus*, he who discoursed of reincarnation and the spindle of the universe.

> Plato thought nature but a spume that plays
> Upon a ghostly paradigm of things.

From these lines one might suppose that the philosopher was at one with the cabbalists and occultists; and yet what Yeats says is true.[128] The protean Plato has passed through yet another transformation.

The theory of forms, MacNeice remarked, 'appeals to anyone whose childhood has been fed on Christianity and his adolescence upon Shelley'; and indeed a revulsion from Plato and a revulsion from Christianity went hand in hand.[129] Plato's fall from grace did not lead to a comparable resurgence of enthusiasm for Aristotle; rather to a diminution of interest in Greek philosophy generally. The new analytical philosophers attached little importance to the past history of their subject; and Collingwood, who continued through the 1930s to insist upon the need for the historical approach, was a voice crying in a wilderness with self-conscious lack of effect. MacNeice for his part found something depressing in the decline of Plato's reputation. In his *Autumn Journal* (1938) he associated it with the fall of the year, the approach of war and the materialism of the Midland city where he lived:[130]

> Good-bye now, Plato and Hegel,
>   The shop is closing down;
> They don't want any philosopher kings in England,
>   There ain't no universals in this man's town.

His instincts were sound: the rise of the dictators was pushing the world towards war; it was also leading men to question Plato's political wisdom. In England the attack began with *Plato Today* (1937) by Richard Crossman, who maintained that 'Plato's philosophy is the most savage and most profound attack upon liberal ideas which history can show'. Crossman hated Plato's views, and yet believed in his eternal relevance as much as ever Jowett had: 'Plato was not simply a Greek who lived in the fourth century B.C. He was also (for good or ill) the inspiration of much modern political thought and action.' And Plato was still to be feared: 'There is a danger that . . . we should swallow Plato's political opinions too easily, and it was partly to meet this danger that *Plato Today* was written. . . . I should not myself agree that the views I have attributed to the modern Plato are . . . absurd . . . the criticisms which he has made of democracy . . . seem to me very difficult to controvert.'[131]

This was perhaps the last moment at which one could find an aspiring statesman wanting to write seriously about Plato; almost the last moment, too, at which one might expect a leading churchman to be well versed in him. For half of the Second World War, however, the Church of England was led by a man who admitted to loving Plato and St. John above all other authors. William Temple was the late inheritor of a Victorian tradition; the dominating influence upon his philosophy was Edward Caird, Jowett's pupil and successor as Master of Balliol. He died in 1944, a year before Popper dealt Plato the blow from which he has not recovered. Popper's design was to destroy the Victorian picture of Plato; yet in a way his work marks the culmination of a Victorian attitude and ideal. In the first place, he greatly admired the Athenian democracy, and was indignant with Plato for attacking it. Secondly, he despatched Aristotle to a subordinate role: 'Aristotle's thought is entirely dominated by Plato. He followed his great teacher as closely as his inartistic temperament permitted, not only in his general political outlook but practically everywhere.' Plato, by contrast, was 'the greatest philosopher of all time'.[132] Popper knew Plato's power, and feared it; the first volume of his work is significantly entitled *The Spell of Plato*. And perhaps he was not quite the last man to dread that spell. Only a few years back the might of the Chinese propaganda machine was unleashed against two thinkers who threatened the revolutionary purity of the People's Republic. The first of these, predictably, was Confucius; Plato was the second.

XI

CHANGE AND DECAY

Turning Points

SOPHOCLES AND PUBLIC ORDER

The second-rate superior minds of a cultivated age . . . are usually in exaggerated opposition against its spirit.

Mill[1]

G OETHE looms in the background of the nineteenth century from its beginning to its close, dimming slowly, a mighty shape. 'Self-culture is the true ideal of man,' Wilde said. 'Goethe saw it, and the immediate debt that we owe to Goethe is greater than the debt we owe to any man since Greek days. The Greeks saw it, and have left us, as their legacy . . ., the conception of the con-templative life.'[2] But was Goethe's goal—the harmonious develop-ment of a many-sided personality—attainable in the nineteenth century? 'To me,' Mill reflected in 1854, 'it seems that nothing can be so alien . . . to the modern mind as Goethe's ideal of life. He wished life . . . to be rounded off and made symmetrical like a Greek temple or a Greek drama. . . . As well might he attempt to cut down Shakespeare or a Gothic cathedral to the Greek model. . . . Not symmetry, but bold, free expansion . . . is demanded by . . . the modern mind.'[3] However, in the 1860s Arnold tried valiantly to re-establish the Greco-German idea; the attempt was earnest, elegant, sensitive, and desperately misconceived.

Culture and Anarchy grew out of the political unrest, potentially the worst in Britain for thirty-five years, that arose in the years leading up to the Second Reform Act. The book began as a collection of articles; when Arnold collected them together, he introduced them with a pair of texts—texts to preach not upon but against. The first was from a speech by Bright, in which he had spoken slightingly of 'literary gentlemen . . ., who are for what they call culture because they . . . have a smattering of two dead languages', and criticized them for their opposition to electoral reform.[4] The second text was from Frederic Harrison: 'Culture . . . sits well on a professor of *belles-lettres*; but as applied to politics, it means simply a turn for small fault-finding, love of selfish ease, and in-decision in action. The man of culture is in politics one of the poorest mortals alive.'[5] This was tiresomely *simpliste*, no doubt; but Arnold unfortunately went some way towards making Harrison's last sentence come true. Public life and direct political action, he con-cluded, were not much permitted to the believer in culture, and should he find himself dragged into a committee-room, 'the speech most proper for [him] to make is Socrates's: *Know thyself!*'[6] There was a priggishness about this—a sort of Greeker-than-thou attitude —which was not likely to conciliate his critics.

The debate between Arnold and his opponents began in mis-understanding. Bright had not attacked classical education as such; rather he had insisted that no kind of knowledge, except political knowledge, could give one man a better title to the franchise than another: 'If . . . a man *scientifically or classically* educated knows nothing of politics, which is often the case, how shall he be more competent to decide who shall sit in this House . . . than men in the humbler classes of society?'[7] Arnold, for his part, agreed that 'the culture that is supposed to plume itself on a smattering of Greek and Latin' was valued only out of ignorance or as an 'engine of . . . class distinction': 'No serious man would call this *culture*, or attach any value to it, as culture, at all.'[8] The pity was that the two sides did not make more effort to understand each other. Arnold lunged out at Bright, and in turn was told by Bright's news-paper, the *Morning Star*, 'To be a man of culture . . . in the modern and slangy sense—we explain for Mr. Arnold's instruction—is to be a small pedantic Tory prig who, knowing very little Latin and less Greek, is proud of declaring that he . . . wants to know nothing else.'[9]

What then did Arnold himself mean by culture? His talent for abstract thought was slight, and he made no real attempt to define his central concept. Instead we are offered a succession of suggestive imprecisions: culture is 'a study of perfection', it 'believes in making reason and the will of God prevail', it is the eternal opponent of fierceness and abstract systems.[10] These various accounts of culture are not definitions, and they are certainly not synonymous with each other; but they are as much as we are given. One thing, how-ever, is clear: to Arnold culture is peculiarly the ideal and the achievement of the Greeks. 'The Greek word *euphuia*, a finely tempered nature, gives exactly the notion of perfection as culture brings us to conceive it. . . . The immense spiritual significance of the Greeks is due to their having been inspired with this central . . . idea of the essential character of human perfection.'[11]

Arnold's account was riddled with faults, attractive though it seems. In the first place, he was wrong about the Greeks: neither in their literature nor in their lives did they attain to the harmony, the radiancy, the 'balance and regulation of mind' that he himself valued so highly. The Rev. F. W. Robertson was among those criticized by Arnold for belittling the Greeks. Christ, he had said, brought the knowledge that God is Love: 'Hence came deep calm— the repose . . . which the Greek never found.'[12] This was the direct contrary of what Winckelmann had said about Greek blitheness: the Brighton preacher challenged the German sage; and the Brighton preacher was right. Restlessness and worldliness, Robertson maintained, were characteristics of Greek life and religion: 'This bright world was all. Its revels—its dances—its theatrical exhibitions—. . . these were blessedness; and the Greek's hell was death. Their poets speak pathetically of the misery of the wrench from all that is dear and bright. The dreadfulness of death is one of the most remarkable things . . . in those ancient writings.'[13] This amateur reader of the classics, without pretensions to scholarship, saw more clearly than his most highly educated contemporaries and anticipated an element of Nietzsche's theory by some twenty years; and if the Greeks, on this account, appear less ideal than formerly, they gain correspondingly in depth and complexity. It is ironical that Arnold, defending the Greeks, made them dull in their perfection, while Robertson, attacking them, made them live.

To an inadequate notion of what Hellenism had been in the past Arnold added an inadequate conception of what culture ought to be in the present; his idea was deficient philosophically as well as historically. He was right to insist that culture was or should be concerned with much more than just aesthetic enjoyment, but unequal to the immensely difficult task of pinning it down. The phrase 'sweetness and light' was fatally equivocal; he constantly confuses aesthetic and moral criteria. Much of the time the phrase is used to represent the application of disinterested reason to political and social questions—something with which no one would wish to quarrel—but at other moments it is the symbol of an artistic ideal, and a weak artistic ideal at that. 'Poetry is at bottom a criticism of life,' he once said; and T. S. Eliot was to retort, in the next century, 'If we mean life as a whole—not that Arnold ever saw life as a whole—. . . can anything that we can say of it ultimately, of that awful mystery, be called criticism?'[14] Balance and proportion and Olympian serenity are fine ideals but they are not the only goals that art may set itself; Arnold, however, would accept no others. 'The bent of Hellenism,' he said, 'is to follow . . . the whole play of the universal order, to be apprehensive of missing any part of it, of sacrificing one part to another.'[15] Yet so many great men have achieved their greatness at the cost of some great lack; the well-rounded man tends to become a don or a critic instead. The great lack seems often, and especially among the Victorians, to be part and parcel of their greatness. Where would Dickens be without his robust vulgarity and sentimentality? where Ruskin without his obsessiveness? where Gladstone with a keen sense of humour? The final question, as Carlyle had said, is 'not how much chaff is in you; but whether you have any wheat'.[16] Incompleteness, as Proust was to observe, was peculiarly the quality of the best nineteenth-century art, and a source of novel beauty.[17] Arnold's anxiety to miss no part of the universal order was perhaps the disguise of weakness; the word 'apprehensive' is significant, so strangely inapplicable to Aeschylus or Thucydides, so apt for himself. But at least he lived up to his ideal, stunting the natural growth of his talent and torturing it like an espalier into unnatural stiffness. He suppressed *Empedocles* and laboured over *Merope*; we must admire his earnestness, if not his judgement.

At moments he seems almost to enjoy being an outsider. Culture takes men out of their class, he argues; the English are divided into Barbarians, Philistines and Populace, but among each of these classes there are 'a certain number of *aliens*'. The danger of this attitude was that it was liable to fix the cultured person in a permanent pose of peevish superiority: he criticized a newspaper called the *Nonconformist* for its motto, 'the Dissidence of Dissent and the Protestantism of the Protestant Religion', yet in a way his motto for culture was rather similar. 'Culture,' he said, 'begets a dissatisfaction'—another significant word—'which is of the highest possible value in stemming the common tide of men's thoughts in a wealthy and industrial community, and which saves the future, as one may hope, from being vulgarised.'[18] Like Mill, he saw the especial value of the Greeks to a mechanized age; unlike Mill, he felt that wealth and industry were *necessarily* the enemies of culture: in his vocabulary, coal, railroads and machinery are words as automatically pejorative as incense or chalice in the literature of the Protestant Truth Society.

Though he held aloof from political action, he was not deterred from laying down the law on a wide range of public questions; this was another source of irritation to his opponents. His mistake was to suppose that if only people were more cultured, they would all agree; culture, he said, is 'possessed by the scientific passion'.[19] Here he was the victim partly of the optimism of the mid-century, when health, knowledge and wisdom seemed to be steadily and indefinitely increasing, and partly of his uncritical worship of Greece: he believed that culture could bring about the sort of perfection for which he hoped because he also believed that in Athens it had already done so. Both these attitudes—to the past and to the future—should have been implausible in the later 1860s. Also, he was perhaps too much influenced by Plato's doctrine that moral and political truths can be seen and known with certainty. Should an inflammatory demagogue be silenced? Should an absurd bequest be upheld?[20] These are difficult questions about which intelligent men may reasonably differ. In claiming that culture made the answers to these problems self-evident he was making it do too much. He was himself delighted to think that 'our poor culture, which is flouted as so unpractical, leads us to the very ideas capable of meeting the great want of our . . . times! We want an authority . . .; culture suggests the idea of *the State*.'[21] Here again the voice of Plato is heard. The *Daily News* retorted, 'You may make [the State] the organ of something or other, but how can you be certain that reason will be the quality which will be embodied in it?'[22] This was a good question, to which Arnold had no adequate answer; indeed we know, with the experience of totalitarian societies behind us, that the *Daily News* was right. Arnold was not himself an entirely satisfactory example of the cool rationality of the cultured. It is odd to appeal for a rigid application of the laws in the name of flexibility, but this is what he did, attacking the 'want of flexibility' in the British race evidenced by their reluctance to lock up Papist-baiters and railing-breakers.[23] Some of his readers must have wondered if culture was not another name for the tyranny of Matthew Arnold's own opinions.

'Suppose we Hellenise . . . with free-trade, as we Hellenised with the Real Estate Intestacy Bill, and with the disestablishment of the Irish Church. . . .' When he wrote this, he failed to see how he was turning Hellenism, and culture (which in his mind had become virtually a synonym for Hellenism), into the watchword of a sect or party. 'Often by Hellenising,' he claimed, 'we seem to subvert stock Conservative notions . . . more effectually than [our Liberal friends] subvert them by Hebraising.'[24] If Hellenism is necessarily opposed both to radicals and Conservatives, it is not left with much room to expand in; the truth is that by giving culture so large a role he made it not more glorious but more trivial. 'The *Times*,' he wrote, 'replying to some foreign strictures on the dress, looks, and behaviour of the English abroad, urges that the English ideal is that every one should be free to do and . . . to look just as he likes. But culture indefatigably tries, not to make what each raw person may like the rule by which he fashions himself; but to draw ever nearer to a sense of what is indeed beautiful . . . and becoming, and to get a raw person to like that.'[25] This is the first example that he gives of the practical effect of culture; the trouble with it is that culture comes to seem a sort of joyless nanny, telling her little charge not to stare, not to fidget, not to stick his fingers in his mouth. And of course it *is* rude to stare, it *is* unhygienic to stick one's fingers in one's mouth; but how disappointing, so soon after those exalted words about 'the study and pursuit of perfection', to find ourselves worrying about the right shirt to wear on the *Promenade des Anglais*. Certainly culture meant more to Arnold than this, and he later referred with disarming good humour to the misconceptions of his adversaries: 'The "religion of culture" . . . is said to be a religion proposing parmaceti, or some scented salve or other, as a cure for human miseries; a religion breathing a spirit of cultivated inaction.'[26] He saw the dangers, but he could not altogether avoid them: culture seems somehow, in his hands, to diminish even the most serious matters. 'The great men of culture,' he wrote—and here he was thinking particularly of the Hellenists Lessing and Herder—'have laboured to divest knowledge of all that was harsh, uncouth, difficult, abstract, professional, exclusive; . . . to make it efficient outside the clique of the cultivated and learned.'[27] This is a strange mixture of primness and large idealism; counteracting his enthusiasm for diffusing culture as widely as possible is a conception of culture that makes the diffusion less and less worth while. Much knowledge is surely of its essence harsh or difficult or abstract; to suppose otherwise is to prefer convenience to truth. Even in aesthetic terms Arnold's hopes are unsatisfying; once we have purged away all the roughness and uncouthness we may find that the grandeur and the sublimity have gone as well.

Religion, in Arnold's hands, is similarly diminished. 'Culture,' he declared, 'is always assigning to system-makers and systems a smaller share in the bent of human destiny than their friends like. . . . But Jacobinism loves a Rabbi . . . it wants . . . his ideas to stand for perfection . . . and for Jacobinism, therefore, culture, eternally passing onwards and seeking,—is . . . an offence.'²⁸ Here is another limitation. Do not the great religions love a Rabbi? Are they *ipso facto* uncultured? And perhaps some systems are true? The sort of culture that is eternally passing onward may well be seeking the sweetness without the light; not solid knowledge but a dilettante titillation of the intellect. Arnold was paving the way for Pater and Wilde.

In the fourth chapter of *Culture and Anarchy* Arnold introduces the terms Hebraism and Hellenism. Though he took them from Heine, he was essentially schematizing the idea, which ran through so much nineteenth-century thought in England, that Greece and Jewry between them had a unique importance in human history, whether as allies in God's plan for the redemption of the world or as rivals contending for the soul of man. Taking Heine as an example of a man who had overvalued Hellenism at the expense of Hebraism, and Robertson as an example of the opposite case, Arnold tried to reconcile the two warring sides: 'In both these cases there is injustice. . . . The aim and end of both Hebraism and Hellenism is . . . the same, and this aim and end is . . . admirable.'²⁹ But at the heart of the matter was a question that demanded to be squarely faced: were the claims of Christianity true or false? Arnold dodged the issue; in consequence he appeared to be a man crying peace where there was no peace, and crying without true passion or conviction. 'The final aim of both Hellenism and Hebraism, as of all great spiritual disciplines, is no doubt the same: man's perfection or salvation.' 'No doubt', 'or'—the little words are revealing. One does not feel that Arnold really believes in salvation; it is not so much that Hellenism is exalted as that the words 'salvation' and 'spiritual' are debased. 'At the bottom of both the Greek and the Hebrew notion,' he continues, 'is . . . in a word, the love of God.' No; not unless we are to reduce the 'love of God' from the sublimity of the Christian conception to virtual triviality. 'The uppermost idea with Hellenism is to see things as they really are; the uppermost idea with Hebraism is conduct and obedience.'³⁰ This account of Hebraism is at best partial. Certainly the moral code of Hebraism is stern and rigorous, but the Old Testament is above all about God, and Arnold's idea of it as merely a system of morality is fundamentally man-centred. He turns it, as he had earlier turned Hellenism, into a governess saying, 'Do this; don't do that.' He cannot feel it, or even imagine others feeling it, as terrible, sublime, the revelation of the Godhead. This defect equally disables his account of Hellenism. He called upon Plato as an ally, declaring that the philosopher had allowed a 'partaking of the divine life' only to 'the lover of pure knowledge, of seeing things as they really are'.[31] This is true, more or less; yet Plato was not so one-sided, or so respectable. Arnold ignored the mystical Plato, the Plato who believed in metempsychosis, the Plato who held that 'our greatest blessings come through madness'.

The terms Hellenism and Hebraism may be understood either symbolically or historically. In the first sense they denote two types of human impulse which may be found, in greater or lesser degree, at any time and in any society; in the second sense they denote the character of the Greek and Jewish cultures as they actually were two thousand years or so ago. In this second sense the Jews were not always Hebraic or the Greeks Hellenic. Arnold's attempt to define his terms is no definition at all, but a confusion between these two senses, and this simple and fatal confusion is at the heart of his analysis:

> We may regard this energy driving at practice, this paramount sense of the obligation of duty, self-control and work . . . as one force. And we may regard the intelligence driving at those ideas which are . . . the basis of right practice, . . . the indomitable impulse to know and adjust them perfectly, as another force. And these two forces we may regard as in some sense rivals,—rivals not by the necessity of their own nature, but as exhibited in . . . man and his history,—and rivals dividing the empire of the world between them. And to give these forces names from the two races of men who have supplied the most signal and splendid manifestations of them, we may call them respectively the forces of Hebraism and Hellenism. Hebraism and Hellenism,—between these two points of influence moves our world.[32]

'To give these forces names'—there is the rub. Are they just handy tags, these names, or is there a historical theory attached to them? Arnold himself has not seen the problem: 'As one passes and repasses from Hellenism,' he murmurs, 'from Plato to St. Paul . . .'; and then two pages later, 'By alternations of Hebraism and Hellenism, of a man's intellectual and moral impulses. . . .' In his last chapter the terms seem to have become purely symbolic: 'Hellenism, . . . or the habit of fixing our mind upon the intelligible law of things . . .'; 'to Hellenise . . . that is, to examine into the nature of real good . . .';

and yet he is still happy to apply the words historically where this enables him to make a telling point: Who will believe, he asks, that the 'delicate and apprehensive genius of the Indo-European race' will find its last word on the question of sexual morality 'in the institutions of a Semitic people, whose wisest king had seven hundred wives and three hundred concubines?'[33] Indeed, he was influenced by his father's racial theory of history: 'Hellenism is of Indo-European growth,' he argued, 'Hebraism is of Semitic growth; and we English, a nation of Indo-European stock, seem to belong naturally to the movement of Hellenism.' This left him with the problem of explaining the 'Hebraising turn' of English and American life; he accounted for it by the 'prominence of the moral fibre' in the Anglo-Saxon race.[34]

Thanks to his confusion between the historical and symbolic meanings of his terms, Arnold's idea of what the Greeks and Jews were actually like becomes flat and partial. The odd consequence is that the one criticism that he does venture to make of the Greeks is arguably unfair. 'Socrates is terribly *at ease in Zion,*' he wrote, paraphrasing Carlyle. Hebraism has 'an awful sense of the impossibility' of being at ease in Zion; Socrates by comparison seems to talk almost 'glibly'.[35] This judgement is perhaps too harsh, but at least it has the merit, or so one might suppose, of emphasizing the awesome majesty of the Judaeo–Christian God. But in fact the result is different. Arnold does his best to keep Christ out of Christianity by presenting it not as a saving gospel but as a moral code: 'Christianity . . . occupied itself, like Hebraism, with the moral side of man exclusively . . . and so far it was but a continuation of Hebraism.' But even this does not satisfy him, for he goes on, 'But it transformed . . . Hebraism by criticizing a fixed rule. . . . What was this but an importation of Hellenism, *as we have defined it*, into Hebraism?' In Chapter 4 St. Paul was taken as the type and representative of Hebraism; now, in Chapter 5, it suits Arnold to picture him as a blend of the two great forces: his remedy for the rigidity of the Jewish law, we are told, was 'an importation of *what we have called Hellenism* into his Hebraism'.[36] The italics in these quotations are not Arnold's; indeed, they expose his equivocation all too clearly. If Hellenism means no more than open-mindedness, then what he said was true, if not very important; but in effect he was implying something much more substantial: that Christianity represented a tempering of the austere Jewish religion by means of the mellow wisdom of the Greeks. Without knowing it, he was making straight the way for the soft religiosity of the aesthetes.

Mallock made Mr. Luke, his satirical travesty of Arnold, speak of 'a certain Galilean peasant . . . who described the highest culture by just the same metaphor, as a hunger and thirst after righteousness. Our notion differs only from his, from the *Zeitgeist* having made it somewhat wider.' This was a cruel burlesque of Arnold's manner, and yet Mallock was prophetic, for this was just the way that others were to talk. Pater admired 'that reasonable Ideal, to which the Old Testament gives the name of *Creator*, which for the philosophers of Greece is the *Eternal Reason*, and in the New Testament the *Father of Men*'; and he praised 'the moderation, the divine moderation of Christ'. Robertson had deplored the Greek worship of the Beautiful: 'What was the consequence? Religion degenerated into the arts.' This too could have been prophetic of the nineteenth century. Pater's idea of a Hellenic Christ with 'Nothing in excess' for his motto is intimately connected with his enjoyment of ' "the beauty of holiness", nay! the elegance of sanctity . . . the aesthetic charm of the catholic church'. Wilde went even further: 'Christ's place indeed is with the poets. . . . Shelley and Sophocles are of his company.'[37]

Even as abstract terms Hellenism and Hebraism are unsatisfactory. In the first place, they led Arnold to make a strict and misleading severance of aesthetic from moral values. He was aware of one objection to his theory: 'To say that we work for sweetness and light, then, is only another way of saying that we work for Hellenism. But, oh! cry many people, sweetness and light are not enough; you must put strength and energy along with them.'[38] He failed— and so no doubt did most of his opponents—to see that there might be purely aesthetic grounds for conjoining energy to sweetness and light. In the later parts of *Culture and Anarchy*, misled by the apparent exclusivity of the terms Hellenism and Hebraism, he tends to turn sweetness and light into aesthetic values and strength and energy into moral values. The truth could equally well be the other way round. His second great mistake was to make Hellenism, and the associated metaphors of sweetness and light, do too much. They represent the aesthetic qualities that he most admired, but they also represent the power of unprejudiced reason; these are two very different things. This confusion was to impair the effectiveness of his arguments. 'It is not at this moment true,' he wrote, 'what the majority of people tell us, that the world wants fire and strength more than sweetness and light, and that things are . . . to be settled first and understood afterwards.'[39] This was sound advice for those who were politically active, but they did not heed it because they

associated it with a type of aesthetic culture that they disliked or
disbelieved in.

The Second Reform Bill was passed in 1867, and in the next year
the new electors swept the Liberals to power with a huge majority.
Gladstone became Prime Minister, the most enthusiastic Hellenist
ever to have held that office. 1867 was also the year of Pater's
essay on Winckelmann, the first rallying-cry—if anything so muted
can be called a rallying-cry—of the new aesthetic Hellenism. But
the times were not so receptive to Greek influences as these superficial indications might suggest. Gladstone was to dominate British
politics for the next quarter of a century; yet he was to become
increasingly like some great whale stranded upon an alien shore, a
lonely survivor from the primeval days when there were still giants
upon the earth. Pater's brand of Hellenism, unlike Gladstone's,
attracted many followers, but with consequences not wholly fortunate. Arnold did not convince Bright and his friends, but he did
convince Pater; in both cases he was perhaps unlucky.

The concluding pages of Pater's essay on Winckelmann are
dominated by the name of Goethe. Like Mill, Pater wonders whether
Goethe's plan of life can be achieved under modern conditions;
unlike Mill, he set it up none the less as a goal to be striven after.
Pater's magnetism could be extraordinary. Few men can have been
more unlike him than the ambitious John Buchan, with his intense
admiration of worldly success; but as an undergraduate he felt a
special pleasure in belonging to the college where Pater had lectured
on Plato. In retrospect, though, he found something defective in his
undergraduate life: 'Some of us were men of the world too young:
humour and balance were prized too highly; a touch of Gothic
extravagance was needed to correct our over-mellow Hellenism.'[40]
This was the risk that Arnold had failed to foresee.

EDUCATION IN THE LATER NINETEENTH CENTURY

Culture and Anarchy was a symptom of two processes, both of
which it encouraged; and though one of these appears to be literary,
the other historical, they are hardly to be separated. In the first
place, Hellenism itself was changing in character; it was becoming
less an active enquiry into the past and more a symbol for a certain
type of aesthetic ideal which aimed at calm, balance and proportion,
or at any rate celebrated these qualities in the art of the past. In
fact, the Hellenism of Winckelmann and Goethe was about to be
revived. Winckelmann's idea had been valuable in its day, but in

the second half of the nineteenth century his theories had been tested and his inadequacies were plain to see. Pater, however, was blind; worse, he misled a whole generation. Arnold was confused and ambiguous about what he meant by Hellenism; but Pater seems never to have considered the possibility of ambiguity at all. He distinguished neither between theory and practice, nor between art and actuality. Greek ideals, Greek art, Greek life—all, for Pater, had been equally pure, clear and calm. Such a belief could only be maintained by closing one's eyes to the evidence, and late Victorian Hellenism became increasingly enfeebled by its failure to face reality. Arnold had once boasted that men who studied the classics constantly were more under the empire of facts than other people; Pater and his followers fell under the empire of fantasy.

At the same time the classics were becoming more and more associated, once again, with certain political or social attitudes. It was unfortunate that Hellenism should seem to be another name for opposition to reform, and certainly unjust to Arnold, whose years of devoted work as a school inspector were of great and lasting value. Here again Pater had a decisive effect by developing Arnold's distrust of political action into a modern form of Epicureanism. The ancient Epicureans had been quietists—'Live secretly' was one of their maxims—and the new Epicureans followed their example. When the word 'aesthete' sprang into existence in the eighties, it bore a pejorative sense: an aesthete was not just a lover of beauty but a man who shrank from the life of action. Unthinking Tories and languid egoists seemed to be the two classes of men who clung to the ancient world.

Cory had seen that a classical education ought to be a training in active and independent thought; and this meant that the ancients should not be approached in too reverential a frame of mind. 'Whilst revering the intellectual freedom of our heathen forefathers,' he wrote, 'we may honestly investigate their many errors; using them at once as patterns and as warnings.'[41] Jackson, the enlightened schoolmaster in Forster's *Longest Journey*, warns Elliot that he must not treat the past as a glorious contrast to the humdrum present: 'Impress on your class that many Greeks and most Romans were frightfully stupid.'[42] But Forster, whose picture of public school education at the turn of the century is largely just, means Jackson to stand out as a shining exception to the general rule. Men like Cory had had to contend with the Victorian tendency towards hero-worship; among old-fashioned dons and schoolmasters this tendency was worsened by a fear of conceding anything to the enemies of classical education, among the aesthetes by Pater's rhapsodic account of antiquity, which collapsed unless the Greeks were assumed to be virtually without fault.

Matthew Arnold's belief that the classics were of particular value in an industrial and scientific age was shared by others who did not feel his anxious distaste for the entire modern world. Mill wanted to call the old world in to redress the balance of the new: classical literature should be studied, he said, 'not as being without faults, but as having contrary faults to those of our own day'; and conversely, ancient states exhibited 'precisely that order of virtues in which a commercial society is apt to be deficient'.[43] When a scheme for the Owens College at Manchester, founded out of the bequest of a wealthy textile manufacturer, was published in 1850, its authors suggested that classical studies would be especially valuable in an industrial district: 'In a locality where men's minds and exertions are mainly devoted to commercial pursuits, it seems particularly desirable to select, as an instrument of mental training, a subject, which, being . . . remote from the . . . daily occupations of the individual, may counteract their tendency to limit . . . the power of applying the mental faculties.'[44] But alas, this heavy, worthy language made the classics sound more of a duty than a pleasure.

It was an unhappy mischance that two of the most influential educators of the nineteenth century were particularly opposed to scientific education. For most of his life, Jowett was sweepingly contemptuous of the sciences; Dr. Arnold was more respectful, but he felt that 'Physical science, if studied at all, seems too great to be studied', and during his reign at Rugby the amount of time devoted to the subject was actually reduced.[45] The Public Schools Commission found that the teaching of science was both slight and inefficient, and steps taken to improve the situation tended to be slow and half-hearted. Headmasters complained that there was no room in the curriculum for a further subject, and they were reluctant to cut down the time given to the classics.

Cory stands out in glorious contrast. This most inspired of classical teachers was not afraid that his subject would suffer from healthy rivalry, and he dared to teach science himself, besides pressing upon his pupils the works of Darwin.[46] Mill argued that classics and the sciences should go hand in hand, insisting that it was 'only the stupid inefficiency of the usual teaching which makes those studies be regarded as competitors instead of allies'. Similar views were expressed in Farrar's *Essays* by Houghton and Sidgwick; indeed, they were commonplace among those men of liberal opinions who were remote from the practical problems of devising a school curriculum.[47] Mill's modesty prevented him from realizing that the width of his own knowledge was the product of exceptional intellect and energy; the growth of specialization was already an inexorable process, and Huxley was being more realistic when he argued, in opposition to Mill, that the student of science could not afford to lose time in trying to acquire a classical education as well.[48] This was in 1880, at the opening of Josiah Mason's Science College, Birmingham, an institution from which the humanities were specifically excluded. Mason had made this stipulation in 1870, when he first set out his plans; the mood of the mercantile philanthropists had changed greatly in the twenty years since the Owens College had been set up.

The sixties were a time of vigorous debate about education. The most aggressive attacker of Newman's liberal ideal was Spencer, whose querulous carpings at everything to do with the ancient world were almost a backhand compliment. There was some truth, though, in his claim that thanks to their early training boys were left for the rest of their lives with a predisposition to depreciate everything modern.[49] By contrast, Spencer himself evinced a particular dislike, almost a hatred, of anything Greek—art, literature and philosophy; this again was an unconscious tribute to the special position of Hellenism in Victorian thought.

Despite its wide influence his *Education* (1861) reveals the virtues of the humane education that he so despised. With the brash assurance of a clever, self-taught man he laid down the law on any and every subject—the page headings included 'Worthlessness of ordinary history', 'How *not* to teach drawing', 'Warm clothing essential' and 'Elements of feminine attraction'—and he later confessed himself unable to comprehend how anyone could possibly hold the view of education opposed to his own.[50] He looked upon the small size of the ancient states with contemptuous indignation: how foolish to waste so much time studying such a 'minute space' of a world which is itself 'but an infinitesimal part of the Universe'. Lowe used the same argument, but it is not a good one. Athens is certainly smaller than the Crab Nebula; but that does not settle the matter.[51]

Spencer was hostile to the whole concept of a liberal education. He argued that the most important of human actions were those necessary for self-preservation, while the least important were 'those miscellaneous activities which fill up the leisure part of life, devoted to the gratification of the tastes and feelings'; education, he held, should have the same priorities.[52] Mill's belief that education

should aim to produce 'cultivated human beings' and Arnold's that
it should inculcate a love of beauty were to him absurdities.[53]
Huxley was less absolute; his assertion was rather that a scientific
education was as good a means of making men cultivated as a
literary one.[54] To this specious claim Arnold was able to make an
effective reply; but while the defenders of the classics were having
the best of the debate, their cause was being defeated in the field.
The Public Schools Commission of 1864 firmly recommended that
classics be kept as the basis of the curriculum, since Greece and
Rome had given birth to 'the most graceful . . . poetry, the finest
eloquence, the deepest philosophy' and so forth.[55] But the Inquiry
into Grammar Schools (1868) took a less idealistic tone. In the north
of England, the commissioners reported, classical education was
unpopular and in all but a few schools Greek had almost disappeared
because parents were keen on money-making and pressed for a
short, utilitarian education. The report was in favour of retaining
Latin, but principally on the prudential ground that it would be
inexpedient to dislodge it until there was a prospect of getting something better. Greek they thought unnecessary except for those few
schools that prepared boys for university.[56] Latin and Greek for the
upper classes, modern studies for the rest—this was a dangerous
position for the classics to be placed in. If they had declined equally
in all schools, their future might paradoxically have been more
assured. As it was, the worst suspicions of men like Spencer seemed
to be increasingly well founded, and the defence of the classics
became more and more associated, in T. S. Eliot's words, with
'sentimental Toryism, combination-rooms, classical quotations in
the House of Commons'.[57]

In the later years of the century the voice of public opinion took
on an ever more strident, anxious tone. Now that other nations
had gone through their own industrial revolutions Britain's pre-
eminence in the world was challenged; and the growing might of
Germany was not only a blow to English self-esteem but a threat
to the peace of Europe. In these circumstances the noisy jingoism
of the time found its most justified outlet in a nervous demand for
greater national efficiency. There were too few technologists, and
it was evident that in the future schools and universities would
have to devote more of their time and resources to the sciences. In
the event the ideals of Newman, Arnold and Mill were mauled but
not wholly discarded. Students today are offered what is essentially
a choice between a scientific training and a form of humane education
that has evolved out of the Victorian liberal idea. It was inevitable

that the humanities would have to give some ground to science; inevitable, too, that classics would have to share the field with other arts subjects such as history, English and philosophy. But the growth of these rival disciplines does not in itself account for the precipitous decline of classical education; no less important were those social and cultural developments which had created the feeling, obscure but powerful, that the study of Greece and Rome was tied up with stuffiness and snobbery. This was hardly a rational feeling; but reason does not often determine the spirit of an age. In 1600 a classical education seemed the key to all wisdom, in 1900 an outmoded irrelevance, but in truth it was scarcely if at all more valuable at the one date than the other.

'The lower classes,' Lowe wrote in 1867, 'ought to be educated . . . that they may . . . defer to a higher cultivation when they meet it; and the higher classes ought to be educated in a very different manner, in order that they may exhibit to the lower classes that higher education to which, if it were shown to them, they would bow down and defer.' At an earlier date this argument would have been used in defence of a classical education; Lowe, however, drew an opposite moral. A workman might be expected to know more about his own work than a politician, but the thought of such a thing filled Lowe with shame: 'So far from being able to assert . . . superiority, I am always tormented with the conception, "What a fool the man must think me. . . ." '[58] The classics must go in order that the populace be kept in their place; the ruling classes were starting to lose their nerve. Meanwhile, assailed on one side and uncertain of support on the other, the defenders of classics were often driven to an intransigence that was not in the best interests of their cause. This is symbolized in one way by the revelation in 1903 that Cambridge University had lost an endowment of £100,000 by its insistence that naval engineers should study Greek; in another by Mackenzie's schooldays at St. Paul's, described in fictional form in *Sinister Street*: 'You stinking Modern beasts! Classics to the rescue!'—and physics and chemistry textbooks scattered in the corridors. Then again there was the Classical v. Modern rugby match: 'Into that game Michael poured . . . detestation for everything that the Modern side stood for. . . . They were at Thermopylae, stemming the Persian charges . . .—they were at Platea with Aristides. . . .'[59] The hostility between science and classics persisted for a long time; how long and with what consequences it is neither pleasant to contemplate nor easy to assess.

The Revolt Against Respectability

MATTERS OF MORALITY

The classics were the staple of education; yet they were always potentially subversive. In Byron's poem Don Juan's mother finds the whole business horribly puzzling, and the boy's 'reverend tutors' (forerunners of Cory's 'possible clergymen') have a hard job to justify the study of indecent authors and an immoral mythology. At Harrow the poet himself had been amused to be given an expurgated edition of Martial, in which the objectionable epigrams were removed from the main text and printed together at the back, so that the smutty schoolboy was spared the trouble of reading the whole volume. George Eliot's Lydgate has enough education to read the indecencies in the school classics; Forster records that Maurice's 'interest in the classics had been slight and obscene'; here fiction accurately reflects real life.[60] The classics were kept as a masculine preserve not least because they initiated young gentlemen into the mysteries discussed in the smoking room or over the port before the company joined the ladies. Don Juan's mother was a respectable female, and that in large measure was why she found the classics so baffling; the masculine mind, gifted with a superior penetration, could understand, even if it could not explain, how they could be at once improper and improving. When Gilbert satirized women's education, he felt an agreeable frisson at the thought of sweet young things in contact with the naughty authors of the ancient world.[61] Melissa asks what authors a girl should read to succeed in classics, and Psyche answers,

> You should read Anacreon,
> Ovid's Metamorphoses,
> Likewise Aristophanes, . . .
> But, if you will be advised,
> You will get them Bowdlerized!

Antinomian individuals could needle the established order through this chink in its armour. There was an organization which went by the attractively simple name of the Society for the Suppression of Vice; in 1875 it decided that 'the book entitled Rabelais' should be suppressed, and Swinburne instantly despatched a letter of protest, written more in pleasure than in anger: 'This august Society might . . . exercise its omnipotence in the suppression of classical literature

. . . from the book entitled Homer to the book entitled Aristophanes the roll of Greek poetry calls aloud for . . . excision.'[62] Later, when there was an outcry over Burton's translation of *The Arabian Nights* Symonds declared, 'When English versions of Theocritus and Ovid, of Plato's *Phaedrus* and the *Ecclesiazusae*, now within the reach of every schoolboy, have been suppressed, then and not till then can a . . . rendering of the *Arabian Nights* be denied . . . to adult readers.'[63] None the less, he had himself the feeling that Greek literature had somehow been disinfected. In his *Studies of the Greek Poets* he suggested that the only age which offered any kind of a parallel to the era of Aristophanes was the Italian Renaissance; for a brief moment 'it seemed as if the Phallic ecstasy might possibly revive', but it was not to be, for while the Greeks had been unconscious of sin, the extravagances of the Renaissance were guilty and morbid: 'What was at the worst bestial in the Greeks has become devilish in the Renaissance . . . the comedies of Aristophanes . . . owe their licence in a great measure to their religious origin.' Contrasting Aristophanes with Rabelais, he claims that the Greek cannot approach the 'grossness peculiar to French Pantagruelism'; Rabelais 'carries us off to Gothic courts', whereas Aristophanes exhibits 'a sort of southern childishness'.[64] Greek smut is clean smut.

In defending Burton, Symonds lumped together Aristophanes, Plato, Theocritus and Ovid, but Plato is very much the odd man out. The three poets, at worst, could only titillate; the philosopher could sway the reader's mind. Among the later Victorians it was homosexuals who took the most interest in Plato's theory of love. In *Maurice* Forster describes how Clive Durham comes while still at school to accept his inversion: 'Never could he forget his emotion at first reading the Phaedrus. He saw there his malady described . . . calmly, as a passion which we can direct . . . towards good or bad. Here was no invitation to licence. He could not believe his good fortune at first. . . . Then he saw that the temperate pagan really did comprehend him, and . . . was offering a new guide for life.' Durham is a creature of fiction, and we may feel that his conversion sounds a little too precious and precocious to be true; but we should be wrong. In 1858 Symonds, then aged 17, came back late from the theatre; idly he picked up Cary's Plato, and turned by chance to the *Phaedrus*. He was spellbound. He read the dialogue right through, and then the *Symposium*. When he finally put the book down, the dawn had already broken; he had not slept, and yet he seemed to be awakening to a new world.[65]

The two stories have striking features in common: the intelligent schoolboy, the homosexuality, and the *Phaedrus*. Yet Forster cannot have known about Symonds's experience; the two incidents are so similar because they are both the products of Victorian conditions. The love that dared not speak its name has now become so insistently communicative that we easily forget how little was known about it a century ago. In 1850, thirty-three boys were expelled from the Woolwich Academy; the father of one of them told a reporter that he had no idea what his son was supposed to have done.[66] There were no sensible little paperbacks then; the Platonic dialogues contained almost the only intelligent discussion of the subject to be found anywhere, and when inverts first lighted upon them, the sense of liberation was overwhelming.

Plato glorified the love of one man for another, but he also preached perfect chastity. Many Victorian inverts shared the high-mindedness of the age, and the philosopher's temperance chimed in harmony with their own beliefs. If Plato set them free, he also imposed a demanding standard, which the best of them were proud to live up to; they were genuinely keen not to let Plato down. Durham takes Plato, in place of the Bible, as a 'guide for life'; ' "To make the most of what I have." Not to crush it down . . ., but to cultivate it in such ways as will not vex either God or Man.' Forster describes his calm and happiness: 'Clive had expanded in this direction ever since he had understood Greek. The love that Socrates bore Phaedo now lay within his reach, love passionate but temperate, such as only finer natures can understand.'[67] Under Plato's influence, Maurice and he do not consummate their love; Maurice does not 'unite' with another man until he meets the gamekeeper Scudder, who is not inhibited by an expensive education. Symonds's development followed a similar pattern. After discovering the *Phaedrus* he plunged into a romantic friendship with a choirboy; their emotions were passionate, but in obedience to Plato, they had done no more than hold hands after more than a year. In 1866 Symonds considered a friend's liaison with a schoolboy; he put the problem in the form of question and answer: 'Is this Eros Greek? No. . . . Is it what Plato would allow? No. . . . What is the source of Arthur's love? Is it intellectual sympathy? No. Is it moral good? No. . . . Is it chiefly aesthetical enjoyment and the pleasure of . . . sensuousness? Yes. Are these likely to produce moral and intellectual strengths? No.'[68] Intellectual sympathy and moral good are Plato's criteria; the affair is condemned simply because it is not, in the strict sense of the word, Platonic. But like Maurice, Symonds fell: in his later years a succession of complaisant young Italians offered him satisfactions that were far from cerebral. Symonds and his old tutor Jowett died in the same year (1893), and shortly afterwards Swinburne, in some *Recollections of the Master of Balliol*, seized the chance of transfixing Symonds with a malevolent aside: he implied that Jowett had perhaps been too indulgent to Plato's doctrine of love, but added that 'the most malignant imbecile' could not compare him with 'such renascent blossoms of the Italian Renascence as the Platonic amorist of blue-breeched gondoliers who is now in Aretino's bosom. The cult of the calamus, as expounded by Mr. Addington Symonds to his fellow-calamites, would have found no acceptance . . . with the translator of Plato.'[69] There is a malicious double allusion in this last sentence. Calamus, meaning 'pen', is the title of a collection of poems by Whitman, soaked in homosexual emotion and much admired by Symonds. The nonce word 'calamite' means, presumably, the user of a pen, but Swinburne evidently means to suggest another word; he dots his 'i's' but crosses only one of his 't's'. He was right to suspect hypocrisy; a year before his death Symonds told his daughter, 'I love beauty with a passion that burns the more I grow old. I love beauty above virtue, and think that nowhere is beauty more eminent than in young men.'[70] He presents this judgement in the tones of a connoisseur, and indeed he adds, 'This love is what people call aesthetic with me', exploiting the ambiguity that had come over this adjective in the age of Pater and Wilde. Indeed, Wilde and Douglas both indulged the illusion that a knowledge of antiquity had contributed to their downfall: the vulgarians in the jury-box, inadequately informed about Greek morality, had crudely misinterpreted the purity of their writings. If anything, the reverse was true: they were self-deceived by their dabblings in Plato. In *The Critic as Artist* Wilde recalled Arnold's remark that there was no Higginbottom by the Ilissus; he might have reflected that there was no Charles Parker, no Alfred Wood. He persuaded himself, or so he claimed, that these wretched youths were the modern equivalents of Lysis and Charmides. A little Plato is a dangerous thing.

The city states of Greece were male-dominated societies. At dinner parties no women were seen except flute-girls; men spent most of the day out of doors, in the streets and marketplaces, where women, or at any any rate women of good family, were not to be seen. At Athens women of the respectable classes lived in a condition not much better than purdah; at Sparta they were freer, but there, for special reasons, the atmosphere of masculine exclusiveness was even more intense. Victorian England bore little real resemblance to ancient Greece, but there was this similarity, that English males of the better classes spent much of their time in institutions from which women were barred: public school and university, army and navy, Parliament, the club. In both Greece and England a great many women fell into one of two types; on the one hand there were wives, mothers and sisters, chaste and worshipful; on the other there was the *hetaera*, the courtesan or the servant girl, inferior in class, an incitement to adventures delightful but sordid.

If heterosexual activity is either the violation of a goddess or an escapade with a whore, it comes to seem exciting but a little degrading. In such a millieu the invert who remained chaste and self-controlled might feel that his emotions were nobler than a normal man's because the disgusting side of love played no part in them. From this belief it was only a short step to the claim that a boy's kiss is purer than a woman's kiss. The English milord in lustful pursuit of a contadina would never dream of claiming that he was motivated by an abstract love of beauty, but Symonds, whose activities were not a whit less physical, sees fit to adopt a tone of self-congratulation. Similarly, the Revd. Edward Lefroy wrote, 'I have an inborn admiration for beauty, of form and figure. It amounts almost to a passion,'—that 'almost' is nice—'and in most football teams I can find one Antinous . . . some folk would say it was . . . sentimentalism to admire any but feminine flesh. But that only proves how base is the carnality, which is now reckoned the only legitimate form. The other is far nobler. . . . Platonic passion in any relationship is better than . . . animalism.'[71] Symonds averred, 'This passage . . . shows in how true a sense he possessed the Greek virtue of temperate self-control'—an equivocal comment.

Lefroy evidently assumed that if love is not consummated it is not carnal. He was not consciously a hypocrite, and Plato was a comfort because he seemed to offer him a way of distinguishing himself from other homosexuals whose behaviour he was too honest not to denounce. He was clearly pure in the technical sense, and no doubt he had persuaded himself that the nature of his emotion was therefore not lustful. In an address with the unhappy title *Muscular Christianity* he attacked Pater and Symonds, suspecting that their use of the term 'nature' might be a way of speaking about man's 'worst passions and most carnal inclinations'. 'The new religion,' he explained, 'seems to differ in a very important respect from Hellenism properly so-called. The Greeks had at least an ideal standard, that which they indicated by the term *to kalon*. Unquestionably they often fell short of it . . .; but there is no inconsistency in the general teaching of their greatest philosophers . . . they would not have tolerated for a moment a philosophy which . . . encouraged the cultivation of merely sensual faculties, without an equal training of man's diviner instincts.' Muscular Christianity, he declared, 'includes all that is brightest in Hellenism, and all that is purest in Hebraism'.[72] There is, no doubt, a weak form of pederastic emotion in which carnal desire is swamped by a mood of wistful adoration and plays only a small part. Perhaps Lefroy's feelings were of such a kind. Needless to say, this sentimentalism is not Plato's conception of a sublime love transcending physical desire.

Lefroy was more scrupulous than many. Plato valued homosexual above heterosexual love; he also distinguished between Aphrodite the daughter of Dione, goddess of earthly love, and Aphrodite Urania, the symbol of a heavenly love from which all earthly passion has been refined away. These two notions, the superiority of homosexual to heterosexual passion and the superiority of heavenly to earthly love, are distinct, but it was not difficult to confuse them. The confusion was encouraged by Carl Heinrich Ulrichs, who in the 1860s invented the terms Urning and Dioning to denote homosexual and heterosexual.[73] The terminology was eagerly adopted by English inverts; they called themselves 'Uranians', and fortified by this consoling word, convinced themselves that they were better than other people; the favourite theme of their numerous poetasteries was that love between males was pure, even holy, 'passing the love of women'.[74] The Gay Liberationists of today maintain that there is no qualitative distinction between inversion and normal sexuality: it is simply a matter of taste. The attitude of Victorian inverts was very different. This was partly, no doubt, because they took on the colour of their surroundings; the blend of moral earnestness and self-satisfaction was typical of the age. But there is a further explanation for the fierce hostility which many Uranians displayed towards the female sex; in Freudian terms it is manifestly the consequence of guilt and self-hate, projected into a hatred of women. To the Uranians Plato came as a godsend, because he seemed to lend philosophical weight to their prejudice.

The public-school world struck even foreigners as Hellenic; friendships flourished there which could easily seem similar to those that Plato described. But here we enter on very uncertain ground. The Victorians described schoolboy friendships with a fulsomeness which we find somewhat embarrassing, as in these two passages from novels of 1832 and 1844:

His face was quite oval, his eyes deep blue: his rich brown curls clustered . . . upon . . . his downy cheek. . . . I beheld him: I loved him. My friendship was a passion. . . . Oh! days of . . . pure felicity, when Musaeus and myself, with our arms around each other's neck, wandered together.

At school, friendship is a passion. . . . All loves of after-life can never bring its rapture, or its wretchedness; no bliss so absorbing, no pangs of jealousy . . . so keen! . . . what bitter estrangements and what melting reconciliations; what scenes of wild recrimination, agitating explanations, passionate correspondence; . . . what earthquakes of the heart . . . are confined in that simple phrase, a schoolboy's friendship!

Both passages are by the same man, and he was neither a weakly schoolmaster nor an epicene clergyman; the author is Disraeli, twice Prime Minister, and the most sophisticated of Victorian Prime Ministers at that.[75] In the first passage it is hard not to detect a tinge of sexual feeling; the second is not so certain; but in any case, a very worldly man was unaware, 130 years ago, of possible implications which are obvious today. Nor was he unusual: Thackeray declared that 'before the female enslaver makes her appearance' every generous boy worships a friend 'whom he cherishes in his heart of hearts; whose sister he proposes to marry'.[76] Dickens's unawareness is even more striking: Steerforth gives Copperfield the nickname Daisy, and regrets that he has no sister, since she would be the sort of pretty, timid little thing that he would like to know.[77] Yet even here a shadow of uncertainty lingers. It is not so much the presence of sex in Dickens that disturbs the modern reader as its absence. There is surely no sexual element, for example, in Nubbles's devoted worship of Little Nell, and, strange to say, it is precisely this lack which makes the relationship, to our sense, so oddly unpleasing. It is possible that Steerforth's feeling, if we may speak of a fictional character as though he were real, was of a sexless, chivalrous type; he certainly wanted to seem a hero in the eyes of others, and his chief motive for taking David up was to feed his own vanity.

To our worldly-wise generation the Victorians may seem pitiably blind, but we can easily be misled. Admittedly we now know that many adolescents pass through a homosexual phase; we also realize that institutions which keep men and women apart can prolong this phase. Much Greek homosexuality in the city states was of this kind, not an ineradicable inversion but an adolescent development abnormally protracted by a dominantly male environment. Freud has enlightened us; but he has also changed the nature of experience. Paradoxically he has added to our inhibitions: we find it hard to describe the pleasures of friendship in the vigorous and enthusiastic language that came naturally to our ancestors, and perhaps we are no longer even capable of forming the passionate but sexless attachments which they enjoyed; if so, the loss is greatly ours. It is often glibly assumed that *Tom Brown's Schooldays* is imbued with unconscious homosexual feeling, but this is most unlikely, because it is evident that Hughes understood the nature of schoolboy vice from his attack on the 'pretty white-handed curly-headed boys, petted and pampered by some of the big fellows, who . . . did all they could to spoil them for . . . this world and the next'.[78] To a later edition Hughes added a footnote: 'A kind and wise critic . . . notes . . .: The "small friend system was not so utterly bad from 1841–1847". Before that, too, there were many noble friendships between big and little boys, but I can't strike out the passage; many boys will know why it is left in.' We must not be too quick to doubt the existence of these 'noble friendships'; the two kinds of relationship, the honourable and the base, existed side by side, and the Uranians had an interest in confusing them. Tom Brown declares, 'Thank goodness, no big fellow ever took to petting me.'[79] There is no need to look askance at his friendship with young Arthur.

In the Greek experience, too, we can recognize a distinction between sexless devotion and homosexual love. The plot of the *Iliad* depends upon the passionate friendship between two males, and yet Gladstone was quite right to insist that there was no trace whatever of unnatural vice in Homer. True, some later Greeks did argue that the friendship of Achilles and Patroclus was sexual, but the theory is fraught with difficulty: the pederastic love of the Greeks was one-sided—the older man was the lover or *erastēs*, the younger the *erōmenos* or beloved—and Achilles could not easily be fitted into either role. So when the Victorians compared their friendships to those of the Greeks, the result could be ambiguous: a reference to Achilles and Patroclus might be either to Homer or to Plato. Some may hardly have known themselves what they meant; how ingenuous or disingenuous was Pater when he described the Spartans taking Castor and Polydeuces as types 'of a clean, youthful friendship, "passing even the love of women" '.[80] In the 1880s Lord Selborne described his youthful friendship with Frederick

Faber: 'The attraction of his looks and manners . . . soon made us friends, and our affection . . . became not only strong, but passionate. There is a place for passion, even in friendship; it was so among the Greeks; and the love of Jonathan for David was "wonderful, passing the love of women".'[81] Selborne was a former Lord Chancellor and a devout high churchman; Faber founded the Brompton Oratory. Did the early friendship between these two eminent and honourable men contain, unconsciously, a sexual element, or was Selborne merely using a fulsome form of language that sounds odd today? We cannot know.

When Hallam Tennyson was collecting material for a life of his father, he asked the Master of Balliol for an account of *In Memoriam*. Jowett stressed the importance of Shakespeare's Sonnets as a source, adding, 'He found the Sonnets a deeper expression of the . . . love which he felt more than . . . his dramas. The love of the Sonnets which he so strikingly expressed was a sort of sympathy with Hellenism.' Jowett had an especial horror of emotional friendships between males, and he must have been well aware that the Greeks were not always chaste and high-minded, and yet he was not afraid to bring Hellenism into the picture. Hallam Tennyson, belonging to a younger generation, was more cautious: when he quoted Jowett's remarks, he excised the second sentence, as well as another in which Jowett observed that it 'would not have been manly or natural' for the poet to have dwelt always on his sorrow.[82] This little episode well illustrates the delicacy needed for an understanding of Victorian emotions; neither the literary analogues nor the nature of the emotion itself can be neatly pinned down. Hellenism can mean almost anything, and to this day there is no general agreement about Shakespeare's Sonnets. And even if they do express homosexual sentiments, we cannot suppose that Tennyson's feelings were similar merely because he used them as a source. Besides, deep emotions by their very nature resist tidy classification, and there is the further complication that like religious experience, friendship can perhaps be described in terms of sexual imagery, or it can be a sublimation of sexual impulses; the two possibilities are quite distinct, even if we are not able to distinguish them. The wise man will not claim to have found any trace of sexual emotion in Tennyson's elegy.

There are Victorian writers, however, who unconsciously reveal themselves with appalling clarity. Farrar is a spectacular example, a man of the highest respectability, headmaster of Marlborough, Dean of Canterbury, happily married with ten children, and author

of a best-selling *Life of Christ*. (It was rumoured that Farrar got
£1,000 for the *Life of Christ*; 'And to think,' said the wags, 'that
Judas was content with thirty pieces of silver.') The three novels
of this pious cleric are pervaded by a clammy, oppressive atmosphere which makes them, in a grotesque way, compelling. The
sense of guilt and nameless fear which they convey recalls, if we may
compare the ridiculous with the sublime, the dark terrors of Greek
tragedy. In *Eric*, Farrar himself draws the comparison: 'Sometimes
the vision of a Nemesis . . . terrified his guilty conscience . . .;
and the conviction of some fearful Erinnys . . . dawning out of the
night of his undetected sins, made his heart beat fast with agony
and fear.' But what is this dimly revealed evil? Surely, we think,
Farrar is warning us against unnatural vice. This supposition seems
the more certain when the saintly Russell condemns the 'big fellows'
who take up little ones; his remarks are prompted by Eric's friendship with an older boy, Upton, 'a fine sturdy fellow of eighteen,
immensely popular . . . for his prowess and good looks . . . little
boys . . . idolised him, and did anything he told them very willingly.
He meant to do no harm, but he did great harm.' The meaning seems
clear, but Farrar has a surprise in store, for the friendship turns
out, almost, it would seem, in the author's own despite, to be a
temporary salvation for both boys. When the climax comes, Greek
literature is inevitably brought in to enrich the emotional atmosphere.
The two boys are standing by a window, with Upton's arm resting
on Eric's shoulder.

> Upton had just been telling Eric the splendid phrase *anērithmon
> gelasma pontou* which he had stumbled upon in an Aeschylus
> lesson . . ., and they were trying which would hit on the best
> rendering of it. Eric stuck up for the literal sublimity of 'the
> innumerable laughter of the sea,' while Upton was trying to
> win him over to 'the many-twinkling smile of ocean.' They
> were enjoying the discussion . . ., when Mr. Gordon entered.
> On this occasion he was particularly angry . . .[83]

Gordon, however, is portrayed as an insensitive man; Rose, the
all-wise, applauds the friendship. Above all, Aeschylus stamps it
with the seal of approval: there can be nothing seriously wrong
with two boys who discuss their Greek studies together. Similarly,
the good boys in *St. Winifred's* can be infallibly distinguished from
the bad by an irrepressible tendency to quote Homer. We can
hardly avoid confusing fiction with reality and concluding that
Farrar does not appreciate what Gordon is so angry about.

Julian Home is a university novel, with less scope for the passionate friendships described in the school stories; but Farrar cannot resist beginning with an account of his hero's schooldays. He goes out of his way to describe Home's friend Lillyston, who plays no part in the rest of the book: 'The school began in fun to call them Achilles and Patroclus . . ., Orestes and Pylades, David and Jonathan, Theseus and Pirithous.'[84] They enjoyed, Farrar says, a 'holy Friendship' and stimulated each other to high effort in a spirit of mutual emulation. This description appears to recall the Sacred Band of Thebes, a crack corps of warriors composed of pairs of lovers, whose passion inspired them to emulous deeds of courage. The extent to which Farrar can ignore the implications of what he writes is extraordinary. Forster describes a class at Cambridge: 'Mr. Cornwallis observed in a flat toneless voice: "Omit: a reference to the unspeakable vice of the Greeks".'[85] Men like Farrar literally omitted it, omitted it so completely that they ended up by understanding neither the Greeks nor themselves.

Others besides Farrar purified their writings with a tincture of Hellas; whenever the name of Theocritus crops up in later Victorian literature, or any reference to Sicily, homosexuality is seldom far to seek. Wilde slipped both the poet and the place into his verses; and he wrote to Douglas from prison, 'Your little book should have brought with it Sicilian and Arcadian airs, not the . . . breath of the convict cell.'[86] In *Sinister Street* Wilmot cries, 'How wonderful to be at school! How Sicilian! Strange youth, you should have been sung by Theocritus.' Among Wilmot's friends, 'Much of the talk . . . concerned itself with the pastoral side of school-life', and he himself gushes, 'Oh fortunate shepherd, to whom will you pipe tomorrow . . .? Oh lucky youth, able to drowse in the tempered sunlight . . ., while your friend splendidly cool in white flannels bats and bowls for your delight.'[87] Evocations of Greek pastoral poetry were particularly appealing when combined with a picture of English lads at their sports. Cory ends his *Invocation*,

> Now lift the lid a moment; now Dorian shepherd, speak:
> Two minds shall flow together, the English and the Greek.

Forster's Rickie Elliot believes Theocritus to be the greatest of Greek poets; besides idealizing the Graeco–Britannic sportiness of Gerald Dawes, he comes to have a deep feeling for Stephen Wonham, who is represented as the modern version of a Theocritean shepherd.[88] Rickie is heterosexual, but we could tell from the novel, without any other evidence, that his creator was not. S. E. Cottam wrote in praise of a pond[89]

> Where English boyhood swims,
> Where all, who have the eyes, can see
> The thews of Grecian limbs.

Lefroy published a volume of sonnets entitled *Echoes from Theocritus*. The mere mention of Theocritus arouses suspicion; suspicion turns to certainty once we discover that the poems include *A Football Player*, *The Cricket-Bowler*, and *A Palaestral Study*. Lefroy was also the author of what Symonds called 'a very characteristic collection of "Addresses to Senior Schoolboys" '. It was Symonds, again, who described *Bill: A Portrait* as 'almost rustic, the music like to that of some old ditty piped by shepherds in the shade'.[90] The curious feature of all this is that the love between men and women is dominant in Theocritus' poetry. Though there are a few allusions to homosexual emotions, few Greek poets seem more unequivocally heterosexual; moreover, he is at times very coarse. The view of him as a celebrator of chaste and sentimental inversion cannot be maintained by anyone who has taken the trouble to read him; and the cause of this strange misrepresentation must be sought elsewhere.

Although Victorian society, or parts of it, extended some degree of toleration to most forms of fornication, homosexual acts were taboo. Towards the end of the century, however, the cachet of the aesthetic movement gave a certain glamour to what before had been literally unthinkable, and well-educated inverts, who in an earlier generation might have been merely appalled by their own nature, began to seek carnal satisfaction. Sexual activity was unsafe in England, but in Italy one was out of danger, and there were plenty of peasant boys and fisher lads who would be happy to oblige. Hence that well-heeled succession of minor littérateurs who expired in Tuscan villas or Venetian palazzi, surprising their relations by the size of the legacies bequeathed to their devoted manservants. Ancient Greece had produced the literary treatments of homosexuality and Italy was where it was practised at the present day; in either case the imagination dwelt upon the Mediterranean world. Greece and Italy came together in Sicily, and Theocritus was dragged in to give a colour of respectability. And Sicily also came to acquire a more specific association, when the German photographer Gloeden settled at Taormina.[91] He specialized in portraits of local youths either naked or posed in vaguely classical

draperies with laurel crowns about their heads; 'Gloeden's celebrated series' achieved great popularity in certain circles, and it
was he, probably, who inspired Wratislaw's poem *To a Sicilian Boy*
and similar mortal verses from other hands. Ancient Greece or
modern Italy? The ambiguity was convenient.

Men like Symonds used the familiar dichotomy between north
and south again and again to contrast a guilt-ridden puritanism with
a joyful and literally unbuttoned paganism; the comparison is
implicit in almost all the homosexual literature that exploits the
idea of Greece. It is the more ironic, therefore, to find another
aspect of the comparison—the contrast between northern manliness
and southern decadence—used to purify English Uranianism.
Robert Cust noted with satisfied surprise 'that the much belauded
Italian model is not the vision of physical beauty that might be
expected . . . the average English lad is quite the equal . . . of the
Italian. Moreover, from his active habits of life he retains his
youthful grace . . . much longer.'[92] And E. E. Bradford wrote in
nervous self-justification:[93]

> Is Boy-Love Greek? Far off across the seas
> The warm desire of Southern men may be:
> But passion freshened by a Northern breeze
> Gains in male vigour and in purity.
> Our yearning tenderness for boys like these
> Has more in it of Christ than Socrates.

The truth is that the Greeks were used or abused to suit the
convenience of the moment. For the most part, however, the Hellenic
tone was employed to becloud emotions whose nature would otherwise be too glaringly plain. A great many slim volumes in this
vein appeared, filled with execrable verse: *Lysis*, *Whimsies* by
Philebus (author of *Young Things*, and *Ladslove Lyrics*), *The Flute
of Sardonyx, Charmides: or 'Oxford Twenty Years Ago'*. The authors
are almost all nonentities, Barford, Bradford, Summers—a procession of dim anxious figures who flit like shadows through the
underworld of Victorian culture. Yet shabby and insignificant
though these people are, they made their mark, for they gave
Hellenism a bad name—literally. In 1880, for example, the Revd.
Richard Tyrwhitt wrote of the Oxford of his youth, 'Vice was less
recondite . . . and did not glide about with the polite hiss of modern
days. There was coarse talk in certain sets, who had not yet been
cultured into Hellenism . . .; but, on the other hand, decency was
considered decent.'[94] Hellenism was no longer a great deep mine in

which men could dig eagerly for unguessed riches; it had become a screen to hide behind, or at best the title of a sect.

DECADENCE

Youth, purity, light—these qualities were often associated with Greece; but there was always the possibility of a different interpretation. As early as 1844 Disraeli invented Sidonia and made him an expert on the 'free ladies of Greece': 'There was . . . not an obscure scholiast, not a passage in a Greek orator, that could throw light on these personages, which was not at his command . . . no man was ever so learned in the female manners of the last centuries of polytheism as Sidonia.'[95] In part this paragon represents the old ideal of the gentleman scholar, but Disraeli's description also marks the beginning of an aesthetic, decadent attitude to the classics, an attitude implicit long before in the posturings of the Dilettanti Society.

Though Matthew Arnold declared the fifth and first centuries to be the modern ages of Greece and Rome, many Victorians, conscious of living in a secondary era, felt that they had more in common with the 'later' periods of antiquity, when culture had passed its acme; it was with a purpose that Lytton and Pater set their novels of Roman life well after the death of Augustus. Just before the Second World War MacNeice was to sum up the decline of Greece:[96]

> And Athens became a mere university city . . .
> And for a thousand years they went on talking,
>   Making such apt remarks,
> A race no longer of heroes but of professors
>   And crooked businessmen and secretaries and clerks
> Who turned out dapper little elegiac verses
>   On the ironies of fate, the transience of all
> Affections, carefully shunning an over-statement
>   But working the dying fall.

MacNeice was giving a satirical twist to the comparisons that had too smugly been drawn between Athens and England. Yes, England *is* like Athens, he implies, but like Athens in its days of decay. Those elegiac verses, so characteristic of English dons and schoolmasters, show the direction of his thoughts; above all, no one 'worked the dying fall' more assiduously than Pater and his imitators.

Pater had an immense influence over the clever young men who felt stifled by the priggishness and stuffiness of their elders; Yeats once said that to his generation *Marius* was the only sacred book. However, Pater's subtle, sensitive ideas could easily be coarsened; when Wotton is tempting Dorian Gray, he says, 'I believe that if one man were to live out his life fully . . . were to give form to every feeling, . . . reality to every dream—I believe that . . . we would forget all the maladies of medievalism, and return to the Hellenic ideal—to something finer, richer, than the Hellenic ideal, it may be.'[97] Pater was, in a way, a follower of Arnold, but many of his own followers were in rebellion against the moral seriousness so conspicuous among Arnold's generation. Wotton (or rather Wilde) interprets Pater's almost earnest advice to get as many pulsations as possible into the given time as the advocacy of a glamorously decadent, elegantly selfish way of life; and this he regards as Hellenic, though even he concedes that his ideal is rather 'richer' than anything the Greeks themselves knew.

Gilbert Murray observed in 1897, 'The "serene and classical" Greek of Winckelmann and Goethe did good service . . . in his day, though now we feel him to be mainly a phantom. He has been succeeded . . . by an aesthetic and fleshly Greek in fine raiment, an abstract Pagan who lives to be contrasted with an equally abstract early Christian or Puritan. . . . He is a phantom too, as unreal as those marble palaces in which he habitually takes his ease.'[98] At first sight the word 'fleshly' seems surprising. This luscious epithet had burgeoned in 1871, when Robert Buchanan had attacked Rossetti and the Pre-Raphaelites in an article entitled 'The Fleshly School of Poetry'. Few men, surely, could be less Hellenic than Rossetti; but ten years later in *Patience*, Gilbert put some distinctly Hellenic language into the mouth of the fleshly poet Bunthorne, who hymns 'the amorous colocynth' and 'The writhing maid, lithe-limbed, Quivering on amaranthine asphodel.'[99] Although Bunthorne's preciosities are mainly inspired by Japan and the Middle Ages, Gilbert's instinct was right: the bitter controversy over fleshly poetry and the outrage aroused by Pater's *Renaissance* were two aspects of a single phenomenon, an angry reaction to a new spirit that was coming into the world. The 1870s witnessed the beginning of the end of 'Victorianism'; Yeats was not far wrong in maintaining that modern poetry began with Pater's description of the Mona Lisa.[100] Pater and Rossetti were very unlike, but their followers combined the fastidious refinement of one with the turbid luxuriance of the other.

Gilbert seems at time to be satirizing *The Picture of Dorian Gray*, but Wilde's novel was written ten years after *Patience*; it is the full, rich flowering of a long, slow growth. Its visual world is an exotic but fastidious blend of Hellenism, japonaiserie and Louis Quinze; the mixing of Pater and Rossetti was facilitated by the eclecticism of the age. If Murray thought, however, that the fleshly Hellenists entirely rejected the Greece of Winckelmann, he was wrong. Though Wilde's Hellenism is gorgeously mingled with curious odours and strange luxuries, Pater's notion that Greek sensuousness does not fever the soul was too convenient to be abandoned. Wilde has his cake and eats it; he portrays a self-consciously decadent society, and yet he prates almost priggishly of purity. 'Decadent' is in itself an ambivalent word: though it often carries a connotation of moral depravity, it can be used in a purely descriptive sense to describe a culture that has passed its zenith. An interest in 'decadent' writers may be simply literary: that respectable Scotsman, J. W. Mackail, O.M. (described by a Glasgow newspaper as the greatest classical scholar to hail from the Isle of Bute) was fascinated by the strange literature of declining Rome; this was a natural reaction against the taste of the mid-century, which had fed so exclusively on so rich a diet: Homer, Aeschylus, Sophocles, Thucydides. It was a relief to come down from the heights for a while and breathe the more relaxing atmosphere of the valleys. Mackail was following in the footsteps of Pater, who displays the poet Flavian pondering upon the charm of Antonine literature, with its 'artificial artlessness'; 'Though it must count, in comparison with that genuine early Greek newness at the beginning, not as the freshness of the open fields, but only of a bunch of field flowers in a heated room.'[101]

Gilbert was not unjust, though, in giving Bunthorne's Hellenism a tone of discreet prurience. Dorian Gray has a fancy for very late Greek writers. Wilde mentions Philostratus and Procopius; the one is innocuous, the other perpetrated the lubricious *Secret History*. A similar doubt hangs over Wilmot's late antique tastes: 'I have spoken . . . of Lucian and Apuleius. There is Suetonius, with his incredibly improper tales that show how beastliness . . . flowers from the deposited muck of a gossip's mind. There is . . . Ausonius, whose ribald verses are like monkish reaction. . . . You must read your Latin authors well, for since you must be decadent, it is better to decay from a good source.' This is mere lip-smacking. The styles of both Gray and Wilmot are modelled on Des Esseintes, in Huysmans' novel *À Rebours*, but with a difference: whereas the imaginary Frenchman combines a deep knowledge of Latin with an inability to construe the simplest sentence in Greek, the Englishmen imbue their decadence with a more or less Hellenic tinge.[102]

There is an element of caricature in Mackenzie's portrait, but his own heady mixture of Anglo-Catholicism, Oxford romance and Cockney sensationalism was to be extravagantly caricatured in its turn by Hamish Miles and Raymond Mortimer in *The Oxford Circus* (1922): Gaveston ffoulis 'collected obscure texts from the Silver Age of every tongue, and the declining decades of every century yielded him their . . . curious fruits. He delighted . . . to pore over . . . the Eroticks of Kottabos the Syracusan. Recumbent upon a score of Liberty cushions, and meshed in the fumes of musk and attar and patchouli, Gaveston would ponder upon the corrupt and fetid beauty of the Sicilian's style.'[103] The burlesque is not subtle; but the parodists were right to blend decadent Hellenism with musk and attar. Pater had spoken of fields, and of flowers in heated rooms, a typically suggestive metaphor, appealing—but unobtrusively—to the senses of sight and smell alike. His whispered evocations were amplified by less introverted personalities. In *The Critic as Artist* Gilbert commends Meleager: 'For he too has flowers in his song, red pomegranate blossom, and irises that smell of myrrh. Dear to him was . . . the odorous eared-spikenard . . . the feet of his love . . . were like lilies set upon lilies. Softer than sleep-laden poppy petals were her lips, softer than violets and as scented.' Symonds, too, enjoyed imagery of scent and flowers: after praising the idyllists for their excessive beauty, he continued, 'Yet we agree with Shelley, who compares their perfume to "the odour of the tuberose, which . . . sickens the spirit with excess of sweetness".'[104] Here was the possibility of voluptuously decadent metaphor: the scent of the flower is sweet, but the stink of festering vegetation is sweet too. In a juvenile poem Hopkins had described himself dreaming of a spring evening: 'A little sickness in the air From too much fragrance everywhere.' He meets Death, who tells him, 'I mark the flowers ere the prime Which I may tell at Autumn-time.'[105] The metaphor could be reversed: perhaps one might catch a whiff of spring from the rotting decay of autumn. Adopting Pater's idea that the Renaissance was a continuation of Hellenism by other means, Symonds pointed to the popularity of Longus and Musaeus in that period, 'so that the accents of the modern Renaissance were an echo of the last utterances of dying Greece'. He described *Hero and Leander* as a 'poem of young love . . . born, like a soul "beneath the ribs of death", in the dotage and decay of Greek art'; 'Romantic grace and pathos were chiefly appreciated by the Greeks in their decline.

It is this circumstance perhaps which caused the tales of *Hero and Leander* and *Daphnis and Chloe* to attract so much attention at the time of the Renaissance . . . are not the colours of the autumn in harmony with the tints of spring?' Symonds is very severe, however, on the epigrammatists of Justinian's time: their poems are 'the very last fruits of the Greek genius, after it had been corrupted by the lusts of Rome and the effeminacy of the East. Very pale and hectic are the hues which give a sort of sickly beauty to their style. . . . But a man need be neither a prude nor a Puritan to turn . . . with loathing from these last autumnal blossoms. . . . The brothel and the grave are all that is left.' Symonds seems to feel strongly on the subject, for elsewhere he extends his condemnatory metaphor to epigrammatists who had lived hundreds of years earlier: 'It is the fashion among a certain class of modern critics to rave about the art of Decadence, to praise the hectic hues of consumption and even the strange livors of corruption more than the roses and the lilies of health. Let them pursue the epigrams of Meleager and of Straton. Of beauty in decay sufficient splendours may be found there.'[106] This description is wildly overdone; the reader who is led by it to 'peruse' the Anthology will find Meleager tame, and Straton merely coarse. The censorious tone carries no conviction. It was not so much that he was hypocritically devouring the perverted poetry he pretended to condemn, as that he ignored it in favour of a fantasy. The decadents did not go to Greek literature to have their experience enlarged; Hellenism had become merely a peg to hang one's preconceptions upon.

Like ffoulis, Symonds associates late Greek literature with the effeminacy of the east; the Hellenism of the decadents languishes in an atmosphere swimming with oriental odours. The air is heavy with metaphor, rich with suggestions of Parisian perfumes and the conservatory during the ball, the rose in the hair and the carnation between the teeth. All this is great fun, no doubt; but somehow the Greeks themselves have been forgotten.

XII

CLASSICAL ART IN THE LATER NINETEENTH CENTURY

W H E N Taine visited England in the 1860s, he was scornful of English painters. Turner was manifestly absurd and as for the rest, they were merely a branch of the Flemish school. 'Heroic painting,' Taine concluded, 'is rare and poor, as likewise figure painting. . . . Noble classical painting, the feeling for a beautiful body, . . . that . . . learned paganism to which David and M. Ingres made themselves the heirs in France has never taken root here.'[1] Only a few years after Taine wrote these words the situation was to be dramatically transformed. In France a group of young artists was to revive the experiments of the despised Turner at representing landscape and light in paint, and to earn for themselves the derisive nickname 'Impressionists'; meanwhile, on the other side of the channel the neoclassical school of Ingres and David, richly sentimentalized, was to enjoy an extraordinary late flowering. Gleyre was the pupil of Ingres; Poynter, the pupil of Gleyre, was President of the Royal Academy until 1918, continuing to turn out paintings of classical scenes at a time when Van Gogh and Cézanne were long dead.

Thomas Hope issued his *Costumes of the Ancients* in 1809 in order to encourage historical painting, which he considered to be the noblest form of the art. He complained that paintings of common life were far more popular: 'Landscapes and low-life groupes will everywhere meet a ready sale.' To Haydon, himself a history painter, the Elgin Marbles were a blinding revelation. He took Wilkie to see them and quite alarmed him by the vehemence of his enthusiasm. Wilkie too observed a 'capital subject' for a picture while standing before the marbles: two boys squirting water at each other. The anecdote puts the quarrel between high art and low art in a nutshell. Thackeray makes the historical painter Gandish as classical as Haydon: 'All studied from the hantique, sir, the glorious hantique. . . . Mr. Fuseli said to me, "Young man, stick to the antique; there's nothing like it".' But he recognizes that he is swimming against the tide: 'Igh art won't do in this country.' And one of his audience whispers, 'High art! I should think it *is* high art! fourteen feet high, at least!'[2] To most people the grand manner in painting seemed as outmoded as the epic style in poetry; as George Eliot claimed, the novel, commonplace and anecdotal, had taken the place of Greek tragedy, and the genre scenes painted by such as Wilkie were the visual equivalent of the novel. George Eliot presented *Adam Bede* as a 'Dutch painting' in prose:[3] Hardy added to the title-page of *Under the Greenwood Tree* the words, 'a rural painting of the Dutch school'. In 1846 Haydon made a last despairing attempt to elevate British taste by displaying his huge paintings of the 'Banishment of Aristides' and 'Nero playing the lyre during the burning of Rome' at the Egyptian Hall; the exhibition was a failure, not least because Tom Thumb the dwarf was drawing large crowds in another part of the building.[4] Low art, in an ironically literal sense, had defeated high art; and Haydon killed himself in despair. The classical style of painting seemed dead for all time; yet within thirty years a new school was to arise more consciously Hellenic than ever before.

In sculpture and the decorative arts the Greek influence was never entirely lost. Regency Hellenism survived, in a debased form, in much of the pottery and metalware shown at the Great Exhibition; like antique amphorae encrusted with barnacles, the chaste forms favoured in the early years of the century were still faintly discernible beneath the fussy knobs and bumps preferred by mid-Victorian taste. Owen Jones suggested in 1853 that the mania for Greek architecture started by Stuart and Revett was barely over;[5] but he was himself preparing the way for Hellenism to return, like Pater's Dionysus, in an altered form. His temper was eclectic: in his lectures he said, 'From the works of Egypt we may learn how to symbolize; from those of Greece we may learn purity of form; . . . from the Moors . . . the great powers of geometrical combinations', and so on;[6] and in his *Grammar of Ornament* he illustrated Greek, Gothic and Islamic forms with strict impartiality. However, his doctrine inevitably favoured Greece in the war against the Goths. In the words of his disciple Lewis Day, writing in 1880,

Owen Jones laid down the law that 'Flowers and other natural objects should not be used as ornaments, but conventional representations founded upon them. . . .' A quarter of a century ago the so-called 'natural' treatment of foliage and flowers was rampant. . . . I think it was mainly owing to . . . Owen Jones that the full tide of our tastelessness was turned. . . . Even his timidity (he was almost morbidly afraid of a touch of nature) was perhaps useful in effecting a clean sweep of all naturalistic ornament whatever.[7]

This is the very antithesis of Ruskin's teaching; Ruskin abominated the 'servility' of Greek ornament, but Day could say, 'There is scarcely a more useful expedient in decoration than that of *repetition.*' Ruskin shouted more loudly than Jones, but it was Jones and his friends who won the day. What is more, posterity has so far judged that Jones deserved to win. When we read Ruskin, we are conscious of confronting a powerful and ingenious mind whose preconceptions are vastly removed from our own. If we read Day, we nod our heads in sage agreement: yes, the decorative arts *were* tasteless in the fifties, and yes, the style of the eighties *is* delightful.

The Pre-Raphaelites, with the exception of Woolner, reacted against 'classical' conventions, and objected to students being made to copy antique statues. Yet by their love of hard edges and clear definition, their hatred of conspicuous brushwork (they nicknamed Reynolds 'Sir Sloshua'), they helped to pave the way for the Hellenic painters. They were much influenced by the Germans of the Nazarene school, and it was a Nazarene, Steinle, who taught Leighton. Architectural tastes, too, became as the century progressed, if not Hellenic, at least more sympathetic to Hellenic ideals. Gothic ceased to be the dominant style for secular buildings in the course of the seventies; the Queen Anne revival enjoyed its vogue in the eighties; and the thirty years preceding the First World War were a time of individualism and experiment, when architectural style ranged from an austere 'stylelessness' to full-blown historicism. The Gothic revival itself grew more 'classical', and the muscular, masculine styles of Street and Butterfield fell into disfavour: Bodley, who had begun as a disciple of Street, cultivated a refined but sumptuous nobility; Pearson built churches of bare and unaffected grandeur. Other architects changed more dramatically. Burges, who had created medieval extravaganzas at Cardiff and Castell Coch, risked a visit to Greece: 'It was not until I was actually on the spot,' he said later, 'that I understood how beautiful Greek architecture was.' He sought for correspondences between the Greek and Gothic spirits, comparing Herodotus with Froissart and Aristophanes with Rabelais. When he built a house for himself in Melbury Road, he combined Greek and Gothic motifs.[8] E. W. Godwin's conversion was more complete: his early work was confidently and conventionally Gothic, but later it was he, more than anyone, who gave visual expression to the aesthetic Hellenism of Pater and Wilde.

But even Godwin's Hellenism was eclectic; Greek prototypes were not to tyrannize the modern artist as they had at the beginning of the century. The walls of his drawing-room in Taviton Street were white; the hangings were grey-blue, with a Japanese pattern. In the centre of the room stood a cast of the Venus de Milo and before it a censer, from which issued a blue and fragrant smoke.[9] An affinity between the arts of Greece and Japan was recognized also by Godwin's mistress, Ellen Terry, who dressed either in Grecian robes or a kimono,[10] and by Albert Moore: in his painting 'Beads', for instance, the fan and jars are more or less Japanese, the figures more or less Greek.

It was an age of idiosyncrasies. The opulent blend of ancient Greece with eighteenth-century France that forms the backdrop for the story of Dorian Gray is discernibly different from Godwin's pure line and pale pastel tones. Different again was Beardsley, whose exquisitely simplified draughtsmanship, like Flaxman's, was much influenced by the Greek vase-painters; but whereas Flaxman had aimed for purity both of style and sentiment, Beardsley's manner was a complex synthesis of many influences combined with acute originality, and the content of his drawings was anything but pure. Equally individual, if less fundamentally original, was Watts, who harked back to another aspect of Regency Hellenism, the romantic titanism inspired by the sculptures of the Parthenon; with the Elgin Marbles in London, he declared, it was unnecessary to travel to Italy.[11] Casts of the famous frieze ran around the walls of his studio; above his chimneypiece, a quaint mixture of gothic fancy and arts-and-crafts homeliness, reposed the great figures from the pediment. Uncomprisingly monumental, they seem awkwardly out of place in this setting, symbolizing perhaps the unease with which Greek art fitted into the Victorian scheme. His own work was meant to fuse northern and southern qualities; he possessed, in the words of Mrs. Russell Barrington, 'the sense of noble Greek serenity emotionalised into passion by the temperament of the Celt'.[12]

Another artist who kept a cast of a Greek frieze in his studio was Walter Crane, for whom the land, literature and political ideals of Greece were inspirations as important as her visual art. His Greek travels prompted him to write conventional poetry about the glories of ancient Hellas (always Hellas, never Greece), contrasting them with the degeneracy of the industrial age or, in Byronic mood, with the desolation of modern Greece. An enthusiastic socialist, he saw in the city state a pattern for the ideal society, democratic in organization and humane in scale.[13] In 1887 he demonstrated the variety of Greek influence on Victorian culture by producing two sumptuous volumes entitled *Echoes of Hellas*, a sort of *Gesamtkunstwerk* uniting art, music, poetry and the theatre. His strong sense of linear design and his ability to compose gracefully within borders of any shape owe much to the example of the Greek vase-painters, and these volumes were printed in black and red to make the resemblance still more plain. The first consists of excerpts from Homer and Aeschylus; the second contains music composed by various hands for a performance of the *Oresteia* at London University.

Unlike some of his contemporaries, Crane did not let his Hellenism destroy his sense of fun. The pages of *The Baby's Opera* and *The Baby's Bouquet*, two collections of nursery rhymes, parody the fashion for the Pompeian and Grecian styles in the decorative arts. One of the rhymes in *The Baby's Opera* recounts an unhappy love story:

> There was a lady loved a swine
>   'Honey!' said she;
> 'Pig-hog, wilt thou be mine?'
>   'Hunc!' said he.

Crane depicts the sty as a Greek temple with a substantial pig carved in the pediment. In the foreground a gracious, drooping lady, classical in dress and hairstyle, bends over a gloriously hoggish hog. He is gently mocking the soft languor of Moore and his kind by confronting it with coarse animality.

Godwin, Watts, Wilde and Crane were vastly dissimilar men, but the diffusion of their various influences made ancient Greece the concern, as it had been a hundred years earlier, of those with advanced ideas about society, art and sexual morality. (Crane, however, though a radical in politics, led a private life of the deepest respectability. His wife forbade him to paint the female nude from the life, and he was obliged to employ a young Italian male, making some rather unconvincing adjustments afterwards. 'Why,' said Leighton, when he saw Crane's *Renascence of Venus*, 'that's Alessandro!')[14] Godwin's aesthetic and social beliefs were inextricably interwoven: as an advocate of female suffrage, he considered that women should not be in bondage to the corset; Greek dress was as rational as it was beautiful.[15] Wilde, actuated no doubt by motives more aesthetic than political, tried to popularize Godwin's ideas: 'Over a substratum of pure wool, such as is supplied by Dr. Jaeger . . ., some modification of Greek costume is perfectly applicable to our climate . . . and our century.'[16] Watts, who might seem to have little in common with Godwin save a love of Greece (and of Ellen Terry), was equally hostile to tight lacing. And Greek sculpture, he thought, could regulate the smallest details of female appearance. Greek statues do not have pointed finger-nails; therefore young ladies must not point their nails. Greek statues of women have rather large feet; therefore tightly pinching shoes should be avoided. The Greeks did not wear high heels; therefore . . .; and so on.[17]

In 1885 some Royal Academicians sponsored a ball to which the ladies were asked to come dressed as Grecian damsels;[18] for a moment it seemed that the age of Thomas Hope might be reborn. Godwin, who had emulated Hope even to the extent of designing a Greek armchair, was sufficiently encouraged to devote most of the next year, his last, to designing the costume and staging for John Todhunter's Hellenic drama, *Helena in Troas*. Arnold and Swinburne had composed their imitations of Attic tragedy without the expectation or even the intention of performance, but now such was the enthusiasm for things Greek that the work of their follower, the imitation of an imitation, was put upon a real stage. This Hellenic occasion brought together two fashionable worlds, the aristocratic and philistine circle of the Prince of Wales, who came to the first performance, and that raffish milieu whose most spectacular member was Oscar Wilde. Never much troubled about being fair when an epigram was possible, Wilde remarked that the verse form of the play owed 'more to the courtesy of the printer than the genius of the poet'; none the less, he persuaded his wife to appear in a minor role.[19]

Symonds was expressing a received view when he wrote, 'Music, dancing, acting, and scenery, with the Greeks, were sculptural, studied, stately; with the moderns they are picturesque, passionate, mobile.'[20] Godwin's intention was to restore the ancient style, and his staging was almost literally 'sculptural': the women of the chorus were posed in the attitudes of the Parthenon frieze, and their costumes of unbleached linen were designed to resemble Pentelic marble. The production was a triumph. Wilde called it 'the most perfect exhibition of a Greek dramatic performance that has as yet been seen in this country'.[21] The young Yeats seemed to be unable to keep it out of the articles which he wrote for American newspapers: 'an immense success' . . . 'the talk of the London season' . . . 'eloquent verse and incomparable staging'.[22] And he judged Todhunter's next play to be even finer.

Helena offered the play-goer a richer and more various experience than he was usually given, a combination of poetry, graceful movement, and, as Yeats believed, a suggestion of yet higher things: 'Its sonorous verse, united to the rhythmical motions of the white-robed chorus, and the solemnity of burning incense, produced a semi-religious effect new to the modern stage. . . . Many people have said to me that the surroundings of *Helena* made them feel religious. Once get your audience in that mood, and you can do anything with it.' But Yeats also felt that much of the play's success was 'due to the wonderful stage—the only exact reproduction of the stage of ancient Athens seen in the world—and the no less wonderful stage management'.[23] This attempt to recreate the ancient stage was not, as it turned out, merely an archaeological exercise; while Todhunter's versification looked back to the past, Godwin's production looked to the future. His abolition of the proscenium arch, his placing the chorus in the midst of the audience and the astringent simplicity of his presentation anticipated twentieth-century developments. Stravinsky was following in Godwin's footsteps when he decreed that the dancers of his *Apollon Musagète* should be monochromatically dressed and limit themselves to 'strictly classical' movements. Nor was Godwin's influence restricted to explicitly Hellenic works: the stagecraft of his son, Edward Gordon Craig, owed much to his father's example.

Towards the end of his life Yeats admitted that he had 'overrated Dr. Todhunter's poetical importance',[24] but it is hard now to see why he should ever have been impressed by those impeccably correct and entirely dull iambics. The explanation is surely that he saw new possibilities opening up before himself. Most people, he lamented, had 'bowed the knee to those two slatterns, farce and melodrama'; but the Athenians had created a theatrical art that was both religious and aesthetic, both cultivated and popular. Yeats persuaded himself that Todhunter and Godwin had shown the way to achieve again that happy state; *Helena* was, as he said, 'an art product, the appeal of a scholar to the scholarly', and yet it 'filled the theatre with the ordinary run of theatre-goers'. Now Todhunter also wrote poems based on Irish mythology. 'They are Greek,' said Yeats, with conscious paradox, '—like the young—as young as nature. *Helena* was as old as mankind.' He agreed that *Helena* held an important place among 'the many hopeful signs of a revival of higher drama', but explained that Todhunter would have been truer to the Hellenic spirit if he had taken an Irish subject.[25] He had not been cynical in advising the playwright to get his audience into a religious mood: he believed that Irish legend still had a living meaning for the Irish people and that plays which drew upon it could restore that unity of art and society which the Greeks had enjoyed. Such were the plays that he proceeded to write. Todhunter has long been forgotten, but during his brief moment of glory he helped to inspire modern poetic drama by pointing the way to Yeats and thus indirectly to T. S. Eliot. The spirit of Hellenism had triumphed again—and yet failed; for the plays of Yeats and Eliot have remained distinguished oddities, obstinately outside the mainstream of English drama.

Greek culture was a target of satire in Gilbert and Sullivan's last collaboration, *The Grand Duke* (1896). Like *Patience* (1881), this new piece mocked the pretensions of those who aspired to be cultured; but whereas in the earlier operetta these aspirations were towards a greenery-yallery medievalism, in the later they are purely Grecian. So far had the new classicism spread in fifteen years. The 'ordinary theatre-goers' came to *Helena in Troas* because they had been prepared for it not only by Godwin and his friends but by other artists more popular and more conventionally respectable.

The grandest of these was Frederic Leighton. Talented, successful, effortlessly charming and superbly handsome, Leighton seemed more like a character out of a novel by Disraeli than a real being. Indeed he *was* a character out of novel by Disraeli, for Mr. Phoebus in *Lothair* was largely based on him. He was also the model for Lord Mellifont in *The Private Life* by Henry James. In Leighton's case life imitated fiction in an almost disturbing fashion. Disraeli describes one of Phoebus's great triumphs, a picture of Hero watching for her lover Leander;[20] Leighton did paint this picture, seventeen years after the novel came out. He was not a peer when James wrote his story; but he was to be ennobled in the last month of his life, the only painter ever to be so honoured.

'The most English of our artists,' Wilfred Meynell called him, '. . . English in birth, blood, and character.' Other critics described this so Hellenic painter more paradoxically: according to Sir Wyke Bayliss, 'Lord Leighton . . . was born on a rough English coast, he lived his life in Hellas, and died in London. That is to say, he was English of the English, Greek of the Greek'; while Mrs. Barrington thought, 'Probably no Englishman ever approached the Greek of the Periclean period so nearly as did Leighton, for the reason that he possessed that combination of intellectual and moral power in a like rare degree. . . . But, being essentially English as well as Greek-like, Leighton pushed this combination of powers to a moral issue.' The same air of paradox runs through a description of his 'Daphnephoria' by W. B. Richmond: 'It . . . could only have been painted in this century, the classic feeling it demonstrates is of to-day, when the severer forms of classic art appeal to the cultivated with more force than formerly. The feeling is Greek, not Roman! more Theocritean than Virgilian; . . . yet highly ideal.'[27] Hardly any criticism could have been more gratifying to Leighton than this, for as he told Steinle, 'I am . . . passionate for the true *Hellenic* art and am touched beyond everything by its noble simplicity . . . the *Roman* is antipathetic to me—I had almost said disgusting.'[28] He steeped himself in the literature as well as the art of ancient Greece; so perfect a person was inevitably an admirable linguist, and well grounded in Latin and Greek by the age of ten.[29] Two of his paintings were suggested to him by the second Idyll of Theocritus;[30] a visit to the Acropolis recalled to him the funeral speech of Pericles; when planning his frieze 'Music', he consulted Swinburne for authoritative advice on Greek mythology.[31] His Hellenism, like the rest of him, had to be flawlessly well-rounded.

Since Greek painting has perished entirely and is known only through a very few Roman imitations of doubtful accuracy, it might seem difficult to create a genuinely Hellenic style of pictorial art. The Victorians were not so easily deterred. 'So it seems a Greek painter must have painted women,' wrote Swinburne of Watts's 'Wife of Pygmalion'. Watts himself, like Ruskin and Symonds, was able to behold the lost statues of Greece with the eye of faith. He was particularly attracted by the Athena of Pheidias: 'I sometimes feel as if I can see it,' he said. 'The fragments give one a great idea of what the Pallas Athene was, probably most spiritual and exceedingly strange'—a description that makes it sound remarkably like one of those grand allegorical figures in which Watts himself specialized.[32] Poynter was able by some mysterious insight to draw detailed comparisons between the developments of the Greek and Italian schools: Polygnotus was the Orcagna of Greek art, producing works 'in a severe style, without perspective . . ., possibly of one colour', while Zeuxis probably combined 'the pictorial and monumental character in about the same degree as the exquisite little picture of the Graces by Raphael . . .; or, may we venture to bring into the comparison, at least as regards simplicity of arrangement and perfection of composition, the *Creation of Adam* and the *Creation of Eve* in the Sistine Chapel?'[33] These speculations combine apparent exactitude with an enormous vagueness: if one can compare an artist equally well with the heroic grandeur of Michelangelo and with Raphael at his most miniature and precise, one might as well admit to ignorance.

Leighton's Hellenism, however, amounted to more than wishful thinking about an unknown past. 'He shared Plato's opinion,' one critic observed, 'that violent passions are unsuitable subjects for art.'[34] His few attempts at representing heightened emotion are certainly unfortunate: 'The Jealousy of Simaetha, the Sorceress' depicts nothing more than a handsome Victorian lady; his 'Bacchante' is absurdly decorous. A few people complained that his pictures were too smooth and the flesh tints of his nudes too pale; but perhaps a certain vapidity of colour and texture were felt to be Hellenic. According to Richmond, 'His technique was exactly in sympathy with the pellucid atmosphere of Greece, and the refined and crisp forms of her landscape.'[35] Who but a Victorian, though, would call the Greek landscape 'refined'?

It was in his composition that Leighton was most Hellenic: again and again he arranged his pictures like the maidens and horsemen on the Parthenon frieze. Still more like a frieze is the manner in which he divides the areas within a painting by exactly horizontal lines. This is exemplified in 'A Syracusan Bride Leading Wild Beasts in Procession . . .'. The figures are all mounted on a marble terrace, the edge of which makes a horizontal line close to the bottom of the picture. In consequence the action seems to be taking place on a stage, and the painting is unhappily reminiscent of a theatrical tableau. The beasts—lion, tiger and leopard—are supposedly tamed by the bride's beauty and chastity, but they appear to be suffering from the effects less of feminine virtue than of taxidermy. Equally stagy, but in a different way, is 'Greek girls playing at Ball': here the horizontal line divides the foreground from a distant landscape of sea and mountains as flat as the backdrop in a theatre. The same formulae are employed again in 'Winding the Skein', and here the staginess is still more obtrusive, because the line dividing foreground from background is formed by the edge of a terrace, recalling those balustrades used in the theatre to separate the playing area at the front from the painted canvas behind.

He was at his best on those rare occasions when he shook off the yoke of Hellenism. Perhaps the best of his oil paintings are 'The Garden of the Hesperides' and 'Flaming June'; mannered in composition, oppressive in colouration, they convey a strong sense of heavy and even sinister languor. But like Matthew Arnold, Leighton struggled against the natural bent of his talent for the sake of being Greek. We may complain that his figures are lifelessly static, but he strove earnestly to make them so; even wild beasts are depicted when they are in a state of exceptional passivity. There is a thorough-going seriousness about his Hellenism that is absent from the other 'classical' painters of the time. Unlike Tadema, say, or Poynter, he seldom designs to allure his public with soft tints or a sentimental theme. He had at least the courage of his highly academic convictions.

He was himself like a Greek sculpture in being unaware of the soul and its maladies. Sexual passion seemed to trouble him not at all. In both his work and his personality he stands oddly alone and apart from Victorian artists, and his paintings never gained from the public the delighted affection that some of his contemporaries enjoyed. But this, paradoxically, was half the secret of his success. Many Victorians, as we have seen, looked down upon the subjective, 'secondary' art of their own times; they worshipped men such as Bach and Homer, unmistakably sublime artists, yet objective and impersonal. Leighton too was objective and impersonal; he ran counter to 'modern' tendencies; he was 'Greek of the Greek'. And yet by very virtue of being in this sense 'un-Victorian' he was fitted to become the perfect example of a Victorian success story—'English of the English'. Cricketers sometimes say that the bowlers win the matches and the batsmen get the knighthoods. Leighton was a 'batsman', a Gentleman rather than a Player, the captain of the team; such vitality as there was in late Victorian art may have lain elsewhere, among the humbler painters of landscape or social life, but it was Leighton who seemed chosen by destiny to become President of the Royal Academy, baronet, and peer. His work inspired not love but (what was better) respect; he might not enchant the eye like a Tissot or a Grimshaw, but one had only to glance at his paintings to appreciate that this was Culture, this was High Art.

The Victorians worshipped genius and undervalued minor art; so the artists of the time were playing for very high stakes: either they would be objects of reverence for future generations, they thought, or they would be completely insignificant. And the historical self-consciousness of the age meant that in any case they tended to think too much about how posterity would regard them. The consequence was that some of them set about creating 'masterpieces', instead of following the direction in which their native talents would naturally have led them; even so witty an artist as Crane turned out large, dreary pictures with classical trappings and allegorical significances. This tendency was not confined to visual artists. Perhaps Hardy's real gifts as a novelist were for depicting the country scene and the humours of rustic life, but he was determined to be the Aeschylus of Wessex. Matthew Arnold deplored the introspective melancholy that was his greatest strength, and composed *Sohrab and Rustum* in a deliberate effort to 'be a poet' of the best sort; there are places where the echoes of Homer seem to have been inserted for the sake of some commentator of the twenty-fifth century, who will annotate the venerable text and record the parallels in the way that classical scholars note the Greek antecedents of Virgil or Horace. Tennyson actually wrote his own notes on the *Idylls of the King*, marking the passages where he had imitated Homer and Pindar.

In the first of Pater's *Imaginary Portraits*, set in the early eighteenth century, a friend of Watteau describes how the painter has decorated a room:

Odd, faint-coloured flowers fill coquettishly the little empty spaces here and there, like ghosts of nosegays left by visitors long ago, which paled thus, sympathetically, at the decease of their old owners; for . . . all this array is really less like a new thing than the last surviving result of all the more lightsome adornments of past times.

In other words, the painter is making something new look antique and faded. These are revealing words, for such an attempt to anticipate the experience of posterity would be strange in the age of Watteau but is eminently characteristic of the nineteenth century. The great merit of the old masters was that they were old: what Samuel Palmer enjoyed in Claude was 'that Golden *Age* into which poetic minds are thrown back, on first sight of one of his genuine *Uncleaned* pictures'.[36] Trollope's Miss Van Siever tells Dalrymple that she cannot care for modern pictures in comparison with ancient ones:[37]

'But I do not in truth mean anything derogatory to the painters of the day. When their pictures are old, they . . . will be nice also.'

'Pictures are like wine, and want age, you think?'

'Yes, and statues too, and buildings above all things. The colours of new paintings are so glaring . . .'

Leighton's admirers were equal to the challenge that such opinions posed. Sir Charles Holroyd reported from the Tate Gallery, 'No pictures here are improving at anything like the rate that Leighton's are; the wax has taken hold of the colours and worked them into the canvas.' 'This', commented James Harlaw, 'is the secret of the brilliance to-day of the great Italian masterpieces—so we may truly call Leighton a great colourist.'[38] Such was the remarkable way in which doubts about Leighton's flesh tones were answered.

Holroyd and Harlaw, writing after Leighton's death, were trying, as it were, to speed up his elevation to the status of old master; but even in his lifetime he had seemed to contemporaries to occupy the kind of heroic position that belongs to the great figures of the past. In James's story the narrator says of Mellifont, 'When he was talked about I always had an odd impression that we were speaking of the dead. . . . His reputation was a kind of gilded obelisk, as if he had been buried beneath it; the body of legend . . . of which he was to be the subject had crystallized in advance.' The trouble was that Leighton knew this himself. When he painted his self-portrait, he used the Parthenon frieze as a background (he too had a cast of part of it let into the wall of his studio). The curling hair upon his brow recalls a Greek statue; the cut of his beard suggests Pericles or even Zeus; he gazes directly at the spectator with a passionless expressionless serenity. In one sense this is one of the least revealing self-portraits ever painted; in another it tells us a great deal about the artist. For this is unmistakably the portrait of a Great Man; it is also the portrait of a figure from the past, a Greek deposited in Victorian London. As a young man Leighton had liked to reconstruct the lives of famous artists: one of his earliest pictures showed Cimabue finding Giotto among his sheep, and he made his name with a painting of Cimabue's Madonna being carried in procession through the streets of Florence. The Madonna is borne aloft above the heads of the populace, though whether as an honour to the Mother of God or as a tribute to the artist's genius is unclear. Cimabue himself, holding the boy Giotto by the hand, walks ahead of his painting. The Florentines are honouring an 'old master' while it is yet new; they have the good fortune to see genius walking, like any mere mortal, through the streets of their city. These were the privileges that Leighton's life and work were to offer the Victorian connoisseur.

His wooden portrayal of Clytemnestra shows him at his pompous worst. Lys Baldry, however, praised its 'statuesque dignity', the 'admirable drawing of the draperies', the 'reticence and scholarly restraint'; and indeed the clichés of academic criticism do seem to leap out of the canvas. It is as though Leighton dutifully set about putting into his pictures, one by one, the elements that *ought* to be found in the work of a master. This is especially evident in his treatment of clothing. Ruskin had argued that drapery carved or painted for its own sake was always base: all noble draperies were the expression either of motion or of gravitation.[39] Leighton's work could almost have been designed to corroborate these improbable assertions: his draperies, wholly unrealistic, seem to have no artistic function, but to be obtruded on the spectator's attention because 'management of draperies' is one of the categories that the academic critic ticks off on his mental scorecard. Leighton's figures are draped rather than dressed, Mrs. Barrington observed, and this approving judgement condemns him; his draperies belong to a realm where Art (with a capital a) has lost contact with life. His method is revealing; 'I can paint a figure in three days,' he once said, 'but it may take me thirty to drape it.'[40] His studies for the 'Captive Andromache' show that he began by painting the figures in the nude. Then, as though pouring treacle over them, he overlaid these slender bodies with a thick shapeless layer of something that he was eventually to work up into the form of clothing. In the final version Andromache has mounds of ponderous drapery heaped upon her; she might almost be encased in plaster. It was just, no doubt, that on another of Leighton's canvasses Helen of Troy, the source of Andromache's troubles, should be subjected to the same sartorial purgatory. Elsewhere, as in 'Daedalus and Icarus' and 'Greek Girls Playing at Ball', he painted draperies caught by the wind, and these are yet more artificial and obtrusive, being crinkled like crêpe paper. As a depictor of the figure he fits perfectly the late Mr. Finching's description of antique sculpture: "There being no medium between expensive quantities of linen badly got up and all in creases and none whatever'—a fair criticism of the late Greco-Roman sculpture so abundant in Italy, but hardly applicable to Greek works of the 'best period'.[41] Ruskin said of drapery, 'An Athenian always sets it to exhibit the action of the body, by flowing with it, or over it, or from it, so as to illustrate both its form and gesture; a Florentine, on the other hand, always uses his drapery to conceal . . . the body, and exhibit mental emotion.'⁴² This acute analysis indicates that in his treatment of clothing the devoutly Hellenic Leighton was fundamentally un-Greek. But he did not use drapery in the Florentine manner either: his draperies exhibit neither emotion nor the absence of emotion; they express nothing whatever.

Ruskin questioned the general opinion that Leighton was a type of the classic ideal, claiming him 'in some degree . . . as a kindred Goth'. He noted that among all the treasures of Greek antiquity, 'you can get no notion of what a Greek little girl was like', but he was pleased to find Leighton 'condescending from the majesties of Olympus to the worship of these unappalling powers, which . . . are as brightly Anglo-Saxon as Hellenic; and painting for us, with a soft charm peculiarly his own, . . . the wonderfulness of childhood.' And perhaps his more ambitious pictures are in the end equally un-Hellenic; there is something soft, something Victorian about the broad healthy features and full-bosomed figures of his women. Maybe Mrs. Barrington was making the same point, in more hagiographic fashion, when she said of his 'Atalanta', 'For noble beauty of the Pheidian type . . ., it would be difficult to find its peer in Modern Art, and yet it was only the worthy record of the beauty of an English girl.' And though he strove to create grand and timeless works, there are indications that he felt a strong pull towards the genre scenes and anecdotal pictures painted by so many of his contemporaries. This shocking truth emerges from the incautious praise of Ernest Rhys: 'Winding the Skein', he wrote, shows 'two Greek maidens as naturally employed as . . . English girls. . . . This idealization of a familiar occupation—so that it is lifted . . . into the permanent sphere of classic art, is characteristic of the whole of Leighton's works. He . . . contrived also to preserve a . . . contemporary feeling in the classic presentment of his themes. He was never archaic.'⁴³

Leighton was 'English of the English' in other ways too. His Nausicaa simpers against her pillar like a Victorian maiden. In the background of 'Daedalus and Icarus' there is a miniature Doric column, perhaps two and a half feet high, with a statuette of Athena on top; it looks like a bibelot on a stand in a Rothschild drawing-room. Leighton could no more escape from the limitations of his age and country than any other artist, and his attempt to turn himself into a Greek was a grievous mistake. In no circumstances could he have produced works of genius, but he might have been a minor artist of considerable merit. His drawing of a lemon tree on Capri is a *tour de force* of precise and complex observation; his woodcuts of biblical scenes are forcefully dramatic; his sketches of Egypt are attractive. But he *would* paint 'masterpieces'.

Alma-Tadema, by contrast, gained from his interest in antiquity. His early pictures of Merovingian subjects, such as 'The Education of the Children of Clovis' and 'Fredegonda at the Death-Bed of Praetextatus', are as boring as their titles suggest; but when he turned to classical scenes, he struck a vein of facile charm that was well suited to such talent as he possessed. Unlike Leighton, he did not try to make himself a Greek or even a Roman; being Dutch by birth, he was perhaps too busy turning himself into an Englishman. Like Fildes or Stone, he was fond of genre scenes; the main difference between him and the others often seems to be merely that he preferred an antique setting to one taken from the seventeenth or eighteenth century. The very titles of his paintings make his anecdotal intentions plain enough: 'Who Is it', 'Shy', 'He Loves Me; He Loves Me Not'. P. C. Standing wrote enthusiastically, 'In "Not at Home" a Roman girl is telling a polite "fib" to a caller, a Roman gentleman, who, half-suspecting, gazes in as if longing to catch a glimpse of the lady for whom he is obviously enquiring.'[44] Does this sound like ancient Rome?

Marble, which he painted with brilliant facility, has a conspicuous place in almost all his works. On his own admission he was inspired with his passion for this material not on classic soil but amid the modern splendours of the smoking-room of a club in Ghent,[45] and indeed many of his pictures suggest that the life of ancient Greece and Rome was that of a Victorian club writ large. Yet he took great pains to get the antiquarian details right; *Blackwood's Magazine* reported from the Academy in 1875, 'As usual, the archaeology is boldly defiant of critical doubts.'[46] But the same exhibition roused Ruskin to indignation:

> The actual facts which Shakespeare knew about Rome were . . ., compared to those which M. Alma-Tadema knows, as the pictures of a child's first story-book compared to Smith's *Dictionary of Antiquities*. But when Shakespeare wrote:
>
> > 'The noble sister of Publicola,
> > The moon of Rome; chaste as the icicle . . .'
>
> he knew Rome herself, to the heart; and M. Alma-Tadema,

after reading his Smith's *Dictionary* through from A to Z, knows nothing of her but her shadow.[47]

Ruskin's instincts were right, but it was peculiarly hard for him to justify them. Twenty-two years earlier he had attacked the very idea of historical painting; for one thing, it was un-Greek:

> Suppose the Greeks, instead of representing their own warriors . . . at Marathon, had left us nothing but their imagination of Egyptian battles; and suppose the Italians . . . had left us nothing but imaginary portraits of Pericles and Miltiades? What fools we should have thought them! . . . and that is precisely what our descendants will feel towards us, so far as our grand historical and classical schools are concerned. What do we care, they will say, what those nineteenth-century people fancied about Greek and Roman history.

For once Ruskin was a true prophet: although we are pleased by the nineteenth-century flavour of Manet and Degas (a taste that he would have deplored), few pictures seem to us more 'Victorian' in a limiting sense than those which attempt to reconstruct the distant past. It was in Ruskin's nature to press his ideas to a dogmatic conclusion: of all the great masters, he said,

> there was *not one* who confessedly did not paint his own present world, plainly and truly. Homer sang what he saw; Phidias carved what he saw. . . . How did Hogarth rise? Not by painting Athenian follies, but London follies. . . . I suppose the most popular painter of the day is Landseer. Do you suppose he studied dogs and eagles out of the Elgin Marbles?[48]

Ruskin believed that historical painting was like Grecian architecture; people pretended to admire it, but secretly it bored them. Landseer, like Gothic architecture, was genuinely popular; therefore he had found the right style for his century. This argument might tell against Leighton; against Tadema, however, it is entirely ineffective, for no one could deny that he was enormously popular. More than any of his contemporaries he appealed to those who did not know much about art but knew what they liked. It is appropriate, somehow, that his biographer, Standing, should have been a universal amateur, author of such diverse works as *On this High Wold*, *Gleanings from Ibsen*, *Guerilla Leaders of the World* and *The Cricketers' Birthday Book*.

Even at the time Ruskin's argument got him into difficulties. It is simply not true, even in the loosest sense, that the great Italians confined themselves to depicting their own times; and in any case he was anxious to except the historical works of the Pre-Raphaelites from his censure. With some awkwardness he extricated himself from the tangle, maintaining that 'where imagination is necessarily trusted to', the Pre-Raphaelites always endeavoured 'to conceive a fact as it really was likely to have happened', trying to 'make . . . their fancy so probable as to seem like memory'.[49] These painters, in other words, seem to have been present themselves at the medieval scenes which they depict; they are reliable reporters, almost photographers. In consequence they enable the spectator too to travel through time; they draw him away from the present and bring him close to the past. In this respect the Pre-Raphaelites were quite unlike the historical painters of the preceding generations, who had deliberately kept the past in the past by presenting it in an obviously ideal and 'generalized' form. Unfortunately for Ruskin, though, they were very like the historical painters of the succeeding decades: almost every picture that Tadema ever painted invites the viewer to step into the canvas and join the ladies and gentlemen. Ruskin had not, as he supposed, distinguished a quality peculiar to the Pre-Raphaelites; rather, he had stumbled upon something that recurs again and again in the art, and indeed the literature, of his time.

The Victorians loved fancy dress. 'The costume of the nineteenth century is detestable,' says Lord Henry Wotton. 'It is so sombre, so depressing.' His friend Dorian Gray falls in love with an actress: 'I have seen her in every age and in every costume. Ordinary women never appeal to one's imagination. They are limited to their century. . . . One knows their minds as easily as one knows their bonnets. . . . But an actress! . . . the only thing worth loving is an actress.'[50] Only an actress could be romantic, because only an actress could spend her life 'dressing up'. Besides, fancy costume had a soothing effect; it distanced one from scenes and emotions that would otherwise be unacceptable. Lamb maintained that the same people who recoiled with disgust from Hogarth's 'Gin Lane' 'would perhaps have looked with complacency' on Poussin's 'Plague at Athens': 'Disease and . . . Terror, in *Athenian garments*, are endurable, and come, as the delicate critics express it, within the "limits of pleasurable sensation".'[51] Sexual emotions, too, could be tamed if they were wrapped up in Greek costume: 'I had drawn you,' Hallward tells Gray, 'as Paris in dainty armour, and as Adonis with huntsman's cloak and polished boar-spear. Crowned with heavy lotus-blossoms you had sat on the prow of Adrian's barge. . . . You had leant over the still pool of some Greek woodland, and seen . . . the marvel of your own face. And it had all been what art should be, unconscious, ideal, and remote.'[52] Remote—that is the significant word. When Hallward finally paints Dorian in modern dress, he reveals to his sitter, and perhaps even to himself, the secret of his love. There may seem to be a contradiction here: on the one hand, the historical painters and novelists were trying to bring their contemporaries to an intimate relationship with the past; on the other, they were using the past to soften passions and actions by the enchantment of distance. The resolution of this paradox is a key to understanding the Victorians' attitude towards the ancient world.

'The affections are immortal'—that was the principle upon which Lytton tried to recreate the life of Pompeii. In its outward features the Roman world looks very different from our own; but if one looked more closely, so Lytton believed, one would discover that human nature had not altered one whit in eighteen hundred years. This was true of small matters as of great; Lytton stressed that he was not idealizing the ancient world, and he is at pains to point out how similar the gossip, flirtations, pretensions and petty snobberies of the Romans were to those of his own time. And yet for all that he does idealize the past: life in Lytton's Pompeii runs as though on greased wheels, with an unnatural smoothness. His characters are modern, but they have been transported into a distant world of painless elegance and order. In fact, they are Englishmen in fancy dress.

Now the Romans were, as everyone agreed, an imperfect people, but the Greeks had been virtually exempt, so it was said, from those blemishes which have marred human arrangements in other times and places. Lytton's hero and heroine are Greek; they are also—one can almost say, therefore—superbly good looking, exquisite in taste, and fervidly democratic. The ancient Greeks are perfect; at the same time, because human nature is unchanging, they are so like us. And so they are insidiously transformed into ourselves acting out our fantasies, clad in lovely loose robes and freed from the small irritations of modern life, slovenly servants, beastly weather, hideous cities, and the tedious restraints of Victorian convention. Almost any period of the past could be used for such escapism, but on the whole antiquity was more suitable than the Christian centuries; and to those of really refined culture Greece was better than Rome. In the New Republic, says Mallock's Mr.

Rose, 'Your feelings will not be jarred by the presence of human vulgarity, or the desolating noise of traffic; nor . . . will your eyes be caught by abominable advertisements. . . . They will rest, instead, here on an exquisite fountain, here on a statue, here on a bust of . . . Aphrodite, glimmering in a laurelled nook.'[53] Many of Tadema's paintings are just as Rose describes: upper-class life with the traffic and the hoardings excluded.

Thackeray detected a strong pictorial element in Lytton's novel, applauding the ingenuity with which he had 'illustrated the place by his text, as if the houses were so many pictures to which he had appended a story'. Lytton himself constantly invited such a response. It is a symptom of the weakness of his imagination that he presents the daily life of Pompeii as a series of static tableaux, as when the villain comes upon Glaucus and Ione seated side by side in the peristyle: 'The scene—the group before Arbaces—was stamped by that . . . ideality of poesy which we yet, not erroneously, imagine to be the distinction of the ancients,—the marble columns, the vases of flowers, the statue . . . closing every vista; and, above all, the two living forms, from which a sculptor might have caught either inspiration or despair!' The splashing of a fountain refreshes the sultry heat of noon; handmaids attend at a little distance; a lyre reposes at Glaucus' feet; in short, we seem to have a scene from Tadema before us.[54]

The resemblance is not purely coincidental. Tadema was turned from Merovingian to classical subjects by his honeymoon in Italy, and the main enticements seem to have been the colour and brilliance of the south and the 'everyday life in olden times' revealed at Pompeii and Herculaneum[55]—the very same attractions that had drawn Lytton. The two men were complementary: the one painted stories, the other wrote pictures. Both were nervously exact with their archaeological accessories, but these nice correctitudes merely heighten the escapist quality of their creations. The most successful fantasies are supplied with an abundance of circumstantial detail, apparently realistic: Ian Fleming's readers know exactly the brand of James Bond's cigarettes and the make of his car, but his actual adventures are incredible, and would seem horribly unpleasant to anyone who took them seriously; the reader is invited not to be James Bond but to dress up as him, like a child playing a game of make-believe. Lytton unconsciously and Tadema perhaps half-consciously create the same effect. 'I venture to believe,' wrote Lytton, 'that scholars themselves will be the most lenient of my judges. Enough if this book . . . should be found a portrait—unskilful,

perhaps, in colouring, faulty in drawing, but not altogether un-
faithful to the features and costume of the age which I have attempted
to paint.' This scenographic attitude is the antithesis of true historical
imagination. By paying so much attention to costume, Lytton
unwittingly gives the impression that his Pompeians are highly
self-conscious about their clothes and customs, whereas the real
Pompeians must have taken such things for granted. Kingsley's
feeling for the past was far stronger, but he too sought to show his
readers their own likenesses 'in toga and tunic, instead of coat and
bonnet'.[56]

One of Tadema's paintings is called 'A Reading from Homer';
an eager listener lies on his stomach gazing up at the reciter. It is
as though he were sprawled on the hearthrug by a Victorian fireside,
but in fact he is lying on bare marble in a position that could only
be appallingly uncomfortable. The figures belong to one era and
the background to another; once again, the effect is of fancy dress.
The very realism with which Tadema paints houses and gardens
actually increases the effect: the marble seems so much more important than the people. Thackeray applauded (a little patronizingly,
it is true) the artist 'who has an aptitude for painting brocade
gowns' and 'bits of armour (with figures inside them)';[57] today
we may feel that the figures should be more important than the
armour. It is revealing that although Tadema is apparently concerned with the accurate recreation of a bygone age, we can seldom
date his scenes even to the nearest century or two. Some of his
settings must be Roman, a few must be Greek, but even these are
not easily distinguished. His 'Sappho' shows a scene on Lesbos
around 600 b.c.; 'In the Rose Garden' and 'Pleading' are set
(presumably) in Italy during one of the imperial centuries of Rome;
but in all three pictures the faces, the mood, even the marble terraces
are virtually the same.

In *Daniel Deronda* George Eliot ironically showed how too great
a concern with roles and costumes might enfeeble the imagination
of intelligent people. Wilde made a similar point: Hallward emphasizes the pretty accoutrements with which he ornaments Gray
because he is trying to conceal from himself a fact of his own nature.
The novelists did not exaggerate; in fact, the artists who painted
fancy-dress pictures tended to live fancy-dress lives. They devoted
infinite care to beautifying their studios, and the books and articles
written about them by their contemporaries usually included full
descriptions of these rooms, complete with illustrations. There are
no messy rags or half-squeezed tubes of paint; these studios are not

workshops but shrines; the artist is hero, the maker of masterpieces, and the faithful are privileged to behold a sacred place. At the same time the art-lover could satisfy his taste for boswellism and enjoy, apparently, a peep at the domestic life of the great man. In one of Tadema's pictures the connoisseur could see Phidias—yes, the great Phidias—at work on the Parthenon; similarly, the subscriber to the *Art Journal* could glimpse the places where painters created the masterpieces of modern times. 'Hars est celare hartem,' says Gandish; Thackeray snobbishly implies that a man who misplaces his aitches and mispronounces the name of Phidias should not aspire to be a grand artist: he cannot live up to the part. Wilde's Lord Henry Wotton takes a different view: 'The only artists I have ever known, who are personally delightful, are bad artists. Good artists . . . are perfectly uninteresting in what they are. A great poet . . . is the most unpoetical of all creatures. But inferior poets are absolutely fascinating.'[58] But did Wilde himself agree? After all, few Victorian writers took more pains to make themselves 'absolutely fascinating' and 'the most poetical of creatures'. 'When you are not on your pedestal,' he was cruelly informed by Lord Alfred Douglas, 'you are not interesting.'[59] Confronted with Leighton, an artist who made sure that his pedestal remained firmly beneath his feet, Henry James came to a conclusion similar to Lord Henry's: the artist who devotes his talent to making his own personality a masterpiece will never create masterpieces in paint. *The Private Life* is a ghost story, a parable about the nature of creativity. Mellifont is entirely a public man; he is less than a whole person, and when he is alone, he simply ceases—literally—to exist. On one occasion he goes off alone to sketch an Alpine scene; but since he does not exist outside company, he cannot begin to paint until he has an audience:

> 'There won't be any sketch.'
> 'Unless we overtake him,' I subjoined. 'In that case we shall find him producing one, in the most graceful attitude, and the queer thing is that it will be brilliant.'

As the narrator and his companion come to look for him, Mellifont materializes out of nowhere:

> He looked neither suspicious nor blank; he looked simply, as he did always, the principal feature of the scene. Naturally he had no sketch to show us, but nothing could better have

rounded off our actual conception of him than the way he fell
into position as we approached. . . . His beautiful little box of
water-colours reposed on a natural table beside him, a ledge of
the bank which showed how inveterately nature ministered to
his convenience. He painted while he talked . . .; and if the
painting was as miscellaneous as the talk, the talk would equally
have graced an album.

James was right; Leighton's style of life was the masterpiece
that his paintings were not. His house (designed by the District
Surveyor of Upper Tooting)[60] was a worthy setting for him, and
here he gave the best parties in London. The showpiece was the
Arab Hall, where the artist and his guests could play at being
Turkish pashas. Art and life in Leighton's case were curiously
dissevered; as a painter he was an earnest Hellenist, but in his own
home there was no trace of Hellenic influence to be found, except
for the inevitable cast of the Elgin Marbles, and that, significantly,
was in his studio, where he exchanged the part of the perfect host
for that of the great classical painter. Tadema adored fancy-dress
balls; Whistler was astonished to behold him barefoot and wreathed
in flowers, wearing a toga and a pair of spectacles.[61] His home,
Townshend House, was not one fantasy world but many. As though
inhabiting Pinewood or Elstree, he could pass from one period piece
to another; there was a Gothic library, a panelled Dutch room, a
drawing-room with columns and onyx windows, and a Pompeian
studio, 'with frescoes from the master's hand'.[62] But in due course
the painter, to use Helen Zimmern's words, 'quitted this beautiful
abode, which had grown too small for his domestic requirements'.[63]
The new 'abode' (that word is somehow fitting) was again eclectic—
a 'delicious blend of old Rome, old Athens, and of the natural
country', according to Standing—but this time there was more
emphasis on Pompeii: Tadema called his library the atrium and his
dining-room the triclinium.[64] 'If you do me the favour to walk into
the Hatrium . . .' said Mr. Gandish;[65] life imitated fiction, and
Tadema was to repeat in his Dutch accent what Gandish had said
in his Cockney.

Thackeray approved of an artist dressing himself up: 'I love his . . .
jaunty velvet jacket. . . . Why should he deny himself his velvet?
It is but a kind of fustian which costs him eighteen-pence a yard.'
He concludes that the painter 'under yonder terrific appearance of
waving cloak . . . and shadowy sombrero, is a good, kindly, simple
creature, got up at a very cheap rate . . . his life is consistent with

his dress: he gives his genius a . . . romantic envelope, which, being removed, you find, not a bravo, but a kind, chirping soul.' Thackeray does not reflect that the earnest, unfashionable endeavours of a Gandish might be preferable to such affectation. When he comes to describe the *vie de Bohème* in Rome, he writes, 'What a gallant, starving, generous, kindly life many of them led! What fun in their grotesque airs, what friendship and gentleness in their poverty!'[66] Starvation is less entertaining than he supposes; these artists are again merely playing charades. Clive Newcome himself is doubly detached from the true bohemian life, for although he moves in these artistic circles, the reader is assured that he can retreat to the 'other society of Rome' whenever he chooses. Thackeray's dispiriting picture may not be due entirely to a failure of imagination: the British artists described in *Trilby* seem equally to be respectable chaps having a bit of a rag, and Du Maurier like Thackeray had known the bohemian life of Paris at first hand. Perhaps the native Frenchmen were more genuine; at any rate, Murger's *La Vie de Bohème*, for all its faults, depicts a seedy, extravagant way of life with a conviction lacking in the English writers, and lacking, it may be, in the English artists themselves.

In many of his pictures Tadema used the same elements as Leighton—maidens, marble and the sea—but he treated them with a winsomeness alien to the older painter. Those melting girlish faces are somehow very modern in their effect, and they are meant to be. The columns, the oleanders and the deep blue sea are painted with a sensuous enjoyment of their colours and textures, and often with an almost photographic realism. One of these paintings is aptly entitled 'Dolce Far Niente'; Tadema's alluring, evocative style is designed to show us that ancient civilization flourished in the idle, idyllic warmth of Mediterranean lands. Prospective purchasers might well be reminded of holidays or honeymoons in Italy, and Tadema's young ladies are, indeed, Victorians transported away from reality into a sunny realm of perpetual holiday. His settings are very like the women's college imagined by Tennyson:[67]

> a court
> Compact of lucid marbles, bossed with lengths
> Of classic frieze, with ample awnings gay
> Betwixt the pillars, and with great urns of flowers.
> The Muses and the Graces, grouped in threes,
> Enringed a billowing fountain in the midst;

And here and there on lattice edges lay
Or book or lute . . .

The marbles, the frieze, the pillars, the statuary, the fountain, all suggest the world of Tadema and Poynter. Yet *The Princess* came out in 1847, long before either of them were launched on their classical careers. But the resemblances are not fortuitous: the poet was presenting an idealized picture of contemporary life, and so in effect were the painters, tempering it with the 'refined ideality' that Lytton so admired. The difference was that whereas *The Princess* was avowedly a fantasy, the others claimed to be recreating the ancient world. Tennyson mentions books and lutes, scattered on the window-sills with, as we surmise, a deceptively casual grace. These too recall the painters; for it is the combination of idyllic elegance with little domestic touches that creates much of their appeal. The ordinary, everyday life of antiquity, as they depict it, is so similar to the life of today, and yet so very different. In 'The Shrine of Venus' Tadema painted what appear to be Victorian girls reclining on a sofa; he is portraying a distant, pagan civilization, and yet how like, one may feel, how very *like* the home life of our own dear queen.

Domesticity, indeed, is the essence of many of his paintings. We are invited to peer through a keyhole at the private lives of Greeks and Romans and enticed into a gossipy curiosity about their feelings and circumstances: why is she looking so pensive? could it be that nice young man . . .? A good number of these pictures contain no male figures, but just a solitary girl or a group of girls together, as if the painter's male clientele could look and see how women behave when they are on their own and unaware that anyone is eavesdropping on their feminine intimacies. For the bolder art-collector he also specialized in pictures of bath-houses which not only gave play to his talent for painting marble but enabled him to introduce young women in various states of fetching undress. It is usually the buildings that give these pictures their titles, as though archaeological reconstruction were the painter's principal aim and the figures merely incidental. 'An Apodyterium' shows a pretty girl taking her clothes off: 'apodyterium' simply means 'undressing room', but the long Greek word adds tone. In 'The Frigidarium' the foreground is occupied by a curtain, momentarily drawn back by a slave to give us, by chance as it were, a distant glimpse of girls bathing. The picture is inquisitive, and yet coy: the quick peek, the furtive glance are an important part of the effect, heightening the spectator's sense of the reality and modernity of the scene. Tadema seems usually to have calculated that discretion is the better part of titillation; an exception is 'In the Tepidarium', which depicts a luscious nude lying with parted lips on a couch and holding up a provocative pair of feathers to cover the last vestige of her modesty. The pose in not so very different from Manet's 'Olympia', but whereas the Frenchman takes a classic composition from Titian and puts it into an unromantic, contemporary setting, Tadema takes a modern cocotte and projects her back into a safely distant past.

Harlaw presents Leighton's 'Bath of Psyche' as a wondrous mixture of high culture and striptease:

'Psyche's' contour is perfect and her form is deliciously rounded. The exquisite pearly fairness of the skin must ever make this rendering of the amorous deity the standard of colour as well as of modelling. . . . This achievement ranks among the finest of the very greatest masters of the nude. Dorothy Dene, Leighton's favourite model, here displays her charms for the admiration of mankind.[68]

Miss Dene went on to the stage, and Harlaw thinks of the painting as a pin-up of an actress. In general Leighton seems to have painted the naked body without any feeling for the sensuous attractions of flesh, but almost from a sense of duty, because it was required that a great classical painter should be a 'great master of the nude'. In consequence, his nudes are among the dullest representations ever painted of a subject not naturally dull.

'Psyche' is an exception, and the affectionately soft, blurry treatment of her face and hair show a freedom of handling rare in Leighton's work. Yet even Psyche, despite what ought to be a teasing, seductive pose, is surprisingly unprovocative. Tadema's propriety was more in doubt, and Helen Zimmern was troubled by 'The Sculptor's Model', which portrayed a naked woman standing in front of a man: 'The work leaves us decidedly cold, and its nudeness is rather unpleasant, because a little lacking in ideality.' Standing, however, insisted robustly, 'The purity of the conception, the wonderful flesh-tints and the slender girlishness of the nude figure, formed a . . . combination of charm before which every note save undivided admiration was silent.'[69] One suspects that 'girlish' and 'lacking in ideality' amount to much the same thing; the nude figure is too much like a real woman. Surely Helen Zimmern is upset precisely because the work does not leave men cold, because the nudeness is all too pleasant. An advantage of classical art was that coquetry could be represented as modesty. Disraeli describes a statue of a woman shown to Lothair: 'Though veiled with drapery which might have become a Goddess of Modesty, admirable art permitted the contour of the perfect form to be traced.' Mr. Phoebus himself, in this respect more like Tadema than Leighton, portrays a figure 'exhibiting in undisguised completeness . . . the female form, and yet the painter had so skilfully availed himself . . . of some gauzelike drapery, which veiled without concealing his design, that the chastest eye might gaze . . . with impunity.'[70]

Poynter was essentially a stuffier version of Tadema: his pictures, filled with marble, mosaic and blue sea, exhibit the splendours of ancient architecture set off by a tender domesticity. He was particularly fond of 'corners' for the sense of casual intimacy that they evoked: 'A Corner of the Villa', for instance, shows a girl feeding pigeons amid surroundings of the usual magnificence. He used the same pose again and again: a maiden is sitting idly at the foot of a marble wall, in a corner; often she is eating fruit. The figure in 'Under the Sea Wall' is just like a Victorian girl having a picnic, except that a Victorian girl did not picnic with one breast exposed. He also cultivated a more grandiose style of historical painting: 'The Ides of March' is classical *grand guignol*—marble and gold, torches flaring, and the lurid light of a comet in the sky. Yet even here the scene is domestic at heart: Calpurnia pleading with Caesar to stay with her, a wife and a husband at home.

The art of Albert Moore is more elusive. He shared Leighton's fondness for frieze-like compositions, but there the resemblance ceased. Thanks to the delicacy and distinctiveness of his palette he was one of the very few English artists appreciated by Whistler; his admirers acknowledged the Greek influences on his work but regarded him, unlike the other classical painters, as a purist. Moore did not give titles to his pictures, it was noted, until he had completed them; they stood or fell on their own merits, without support from the evocative power of history or mythology. None the less, one may sense in his work various sentimental tugs at the emotions which are perhaps the more insidious for being partly disguised. Most of his works are set in a timeless, ideal world, and yet, though his mood is so different from Tadema's, his subjects are often similar; he likes to show women in private, domestic settings, at their toilet, talking together, dressing and undressing. The artist peeps into the boudoir, or the harem. Moore's paintings are suffused with vague intimations of Mediterranean joys; several of them are named after luscious fruits—'Pomegranates', 'Apricots', 'Oranges': 'Kennst du das Land, wo die Zitronen blühn. . . .' The heavy, odorous luxuriance of the south is suggested by another title, 'Jasmine', and that suggestion is reinforced by the subject of the picture, a slumbering girl. Moore loved to paint his women asleep or half-asleep; like Pater, he is a little weary. But the weariness is always pleasurable, as in 'A Summer Night', where the languorous semi-nudity of the figures tells us that the day has been hot and the evening is still warm. The still, moonlit sea in the background conveys the same message; we know, somehow, that its presence refreshes a drowsy atmosphere in which the torrid heat of day yet lingers. Indeed, since the draperies and the frieze-like composition are loosely Grecian, do we doubt that it is the Mediterranean? Moore has something in common with J. F. Lewis, another delicate and individual craftsman, who lived for some years in Egypt and whose pictures of Ottoman ladies and gentlemen relaxing in cool green interiors deliciously dappled with broken sunlight transported a delighted English public to an exotic, scorching and yet comfortable clime. Both painters held out a beaker full of the warm south, and the art lover drank it down greedily.

In his *Sketches in Italy and Greece* Symonds unconsciously exposed the way in which some of the classical painters worked on their admirers. He described the quarries where the Athenians captured on the Sicilian Expedition were imprisoned, and observed, 'The dames of Syracuse stood doubtless . . . above. . . . What the Gorgo of Theocritus might have said to her friend Praxinoe . . . would be the subject for an idyll *à la* Browning.'[71] Symonds's historical imagination is paralysed; he sees the scene not as it was but as it might appear in literature. 'A great painter', he adds, 'combining Doré's power . . . with . . . the colouring of Alma Tadema, might possibly realize this agony of the Athenian captives.' He then gives this painter detailed instructions about the time of day, the shadows, the vegetation, the laughing crowds of Syracusans up above, and continues,

> In the full foreground there are placed two figures. A young Athenian has just died of fever. . . . Beside him kneels an older warrior. . . . He stares with wide despair-smitten eyes straight out, as though he had lately been stretched upon the corpse. . . . They have stood together . . . through the battle of Epipolae, through . . . the slaughter at . . . the Asinarus. But . . . death

has found the younger. Perhaps the friend beside him remembers some cool wrestling-ground in far-off Athens, or
some procession up the steps of the Acropolis, where first they
met.

What is so revealing about this passage is the assumption that a
painting can express so much sentimental anecdote; we look at a
picture and we supply a story.

It is true that much of the greatest art has taken human suffering
for its theme and made it in some sense pleasing to those who see,
hear or read of it; yet there is something peculiarly unattractive
about the way in which Symonds uses the Athenian agony to adorn
the walls not of a real but of an imaginary Royal Academy. To
transform the woes of the past into art is one matter: to assess their
intrinsically artistic quality is another. The man who applies
aesthetic criteria when he contemplates the sufferings of dead
generations may soon find himself estimating the sorrows of his
own time in the same manner. This was Wilde's mistake:

> I used to say [he wrote] that I thought I could bear a real
> tragedy if it came to me with a purple pall and a mask of noble
> sorrow, but that the dreadful thing about modernity was that
> it put Tragedy into the raiment of Comedy, so that the great
> realities seemed commonplace or grotesque. . . . It is quite
> true about modernity. . . . Everything about my tragedy has
> been hideous, mean, repellent, lacking in style.[72]

Wilde might justly say that his sorrows were great; but surely
there was a poverty of spirit in complaining that they were inelegant.

> 'Sue [says Jude the Obscure], you seem . . . to be one of the
> women of some grand old civilization . . . rather than a denizen
> of a mere Christian country. I almost expect you to say . . .
> that you . . . have been listening to Aspasia's eloquence, or have
> been watching Praxiteles chiselling away at his latest Venus,
> while Phryne made complaint that she was tired of posing.'[73]

Jude's picture of the ancient world, a combination of classical
grandeur with a glimpse of an artist's studio and an anecdote,
recalls Tadema. Hardy seems to approve of his hero's language;
yet is there not something lacking in a man for whom experience
is inadequate unless it is robed in the raiment of antiquity? The

attitudes of a fictional creature may not seem very important; however, Wilde's fate indicates that the ways in which we experience art and life are more closely related than we commonly suppose. It is evident from his words that he had used the masterpieces of the tragic stage as a warm bath for his emotions to wallow in; and in the end, when his own life turned into tragedy, he was unable to treat it otherwise.

Flecker was another writer who liked costume drama, but he indulged this fondness with cool self-awareness. The orientals in *Hassan* are Edwardians in fancy dress pretending to be orientals, and the audience is meant to realize this; the florid language and turbid emotions of the characters are presented with a certain detachment. His particular brands of Hellenism and orientalism went naturally together: both classical antiquity and the mysterious east provided suitable settings for escapist fantasy. Indeed, a picture like Edwin Long's 'Babylonian Marriage Market' could belong equally to either world. Escapism was invading all the arts, even music. Laurence Hope and Amy Woodforde-Finden were both wives of Indian Army officers; the former wrote 'Indian Love Lyrics' of a lurid eroticism ('No woman,' said the *Spectator*, 'has written lines as full of a strange primeval savagery'), and the latter set them for voice and piano. Her voluptuous melodies and plangent harmonies became immensely popular, and in the earlier years of this century many a drawing-room tenor urged his audiences to stab him or throttle him with pink tipped hands. A host of inferior imitators turned out songs about Arabian passions and Syrian amours; Mrs. Woodforde-Finden had evidently struck a vein of gold. No doubt Greece would have been drawn upon as well, if only the Greeks had supplied a musical tradition suitable for adaptation; some of Laurence Hope's lyrics are like a milder version of Sappho as interpreted by Swinburne. The east performed in the realm of song the function exercised in the visual arts by the ancient world: it permitted the introduction of themes that would otherwise be unacceptable in polite society.

By the time King Edward died the pursuit of Hellenism in the visual arts was almost ended. When Voysey wrote *Reason as a basis of art* in 1906, he assumed that everyone laughed at Grecian clothing: 'It is easy to trace in modern costume,' he said in Ruskinian tones, 'thoughtlessness, ostentation . . . and a want of reverence. . . . When some good people have felt repelled by these qualities in our dress, they have sought to imitate . . . the Greeks and Romans, and wonder why the ancient symbols which were in their time true expressions,

are now in . . . our London streets merely grotesque.' Yet Voysey
feared that the Greek Revival was returning again, and his purpose
was to combat this threat:

> If you would build yourself a house in Regent Street, and
> honestly adhere to your own natural . . . characteristics, you
> will be called an . . . egotist. . . . Pretend that you are a Greek,
> with Grecian taste, in a Grecian climate, and faithfully follow
> like an ape the expression your splendid education has given
> you to copy, and you will be . . . honoured.

Voysey again adapts one of Ruskin's arguments, but now it is used
to advocate not gothic but 'modern' style:

> No doubt what you build will be a true expression of . . . what
> you like. . . . But the question remains, is such a 'liking' founded
> on reason, conscience, and love. Is it an honest expression? . . .
> Take the early Greek and Roman architectural enrichments:
> . . . they originally possessed a symbolic significance. . . . In
> our days we repeat the forms, and neither know nor care for
> their original meaning . . .[74]

Voysey's fears were not as groundless as they may now seem.
In that same year the R.I.B.A., which had never before awarded its
gold medal outside the ranks of the profession, bestowed it upon
Tadema, for encouraging architecture through his paintings.[75] In
Scotland the Greek tradition had never wholly perished. 'Greek'
Thomson died in 1875, but James Sellars continued to build in his
manner; a few years later the young J. J. Burnet designed the Fine
Art Institute of Glasgow in what was unmistakably a Greek style,
though tempered with a few Beaux Arts details, and even as Voysey
was writing, was adding the Edward VII Galleries to the British
Museum, blending Edwardian opulence with Greek monumentality. In England the Gothic Revival was fading away, and its
last practitioners did not share Pugin's hostility to all things Greek:
in a lecture of 1885 Bodley praised 'that marvellous time when
Greece . . . brought order out of the chaos of barbaric work, and,
suddenly, became the land of all that was beautiful in art'. In 1900
Beresford Pite observed that 'erstwhile ardent Gothic Revivalists
now acclaim . . . Professor Cockerell's works'; and not only Gothic
Revivalists, since a few months before Cockerell had been the
subject of a laudatory lecture by J. M. Brydon, another Scot and a

master of the newly fashionable baroque style.[76] Pite foresaw the
possibility of a second Greek Revival, arguing that the original
Greek Revival, unlike its Gothic counterpart, had 'died a school'
with rules and principles worked out and written down, ready for
use again whenever the architects chose.[77] Seven years later, when
he was commissioned to design an office block in Euston Square, he
did his best to fulfil his own prophecy: the building is Greek, but
eclectically Greek; again, Cockerell has been a guiding light.

The second Greek Revival withered away, and today it can easily
look like a passing vagary of taste, the product of an insular nation's
artistic timidity; the gothic style was played out, it may seem, but
the British were still looking for some way of clinging to historicism.
This is at best a half truth. The 'Modern School' was attempting, in
Pite's words, 'to oust affectation of style by an unaffected stylelessness of difficult simplicity'.[78] He saw Godwin, on whom he showered
his highest praise, as their founding father; but though Godwin
opposed architectural revivalism, he was in a general sense influenced
by Greek principles in everything he did. It is no coincidence that
the 'free style' of the later nineteenth and early twentieth centuries
was most widely and successfully practised in Glasgow, the city in
which the Greek Revival had lasted longest. 'Stylelessness' is
incompatible with gothic design; but the boldest of the neoclassical
architects had come close to its a century earlier; more recently
Thomson had shown that Greek forms need not be tamely imitated
but could be developed into a distinctively new architecture of
idiosyncratic vigour. The elements of classical proportion and
design, reduced to their essentials, can often be detected in the
progressive architecture of the early twentieth century; Heal's
Department Store, designed in 1916, is a handsome example. It
may be significant that Burnet at the end of his career was one of
the first British architects to assimilate the lessons of Chicago.
When Le Corbusier wrote *Vers une Architecture*, he stressed the
close relationship between ancient Greek architecture and his own.
He added that 'Phidias would have loved to live in this standardized
age . . . his vision would have seen in our epoch the conclusive
result of his labours'—[79] a judgement that seems rather hard on
Phidias.

The R.I.B.A. was not prescient in 1906: in the future Tadema
would influence nothing better than the Hollywood epic. But his
classicism was factitious; the true Greek architecture and its offspring the Greek Revival did play a part as a hidden but living force
in forming the principles of the modern movement. And in a larger,

vaguer sense all architects are in debt to Greece; Voysey ended his piece with a long quotation from Plato, to emphasize that he opposed the modern use of antique forms in the name of a Greek ideal: reason.

XIII

THE EMPIRE
AND THE WAR

In the sixth book of the *Aeneid* Anchises unfolds the destiny of his descendants: to the Greeks will belong the great achievements of art and science and thought, but the Romans are to be an imperial people. *Excudent alii spirantia mollius aera.* . . . Others shall fashion bronzes so fine that they seem to breathe, shall carve great statues, plead with more eloquence, and calculate the movements of the heavens. The Roman will have a different task: to rule peoples with *imperium* and accustom them to peace, to spare the conquered and put down the proud.[1]

When an Englishman of the last century read these central words of the *Aeneid*, the central words of all Latin poetry, how could he fail to think of his own country? The French and Italians might be more artistic, the Germans more intellectual, but to the English fortune or, as the later Victorians increasingly believed, Destiny had assigned the splendours and burdens of empire. Virgil's words were quoted by Robertson in his sermons, with a warning to the English not to learn domestic maxims from the Continent, as Rome had from Greece;[2] they were quoted again in J. A. Cramb's *Origins and Destiny of Imperial Britain.*[3] Throughout the century the English combined a large complacency concerning their political and military achievements with a strange modesty about their artistic powers. Such humility was excessive in this of all periods, when French taste had decayed and the fire of Italian genius had gone out, while in the early years of Victoria's reign the son of a Covent Garden barber was painting what are arguably the greatest paintings of the century, perhaps the greatest since Rembrandt; but from Hazlitt to Disraeli, from Ruskin to Symonds, the coarseness of northern man in aesthetic matters is a recurrent theme. Lytton was thinking of his compatriots when he wrote in his Pompeian novel that it was the mode among the Romans 'to affect a little contempt for the very birth which, in reality, made them so arrogant . . . to imitate the Greeks, and yet to laugh at their own clumsy imitation'.[4] Newman quotes from Virgil's lines in *Callista*, adding that in the third century the northern race of Goths were becoming the apparent heirs to the power which was slipping from Rome's grasp; and he says of Jucundus, a pagan with as it were Broad Church tendencies, 'He stood upon the established order of things, on the traditions of Rome, and of the laws of the empire. . . . The Greeks were a very clever people, unrivalled in the fine arts; let them keep to their strong point; they were inimitable with the chisel, the brush, the trowel . . .; but he was not prepared to think much of their *calamus* or *stylus*, poetry excepted.'[5] Kingsley, too, alludes to Virgil in *Hypatia*, when a Greek shows the monk Philammon the monuments of Alexandria: 'Did Christians build that Museum . . ., or design its statues and frescoes. . . . Did they pile up . . . that Exchange? or fill that Temple . . . with breathing brass and blushing marble?'[6] Breathing brass—that strange phrase is straight out of the *Aeneid*. Scorned by the romantics, Virgil returned to favour towards the close of the century, not least because he had been, as Lord Bryce said, 'the national poet of the Empire, in whom imperial patriotism found its highest expression'.[7]

Among the great proconsuls, among the imperial entrepreneurs and adventurers, there were many who were devoted to the literature of the ancient world. We glimpse them in countless memoirs: Rhodes with his Aristotle and his Marcus Aurelius, Lawrence with his pocket *Odyssey* or alone in the desert with Aristophanes, Buchan turning to Euripides in the veld, Storrs in Egypt rising at 6.30 to read Homer before breakfast, or Cromer and Boyle swapping classical quotations over dinner at the British Agency in Cairo.[8] Buchan described Milner as 'deeply versed in the classics . . . one of the finest scholars of his age'; 'Here was Plato's philosopher-turned-king.'[9] Milner himself thought in terms of Greek tragedy when he was sent on his fateful mission to South Africa: 'I run a great risk of growing conceited and, if I had not such a profound *sebas* [reverence] of the High Gods . . . I might be exposed to the danger of failure from over-confidence.'[10] When Rhodes went on his embassy to Lobengula, he surprisingly took with him the cultivated, scholarly Rochfort Maguire, a Fellow of All Souls, partly in the hope that he would teach the classics to Matabele

Thompson on the journey.[11] In consequence Maguire was in at the foundation of the British South Africa Company and went on to become its president; this is one of the few instances of the classics making a man rich. Among his successors in the presidency was Dougal Malcolm, another Fellow of All Souls, a tough businessman who devoted his leisure hours to the composition of exquisite Greek epigrams. In the combination of scholar and man of action there was an element of romance which in some cases was no doubt consciously cultivated. There was perhaps a touch of Alcibiades in such men; or at least they might have liked to think so.

But the usual, the inevitable comparison was with ancient Rome. It had been inescapable ever since 1850, when Palmerston, defending his action in the Don Pacifico affair, had quoted the words, 'Civis Romanus sum.' The phrase *imperium et libertas* was much bandied about; it seemed to have a good Roman ring, but had actually been coined by Disraeli in 1851—an inspired misquotation of Tacitus. By 1870 J. R. Seeley was noticing that the admiration of a previous generation for Brutus was giving way to a new respect for Caesar, who was now regarded by some as 'the greatest Liberal leader that ever lived';[12] this was a feeling that the growth of Liberal Imperialism could only strengthen. Between 1900 and the First World War both Bryce and the diplomat Sir Charles Lucas devoted whole books to exploring the similarities and differences between the Roman and British empires,[13] while the thesis of Cromer's *Ancient and Modern Imperialism* was that the comparisons must all be with Rome, since 'the Imperial idea [was] foreign to the Greek mind'.[14] The parallels were no less obvious to such enemies of imperialism as J. M. Robertson and the economist J. A. Hobson, who castigated the economic parasitism and moral enfeeblement produced by both empires.[15] It is a sign that an idea is pervasive when it is accepted on both sides of a dispute. None the less, there was also a strong if latent desire to compare imperial Britain with ancient Greece. It was present even in Rhodes, who liked to be told that his face resembled a Roman emperor's, and for whom 'Remember always that you are a Roman' was a favourite saying: he proposed to put up replicas of Doric temples at Cape Town and Kimberley, choosing the one style of Greek architecture that the Romans had never copied.[16] It was a commonplace to say that the British Empire was really two empires, consisting on the one hand of the settlement colonies, in which the population was largely British in origin, on the other of subject peoples governed more or less despotically. As early as 1869 Adderley was describing these as the Empire's

'Grecian' and 'Roman' elements.[17] Freeman took the sense of unity that the Greeks retained, despite political and geographical separation, as a model for the kind of unity that he hoped to see established among the English-speaking peoples. He wished that there were some term to cover them all, as the Greeks had had the term 'Hellene',[18] and grew indignant when Englishmen and Americans referred to each other as foreigners. Not everyone cared for such analogies: Seeley thought that people misled themselves by comparing the relation of Britain to Canada with that of Greece to Sicily: 'We are unconsciously influenced by a historical parallel which when examined turns out to be inapplicable.' It was not that he was indifferent to Greek history—indeed, he explained that he modelled his method upon Thucydides—but as he shrewdly remarked, one urgent reason why politicians should study history was to guard against the false analogies which deceive those who are ignorant of the subject.[19] Whereas comparison between Britain and Rome was unavoidable but not necessarily welcome, since many people regarded Roman civilization with a mild contempt, comparison between Britain and Greece was more in the nature of a temptation directed to the emotions, a strong and perhaps, as Seeley suggested, an unconscious influence. It is significant that Seeley imagines the opponents of imperialism as trying to contrast the Greek and British forms of colonization in words such as these: 'The Goth never relaxes for any distance his barbarous system of constraint; the mild intelligent Greek . . . perceives that the grown-up child has a right to be independent, and so he blesses him and bids him farewell.'[20] This argument struck home precisely because Englishmen wanted to see themselves as modern Athenians. They felt virtually no temptation to compare their empire with that of Macedon, though there were sporadic attempts to romanticize the aims of Alexander himself. To an extent Grote's influence lingered on: Athens was still the model, but an Athens rather different from the radical democracy that the whigs and utilitarians had admired.

The pomp of late Victorian civilization, half vulgar, half magnificent, looked overblown and ripe almost to rottenness, its spirit fittingly reflected in those tumescent, pseudo-baroque palazzi piled up by bureaucrats and bankers in Britain and across half the globe. Imperialist sentiment was in part the product of an immense pride and self-confidence; yet it was also created, or at least infected, by the nervousness, the menacing sense of decadence that invaded the public mood towards the close of the century and imparted to much of the rhetoric of empire a certain dark splendour. Kipling was haunted by the knowledge that cities and thrones and powers stand in time's eye for less than a day, and the stories of Roman Britain that he put into *Puck of Pook's Hill* are set in the fifth century after Christ, when a decaying empire was crumbling in the fist of the barbarian. After Marcus Aurelius, Rhodes's favourite reading was Gibbon's *Decline and Fall*.[21] In an atmosphere of apocalyptic jingoism the analogy with Rome acquired a new force: there too had been the braggart architecture, the vast wealth, the decay of morality and religion, the puzzling mixture of decadence and majesty. But the anxious mood also gave force to the comparison with Greece: the Romans of the first century had differed from the British in being wholly unaware that their empire would ever come to an end, but the Athenian power had looked fragile and impermanent even at its times of greatest success. Sparta in the fifth century and Macedon in the fourth had threatened it as Germany now threatened Britain. Two passages of Thucydides convinced Freeman that the problem of India was irresoluble; the first was Cleon's claim that it is impossible for a democracy to rule over others, and the other was Pericles' observation that the Athenian empire was a tyranny, which it seemed unjust to have taken, but perilous to let go. Seeley, for all his distrust of historical parallels, could not resist comparing the rise of Macedon to the rise of Russia and the United States in his own time; in both periods, he argued, a new type of state was coming into being on a scale never seen before, and the decline of Athens showed that England must now adopt the policy of imperial federation if she was not to be swamped. In the 1930s MacNeice, wondering whether to settle in America, found himself reflecting that it had been bad for England to live off the empire; 'She was like fifth-century Athens, able to maintain free speech and a comparatively high standard of living, but only on the basis of gagged and impoverished subject peoples.'[22]

The advent of war gave an additional power to the comparison with Greece in both its aspects, the proud and the pessimistic. Julian Grenfell's mother had a premonition of death the day before he was fatally wounded; but she dried her tears and said, 'Well, they could do no more than die for their country—since the days of Athens.'[23] Buchan recalled that between 1914 and 1918 he had 'read and re-read Thucydides, for he also had lived among crumbling institutions'.[24] Comparisons between Britain and Athens might be merely the expression of a simple patriotism, but they could also be a way of voicing the fears that men did not care to admit openly, and perhaps not even to themselves. In his book on Demosthenes, Pickard-Cambridge argued that his subject's claim to be ranked as a hero rested on a constant adherence to the cause of Hellenic freedom; the best features of the Athenian character, he explained, were bound up with political liberty, 'Nor is it an absurd contention that the life of the individual is . . . ennobled by membership of an imperial nation.' That he had his own country in mind is confirmed by a footnote asserting that British imperialism contained an element of nobility beyond the Athenian range of conception. This sounds like the language of complacency, but as he drew out his analogy, could he have escaped the reflection that Demosthenes was defeated and his city humbled? The book was called *Demosthenes and the last days of Greek freedom*, and it came out in 1914.[25]

Already during the Boer War Cramb was comparing the situation to the crisis of the fifth century:

> The defeat of Athens at Syracuse, involving inevitably the fall of her empire, was a disaster to humanity . . . the one state which Hellas ever produced capable at once of government and of a lofty ideal, intellectual and political, was a ruin. . . . A disaster in South Africa would have been just such a disaster . . ., but on a wider . . . scale. For this empire is built upon a design more liberal even than that of Athens . . .

The bombast is there, but so too is the smell of fear; 'There is,' he says, 'perhaps not a single heart in this Empire which does not at moments start as at some menacing . . . sound, a foreboding of evil. . . .' He likens the destiny of the race to the 'Nemesis of Greek Tragedy', and quotes darkly from the 'embittered wisdom' of Aeschylus and Sophocles.[26]

Eighteen years later, in a lecture delivered four days before the armistice, Gilbert Murray remarked on the impressive similarities between the present conflict and the Peloponnesian War; both, he suggested, were struggles between Sea-power and Land-power, between the principles of democracy and military monarchy; and the Germans had even adopted the Spartans' 'terrorist policy of sinking all craft whatsoever'. And once again we can detect oblique indications of Murray's anxieties in the recent years. He noted in Athens 'a division of parties curiously similar to our own. There were no pro-Spartans . . ., just as there are no pro-Germans . . . with us. There was roughly a Peace by Negotiation party, led by Nicias, and a Knock-out-Blow party led by Cleon.'[27] Murray implies that Nicias was rather like Lansdowne; clearly he must have wondered, in the aftermath of the Lansdowne letter, whether Britain, like Athens, was not throwing away the one chance of avoiding catastrophe. He does not venture to suggest that defeat had ever been a possibility, but he does allow himself the observation that 'the democratic sea-empire of Athens suffered much from its lack of cohesion and its dependence on sea-borne resources, while the military land-empire of the Peloponnesians gained from its compact and central position'.[28] Later, in the course of a yet more desperate conflict, Murray was to think again of Athens. War affects even the least nationalistic of men, and in 1941 he dwelt proudly on the striking resemblances between the English and the Athenians in their taste for literature and their love of sport, their inspired amateurism and wide tolerance; 'Free Speech, Liberty, Equality before the Law, all the familiar Greek watchwords are our watchwords also.' And once more the note of uneasiness is also heard. Like Adderley, Murray thinks that 'at home England is Greek, in the Empire she is Roman'; and like Freeman, he recalls the warning words of Cleon. Again, he finds the *Philippics* of Demosthenes, vainly urging the Athenians to prepare themselves against Macedon before it is too late, grimly reminiscent of Churchill's speeches against appeasement and the deaf ears on which they fell.[29]

Murray alluded in his lecture of 1918 to the most poignant way in which the Athenians at Syracuse and the English in the trenches were alike: in both cases the golden youth of a rich, imperial nation set out to war in high spirits, buoyed up by a confident, uncomplicated patriotism, and found themselves plunged into an unimagined hell. To the British officers and their friends the heroic resonances of ancient Greece might serve as a palliation of the horror, a sort of noble lie; 'We are like the young *phulakes* [guardians],' S. H. Hewett wrote from France, eagerly commending the close comradeship of warfare.[30] Buchan saw his countrymen as 'latter-day Spartans who stood their ground in a more fateful Thermopylae', and the same notion was implied by the words on a communal grave—'The Devonshires held this trench. The Devonshires hold it still'[31]—consciously reminiscent of Simonides' epitaph —'Stranger, tell the Spartans that we lie here, obeying their command'—where the present participle suggests that the dead of Thermopylae, like the later Devonshires, are obedient even in the grave.

Kipling, too, thought of his *Epitaphs of War* as 'cribs' from the Greek;[32] they contain a bitterness and hatred absent from his models, but perhaps his failure to be Hellenic is fitting, expressive

as it is of the gulf between antique chivalry and modern war. Yet
the comparison with Greece was inevitable, if only because the
imaginations of so many officers had fed upon Greek literature.
On his deathbed Grenfell recited childhood prayers and lines from
Euripides; Hellas, like the memory of his infantine Christianity, had
sunk deep into him, to become part of the furniture of his mind.
Fragments of Greek are embedded in letters and diaries written at
the front: 'I do hope you aren't having a *thumophthoros* times at
inspections,' said D. O. Barnett, '. . . If there is any soul *eudaimōn*
in this world, it is me—real happiness . . ., *ousa eudaimonia*'; while
Hewett, hearing a rumour that the French had taken Péronne,
recalled (and quoted) Demosthenes' account of how the news came
to Athens that Elateia was captured.[33] These three were all Balliol
men, the heirs of Jowett; countless others, less privileged, tried to
distract themselves with *The Spirit of Man*, an anthology compiled
for fighting men by Bridges, who said of it, 'The authors who show
most solid are Plato, Aristotle, Homer, Shelley'[34]—three Greeks
and a Hellenist (the extracts of Shelley are mostly from *Prometheus
Unbound*). Bridges observed in his preface that amid hate and filth
and slaughter we can 'seek comfort only in the quiet confidence of
our souls; and we look instinctively to the seers and poets of mankind'. One of the attractions of the Greeks, perhaps, was that the
modern scholar could easily imagine a kinship between them and
himself, and yet they were far away in an enchanted distance, free
from the bonds of time and hideous circumstance. Storrs sensed
that Homer was both near and remote when he recollected the many
men during the war who were 'transported far beyond their fatigues
and anxieties by following those of Patroclus and Odysseus';[35] and
a similar feeling flooded through A. D. Gillespie as he listened to a
nightingale singing in Flanders and 'thought of all the men and
women who had listened to that song, just as . . . after Tom was
killed I found myself thinking perpetually of all the men who had
been killed in battle—Hector and Achilles and all the heroes of long
ago, who were once so strong and active, and are now so quiet'.[36]

    Homer, indeed, more than any other poet was in the minds of
fighting men. Back in 1900 Cramb had described with gruesome
enthusiasm the entry to Valhalla of the young English killed in
South Africa, 'smiling, the blood yet trickling from their wounds!
Behold, Achilles turns, unbending from his deep disdain.'[37] This
sounds like the rhetoric of the non-combatant; yet the mood that
inspired it also inspired the younger men who were to die for it.
Brooke's sonnets spoke for a generation; in 1914 even Wilfred

Owen was praising the 'Spring [that] bloomed in early Greece', and looking forward to a blood-sacrifice which would bring it back again.[38] In his one famous poem Grenfell celebrated the 'joy of battle'[39]—the *charmē* of which Homer had sung; and the fragments which Brooke scribbled on his fatal voyage show how he saw the war in Homeric terms:[40]

> They say Achilles in the darkness stirred . . .

> And Priam and his fifty sons
> Wake all amazed, and hear the guns,
>   And shake for Troy again.

'We'll be among the Cyclades,' he wrote home. 'There I shall recite Sappho and Homer, and the winds of history will follow us all the way.' It was indeed impossible not to think of the *Iliad*, for Troy and the Gallipoli peninsula face each other across the Dardanelles; and when Brooke, with a terrible appropriateness, died on Scyros, one comparison was inevitable: as Charles Lister wrote after seeing him buried, 'The Island of Achilles is . . . a suitable resting-place for those bound for the plains of Troy.' Perfect in physical beauty, perfect in the setting of his death, Brooke was fated to be likened to the heroes of epic or romance; but even when men died in less cruelly apt circumstances, their friends often found the temptation to dignify them with the aura of heroic poetry irresistible. Buchan wrote of Jack Wortley, 'The much-enduring Ulysses was not to come to port in Ithaca . . . he had fallen in the first few hours of the action'; and Ronald Knox said that the many friends who mourned Patrick Shaw-Stewart would feel 'that something is lacking to the Epic cycle which includes the *aristeia* of Charles Lister and the Grenfells, if the tale stops short at *Taphon Hektoros*'.[41] The same spirit animated Maurice Baring's commemoration of Lord Lucas, killed with the Royal Flying Corps:[42]

> You had died fighting, fighting against odds,
> Such as in war the gods
> Aethereal dared when all the world was young;
> Such fighting as blind Homer never sung,
> Nor Hector nor Achilles never knew;
> High in the empty blue.

The Great War was such fighting as Achilles never knew in a

more brutal sense than Baring intended. A hundred years earlier Byron had warned of the foulness of modern warfare, and the truth of that warning was to strike home at last. Shaw-Stewart had read his beloved *Iliad* on the voyage to Gallipoli and sent back letters full of humour and high spirits; but when he reached the scene of battle, his mood changed:[43]

> O hell of ships and cities
>> Hell of men like me,
> Fatal second Helen,
>> Why must I follow thee?
>
> Achilles came to Troyland
>> And I to Chersonese:
> He turned from wrath to battle,
>> And I from three days' peace.
>
> Was it so hard, Achilles,
>> So very hard to die?
> Thou knowest and I know not—
>> So much the happier I.
>
> I will go back this morning
>> From Imbros over the sea;
> Stand in the trench, Achilles,
>> Flame-capped, and fight for me.

In this poem he seems to be clinging to Homer for support, half proudly, half desperately. Some men noticed—what seems so obvious to us—that though Homer glorified war as much as any poet has ever done, he saw its tragedy and cruelty too with a clarity that has not been surpassed; for others the disillusionment was complete. 'To speak of glory seemed a horrid impiety,' Buchan thought. 'That was perhaps why I could not open Homer.'[44] Sassoon preferred the dour endurance of the common soldier to 'fool-heroes' with their talk of glory,[45] and the war poets whose work has meant most to readers in the last fifty years have nothing to say about Hector or Achilles. There could be no epic of the Great War, or at least not in the conventional sense. Herbert Read judged David Jones's *In Parenthesis* 'as near a great epic of the war as ever the war generation will reach'.[46] Like the *Idylls of the King*, it is splintered and fragmentary; but Jones, like Tennyson, is conscious of belonging to a tradition of heroic poetry. His models are principally the medieval epics of France and Wales; yet there are also formal similes of the Homeric type and even a 'Homeric' catalogue of warriors:[47]

> Anglo-Welsh from Queens Ferry
> rosary-wallahs from Pembrey Dock . . .
> and two lovers from Ebury Bridge . . .
> that men called the Lily-white boys.

The tiny pathetic snatch of personal detail is like the *Iliad*; the passage gains in force if we hear the distant echo of Homeric thunder. And yet that echo must remain very distant: the places are unromantic, the people commonplace, the fighting ugly and unglamorous. However, Jones has the advantage in this, that whereas Homer ignores the common people, the modern 'epic' has room for them and their sufferings. There was a flaw in the Homeric ideal, which the war exposed: it spoke only to an élite. The talk of chivalrous heroism, of renewal through battle and self-sacrifice, was a luxury with which a too privileged class had fatally indulged itself.

The men who were naturally and worthily commemorated in Hellenic terms were those who were exceptional by reason of birth or talent or beauty. Some of these nonpareils seem now as though they had stepped from the pages of a novel. There was Raymond Asquith, as astonishing in real life as Beerbohm's imaginary Duke of Dorset, and like Dorset fated to die young and unnaturally; 'He was a fine classical scholar,' we are told, 'at once learned and precise . . .; he wrote good poetry, Greek, Latin and English; he had the most . . . luminous critical sense.'[48] There was Shaw-Stewart, of All Souls and Baring Brothers, who during his Eton schooldays had held a debating society spellbound reciting from the last book of the *Iliad*[49]—including those lines which had moved the fictional George Arthur to tears in *Tom Brown's Schooldays*. And there was Brooke. Frances Cornford had described him back in 1910 as a 'young Apollo, golden-haired'; after his death Lister wrote in melancholy reminiscence of his 'dazzling purity of mind and work, clean cut, classical, and unaffected . . . like his face'.[50] Others, too, seemed in the affectionate memories of their friends to have been gifted with a Hellenic grace. Edward Marsh recalled that Edward Horner's head 'was of a Greek type most like the Hermes of Praxiteles, with perfect modelling of forehead, mouth and chin'; Buchan suggested that the war brought the real Raymond Asquith to light, 'as the removal of Byzantine ornament may reveal the grave handiwork of Pheidias'.[51] Such comparisons are part sophisticated, part simple; on the one hand they are the product of long subjection to a classical education, on the other they echo, rather touchingly, a cliché of popular fiction. This cliché is exposed with innocent clarity in that idyll of late Victorian life, *The Young Visiters*: 'I certainly love you madly you are to me like a Heathen god she cried looking at his manly form and handsome flashing face I will indeed marry you.'[52] But the Apolline splendour of Edwardian England was to be extinguished; 'Phoebus Apollo' were the last words that Grenfell spoke apart from his father's name,[53] and that dying murmur has acquired a symbolic force.

The young men who sailed to Gallipoli reported the same emotions and experiences as Byron and his contemporaries a hundred years before. Brooke wrote that his eyes had fallen 'on the holy Land of Attica'; Lister found it exhilarating to recall the raft of Odysseus and to see Samothrace, 'where Poseidon sat to look on at the fighting on the plains of Troy'. Shaw-Stewart was entranced by the 'association-saturated spots' that he visited: '[The] flower of sentimentality . . . expands childishly [in me] on classical soil. It is really delightful . . . to bathe . . . in the Hellespont, looking straight over to Troy . . ., to be fighting for the command of Aegospotami, and to restate Miltiades's problem of the lines of Bulair.'[54] But when Knox visited these scenes after the war, he felt that the old associations, unchanged for so long, had been abruptly and irrevocably destroyed: 'The great Pan is dead, and the world of which he is the symbol; we can never recapture it. And I knew that when I saw the Hellespont. It did not remind me of the ship Argo, nor of the agony of Troy. . . . It was peopled for me instead by those who fought and died there fifteen years ago, men of my own country and of my own speech.'[55] The visitor approaching Troy today is puzzled to see the flat landscape dominated by a concrete structure—a silo? a power-station?—huge, stark, self-consciously modernistic; it is Ataturk's monument to the Turkish dead.

For Yeats it was not Pan but Homer who was the symbol of the old, vanishing order. In *Ancestral Houses*, with words as eloquent as any written this century, he evoked the aristocratic world of privilege lightly worn:

> Surely among a rich man's flowering lawns,
> Amid the rustle of his planted hills,

> Life overflows without ambitious pains,
> And rains down life until the basin spills . . .

Then in the second stanza the mood darkens:

> Mere dreams, mere dreams! Yet Homer had not sung
> Had he not found it certain beyond dreams
> That out of life's own self-delight had sprung
> The abounding glittering jet; though now it seems
> As if some marvellous empty sea-shell flung
> Out of the obscure dark of the rich streams,
> And not a fountain, were the symbol which
> Shadows the inherited glory of the rich.

Mere dreams indeed. Homer's was the right name to invoke, for
the war had destroyed the Homeric ideal and social changes were
destroying the way of life which had brought that ideal to birth.

G. M. Young in the thirties found himself looking back on the
Victorians as a generation of heroes, praising the 'epic quality' of
their warfare against human distress and writing, in parody of
Homer, about 'wide-wayed Liverpool' and 'hundred-gated Leeds'.[56]
But it was early Victorian England that drew these phrases from
him; he described the later part of the century in different terms.
And certainly, whether we consider art or moral beliefs or social
and economic conditions, we find that the processes which have
given the twentieth century its distinctive character had already
begun before the war broke out. One such process, a small one
among others of far greater significance, was a change in the nature
of Greek scholarship in England, starting with James Frazer,
continuing with the writings of Jane Harrison and Gilbert Murray,
and further encouraged by the belated impact of Nietzsche in the
first decade of this century. Large mistakes were made; but these
developments were for the health of classical studies. They inspired
a chastening sense of our limitations; we are better aware than our
ancestors of the gulf that separates us from antiquity. As MacNeice
wrote in 1938,[57]

> . . . how one can imagine oneself among them
>   I do not know;
> It was all so unimaginably different
>   And all so long ago.

And yet this claim to a sense of baffled incomprehension is something of a pretence, or an exaggeration; MacNeice did in fact
allow his imagination to play upon the past. He rejects the idea
that the Greeks were 'models of . . . lucidity, dignity, sanity', and
scoffs at its typical proponent, 'the humanist in his room with
Jacobean panels . . . looking on a lazy quad' (Sir Richard Livingstone,
I presume). But in its place he puts another and more living picture:

> . . . when I should remember the paragons of Hellas
>   I think instead
> Of the crooks, the adventurers, the opportunists,
>   The careless athletes and the fancy boys,
> The hair-splitters, the pedants, the hard-boiled sceptics
>   And the Agora and the noise
> Of the demagogues and the quacks; and the women pouring
>   Libations over graves
> And the trimmers at Delphi and the dummies at Sparta and lastly
>   I think of the slaves.

Greek scholarship has flourished in this century, and never
perhaps has antiquity been so well worth studying as it is today;
but scholars in themselves cannot exercise a wide influence unless
the greater world chooses to listen to them. At the beginning of the
nineteenth century scholarship and poetry were regarded as allies,
a hundred years later as rivals. Housman was the most eminent
Latinist of his day, but he kept his scholarship and his poetry rigidly
apart, allowing neither to fertilize the other. Beazley became the
greatest of all experts on Greek vase-painting, but not before
Flecker had urged him to abandon his studies on the ground that
they would destroy his poetic gift.[58] T. E. Lawrence agreed: 'If it
hadn't been for that accursed Greek art he'd have been a very fine
poet.'[59] To be sure, there are Hellenic references in such poets as
Yeats and Eliot, but they are usually superficial, the result of
reading some stimulating book—Nietzsche on tragedy, or Norwood
on comedy—rather than the product of a long immersion in the
ancient world. Meanwhile Greek sculpture, once passionately loved
by the poets, was becoming distinctly unpopular. Roger Fry, the
most influential art critic of his time, launched what he called 'a
frank attempt to dethrone Greek art altogether';[60] and the man
who was to become the most influential art critic of our own day,
Kenneth Clark, confessed to finding Fry's iconoclasm 'a real relief';
'I believe,' he added, 'that others who are persuaded by these

lectures to look at Greek art with a free and innocent eye will experience one of the great pleasures of life, liberation from an unconscious insincerity.'[61]

These changes in aesthetic fashion would have occurred even if there had been no Great War; none the less, the war did greatly affect the Hellenic element in our culture by accelerating and in part creating the circumstances that have led to the decline in classical education. It was not wholly inappropriate that the Hellenic Society should meet in 1916 to consider 'the crisis through which Hellenic Studies are now passing',[62] nor that Lloyd George in the year of the Versailles treaty should set up a committee to inquire into the position of the classics in British education. The committee found their witnesses united in their support: men of eminence and influence, they reported, were no longer attacking classical education as they had in the past; scientists insisted on the value of a preliminary training in classics for their pupils; representatives of the Labour Party pressed for more Latin and Greek in the schools attended by children of the working class. 'Ancient thought,' the report concluded,

> is inwoven in the fabric of our modern life. . . . That it would be a national disaster if classical studies were to disappear from our education . . . is conceded by men of every school.

The committee was optimistic too about the future:

> It is the task of everyone who has derived anything of . . . happiness from the study of classical learning to take a part in enlightening public opinion, and we [are] convinced that the endeavour will not be in vain. . . . The economic, political, social and moral welfare of the community depend mainly on the development of a national system of education which, while securing for every child . . . the equipment necessary for playing his part amid . . . modern society, will also provide his leisure with ennobling occupation and his life with a spiritual ideal. And we would submit that in such an education the study of the [remains] of Greece and Rome cannot be replaced by any other which . . . is so comprehensive and so effectual.[63]

The report came out in 1921, but the ideas and the optimism and even the language are the late products of a Victorian creed. The committee might well have been echoing the words used by Matthew

Arnold in 1882, words which sum up the hope and beliefs of a whole century: 'The instinct for beauty,' he wrote,

> is set in human nature, as surely as the instinct for conduct. If the instinct for beauty is served by Greek literature and art as it is served by no other literature and art, we may trust to the instinct of self-preservation in humanity for keeping Greek as part of our culture. We may trust to it for even making the study of Greek more prevalent than it is now.[64]

We must still insist on the importance of studying the ancient world for a balanced understanding of our past, and of ourselves; but Arnold's simple trust is no longer so easy to come by. Most of the Victorians looked towards the future with confidence: mankind at heart was both rational and good; in the twentieth century culture and reason and happiness would continually flourish and expand; and in this enlightened age the language and civilization of ancient Greece would surely be ever more widely studied, ever more vigorously enjoyed. Mere dreams.

NOTES

NOTES

Chapter 1 The Origins of Hellenism

1. Stuart and Revett, *The Antiquities of Athens* I (1762), p. vi f.
2. L. Lawrence, 'Stuart and Revett . . .', JWI II (1938–9), 130.
3. T. Spencer, *Fair Greece, Sad Relic* (1954), p. 161.
4. Virg. *Ecl.* 6. 1; Hor. *Epist.* 1. 19. 23 ff.
5. Stuart and Revett I, pp. iv, ii.
6. Ib. I, p. v.
7. *Childe Harold's Pilgrimage*, canto 2, st. 88.
8. *A Journey to the Western Islands of Scotland*, 'Inch Kenneth'.
9. Stuart and Revett I, p. v; J. M. Crook, *The Greek Revival* (1972), p. 15.
10. Stuart and Revett I, p. iii.
11. Ib. I, p. x; II, 'advertisement'.
12. L. Cust, *History of the Society of Dilettanti* (1914), pp. 265, 7, 51.
13. Ib., p. 77.
14. Stuart and Revett I, pp. vii, v.
15. Ib., III, p. 37.
16. Lawrence, 128; Jones, *Lectures . . . on the Great Exhibition*, p. 290.
17. *The Ruins of Palmyra* (1753), introduction.
18. *The Correspondence of Alexander Pope*, ed. G. Sherburn (Oxford, 1956) I, p. 493; Wood, *An Essay on . . . Homer*, 'To the Reader'.
19. *The Iliad of Homer* I (1715), preface.
20. *An Essay on the Original Genius and Writings of Homer* (edn. of 1775), pp. 91, 77 ff.
21. H. Honour, *Neo-classicism* (1968), p. 63; Cowper's *Iliad* (1791), pp. vi f., x; G. O. Trevelyan, *Life and Letters of Lord Macaulay*, ch. 4.
22. *Essay on . . . Homer*, p. 76.
23. *Description of the Plain of Troy*, tr. A. Dalzel (Edinburgh, 1791), p. 41.
24. Chandler, *The History of Ilium or Troy* (1802), p. 13; Byron, *Don Juan*, canto 4, st. 77; *Childe Harold's Pilgrimage*, canto 3, st. 91; *Don Juan*, canto 4, st. 101.
25. Crook, p. 72; Adam, op. cit. (1764), p. 4.
26. Crook, p. 82; Laugier, op. cit., ch. 1.
27. Stuart and Revett III, p. xii.
28. Ib., p. xiii ff.
29. D. Watkin, *The Life and Work of C. R. Cockerell* (1974), pp. 9, 7.

30. Shelley, *Ode to Liberty*, l. 61 ff.; Crook, p. 45.
31. Keats, *On Seeing the Elgin Marbles*; 'A Journey through France and Italy' (*The Complete Works of William Hazlitt*, ed. P. P. Howe (1932–4), XVI, p. 66).
32. W. Gaunt, *Victorian Olympus* (1952), p. 17; Shelley, *Hellas*, preface; Macaulay, 'Mitford's History of Greece'.
33. *The Rights of Man*, pt. 2, ch. 3.
34. Macaulay, loc. cit.; Byron, *Don Juan*, canto 12, st. 19; Mill, *Autobiography*, ch. 1.
35. E. Rawson, *The Spartan Tradition in European Thought* (Oxford, 1969), p. 357.
36. *Complete Prose Works*, ed. R. H. Super (Ann Arbor, 1960–77), V, p. 285.
37. *The Collected Works of John Stuart Mill*, ed. J. M. Robson, etc. (Toronto, 1963), XI, p. 273; *Don Juan*, canto 3, st. 86.
38. *T.L.S.*, 1974, p. 767.
39. Crook, p. 42.
40. Shelley, *Hellas*, preface; *The Swinburne Letters*, ed. C. Y. Lang (New Haven, 1959–62), III, p. 56; Symonds, *Studies of the Greek Poets*, ch. 25; Kingsley, *The Heroes*, preface; Ruskin, *The Crown of Wild Olive*, § 90.
41. Hazlitt, 'On Antiquity' (Howe XII, p. 253); Wilde, *The Critic as Artist*.
42. *To Homer*.
43. *The Stones of Venice* I, ch. 2, § 12; *Lectures on Architecture and Painting*, § 24.
44. *Contrasts* (2nd edn., 1841), p. 17.
45. *The Letters and Diaries of John Henry Newman* XII, ed. C. S. Dessain (1962), pp. 221, 326.
46. Crook, p. 129.
47. *Instances of Accessory Art*.
48. *The Stones of Venice* II, ch. 6, § 6; *Praeterita* II, § 199.
49. Op. cit., ch. 3, § 15.
50. Ib., ch. 3, § 21.
51. Ib., ch. 4, § 19.
52. *The Stones of Venice* I, ch. 1, §§ 17, 19.
53. 'The English Renaissance of Art'.

Chapter 2 The Death of Poetry

1. *The Captive*, tr. C. K. Scott Moncrieff, I, p. 211.
2. Bk. 2, l. 717 ff.
3. *Lives of the Poets*, 'Milton'.
4. *Hellas*, preface.
5. J. P. Eckermann, *Conversations with Goethe*, tr. J. Oxenford, 5th July, 1827.

6. *Studies in Literature*, 2nd series (Cambridge, 1922), 'Byron'.
7. L. 189 ff.
8. Canto 1, st. 200.
9. Canto 14, st. 99.
10. Canto 7, st. 78.
11. Canto 9, st. 4; canto 8, st. 90.
12. Canto 7, st. 80.
13. *Dipsychus*, pt. 2, sc. 4.
14. *Lothair*, ch. 17.
15. *Aurora Leigh*, bk. 5, l. 139 ff.
16. Ib., bk. 5, l. 154 ff.
17. J. Froude, *Thomas Carlyle: A history of the first forty years* . . . (1882) II, pp. 97, 209.
18. *The French Revolution* III, bk. 7, ch. 7.
19. Froude II, p. 98.
20. *Aurora Leigh*, bk. 5, l. 203 ff.
21. *Modern Painters* V (pt. 9), ch. 9.
22. *Autobiography*, ch. 2.
23. Ib., ch. 4.
24. Ib.
25. I. Jack, *English Literature 1815–32* (Oxford, 1963), p. 421.
26. *England and the English*, ed. S. Meacham (Chicago, 1970), p. 286 f.
27. *Letters and Literary Remains of Edward FitzGerald*, ed. W. A. Wright (1889), I, p. 181.
28. Bk. 1, ch. 3.
29. Preface to *Poems* (1853) (*Prose Works*, ed. Super, I, p. 14.)
30. *The Epic*, l. 27 ff.
31. H. Tennyson, *Alfred Lord Tennyson* (1897) I, p. 304.
32. Sect. 48.
33. Sect. 57.
34. Sects. 77, 57.
35. Sect. 54.
36. 'Epilogue', ll. 27 f., 31 f., 140 ff.
37. *The Poems of Tennyson*, ed. C. Ricks (1969), ad loc.
38. *The Passing of Arthur*, l. 428 ff.
39. H. Tennyson, II, p. 130.
40. Ricks, p. 1467.
41. H. Tennyson, loc. cit.
42. Ib.
43. Super I, p. 134 f.
44. Ll. 178 f., 233 ff. (cf. *Il.* 24. 486 ff.), 241 (cf. *Il.* 23. 18) 187 ff.
45. L. 541 ff. (cf. *Il.* 16. 844 f.).
46. *The Letters of Matthew Arnold to Arthur Hugh Clough*, ed. H. F. Lowry (1932), p. 145.

Chapter 3 Self-Consciousness

1. *As You Like It*, act 4, sc. 1.
2. Hor. *Odes* 4. 14. 47; 1. 35. 29; Cat. 11. 11 f.; Virg. *Ecl.* 1. 64 ff.
3. *To Virgil*, l. 19; *Dover Beach*, l. 20.
4. Ruskin, *Praeterita* II, § 22; Clough, *Resignation—to Faustus*; Arnold, *Stanzas from the Grande Chartreuse*, l. 80 ff.
5. *Wilhelm Meisters Lehrjahre*, bk. 3, ch. 1.
6. *Brot und Wein*, l. 55 ff.
7. Lecture 1 (tr. J. Black).
8. *The Newcomes*, ch. 35; *Childe Harold's Pilgrimage*, bk. 4, st. 79.
9. *Extracts from the Letters and Journals of William Cory*, ed. F. Warre Cornish (Oxford, 1897), p. 312; *Lothair*, ch. 48.
10. *Studies of the Greek Poets*, chs. 21, 24.
11. Pt. 5, ch. 18; pt. 2, ch. 15.
12. Symonds, ch. 24; G. O. Trevelyan, *Life of Macaulay*, ch. 7.
13. *Beppo*, st. 47; *Thyrsis*, l. 81 ff.
14. Ch. 28.
15. *Little Dorrit*, bk. 2, ch. 9.
16. Chs. 8, 17.
17. *Marius the Epicurean*, ch. 2.
18. Ch. 40.
19. Ch. 17.
20. Ch. 40.
21. *Imaginary Portraits, Duke Carl of Rosenmold*.
22. *The Lord of the Rings*, bk. 4, ch. 4.
23. *The Stones of Venice* II, ch. 4, § 10 ff.
24. Ib., § 35.
25. Ib., ch. 6, § 7 f.; Byron, *The Giaour*, ll. 15, 28.
26. *Childe Harold*, bk. 2, st. 38.
27. Act 1, sc. 2; act 2, sc. 1; act 3, sc. 3; act 4, sc. 1.
28. *The Spirit of the Age* (Chicago, 1942), p. 1.
29. *An Invocation*.
30. *Imaginary Conversations*, 'Pericles and Sophocles'.
31. 'Schlegel on the Drama' (*Complete Works*, ed. Howe, XVI, p. 66).
32. *Marius*, ch. 12.
33. Ch. 6.
34. P. Grosskurth, *John Addington Symonds* (1964), p. 245.
35. *Roderick Hudson*, ch. 5; *Marius*, ch. 11.
36. Ch. 6.
37. *The Picture of Dorian Gray*, ch. 2; *Marius*, ch. 4.
38. Ch. 6.
39. Chs. 10, 22.
40. Chs. 18, 22.
41. *The Works of Thomas Carlyle*, ed. H. D. Traill (1896–9) XXVIII, p. 37.
42. *Grande Chartreuse*, ll. 157 f., 85 ff.; Carlyle XXVIII, p. 32; Mill,

The Spirit of the Age, p. 6; H. Tennyson, *Alfred Lord Tennyson* II, p. 337.

43. Keats, *On Seeing the Elgin Marbles*; George Eliot, *Scenes of Clerical Life, Janet's Repentance*, ch. 14.
44. M. Praz, *The Romantic Agony* (2nd edn., 1970), p. 14; E. M. Butler, *The Tyranny of Greece over Germany* (Cambridge, 1935), p. 134.
45. *The Ancient Sage*, ll. 219, 223 ff.
46. *Marius*, chs. 5, 6.
47. *Latin Literature*, pt. 3, ch. 5.

Chapter 4   The Nineteenth-Century Background

1. A. P. Stanley, *The Life . . . of Thomas Arnold, D.D.* (1844) I, p. 123.
2. M. Sanderson, *The Universities in the Nineteenth Century* (1975), p. 38.
3. *The Works of the Rev. Sydney Smith* (1859) I, p. 173.
4. E.g. Mill, 'Civilization' (*The Collected Works of John Stuart Mill*, ed. J. M. Robson etc. (Toronto, 1963–) XVIII, esp. p. 145).
5. *The Idea of a University*, ed. C. F. Harrold (New York, 1947), p. 123.
6. M. L. Clarke, *Classical Education in Britain, 1500–1900* (Cambridge, 1959), pp. 98, 121.
7. Bk. 3, ch. 15.
8. *Miscellaneous Works* (1845), p. 350.
9. Stanley I, p. 5.
10. Clarke, p. 80; Stanley I, pp. 17, 188 f.
11. Mill, *Collected Works* XVI, p. 1288; *Taine's Notes on England*, tr. E. Hyams (1957), pp. 112, 105.
12. *The Stones of Venice* III, appendix 7.
13. Stanley I, p. 129; *Miscellaneous Works*, pp. 349, 396.
14. *Endymion*, ch. 76; J. Clive, *Thomas Babington Macaulay* (1973), p. 69.
15. Lytton, *The Last Days of Pompeii*, bk. 2, ch. 4; D. Forbes, *The Liberal Anglican Idea of History* (Cambridge, 1952), p. 14.
16. Forbes, pp. 14, 92; G. Faber, *Oxford Apostles*, ch. 7, sect. 3; Gladstone, *Studies on Homer and the Homeric Age* (Oxford, 1858), III, p. 1.
17. *Essays on a Liberal Education*, ed. F. W. Farrar (1867), p. 382.
18. *The Newcomes*, ch. 5; *Pendennis*, ch. 18; *Dombey and Son*, ch. 11; *The Mill on the Floss*, bk. 2, ch. 3.
19. Bk. 2, ch. 1.
20. *Middlemarch*, chs. 11, 7; Alan St. Aubyn, *The Junior Dean* (1891) II, p. 225; Smith, *Works* I, pp. 178, 180.
21. *Don Juan*, canto 11, st. 52; *The Last Chronicle of Barset*, ch. 1.
22. Op. cit., p. 22.
23. Farrar, op. cit., pp. 78, 369 ff.
24. Ch. 29.
25. *Aratra Pentelici*, § 78.
26. *The Adventures of Mr. Verdant Green*, pt. 1, ch. 11.

27. F. Mehring, *Karl Marx*, tr. E. Fitzgerald (1936), p. 503.
28. Mill, *Collected Works* XVIII, p. 145; Arnold, Preface to *Poems* (1853) (*Prose Works*, ed. Super, I, p. 13).
29. *Miscellaneous Works*, p. 350; Stanley I, p. 122.
30. G. Costigan, 'William Johnson Cory', *Cornhill* 1972, p. 242 f.
31. Farrar, pp. 338, 315, 316 f.
32. *The Life of Richard Cobden* (1881) II, p. 481 f.
33. G. Faber, *Jowett* (2nd edn., 1958), pp. 222, 339.
34. *Scenes from Clerical Life, Janet's Repentance*, ch. 6; *Felix Holt the Radical*, ch. 2.
35. Ch. 41.
36. Sanderson, p. 36.
37. *Works* I, p. 173.
38. Ib., I, p. 170.
39. *Chapters on the Poets of Ancient Greece* (1841), pp. 49, 69.
40. Ch. 22.
41. *Lectures on Architecture and Painting*, §§ 118, 112, 114, 120.
42. E. Russell, *That Reminds Me*—(1899), p. 123 f.
43. QR CXIII (1863), p. 95 f.
44. 'The Intelligent Study of Holy Scripture' (1855).
45. *Essays and Reviews*, p. 17 f.
46. *Essays on the History of Religious Thought in the West* (1891), pp. 93 f., 140.
47. *The Gospel of Life*, p. 113; Kingsley, *The Heroes*, preface.
48. *The Richmond Papers*, ed. A. Stirling (1926), p. 412.
49. *The George Eliot Letters*, ed. G. Haight (1954–6), VI, p. 302; *Apologia pro Vita Sua*, ch. 1.
50. Op. cit., p. 230.
51. *Essays Ancient and Modern* (1936), pp. 172, 174.
52. *Marius*, ch. 6; Macaulay, *Essays*, 'Machiavelli'.
53. Symonds, *Studies of the Greek Poets*, ch. 1; Arnold, 'On the Modern Element in Literature' (*Prose Works*, ed. Super, I, p. 23).
54. 'History'.
55. *The Collected Works of John Stuart Mill*, ed. J. M. Robson etc. (Toronto, 1963–).
56. *Essays and Reviews*, p. 18.
57. Arnold, op. cit. (Super I, p. 30); Ruskin, *Praeterita* I, § 237.
58. 'Flaxman's Lectures on Sculpture' (*Complete Works*, ed. P. P. Howe, XVI, p. 352).
59. *History of Ancient Art*, bk. 8.
60. Symonds, op. cit., ch. 14; Schlegel, *Lectures on the Drama*, lecture 6; Symonds, chs. 13, 14.
61. *Memoirs of . . . Wren* (1823), p. xiii f.
62. Op. cit. I, ch. 1, §§ 4, 5.
63. Op. cit., § 116.
64. *Praeterita* II, §§ 29, 30; I, § 189; III, § 67, 84; II, § 99.

65. Pater, *The Renaissance*, preface; Ruskin, *The Stones of Venice* I, ch. 1, § 30; III, ch. 3, § 67; I, ch. 1, § 24.
66. Ib. I, ch. 1, § 30.
67. *The Renaissance*, preface.
68. Op. cit., chs. 11, 13.
69. Op. cit., 'Winckelmann'.
70. *Alton Locke*, ch. 26; Macaulay, *Essays*, 'Milton'.
71. Ruskin, *Modern Painters* III (pt. 4), ch. 12, § 6; A. P. Stanley, *The Life . . . of Thomas Arnold* (1844) I, p. 133; G. O. Trevelyan, *The Life . . . of Lord Macaulay*, ch. 12; Woolf, 'On Not Knowing Greek' (*Collected Essays* (1966–7) I, p. 12).
72. Stanley I, p. 134; *Modern Painters* III (pt. 4), ch. 8, § 10.
73. *Miscellaneous Works* (1845), p. 396 f.
74. *Essays on a Liberal Education*, ed. F. W. Farrar (1867), p. 327.
75. *Marius*, ch. 4; *Mad as the Mist and Snow*.
76. *Praeterita* I, § 81; *Middlemarch*, ch. 10; *Pericles and Aspasia*, letters 141, 145, 154; *Imaginary Conversations*, 'Pericles and Sophocles'.
77. *The Last Days of Pompeii*, bk. 5, ch. 2.
78. *A History of the Literature of Ancient Greece* (1858) I, p. 1.
79. Bk. 1, introduction.
80. *Charicles*, tr. F. Metcalfe (3rd edn., 1866), p. viii.
81. P. Grosskurth, *John Addington Symonds* (1964), p. 80.
82. D. Forbes, *The Liberal Anglican Idea of History* (Cambridge, 1952), p. 96.
83. Bk. 3, ch. 2.
84. Ch. 30.
85. Preface.
86. Bk. 1, chs. 3, 7.
87. Bk. 1, ch. 3.
88. Bk. 4, ch. 2.
89. Trevelyan, ch. 16.
90. Op. cit., chs. 18, 8.
91. Wilde, *De Profundis*; Pater, *Marius*, ch. 18; *The Note-Books of Samuel Butler*, ed. H. F. Jones (1912), p. 193.

Chapter 5 Tragedy

1. Op. cit. (1891) II, p. 224.
2. Lecture 3 (tr. J. Black).
3. Lecture 6.
4. *Studies of the Greek Poets*, ch. 12.
5. Symonds, loc. cit.; *The Swinburne Letters*, ed. C. Y. Lang (New Haven, 1959–62), IV, p. 193; Tovey, *Essays in Musical Analysis* (1935) I, p. 32; Woolf, *Collected Essays* (1966–7) I, pp. 7, 10; Ruskin, *The Stones of Venice* III, ch. 3, § 67; II, ch. 4, § 35.

6. Op. cit., ch. 11.
7. *Odes*, 4. 2. 5 ff.
8. *Further Letters of Gerard Manley Hopkins* . . ., ed. C. C. Abbott (2nd edn., 1956), p. 276.
9. *The Letters of Gerard Manley Hopkins to Robert Bridges*, ed. C. C. Abbott (1935), pp. 157, 49.
10. Byron, *Letters and Journals*, ed. R. Prothero (1898–1901), IV, p. 174.
11. *Letters* III, p. 55.
12. Ib. VI, p. 85; III, p. 55.
13. Ib. VI, p. 147.
14. 'The Study of Poetry' (*Prose Works*, ed. Super, IX, p. 161); *Culture and Anarchy*, ch. 1 (Super V, p. 100).
15. *Merope*, preface.
16. 'Pagan and Mediaeval Religious Sentiment' (Super III, p. 321).
17. Macaulay, *Essays*, 'Milton'; Forster, *The Longest Journey*, ch. 17.
18. Newman, *The Idea of a University*, ed. C. F. Harrold (New York, 1947), p. 225; *Keble's Lectures on Poetry*, tr. E. K. Francis (Oxford, 1912) II, pp. 226, 252.
19. Pater, *Greek Studies*, 'The Bacchanals of Euripides'; F. A. Paley, *Euripides* . . . (2nd edn., 1874) II, p. 413 f.
20. Jowett, *The Dialogues of Plato* (3rd edn., Oxford, 1892) II, p. 313; E. Abbott, *Hellenica* (1880), p. vi; L. Campbell, *Religion in Greek Literature* (1898), p. 281.
21. *Judaism (A Tragic Chorus)*.
22. *The Table Talk* . . . *of Samuel Taylor Coleridge* (1917), p. 56; Gladstone, *Studies on Homer and the Homeric Age* (Oxford, 1858) II, p. 7; Alford, *Chapters on the Poets of Ancient Greece* (1841), p. 104.
23. Symonds, op. cit., ch. 1; Tyrrell, *Euripidou Bakhai* (1871), p. xxv.
24. Woolf, op. cit. I, p. 3; Coleridge, *Table Talk*, p. 112; Forster, op. cit., ch. 26.
25. *Tess of the d'Urbervilles*, ch. 59; *Jude*, pt. 5, ch. 4; Swinburne, *Letters* VI, p. 91.
26. *To Dorothy Wellesley*.
27. A. N. Jeffares, *A Commentary on the Collected Poems of W. B. Yeats* (1968), ad loc.
28. *The Letters of John Addington Symonds*, ed. H. M. Schueller and R. L. Peters (Detroit, 1967–9) II, p. 148.
29. *Letters* II, p. 302.
30. Op. cit., ch. 17.
31. G. O. Trevelyan, *The Life* . . . *of Lord Macaulay*, ch. 6.
32. Ib., appendix 2.
33. Jeffares, p. 312.
34. Trevelyan, ch. 6.
35. *De Profundis*.
36. Ib. (cf. Eur. *I.T.* 1193).
37. Trevelyan, ch. 14.

38. *The Last Chronicle of Barset*, chs. 13, 17.
39. Ib., ch. 62.
40. *Merope*, preface.
41. *De Quincey as Critic*, ed. J. E. Jordan (1973), pp. 180 f., 167; Lewes, *Goethe*, bk. 5, ch. 3.
42. *Merope*, preface.
43. 'Schlegel on the Drama' (*Complete Works*, ed. P. P. Howe, XVI, p. 76).
44. Jordan, p. 181.
45. *The Birth of Tragedy*, sect. 7.
46. Hazlitt, op. cit. (Howe XVI, p. 73); Trevelyan, ch. 15.
47. *Hellas*, preface.
48. Ib., l. 54 ff.
49. Act 3, sc. 4, l. 98 ff.
50. L. 553 ff.
51. L. 690 f.
52. *The Letters . . . to Robert Bridges*, pp. 202 f., 210.
53. Ib., pp. 147, 201; *The Correspondence of Gerard Manley Hopkins and Richard Watson Dixon*, ed. C. C. Abbott (1935), p. 106.
54. *Letters* I, p. 115; III, p. 55; V, p. 153; III, pp. 58, 55.
55. Reginald Lord Esher, *Ionicus* (1923), p. 115.
56. Sonnet, *To a Friend*; 'On the Modern Element in Literature' (Super I, p. 28).
57. 'Winckelmann'.
58. *Maurice*, ch. 6; Browning, *Balaustion's Adventure*.
59. *Table Talk*, p. 262.
60. *Wine of Cyprus*.
61. Coleridge, *Table Talk*, p. 252; Alford, op. cit., p. 159; Pater, *Greek Studies*, 'The Bacchanals of Euripides'.
62. *The Letters of Thomas Babington Macaulay*, ed. T. Pinney (Cambridge, 1974) I, p. 77 f.; *Essays*, 'Milton'; Trevelyan, ch. 6.
63. *Merope*, l. 890 ff.
64. Trevelyan, ch. 6.
65. *Letters* III, p. 99; cf. V, p. 105.
66. *Erechtheus*, l. 532 f.
67. *Greek Studies*, loc. cit.
68. Livingstone, *The Pageant of Greece* (Oxford, 1923), p. 123; Norwood, *Euripides and Mr. Bernard Shaw* (1913), pp. 7, 32; Verrall, *Euripides the Rationalist* (Cambridge, 1895), p. 138.
69. Sect. 11.
70. D. S. Thatcher, *Nietzsche in England 1890–1914* (Toronto, 1970), p. 211.
71. *Wagner on Music and Drama*, ed. A. Goldman and E. Sprinchorn, p. 82 ff.
72. *The Pleasures of Literature* (1938), p. 137.

Chapter 6 George Eliot and the Greeks

1. *David Copperfield*, ch. 18.
2. Ch. 11.
3. *Amos Barton*, ch. 2.
4. *The George Eliot Letters*, ed. G. Haight (1954–6), VII, p. 39, V, p. 464.
5. *Amos Barton*, chs. 7, 5.
6. Ch. 2.
7. Ch. 6.
8. Ch. 4.
9. *Letters* III, p. 356.
10. Ch. 13.
11. Chs. 3, 12.
12. Chs. 1, 4.
13. Ch. 17.
14. Ch. 5.
15. Ch. 3.
16. Chs. 5, 9, 15.
17. Ch. 12.
18. Ch. 5.
19. Ch. 16.
20. *Prom.* 890.
21. Ch. 22.
22. *Med.* 1156 ff.
23. Ch. 36.
24. Ch. 22.
25. Ch. 28.
26. Ch. 29.
27. Ch. 53.
28. Chs. 33, 4.
29. Ch. 56.
30. Bk. 1, ch. 7.
31. Bk. 1, ch. 10.
32. Bk. 4, ch. 1.
33. Bk. 5, ch. 4.
34. Bk. 5, ch. 2.
35. Bk. 1, ch. 3.
36. Bk. 2, ch. 1.
37. Bk. 1, ch. 13.
38. Ch. 38.
39. Ch. 11.
40. *Ag.* 758 ff.
41. 'Proem'.
42. Ch. 3.
43. Ch. 6.
44. Chs. 3, 6.

45. Ch. 6.
46. Ib.
47. Ch. 39.
48. Chs. 42, 48.
49. Ch. 49.
50. Ch. 47.
51. Bk. 3, ch. 8.
52. Chs. 1, 39.
53. Ch. 1.
54. Chs. 5, 2.
55. Ch. 2.
56. *Med.* 1029 f.
57. Ch. 36.
58. Ch. 39.
59. *Med.* 230 ff.
60. Ch. 39.
61. *Med.* 38 f.; 103 f.; 119 f.
62. Ch. 39.
63. Ch. 42.
64. *Med.* 471 f.
65. Ch. 44.
66. Ch. 19
67. 'Finale'.
68. Ch. 3.
69. Ch. 15.
70. Ch. 42.
71. Ch. 3.
72. *Essays* (Oxford, 1889) II, p. 166.
73. Ch. 2.
74. Ch. 20.
75. Chs. 3, 22.
76. Ch. 10.
77. Ch. 5.
78. Ch. 16.
79. Ib.
80. Ch. 16.
81. Ch. 38.
82. Ch. 42.
83. Ch. 43.
84. Ch. 41.
85. Ch. 63.
86. Ch. 3.
87. Ch. 6.
88. Ib.
89. Ib.
90. Ch. 45.

Chapter 7   The Consequences of Sculpture

1. *The New Republic*, bk. 4, ch. 1.
2. H. Honour, *Neo-classicism* (1968), p. 114.
3. *Don Juan*, canto 2, st. 194; *Dolores*, l. 49 ff.
4. *The Note-Books of Samuel Butler*, ed. H. F. Jones (1912), p. 388 f.
5. *Don Juan*, canto 1, st. 41; *The Grand Duke*, act 2.
6. Bentham, *Chrestomathia* (*The Works of Jeremy Bentham*, ed. J. Bowring (Edinburgh, 1843) VIII, p. 43); Ruskin, *Modern Painters* II (pt. 3), sect. 1, ch. 14, § 25; Mrs. R. Barrington, *The Life . . . of Frederic Leighton* (1906) II, p. 29.
7. *Middlemarch*, ch. 9.
8. *The Richmond Papers*, ed. A. Stirling (1926), p. 63; Alford, *Chapters on the Poets of Ancient Greece* (1841), p. 5 f.
9. *Modern Painters*, loc. cit.
10. P. Grosskurth, *John Addington Symonds* (1964), p. 19.
11. *The Junior Dean* (1891) II, p. 232.
12. *The Renaissance*, 'Winckelmann'.
13. *Hiram Powers' Greek Slave*.
14. M. Lutyens, *Effie in Venice* (1965), p. 20 f.
15. Hazlitt, 'Flaxman's Lectures on Sculpture' (*Complete Works*, ed. P. P. Howe, XVI, p. 353).
16. Pater, *Greek Studies*, 'The Age of Athletic Prizemen'; James, *Roderick Hudson*, chs. 11, 6.
17. Ruskin, *Aratra Pentelici*, § 61; James, ch. 15; Ruskin, op. cit., § 21; Pater, *The Renaissance*, 'Winckelmann'.
18. *Don Juan*, canto 13, st. 110; *The Old Curiosity Shop*, ch. 27.
19. *Felix Holt the Radical*, ch. 43.
20. Ch. 43.
21. Woolf, *Collected Essays* (1966–7) I, p. 5; Flecker, *Oak and Olive*.
22. Ch. 20.
23. W. Gaunt, *Victorian Olympus* (1952), p. 99; Walpole to Mary Berry, Aug. 1791; Blake, *Complete Writings*, ed. G. Keynes (Oxford, 1966), p. 451.
24. Pater, *The Renaissance*, 'Leonardo da Vinci'; Wilde, ch. 1.
25. Chs. 2, 13.
26. Ch. 3.
27. Ch. 22.
28. *Roman Elegies*, no. 5.
29. *The Renaissance*, 'Winckelmann'; *Imaginary Conversations*, 'Aesop and Rhodope'.
30. *The Statues*; *Explorations* (1962), p. 451.
31. *The Complete Works of Algernon Charles Swinburne*, ed. E. Gosse and T. J. Wise (1925–7), XV, p. 197; *The Newcomes*, ch. 25.
32. *Liber Amoris*, pts. 3, 2 (Howe IX, pp. 137 f., 143, 133); Byron, *Don Juan*, canto 6, st. 43; Pater, *The Renaissance*, 'Winckelmann'; Gilbert, *Princess Ida*, act 2.

33. *Miss Brown* (Edinburgh, 1884) I, pp. 121, 124; II, pp. 238 f., 310; *Earl Lavender* (1895), p. 129.
34. E. M. Butler, *The Tyranny of Greece over Germany* (Cambridge, 1935); Leighton, *Addresses Delivered to the Students of the Royal Academy* (1896), p. 89; Pater, *Marius the Epicurean*, ch. 21; Kingsley, *Alton Locke*, ch. 6; Disraeli, *Lothair*, ch. 8.
35. *Framley Parsonage*, ch. 43; *Middlemarch*, chs. 12, 63.
36. *Marius*, ch. 2; *The Renaissance*, 'Winckelmann'.
37. *The Renaissance*, loc. cit.; Schlegel, *Lectures on the Drama*, lecture 1; *The Last Days of Pompeii*, bk. 1, ch. 3.
38. *The Renaissance*, 'Winckelmann'; 'Leonardo da Vinci'.
39. *The Portrait of a Lady*, ch. 28.
40. *Marius*, ch. 2; *Adonais*, st. 52.
41. *The Renaissance*, 'Winckelmann'.
42. H. Tennyson, *Alfred Lord Tennyson* (1897) II, p. 127.
43. Mackenzie, bk. 2, ch. 3; Wilde, ch. 3.
44. Op. cit. (1874), pp. 168, 231.
45. Chs. 24, 21.
46. *Wilhelm Meisters Lehrjahre*, bk. 8, ch. 3.
47. Ch. 2.

Chapter 8   The Interpretation of Greece

1. *The Table Talk . . . of . . . Coleridge* (1917), p. 184; Kingsley, *The Heroes*, preface; *The Works of . . . Smith* (1859) I, p. 169; Wilde, *De Profundis*; Lytton, bk. 1, ch. 7; Macaulay, 'Thoughts on the Advancement of Academical Education . . .', *Ed. Rev.* XLIII (1826), 331.
2. E. M. Butler, *The Tyranny of Greece over Germany* (Cambridge, 1935), p. 11.
3. *Romola*, ch. 38; *Jude*, pt. 1, ch. 7.
4. Pt. 2, ch. 3.
5. J. E. Sandys, *A History of Classical Scholarship* (Cambridge 1903–8) III, p. 234.
6. MacNeice, *The Strings Are False* (1965), p. 87; Woolf, *Collected Essays* (1966–7) I, p. 11 f.
7. *Seven Men*, 'Enoch Soames'.
8. *The Renaissance*, 'The Poetry of Michelangelo'.
9. *The Old Vicarage, Grantchester*.
10. *De Profundis*.
11. *Childe Harold's Pilgrimage*, canto 2, st. 89; *Extracts from the Letters and Journal of William Cory*, ed. F. Warre Cornish (Oxford, 1897), p. 282.
12. Op. cit., p. 111.

13. *The Princess*, sect. 7, l. 167.
14. Arnold, *On Translating Homer* (*Prose Works*, ed. Super, I, p. 150); Grote, *History of Greece*, prefatory note; G. O. Trevelyan, *The Life . . . of Lord Macaulay*, ch. 11; Arnold, ib.
15. Browning, *Aristophanes' Apology*.
16. *Don Juan*, canto 8, st. 39; *The Newcomes*, ch. 31; Mallock, *The New Republic*, bk. 4, ch. 1.
17. Super III, p. 272 f.
18. W. J. Bate, *The Burden of the Past . . .* (1971), p. 74.
19. *Cranford*, ch. 15.
20. Ch. 2 (Super V, p. 116).
21. *In Parenthesis* (1937), p. 160 f.
22. 'On Mitford's History of Greece'.
23. Buckle, *History of Civilization in England* I, ch. 2; *Romola*, ch. 6.
24. *Thoughts of a Briton on the Subjugation of Switzerland*.
25. Grote, *History of Greece*, pt. 2, ch. 1; Tozer, *Lectures on the Geography of Greece* (1873), p. 177; Symonds, *Sketches in Italy and Greece* (1874), p. 207.
26. Gillies, *The History of Ancient Greece* (1786) I, p. 36; Aristotle *Pol.* 1327 b.
27. See Arnold, 'The Function of Criticism . . .' (Super III, p. 272).
28. Pater, *The Renaissance*, 'Winckelmann'; Disraeli, *Lothair*, ch. 8; Robertson, *Sermons on Christian Doctrine* (1906), p. 298.
29. *Don Juan*, canto 1, st. 63.
30. *Childe Harold's Pilgrimage*, canto 2, st. 73; Symonds, op. cit., p. 207 f.
31. *Introductory Lectures on Modern History* (Oxford, 1842), pp. 36 f., 33.
32. Leighton, *Addresses Delivered to the Students of the Royal Academy* (1896), address of 1883; Disraeli, *Sybil, passim*.
33. Ar. *Lys.* 998 ff.
34. *Taine's Notes on England*, tr. E. Hyams (1957), p. 286; Mueller, *Dorians*, bk. 4, ch. 1, sect. 4.
35. Arnold, 'A New History of Greece' (Super V, p. 263); Pater, *Plato and Platonism*, chs. 8, 1.
36. Pater, ib., ch. 8.
37. Buckle, loc. cit.
38. *Contarini Fleming*, pt. 5, ch. 8; Tozer, op. cit., p. 175.
39. Pater, op. cit., ch. 8.
40. *Writings on Art*, ed. D. Irwin (1972), p. 73.
41. Plato, *Tim.* 22b.
42. Pater, *The Renaissance*, 'Winckelmann'; *Greek Studies*, 'The Age of Athletic Prizemen'; Symonds, *Studies of the Greek Poets*, ch. 21.
43. *Marius the Epicurean*, ch. 22.
44. *Essays and Reviews*, p. 4.
45. Ib., pp. 24, 27.
46. Kovalevsky's description (S. S. Prawer, *Karl Marx and World Literature* (Oxford, 1966), p. 395).

47. Symonds, *Studies* . . ., ch. 1; *Essays and Reviews*, p. 27; Jebb, *Essays and Addresses* (Cambridge, 1907), p. 560; Pater, *Greek Studies*, loc. cit.
48. 'On Antiquity' (*Complete Works*, ed. P. P. Howe, XII, p. 254 f.).
49. *The Renaissance*, 'Winckelmann'.
50. Pater, *Greek Studies*, loc. cit.; Jebb, op. cit., p. 570; Jenkyns, *A Lecture on the Advantages of Classical Studies* (Durham, 1834), p. 10 f.
51. *Studies* . . ., chs. 24, 21.
52. *The Renaissance*, 'Winckelmann'; Hazlitt, 'Schlegel on the Drama' (Howe XVI, p. 64); Symonds, *Sketches* . . . p. 216 f.; Pater, *Plato and Platonism*, ch. 8.
53. Woolf, op. cit. I, p. 3; Symonds, *Studies* . . ., ch. 17.
54. *The Dynasts*, preface.
55. Plut. *Demetr.* 12.
56. Symonds, *Studies* . . ., chs. 18, 10; Ruskin, *Aratra Pentelici*, § 200; Pater, *The Renaissance*, 'Sandro Botticelli'; Mallock, op. cit., bk. 3, ch. 4.
57. Edn. of Beethoven, op. 110 ad loc.; *Essays in Musical Analysis* (1935–9) I, p. 195.
58. Op. cit., p. 569.
59. *The Renaissance*, 'Winckelmann'.
60. R. Hill (ed.), *The Symphony* (1949), p. 349.
61. *The Renaissance*, 'Winckelmann'.
62. *A Musical Instrument*.
63. *Flush or Faunus*.
64. *The Dead Pan*, headnote.
65. 'The world is too much with us . . .'
66. *Childe Harold's Pilgrimage*, canto 2, sts. 53, 85, 88, 87.
67. *Hellas*, l. 230 ff.; *Shelley at Oxford*, ed. W. S. Scott (1944), pp. 64 f., 61; *The Athenians*, ed. Scott (1943), p. 44.
68. *The Queen of the Air*, preface.
69. *Modern Painters* III (pt. 4), ch. 12, § 5; ch. 13, § 1 f.
70. Ib. III, ch. 13, § 3; Symonds, *Studies of the Greek Poets*, ch. 24.
71. *Modern Painters* III, ch. 13, § 15 ff.
72. Ib., § 4.
73. Ib., § 5.
74. *Sesame and Lilies*, § 35.
75. Ib., § 84.
76. *Fors Clavigera*, letter 5.
77. *Praeterita* III, § 84.
78. *Modern Painters* III, ch. 4, § 5.
79. Op. cit., § 3.
80. Ib., § 32.
81. *Praeterita* III, § 70; *The Queen of the Air*, § 75 f.
82. *Modern Painters*, III ch. 13, § 7.
83. Ib., § 8.
84. Ib., § 13.
85. *Praeterita* III, § 84; I, § 75.

86. *Sketches in Italy and Greece* (1874), p. 21.
87. Wilde, *De Profundis*; Symonds, *Sketches* . . ., p. 6 f.
88. Op. cit., *The City of Lucca*, ch. 6 (tr. C. G. Leland).
89. In *Imaginary Portraits* and *Miscellaneous Studies*.
90. In *Seven Men*.
91. *Studies* . . ., ch. 21.
92. *Little Gidding*, sect. 1.
93. *Explorations* (1962), p. 438.
94. Chs. 7, 35.
95. *Pan*.
96. *The Song of the Happy Shepherd*.

Chapter 9 Homer and the Homeric Ideal

1. Shaw, *Dramatic Opinions and Essays* (1907) II, p. 52; Gladstone, *Studies on Homer and the Homeric Age* (Oxford, 1858) I, p. 13; Shelley, 'Discourse on the Manners of the Ancients'; J. A. Froude, *Thomas Carlyle: A history of the first forty years* . . . (1882) II, p. 97; Froude, *Short Studies on Great Subjects*, 'Homer'.
2. J. Clive, *Thomas Babington Macaulay* (1973), p. 25; A. P. Stanley, *The Life* . . . *of Thomas Arnold* (1844) I, p. 3; Kinglake, *Eothen*, ch. 4; Ruskin, *Praeterita* I, § 1; George Eliot, *The Mill on the Floss*, bk. 2, ch. 3; Mackenzie, *Sinister Street*, bk. 1, ch. 8.
3. E. T. MacDermot, *History of the Great Western Railway* (1927), p. 874; Froude, *Short Studies* . . ., loc. cit.
4. Hunt, *Foliage*, preface; Lamb, letter of 13th June, 1809.
5. *The Poems of John Keats*, ed. M. Allott (1970), ad loc.
6. Arnold, *On Translating Homer* (Super I, p. 111); Ruskin, *Modern Painters* III (pt. 4), ch. 12, § 6.
7. Macaulay, *Essays*, 'Moore's Life of Byron'; Gladstone, op. cit. III, p. 512.
8. 'To one who has been long in city pent', l.1 ff.; *On First Looking into Chapman's Homer*, l. 5 f.
9. Symonds, *Studies of the Greek Poets*, ch. 1; *Letters of Matthew Arnold* . . . *to* . . . *Clough*, ed. H. F. Lowry (1932), p. 146; *On Translating Homer*, 'Last Words' (Super I, p. 216).
10. *Aspects of Poetry* (Oxford, 1881), p. 405 f.
11. *The Swinburne Letters*, ed. C. Y. Lang (New Haven, 1959–62), II, p. 326.
12. Newman, 'Homeric Translation in Theory and Practice'; Landor, *Pericles and Aspasia*, letter 8.
13. *Biographia Literaria*, ch. 14.
14. Froude, *Thomas Carlyle* . . . *the first forty years* II, p. 404 ff.
15. Arnold, *On Translating Homer* (Super I, p. 167); Landor, loc. cit.; Pater, op. cit., ch. 6.

16. *On Translating Homer* (Super I, p. 120).
17. Ib. (Super I, p. 102); *The Collected Works of Walter Bagehot*, ed. N. St John-Stevas (1965–   ), I, p. 303.
18. Op. cit.
19. *On Translating Homer* (Super I, pp. 121, 119, 128, 168, 111, 168, 113, 191, 142).
20. Ib., 'Last Words' (Super I, p. 189 ff.).
21. Ib. (Super I, p. 190).
22. Ch. 10.
23. Op. cit. III, p. 616.
24. G. O. Trevelyan, *The Life . . . of Lord Macaulay*, chs. 6, 11.
25. J. Morley, *The Life of William Ewart Gladstone* (1903) II, p. 353.
26. Ib. II, p. 477; III, p. 385.
27. Ward, *A Writer's Recollections* (1918), p. 238.
28. Morley II, p. 523.
29. Op. cit. II, pp. 481, 489, 507 f., 493; III, p. 105 f.
30. P. Magnus, *Gladstone* (1954), p. 34; Morley I, p. 594.
31. Gladstone, op. cit. I, p. 11 f.; Newman, *The Iliad of Homer* (1856), p. iv.
32. Op. cit. III, pp. 3, 31, 74 f.
33. Gladstone, op. cit. III, pp. 94 f., 76; Doyle, *Lectures on Poetry . . .* (2nd series, 1877), p. 148; Disraeli, *Lord George Bentinck*, ch. 16.
34. Magnus, p. 257.
35. *Praeterita* I, §§ 3, 7.
36. *Gleanings of Past Years . . .* (1879) VII, p. 36.
37. *Studies on Homer . . .* I, p. 6; II, p. 37 ff.
38. Ib. II, p. 4 f.
39. Ib. II, p. 37.
40. Ib. II, pp. 46, 55 ff., 131, 111, 140, 153, 172, 54, 342.
41. Kingsley, *The Heroes*, preface; Arnold, 'Curtius's "History of Greece"' (Super V, p. 271).
42. *Studies on Homer . . .* II, pp. 465, 466, 479, 269.
43. Ib. II, p. 513 ff.
44. Ib. III, p. 580.
45. Ib. II, p. 2 f.
46. *Pendennis*, chs. 5, 36.
47. Trevelyan, ch. 12.
48. *Julian Home*, ch. 26.
49. *Don Juan*, canto 1, st. 63.
50. E.g. *The Mill on the Floss*, bk. 3, ch. 3; *Daniel Deronda*, ch. 22.
51. Sect. 2.
52. Trevelyan, chs. 8, 9.
53. Suetonius, *Vita Vergili* 46.
54. *Miscellaneous Works* (1845), p. 350.
55. R. M. Ogilvie, *Latin and Greek* (1964), p. 156.
56. Trevelyan, ch. 4.

57. Ogilvie, p. 160.
58. *The Last Chronicle of Barset*, ch. 80.
59. *On Translating Homer* (Super I, p. 127).
60. M. L. Clarke, *George Grote* (1962), p. 110; *The George Eliot Letters*, ed. G. Haight (1954–6), IV, p. 424.
61. Trevelyan, ch. 12.
62. Keble's *Lectures on Poetry*, tr. E. Francis (Oxford, 1912), I, pp. 196, 275; Ruskin, *Praeterita* I, § 1; *Modern Painters* III (pt. 4), ch. 12, § 6; Mure, *A Critical History of the . . . Literature of Antient Greece* (2nd edn., 1854–9) II, p. 231; Froude, *Short Studies . . .*, 'Homer'.
63. Gladstone, *Studies on Homer . . .* III, p. 555; Mure I, p. 274; Symonds, *Studies of the Greek Poets*, ch. 3.
64. Shairp, p. 381; Froude, *Short Studies . . .*, loc. cit.; Ruskin, *Modern Painters* III, ch. 7, § 4.
65. *Studies on Homer . . .* II, p. 504 f.
66. *Julian Home*, ch. 18.
67. *The Note-Books of Samuel Butler*, ed. H. F. Jones (1912), pp. 193, 393; *The Authoress of the Odyssey*.
68. *Studies on Homer* III, p. 555 f.
69. *Il.* 2. 211 ff.
70. Ib. 265 ff.
71. *Studies on Homer* III, pp. 124, 129.
72. Op. cit., l. 39 ff.
73. Ch. 64.
74. *Nicholas Nickleby*, ch. 13; *Our Mutual Friend*, bk. 4, ch. 14.
75. Ch. 12.
76. G. Faber, *Jowett* (2nd edn., 1958), p. 65.
77. Pt. 1, ch. 3.
78. Pt. 2, ch. 4.
79. Pt. 1, ch. 13.
80. *Il.* 2. 269.
81. *Letters* IV, p. 45 f.
82. Pt. 2, ch. 5.
83. The lines are *Il.* 24. 771 f.
84. Pt. 2, ch. 6.
85. *Il.* 11. 784; 9. 443.
86. Pt. 2, ch. 8.
87. Ch. 41.
88. Butler, *The Way of All Flesh*, ch. 19; Newman, *The Idea of a University*, ed. C. F. Harrold (New York, 1947), p. 224 f.; Gladstone, *Studies on Homer* III, p. 47.
89. *Taine's Notes on England*, tr. E. Hyams (1957), p. 103.
90. Ch. 3.
91. *Julian Home*, ch. 25.
92. *Gleanings of Past Years* (1879) VII, p. 74.

93. Reade, *Hard Cash*, prologue; Hughes, *Tom Brown at Oxford*, chs. 5, 10.
94. Ch. 3.
95. Faber, p. 65.
96. *The Life . . . of Thomas Arnold* (1844) I, p. 117.
97. Ch. 13.
98. C. R. L. Fletcher, *Edmond Warre* (1922), p. 135 (cf. p. 272 ff.).
99. *Beppo*, st. 75.
100. *Studies of the Greek Poets*, ch. 13.
101. *Lothair*, chs. 76, 29.
102. Ch. 3.
103. Ch. 4.
104. *Culture and Anarchy*, ch. 5 (*Prose Works*, ed. Super, V, p. 190).
105. Ib., ch. 3 (Super V, p. 141).
106. Ib. (Super V, p. 142).
107. 'Pagan and Mediaeval Religious Sentiment' (Super III, p. 228).
108. Livingstone, *The Greek Genius and Its Meaning to Us* (2nd edn., Oxford, 1915), p. 137 f.; Taine, op. cit., p. 111; Mackenzie, *Sinister Street*, bk. 2, ch. 11; bk. 3, ch. 1.
109. *Essays and Introductions* (1961), p. 248.
110. *Enemies of Promise*, ch. 24.
111. Op. cit., ch. 24.
112. Graham, *A Private in the Guards* (1919), p. 80 f.; Proust, *Time Regained*, tr. A. Mayor (1970), p. 145.

Chapter 10 Plato

1. Op. cit. (5th edn., 1966), p. viii.
2. *The Table Talk . . . of Samuel Taylor Coleridge* (1917), p. 118.
3. Pater, *Marius*, ch. 20; J. Notopoulos, *The Platonism of Shelley* (Durham, North Carolina, 1949), p. 17.
4. Mill, *Autobiography*, ch. 4.
5. *System of Logic*, bk. 6, ch. 11, § 3.
6. *Table Talk*, p. 82 f.
7. E. Abbott and L. Campbell, *The Life and Letters of Benjamin Jowett* (1897) I, p. 261.
8. Stanley, *The Life . . . of Thomas Arnold* (1844) I, p. 17.
9. Op. cit., ed. C. F. Harrold (New York, 1947), p. 97.
10. Symonds, *In the Key of Blue* (1893), p. 42.
11. H. Spiegelberg (ed.), *The Socratic Enigma* (New York, etc., 1964), pp. 188 f., 93.
12. *The Philosophical Lectures*, ed. K. Coburn (1949), p. 140.
13. *The George Eliot Letters*, ed. G. Haight (1954–6), VI, p. 407.
14. *The Deformed Transformed*, pt. 1, sc. 1, l. 221 f.; *Don Juan*, canto 6, init.

15. P. Gay, *The Enlightenment* (1973), p. 82; Hume, *An Enquiry concerning the Principles of Morals*, sect. 7.
16. *Extracts from the Letters and Journals of William Cory*, ed. F. Warre Cornish (Oxford, 1897), p. 193.
17. *Culture and Anarchy*, 'Conclusion' (Super V, p. 228 f.).
18. Ib., ch. 5 (Super V, p. 184).
19. *Autobiography*, ch. 4.
20. *The Collected Works of John Stuart Mill*, ed. J. M. Robson, etc. (Toronto, 1963–), XI, p. 309; *On Liberty*, ch. 2 (*Collected Works* XVIII, p. 235).
21. *Deontology*, ed. J. Bowring (1834), I, p. 39 f.
22. *Culture and Anarchy*, ch. 1 (Super V, p. 111); Mill, 'Bentham' (*Collected Works* X, p. 90).
23. *Essays*, 'Lord Bacon'.
24. *An Autobiography* (1904) I, p. 442.
25. *Autobiography*, ch. 2.
26. T. J. Hogg, etc., *The Life of Shelley*, ed. H. Wolfe (1933), I, p. 70.
27. Notopoulos, p. 30.
28. Hogg I, pp. 73, 147 f.
29. Notopoulos, pp. 64, 66.
30. E. J. Trelawney, *Recollections of . . . Shelley and Byron* (Hogg II, p. 209 f.).
31. Bk. 6, ch. 12.
32. Trelawney (Hogg II, p. 206).
33. *Principles of Logic* (1922) II, p. 591.
34. *The Complete Works of Percy Bysshe Shelley*, ed. R. Ingpen and W. Peck (1926–30), IX, p. 340.
35. *Epipsychidion*, l. 509 ff.
36. Op. cit., l. 44 ff.
37. *Rep.* 514–15.
38. *Rep.* 616e–617a.
39. *Adonais*, st. 52.
40. Ib., st. 38.
41. Ib., st. 39.
42. Ib., sts. 40, 41, 43.
43. *The Swinburne Letters*, ed. C. Y. Lang (New Haven, 1959–62), V, p. 122.
44. Ingpen and Peck X, p. 401.
45. Op. cit., l. 149 ff.
46. Ib., ll. 115 f., 77 ff.
47. G. O. Trevelyan, *The Life . . . of Lord Macaulay*, ch. 16; Jowett, *The Dialogues of Plato* (2nd edn., Oxford, 1875) III, p. 150; Cory, op. cit., p. 546.
48. *Alice*, ch. 6; *Crat.* 405 c.
49. Trevelyan, ch. 13.
50. Ib., chs. 16, 13.

51. *Collected Works* XII, p. 311.
52. Trevelyan, chs. 13, 16.
53. Ib., ch. 16.
54. Ib.
55. Ib.
56. *Mill's Ethical Writings*, ed. J. B. Schneewind (New York, 1965), p. 77.
57. *Hellas*, prologue, l. 94 f.
58. *Autobiography*, ch. 3.
59. Ib., ch. 2.
60. *On Liberty*, ch. 3 (*Collected Works* XVIII, p. 266).
61. *Autobiography*, ch. 1.
62. Ib., first draft.
63. Op. cit., ch. 39.
64. Ib., chs. 20, 39.
65. *My Apprenticeship*, ch. 2.
66. *Essays in the History of Religious Thought in the West* (1891), p. 48.
67. *Miscellaneous Writings* (1845), p. 398.
68. M. L. Clarke, *George Grote* (1962), p. 118.
69. Ib.
70. *Tom Brown at Oxford*, ch. 19.
71. *The Works of John Ruskin*, ed. E. T. Cook and A. Wedderburn (1903–1912), XXIV, p. xliv.
72. *The Stones of Venice* II, ch. 8, § 49.
73. Op. cit., ch. 15.
74. Notopoulos, p. 65.
75. Op. cit. III, p. 1 f.
76. *The Crown of Wild Olive*, § 142.
77. Bk. 2, ch. 2.
78. *Gleanings of Past Years* (1879) VII, p. 76.
79. Trevelyan, ch. 16.
80. *Primary and Classical Education* (Edinburgh, 1867), p. 3 ff.
81. P. Magnus, *Gladstone* (1954), p. 257; Trevelyan, ch. 16.
82. *Autobiography*, chs. 6, 7.
83. *Process and Reality* (Cambridge, 1929), p. 53.
84. *Theory of Legislation*, tr. R. Hildreth (1876), p. 3.
85. J. Passmore, *A Hundred Years of Philosophy* (2nd edn., 1966), p. 49.
86. *An Autobiography* (1939), ch. 3.
87. *Culture and Anarchy*, chs. 5, 1 (Super V, pp. 179, 106).
88. Bk. 3, ch. 7.
89. G. Faber, *Jowett* (2nd edn., 1958), p. 169.
90. Ib., pp. 418, 167.
91. Ib., p. 420.
92. G. Costigan, 'William Johnson Cory . . .', *Cornhill* 1972, pp. 238, 240.
93. *Letters and Journals*, p. 112; *Essays on a Liberal Education*, ed. F. W. Farrar (1867), p. 344.

94. Stanley I, pp. 126, 129.
95. Faber, p. 145.
96. Ib., p. 170.
97. Bk. 2, ch. 1.
98. *The Swinburne Letters* IV, p. 144; Jowett, op. cit. I, p. 427.
99. Op. cit. II, p. 302.
100. Ib. II, p. 314; III, p. 177.
101. Ib. II, p. 91 f.
102. Ib. III, pp. 150, 154.
103. *The Renaissance*, 'Pico della Mirandola', Jowett, op. cit. IV, p. 5.
104. *Marius*, ch. 3.
105. Ch. 9.
106. Ch. 8.
107. A. C. Benson, *Walter Pater* (1906), p. 162.
108. MacNeice, *The Strings are False* (1965), p. 231; Pater, *Plato and Platonism*, ch. 1.
109. Ib.
110. Chs. 9, 3.
111. Ch. 2.
112. Ch. 10.
113. Ch. 6.
114. Ib.
115. Ib.
116. *The Renaissance*, 'The Poetry of Michelangelo'.
117. *Plato and Platonism*, ch. 1.
118. Ch. 9.
119. Ch. 10.
120. Chs. 3, 2.
121. Chs. 6, 10.
122. Ch. 7.
123. Ch. 10.
124. Ch. 4.
125. Chs. 9, 1.
126. D.N.B., on Pater.
127. *Surprised by Joy*, ch. 13.
128. *Among School Children*.
129. *The Strings Are False*, p. 125.
130. Op. cit., sect. 13.
131. Op. cit., chs. 4, 12.
132. Op. cit., chs. 11, 6.

Chapter 11 Change and Decay

1. *The Collected Works of John Stuart Mill*, ed. J. M. Robson, etc. (Toronto, 1963–) XI, p. 303.

2. *The Critic as Artist.*
3. *The Letters of John Stuart Mill*, ed. H. Elliot (1910), II, p. 368.
4. *The Complete Prose Works of Matthew Arnold*, ed. R. H. Super (Ann Arbor, 1960–77), V, p. 417.
5. Arnold, *Culture and Anarchy*, 'Introduction' (Super V, p. 87).
6. 'Conclusion' and 'Introduction' (Super V, pp. 226, 88).
7. Super V, p. 417 (italics added).
8. Op. cit., ch. 1 (Super V, p. 90).
9. Super V, p. 423.
10. Op. cit., ch. 1 (Super V, pp. 93, 109).
11. Ib. (Super V, p. 99).
12. *Sermons on Christian Doctrine* (1906), p. 284.
13. Ib., p. 287.
14. *The Use of Poetry and the Use of Criticism* (2nd edn., 1964), p. 111.
15. Op. cit., ch. 4 (Super V, p. 165).
16. *On Heroes and Hero-Worship*, lecture 2.
17. *The Captive*, tr. C. K. Scott Moncrieff, I, p. 211.
18. Op. cit., chs. 3, 1 (Super V, pp. 146, 101, 98).
19. Ch. 1 (Super V, p. 92).
20. Ch. 2 (Super V, p. 120 f.).
21. Ch. 2 (Super V, p. 135).
22. See ch. 3 (Super V, p. 158).
23. Ch. 3 (Super V, p. 160).
24. Ch. 6 (Super V, pp. 209, 220).
25. Ch. 1 (Super V, p. 96).
26. Ch. 2 (Super V, p. 115).
27. Ch. 1 (Super V, p. 113).
28. Ib. (Super V, pp. 109, 111).
29. Ch. 4 (Super V, p. 164).
30. Ib. (Super V, p. 164 f.).
31. Ib. (Super V, p. 167).
32. Ib. (Super V, p. 163 f.).
33. Chs. 4, 7 (Super V, pp. 169, 171, 219 f., 208).
34. Ch. 4 (Super V, p. 173 f.).
35. Ib. (Super V, p. 167 f.).
36. Ch. 5 (Super V, p. 187 f.).
37. Mallock, *The New Republic*, bk. 3, ch. 2; Pater, *Marius*, chs. 19, 22; Robertson, op. cit., p. 288; Pater, op. cit., ch. 22; Wilde, *De Profundis.*
38. Op. cit., ch. 5 (Super V, p. 178).
39. 'Conclusion' (Super V, p. 224).
40. Buchan, *Memory Hold-the-Door* (1940), p. 47; *These for Remembrance* (1919), p. 64.
41. *Essays on a Liberal Education*, ed. F. W. Farrar (1867), p. 363.
42. Ch. 17.
43. *Collected Works* XVIII, p. 195.

44. M. Sanderson, *The Universities in the Nineteenth Century* (1975), p. 91 f.
45. G. Faber, *Jowett* (2nd edn., 1958), p. 81; D. Newsome, *Godliness and Good Learning* (1961), p. 68; T. W. Bamford, *Thomas Arnold* (1960), p. 117 ff.
46. Farrar, p. 320; G. Costigan, 'William Johnson Cory', *Cornhill* 1972, p. 242.
47. Mill, *Autobiography*, ch. 7; Farrar, pp. 381, 127 f.
48. Sanderson, pp. 137, 120.
49. *An Autobiography* (1904) I, p. 442.
50. Ib. II, p. 36.
51. Ib. II, p. 37; Lowe, *Primary and Classical Education* (Edinburgh, 1867), p. 22.
52. *Education* (1861), ch. 1, esp. p. 9.
53. Sanderson, p. 127; Arnold, 'Literature and Science' (Super X, p. 53 ff.).
54. Sanderson, p. 137.
55. Report of the Clarendon Commission I, p. 28.
56. M. L. Clarke, *Classical Education in Britain, 1500–1900* (Cambridge, 1959), pp. 87, 95.
57. *Essays Ancient and Modern* (1936), p. 172.
58. Op. cit., p. 32.
59. Sanderson, p. 211; Mackenzie, op. cit., bk. 2, chs. 4, 11.
60. *Middlemarch*, ch. 15; *Maurice*, ch. 21.
61. *Princess Ida*, act 2.
62. *The Swinburne Letters*, ed. C. Y. Lang (New Haven, 1959–62), III, p. 32.
63. P. Grosskurth, *John Addington Symonds* (1964), p. 269.
64. *Studies of the Greek Poets*, ch. 18.
65. *Maurice*, ch. 12; Grosskurth, p. 34.
66. T. d'A. Smith, *Love in Earnest* (1970), p. 5.
67. *Maurice*, chs. 12, 18.
68. Grosskurth, pp. 43, 108.
69. G. Faber, *Jowett* (2nd edn., 1958), p. 370.
70. Grosskurth, p. 271.
71. Symonds, *In the Key of Blue* (1893), p. 91.
72. Ib., p. 93 f.
73. Grosskurth, p. 279 f.
74. Smith, p. 175 ff.
75. *Contarini Fleming*, ch. 7; *Coningsby*, bk. 1, ch. 9.
76. *The Newcomes*, ch. 12.
77. *David Copperfield*, ch. 6.
78. Pt. 2, ch. 2.
79. Ib.
80. *Plato and Platonism*, ch. 8.
81. *Memorials Part I* (1896) I, p. 136.
82. *The Poems of Tennyson*, ed. C. Ricks (1969), p. 860.

83. *Eric*, pt. 2, ch. 8; pt. 1, chs. 8, 11.
84. Ch. 3.
85. *Maurice*, ch. 7.
86. *De Profundis.*
87. Bk. 2, chs. 8, 9.
88. *The Longest Journey*, chs. 1, 3, 10, 12.
89. Smith, p. 171.
90. *In the Key of Blue*, pp. 97, 88.
91. Smith, p. 62.
92. Ib., p. 64.
93. Ib., p. 3.
94. *Hugh Heron, Ch. Ch.* (1880), p. 51.
95. *Coningsby*, bk. 6, ch. 2.
96. *Autumn Journal*, sect. 9.
97. *The Picture of Dorian Gray*, ch. 2.
98. *A History of Ancient Greek Literature* (1897), preface.
99. *Patience*, act 1.
100. *The Oxford Book of Modern Verse* (Oxford, 1936), pp. viii, 1.
101. *Marius*, ch. 6.
102. Wilde, op. cit., ch. 11; *Sinister Street*, bk. 2, ch. 9; Huysmans, *À Rebours*, prologue.
103. Op. cit., p. 104 f.
104. *Studies of the Greek Poets*, ch. 1.
105. *Spring and Death.*
106. *Studies of the Greek Poets*, chs. 1, 23, 21, 1.

Chapter 12 Classical Art in the later Nineteenth Century

1. *Taine's Notes on England*, tr. E. Hyams (1957), p. 258.
2. Hope, op. cit., p. 1 f.; Haydon, *Autobiography*, ch. 9; Thackeray, *The Newcomes*, ch. 17.
3. Op. cit., ch. 17.
4. D.N.B., on Haydon.
5. *Lectures . . . on the Great Exhibition* (1854), p. 290.
6. Ib., p. 297.
7. *Instances of Accessory Art* (1880).
8. D. Harbron, *The Conscious Stone* (1949), p. 24; W. Gaunt, *Victorian Olympus* (1952), p. 142.
9. Harbron, p. 95.
10. Ib., p. 75.
11. Gaunt, p. 86.
12. *Essays on the Purpose of Art* (1911), p. 368.
13. See Crane, *Renascence* (1891); *Ideals in Art* (1905); *An Artist's Reminiscences* (1907).
14. Gaunt, p. 126.

15. Harbron, p. 162.
16. Ib., p. 165.
17. M. S. Watts, *George Frederic Watts* (1912) III, p. 202 ff.
18. Gaunt, p. 144.
19. Harbron, p. 176 ff.
20. Symonds, *Studies of the Greek Poets*, ch. 17.
21. Harbron, loc. cit.
22. *Letters to the New Island*, ed. H. Reynolds (Oxford, 1934), pp. 132, 113, 105.
23. Ib., pp. 113, 134, 132.
24. Ib., p. viii.
25. Ib., pp. 114, 175, 132, 191, 175.
26. Ch. 35.
27. Meynell, *Some Modern Artists and Their Work* (1883), p. 37; Bayliss, *Five Great Painters of the Victorian Era* (1902), p. 31; Barrington, *The Life, Letters and Work of Frederic Leighton* (1906) I, p. 24 f.; Richmond, *Leighton, Millais and William Morris* (1898), p. 20.
28. Gaunt, p. 140.
29. Ib., p. 27.
30. 'A Syracusan Bride . . .' and 'The Jealousy of Simoetha . . .'
31. Gaunt, p. 92; *The Swinburne Letters*, ed. C. Y. Lang (New Haven, 1959–62), V, p. 122.
32. *The Complete Works of . . . Swinburne*, ed. E. Gosse and T. J. Wise (1925–7), XV, p. 197; M. S. Watts II, p. 81.
33. *Lectures on Art* (1897), p. 288.
34. Mrs. Lang quoted by E. Rhys, *Frederic Lord Leighton* (3rd edn., 1900), p. 8.
35. Op. cit., p. 19.
36. A. H. Palmer, *The Life . . . of Samuel Palmer* (new edn., 1972), p. 250.
37. *The Last Chronicle of Barset*, ch. 24.
38. J. Harlaw, *The Charm of Leighton* (1913), p. 45.
39. Baldry, *Leighton* (1908), p. 33; Ruskin, *The Seven Lamps of Architecture*, ch. 4, § 11.
40. Barrington, *Essays . . .*, p. 322; Harlaw, p. 38.
41. *Little Dorrit*, bk. 2, ch. 9.
42. *Aratra Pentelici*, § 111.
43. Ruskin, *The Art of England*, §§ 75, 106; Barrington, *The Life . . . of . . . Leighton* II, p. 262; Rhys, op. cit., p. 37.
44. Standing, *Sir Lawrence Alma-Tadema* (1905), p. 69.
45. Gaunt, p. 75.
46. Standing, p. 56.
47. *Academy Notes*, 1875.
48. *Lectures on Architecture and Painting*, § 129 f.
49. Ib., § 132.
50. *The Picture of Dorian Gray*, chs. 2, 4.
51. 'On the genius . . . of Hogarth'.

52. *The Picture of Dorian Gray*, ch. 9.
53. *The New Republic*, bk. 4, ch. 1.
54. Thackeray, *The Newcomes*, ch. 39; Lytton, *The Last Days of Pompeii*, bk. 1, ch. 6.
55. Gaunt, p. 75.
56. Lytton, preface; Kingsley, *Hypatia*, ch. 30.
57. Op. cit., ch. 17.
58. Thackeray, ib.; Wilde, ch. 4.
59. Wilde, *De Profundis*.
60. R. Blomfield, *Richard Norman Shaw* . . . (1940), p. 42.
61. R. Ash, *Alma-Tadema* (1973), p. 24.
62. Zimmern, p. 30.
63. Ib.
64. Standing, p. 40; Gaunt, p. 121.
65. Thackeray, ch. 17.
66. Chs. 17, 39.
67. *The Princess*, pt. 2. l. 9 ff.
68. Harlaw, p. 29.
69. Standing, p. 58.
70. *Lothair*, chs. 29, 35.
71. *Sketches in Italy and Greece*, p. 186.
72. *De Profundis*.
73. Hardy, *Jude the Obscure*, pt. 5, ch. 3.
74. Op. cit., pp. 21, 9.
75. Ash, p. 44.
76. *Journ. R.I.B.A.* VII (1900), 131 (Bodley); ib. VIII (1901), 80 (Pite); ib. VII (1900), 349 ff. (Brydon).
77. Ib. VIII (1901), 78
78. Ib., 82.
79. *Towards a New Architecture*, tr. F. Etchells (1927), p. 145.

Chapter 13   The Empire and the War

1. *Aen.* 6. 847 ff.
2. *Sermons on Christian Doctrine* (1906), p. 298.
3. Op. cit. (2nd edn., 1915), p. 44.
4. *The Last Days of Pompeii*, bk. 1, ch. 2.
5. Chs. 6, 8.
6. Ch. 5.
7. *Studies in History and Jurisprudence* (1901) I, p. 72.
8. J. G. Lockhart and C. M. Woodhouse, *Rhodes* (1963), pp. 22, 64; R. Storrs, *Orientations* (new edn., 1943), p. 10; Buchan, *Memory Hold-the-Door* (1940), p. 117; Storrs, loc. cit.; J. Marlowe, *Cromer in Egypt* (1970), p. 234.
9. Op. cit., p. 97.

10. D.N.B.
11. Lockhart and Woodhouse, p. 141 f.
12. *Lectures and Essays* (1870), p. 1 f.
13. Bryce, *The Ancient Roman Empire and the British Empire in India* (1914); Lucas, *Greater Rome and Greater Britain* (Oxford, 1912).
14. Op. cit. (1910), p. 11.
15. Hobson, *Imperialism* (1902), esp. p. 387 ff.; cf. Robertson, *Patriotism and Empire* (1899).
16. Lockhart and Woodhouse, pp. 31, 22.
17. R. F. Betts, 'The allusion to Rome in British imperialist thought . . .', *Vict. Stud.* XV (1971), 154
18. W. Stephens, *The Life and Letters of Edward A. Freeman* (1895) II, p. 180.
19. *The Expansion of England* (1883), pp. 297, 6 f.
20. Ib., p. 39 f.
21. Lockhart and Woodhouse, p. 64.
22. Stephens I, p. 236; *The Expansion of England*, p. 301; MacNeice, *The Strings Are False* (1965), p. 208.
23. N. Mosley, *Julian Grenfell* (1976), p. 262.
24. Op. cit., p. 167.
25. Op. cit., pp. 489, 493.
26. Op. cit., pp. 95 f., 108, 121, 16, 21.
27. *Essays and Addresses* (1921), p. 31 ff.
28. Ib., p. 33.
29. *Greek Studies* (Oxford, 1946), pp. 192 ff., 197, 198, 200.
30. *A Scholar's Letters from the Front* (1918), p. 20.
31. Buchan, *These for Remembrance* (1919), p. 31; P. Fussell, *The Great War and Modern Memory* (New York, 1975), p. 180.
32. Fussell, loc. cit.
33. Mosley, p. 263; *Denis Oliver Barnett* (1915); Hewett, p. 110.
34. J. Hone, *W. B. Yeats* (1942), p. 292.
35. Storrs, p. 520.
36. G. Chapman (ed.), *Vain Glory* (1937), p. 160.
37. Op. cit., p. 24.
38. *1914.*
39. *Into Battle.*
40. *Other Fragments.*
41. *The Letters of Rupert Brooke*, ed. G. Keynes (1968), p. 668; *Charles Lister* (1917), p. 164; Buchan, *These for Remembrance*, p. 58; Knox, *Patrick Shaw-Stewart* (1920), p. 2 f.
42. *In Memoriam, A.H.*
43. Knox, p. 160.
44. *Memory Hold-the-Door*, p. 167.
45. *A Whispered Tale.*
46. J. H. Johnson, *English Poetry of the First World War* (Princeton, 1964), p. 284.

47. *In Parenthesis* (1937), pp. 61, 160 f.
48. Buchan, *These for Remembrance*, p. 31.
49. Knox, p. 31 f.
50. *Charles Lister*, p. 164.
51. Marsh, *A Number of People* (1939), p. 178; Buchan, *These for Remembrance*, p. 80.
52. Ch. 9.
53. Mosley, p. 265.
54. Brooke, *Letters*, p. 670; *Charles Lister*, p. 141; Knox, pp. 127, 142.
55. *Literary Distractions* (1958), p. 20.
56. *Portrait of an Age*, sects. 6, 4.
57. *Autumn Journal*, sect. 9.
58. *Invitation*.
59. J. Sherwood, *No Golden Journey* (1973), p. 34.
60. *Last Lectures* (Cambridge, 1939), p. 72.
61. Ib., p. xxviii.
62. *Journ. Hell. Stud.* XXXVI (1916), p. lviii.
63. *Report of the committee . . . to inquire into the position of classics* (1921), pp. 18, 17, 21, 267 f.
64. 'Literature and Science' (Prose Works, ed. Super, X, p. 71).

INDEX